Doll Values

— ANTIQUE TO MODERN —

SEVENTH EDITION

PATSY MOYER

COLLECTOR BOOKS

A Division of Schroeder Publishing Co., Inc.

On the Cover:

16" wooden Shoenhut with carved bonnet, $3,700.00.

16" bisque Circle Dot Bru, $8,000.00.

17" 1957 vinyl Ideal Shirley Temple, $200.00.

18" Izannah Walker, $3,400.00.

Cover design by Beth Summers
Book design by Holly C. Long

Collector Books
P.O. Box 3009
Paducah, KY 42002-3009

www.collectorbooks.com

Copyright © 2003 Patsy Moyer

The current values in this book should be used only as a guide. They are not intended to set prices, which vary from one section of the country to another. Auction prices, as well as dealer prices, vary greatly and are affected by availability, condition, and demand. Neither the author nor the publisher assumes responsibility for any losses that might be incurred as a result of consulting this guide.

Searching for a Publisher?

We are always looking for people knowledgeable within their fields. If you feel that there is a real need for a book on your collectible subject and have a large comprehensive collection, contact Collector Books.

Credits

My special thanks to a great group of collectors who show their love of collecting by sharing their dolls with others.

Sue Amidon, Jo Barckley, Atelier Bets van Boxel, Sue Ann Blott, Dorothy Bohlin, Travis Cannon, Stephanie Cauley, Ana Lisa Cervantez, Martha Cramer, Marilyn Cross, Debbie Crume, Ellen Cummings, Jane Darin, Sally DeSmet, Betty Eppinger, Toni Ferry, Elizabeth Fielding, Cornelia Ford, Shirley Funsten, Sondra Gast, Cherie Gervais, Hakes Americana, Kathy Hippensteel, Linda Holton, Barbara Hull, Vickie Johnson, Sandy Johnson-Barts, Iva Mae Jones, Sharon Kolibaba, Kathleen Kelly, Lebba Knopp, Anita Ladensack, Denise Lemmon, Marguerite Long, Connie Lee Martin, Valerie McArdle, McMasters Harris Doll Auctions, Christine McWilliams, Marge Meisinger, Chad Moyer, Sarah Munsey, Donna Nance, Dorisanne Osborne, Joan Radke, Inge Ramey, Pat Rather, Ginger Reid, Debra Ruberto, Sheryl Schmidt, Mary Alice Sheflow, Nelda Sheldon, Shirley's Doll House, Sherryl Shirran, Elizabeth Surber, Linda Lee Sutton, Leslie Tannenbaum, JoAnn Threadgill, Jean Thompson, Kate Treber, Mary Lu Trowbridge, Carol Van Verst-Rugg, Vogue Doll Company, Kay Walimaa, Ann Wencel, Thelma Williams, Oleta Woodside, Patricia Wright, Betty Yadon and a very special thank you to fellow author, Carol Stover, who graciously provided expertise, photographs, and suggestions when needed.

Welcome to the world of doll collecting. For as long as there have been little girls who played with dolls, there have been people who so treasured those playthings they wanted to keep them forever. In this book, we present an overview of doll collecting, the doll market, and resources associated with dolls. You are encouraged to seek more knowledge to help you understand more about dolls so you can make wise decisions as you acquire your collection.

This book is divided into two sections, ANTIQUE and MODERN as general ways to separate dolls made of older materials like bisque, wax, cloth, and wood, and dolls made of newer materials such as composition, hard plastic, and vinyl. This immediately becomes confusing to the novice, because some of the composition modern dolls are as old as the bisque dolls in the antique section. We do this only to help the reader who can save time by looking for older dolls in the front antique section and newer dolls in the back modern section. A new classification is emerging that refers to dolls made in the last 30 years as "collectible." In this book, collectible dolls are grouped with modern.

Appendixes are included at the back of the book. There are several. First a bibliography lists many of the doll book references I find helpful. Next, the collector's network lists special interest groups and individuals. Then there are four indexes to help you identify the marks often found on the back of the head or torso of your doll. The first is the symbol index with text describing the symbol and then the company who uses that symbol. Next is a letter index that lists letters that may help you discover the company that made the doll. Next is the mold mark index listing mold numbers and then the page number in this book with an example and the name of the companies that used those mold numbers. Finally there is the name index which lists the names of the dolls and the names of the doll companies.

Many published references have been used for descriptions and marks. Every effort was made to check early advertising, where possible, but the main references are Johanna Anderton; John Axe; Dorothy, Jane, and Ann Coleman; Jurgen and Marianne Cieslik; Jan Foulke; Judith Izen; Pam and Polly Judd; Ursula Mertz; and Patricia N. Schoonmaker. My thanks to these respected authorities and others who have contributed so much in research to collectors.

The dolls in each section are listed alphabetically by manufacturer or type, including a brief history, marks, description, and prices. Dolls are identified by the type of material used on the head — for example; if the head is hard plastic, the doll is referred to as hard plastic, even though the body may be of another material. They may be further classified as a category, such as Oriental, black, or souvenir dolls. Most black and brown dolls are grouped in the category Black. Souvenir dolls are from special occasions, functions, or events that all who attend receive. We have tried to use the general categories set forth in prior issues of this book, but have taken the liberty to add new categories or delete some of them. Your suggestions will be considered if enough data is available to research. We will continue to refine categories, descriptions, and data.

In addition to separating dolls generally into antique and modern sections, we have also **grouped them by manufacturer or type.** Modern manufacturers might be Alexander, Mattel, and Remco. Types are another way dolls can be grouped. Although Barbie doll is a Mattel doll, she has such a following that she has her own category. Another modern category is artist dolls; this category is for dolls of any medium created for sale to the public, whether they are one-of-a-kind works of art or numbered limited editions. They reflect dolls that are not mass produced, but may be produced in numbers.

Where practical, we have also **classified dolls by material,** such as bisque, cloth, composition, hard plastic, porcelain, and vinyl. Look for all-cloth dolls except Lenci, Käthe Kruse, and Steiff under the category Cloth. For the novice collector, decide what material the head of your doll is, remembering that antique dolls are generally made of bisque, china, cloth, papier-mâché, wax, or wood. Modern dolls may be made of composition, porcelain, hard plastic, vinyl, or some other material. Look for little known manufacturers in broad categories such as bisque, German, hard plastic, or vinyl.

Some of the things to consider in evaluating a doll are **quality, condition, rarity, originality, and desirability.** These can vary considerably as any two collectors may rate one or more of these attributes differently or two identical dolls can differ greatly with those same factors. All of these things are desirable factors to keep in mind. Since doll collectors mostly have limited budgets, it is smart buyers who familiarize themselves with as much about the subject as is available. This guide is a good starting place and is written with the novice as well as the more experienced collector in mind.

All dolls were not born equal. Dolls from the same mold can vary because of the conditions at the time of their manufacture. Successful production techniques developed over time; some of which arose only with the passage of time. Bisque dolls could be made with different grades of porcelain giving a range from fine to poor quality. Humidity and temperature could affect the production techniques of composition made up of various formulas of glue, wood pulp, sawdust, and other ingredients, causing their finish to later crack or peel. The formula used for some rubber and early plastic dolls caused them to turn darker colors or become sticky. The durability of the material did not show up immediately — only after the passage of time.

It is important for the collector to become aware of the many different factors that influence the manufacture, durability, popularity, and availability of a doll. Many influences can affect your decision to choose a particular doll to add to your collection. It takes time and effort before you can know the particular subtle differences in the exact same model of one doll, much less the endless variations and levels of differences that can exist in a particular era, category, or type of doll. This guide will serve as the starting point for your search for knowledge in the areas you choose to pursue.

Quality is an important consideration when purchasing a doll. Buy the best doll you can afford. Look at enough dolls so that you can tell the difference in a poorly finished or painted doll and one that has been artistically done. The head is the most important part of the doll. Signs of quality include good coloring; original clothing, wig, and body; and a pleasing appearance.

The condition of the doll is a very important factor in pricing a doll. A beautiful doll re-dressed, dirty, and missing a wig should not be priced as high as a beautiful doll with original clothing, a well-done wig, and clean and unrepaired body. Only consider composition dolls that have cracks, peeling paint, or lifting of paint *if* they have added incentives, such as wonderful coloring, original clothes, boxes, and tags. Look for a smooth finish with rosy cheek color on the face as well as bright crisp clothing.

Originality is also important. Original clothing is an advantage on any dolls, but especially if the clothing is in good condition. It is becoming more difficult to find a completely original doll, so dolls found with original clothing may double or triple in price.

Also important is the correct body with the correct head and original wig on the doll. Patricia Schoonmaker once told me that we are only caretakers of our dolls for awhile — they then are passed on to someone else to care for. As some older dolls come on the market, they may be found on different bodies as they were acquired before the importance of originality became known and the ability to identify the correct body became available.

Rarity is another consideration in dolls. Many dolls were made by the thousands. Some dolls were not made in such quantity. If a doll was of high quality, beautiful, and not many were made, it may be more desirable and higher priced. Age can play a factor in pricing dolls, but not age alone. Modern dolls such as Shirley Temple dolls or Barbie® dolls can out price some older antique dolls.

Desirability is another factor in choosing a doll. Some dolls may be rare in original clothing, and still just not appeal to others. Beauty can be in the eye of the beholder; but some dolls are just not as appealing as others because they were poorly made or unattractive from the start. A well-made doll of quality is generally the one sought after, even in dirty, not original condition. A poorly made doll of inferior quality will always be a poorly made doll whether it is in top condition or cracked and damaged.

The pricing in this book is based on a number of factors including information from informed collectors, doll shows and sales, auctions, and doll-related publications. These factors have led us to build a database of actual sales. The pricing in this book is based on 12,000 to 16,000 dolls. You will see what actually is happening in the auction marketplace. Although any one auction's prices may vary widely; tracking the results over a period of time does reveal some consistency. The rarity and desirability of the same doll will fluctuate from area to area and with time. When a limited number of a certain doll is in the database, I have added the notation, "Too few in database for reliable range." I have arbitrarily set this figure at less than five dolls and the figure may change.

Demand sets the price. If a buyer has just won the lottery or has their own gold mine, the average buyer cannot compete with them. The good news is that these buyers usually cannot cover every collector, shop, or show that may have dolls for sale. The limited few that do have big bucks, cannot be everywhere at once. So the prudent may wish to back off, when the "high rollers" appear. Persons who have the ready cash have the right to spend it wherever they wish. If they want a particular doll and have the means to acquire it, more power to them. Many of these collectors share their dolls via museums, lectures, and exhibits, and that is wonderful. Extraordinary dolls may command higher prices because of all of the above factors.

So what price is too much to pay for a doll? That is a personal decision left entirely up to you and your bank account. The one great thing about collecting is that you are free to make your own choices of what you can afford and what you want to spend. You owe no explanation to others. You may, however, wish to arm yourself with knowledge if your funds are limited, so you can get the most for your money. Perhaps the greatest influence on doll collecting today is the Internet. Auction sites, like eBay have opened up the field of collecting worldwide and brought forth a rapidly changing market place, making the doll market extremely volatile. Items you may have hunted for years are now at your fingertips. Sellers and buyers may have varying degrees of expertise, and it is necessary to constantly do research to be sure what you are getting is what you are seeking.

Doll collecting need not be a short term intense pursuit. More often it becomes a long-term hobby of gathering things to love around you and good values as well. And after some years of loving enjoyment, one might look around and, in the process of collecting dolls, realize they have accumulated a solid investment as well — much as collecting fine art. Wise collectors will document their collection so their estate will show the gains from their endeavors.

This guide makes no attempt to set price standards and should not be considered the final authority. It is simply meant to report prices realized in areas that can be tracked and reported. Every effort has been made to present an unbiased and impartial viewpoint to the collector of the results found in the areas researched. But remember, this is a compilation of data, and can only represent input from the various sources used. The goals are to bring together information from many sources to give collectors an additional viewpoint so that they can make their own personal choice. Collectors have the final decision in buying or selling a doll; it is their decision alone.

The number of categories is immense and no one can be familiar with all of the changing and different areas. For this reason, I have consulted with a broad group of collectors who keep up to date with the market in their particular fields. Some of these collectors have agreed to provide their names and addresses as references in certain areas. These can be found in the Collectors' Network section at the back of the book. If you would like to become part of this network and are willing to share your knowledge with others in your particular field, please send your name, address, field of specialty, and references to: P.O. Box 311, Deming, NM 88031. Please also include your e-mail or website address, if you have one.

The more collectors share, the more we all gain from the experience. If you have questions, you may write the individual collector listed. It is common courtesy to send a self-addressed stamped envelope if you wish to receive a reply to your question. If you would like to see other categories added to this guide, please drop us a line and tell us your areas of interest. If possible, we will add categories when there is enough interest and data is available. We would like to hear from you.

The collector needs to be well informed to make a proper judgment when spending his/her hard earned money buying a doll. The more information accumulated, the better the judgment. Collectors can turn to a national organization whose goals are education, research, preservation, and enjoyment of dolls. The United Federation of Doll Clubs can tell you if a doll club in your area is accepting members or tell you how to become a member-at-large. You may write for more information at:

United Federation of Doll Clubs, Inc.
10900 North Pomona Avenue
Kansas City, MO 64153
816-891-7040
Fax: 816-891-8360

There are also many smaller groups that focus on particular dolls or on some aspect of doll collecting. A list of some of those groups and their interests is located in the Collectors' Network at the back of the book. You gain more knowledge, and the collecting experience is more enjoyable when you participate with others.

Happy collecting!

Antique and Older Dolls

14" bisque Portrait Jumeau, marks: "5"
on back of head, bisque socket head,
light blue paperweight eyes, blond
feathered brows, painted upper and
lower lashes, accented nostrils, closed
mouth, pierced ears, mohair wig, jointed wood and composition body with
straight wrists, separate balls at shoulders, elbows, hips, and knees, maroon
wool dress with lace overlay on the
bodice and sleeves, matching chapeau,
underclothing, old socks and red velvet
composition-era shoes, $4,100.00. Cour-
tesy McMasters Harris Doll Auctions.

17" Bru Jne, marks: "Bru Jne//5" on
back of head, "Bru" on left shoulder,
"No 5" on right shoulder, and on top
of arms, shoes marked "7//Bru Jne//
Paris," bisque socket head on bisque
shoulder plate, blue paperweight eyes,
two-tone feathered brows and accented nostrils, painted upper and lower
lashes, closed mouth, pierced ears,
replaced mohair wig, kid body with
bisque lower arms, re-dressed in
aqua silk dress with beige collar and
lace, new underclothing and socks,
$9,500.00. Courtesy McMasters Harris
Doll Auctions.

19" early china with molded
hat, marks in red inside
shoulder plate, painted blue
eyes with red accent line,
single stroke brows, accented
nostrils, closed mouth, molded side hair loops, molded
hat trimmed with feathers,
cloth body jointed at shoulders, hips, and knees,
dressed in antique white
shirt, gathered top, chemise,
half slip, and pantalettes,
$15,000.00. Courtesy McMas-
ters Harris Doll Auctions.

Alexandre, Henri

1888 – 1892, Paris. Bisque head, paperweight eyes, closed mouth with a white space between the lips, fat cheeks, and early French bodies with straight wrists.

First price indicates doll in good condition, but with flaws or nude; second price indicates doll in excellent condition, in original clothes, or appropriately dressed.

17"	$4,350.00	$5,800.00
19"	$4,950.00	$6,500.00
21"	$5,300.00	$7,100.00

BÉBÉ PHÉNIX, 1889 – 1900+

Phénix trademark first used by Alexandre, then Bébé Phénix in 1895 was used by Mme. Lafosse and then Jules Mettais, both worked for Jules Steiner. Bisque head, closed mouth, paperweight eyes, pierced ears, composition body.

Child, closed mouth

10"	$1,375.00	$1,800.00
14"	$2,175.00	$2,900.00
17"	$2,925.00	$3,800.00
18"	$3,400.00	$4,300.00
20"	$3,900.00	$5,100.00
22"	$4,100.00	$5,400.00
24"	$4,200.00	$5,600.00

Child, open mouth

17"	$1,500.00	$2,100.00
19"	$1,650.00	$2,300.00
22"	$1,800.00	$2,400.00
25"	$2,000.00	$2,700.00

All-Bisque, French

1880+. Jointed neck, shoulders, hips; delicate body with slender arms and legs, glass eyes, molded shoes or boots and stockings. Many all-bisque once thought to be of French manufacture are now believed to have been made in Germany expressly for the French market.

First price indicates doll in good condition, with some flaws, undressed; second price is for doll in excellent condition, with original or appropriate clothing. Allow more for original clothes and tags, less for chips or repairs.

Glass eyes, swivel head, molded shoes or boots

2½"	$525.00	$725.00
5"	$2,175.00	$1,000.00
7"	$2,925.00	$1,750.00

Child, closed mouth

5"	$1,575.00	$2,100.00
6"	$1,875.00	$2,500.00
7"	$2,175.00	$2,900.00

Too few in database for reliable range.

Five-strap boots, glass eyes, swivel neck

6"	$1,500.00	$2,100.00

Painted eyes

2½"	$170.00	$225.00
4"	$425.00	$550.00

Circa 1910 – 1920, glass eyes, molded socks, boots

5"	$300.00	$400.00
7"	$400.00	$550.00

Too few in database for reliable range.

Marked E.D., F.G., or similar French makers

7"	$1,875.00	$2,500.00+

Marked S.F.B.J., Unis, or similar French makers

6"	$475.00	$625.00

4½" all-bisque French-type, unmarked, original blond mohair wig, bisque socket head with fine features, set blue glass eyes, single stroke brows, painted upper and lower lashes, closed mouth, slender body jointed at shoulders and hips, molded and painted socks and two-strap shoes with molded heels, antique pink plaid dress, underclothing, pink lace-trimmed bonnet, circa 1880+, $400.00. Courtesy McMasters Harris Doll Auctions.

6" all-bisque baby, boxed, marks: "6/0" on bottom of shoes, "Trade-Mark//HH//D. Commission//Confection//Pup pe//Ctm//Couleur," bisque head with stiff neck, painted brown eyes, single stroke wavy brows, accented nostrils, open-closed mouth, lightly molded and brush-stroked hair, jointed at shoulders and hips, dressed in original red knit two-piece outfit with striped collar and belt, original knit socks and brown leather shoes, $550.00. Courtesy McMasters Harris Doll Auctions.

Many German firms made all-bisque dolls in smaller sizes from 1860 until 1930. Some were made by well-known firms such as Amberg; Alt, Beck & Gottschalck; Bähr & Pröschild; Hertel Schwab & Co.; Kämmer & Reinhart; J.D. Kestner; Kling; Limbach; Bruno Schmidt; and Simon & Halbig, and may have corresponding mold marks. Some are only marked "Made in Germany" and/or may have a paper label. They are often marked inside the arms and legs with matching mold numbers.

First price indicates doll in good condition, with some flaws or nude; second price is for doll in excellent condition, original clothes, or well dressed. More for labels, less for chips and repairs.

For All-Bisque, Black or Brown, see Black or Brown Section.

BABIES, CA. 1900+

Rigid neck (molded to torso), jointed shoulders and hips only, bent limbs, painted hair

Glass eyes

3"	$200.00	$250.00
5"	$250.00	$350.00

Painted eyes

3½"	$65.00	$90.00
6"	$150.00	$200.00

Swivel necks (socket neck), jointed shoulders and hips, wigs or painted hair

Glass eyes

4"	$175.00	$300.00
6"	$300.00	$475.00
8"	$450.00	$600.00

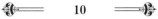

Painted eyes

3"	$145.00	$195.00
5"	$245.00	$325.00
7"	$175.00	$350.00

Babies with Character Face, ca. 1910+
Jointed shoulders and hips, molded hair
Glass eyes

5"	$325.00	$450.00
7"	$400.00	$525.00

Painted eyes

5"	$165.00	$225.00
7"	$225.00	$300.00

Swivel neck, glass eyes

5"	$375.00	$550.00
10"	$750.00	$1,000.00

Swivel neck, painted eyes

5"	$250.00	$325.00
7"	$375.00	$500.00

Mold 391, 830, 833, and others

6"	$350.00	$450.00
8"	$500.00	$650.00

Baby Bo Kaye, mold 1394
Designed by Kallus, distributed by Borgfeldt

5"	$850.00	$1,125.00
7"	$1,050.00	$1,425.00

Baby Bud, glass eyes, wig

6 – 7"	$975.00	$1,300.00

Baby Darling, mold 497, Kestner, 178
One-piece body, painted eyes

6"	$500.00	$600.00
8"	$600.00	$700.00
10"	$635.00	$825.00

Swivel neck, glass eyes, more for toddler body

6"	$450.00	$600.00
8"	$625.00	$825.00

Baby Peggy Montgomery
Made by Louis Amberg, paper label, pink bisque with molded hair, painted brown eyes, closed mouth, jointed at shoulders and hips, molded and painted shoes/socks

3½"	$225.00	$400.00
5½"	$450.00	$600.00

Bonnie Babe, 1926+, designed by Georgene Averill
Glass eyes, swivel neck, wig, jointed arms and legs

4½"	$500.00	$650.00
7"	$600.00	$800.00
8"	$750.00	$1,000.00

Molded-on clothes, dome head, swivel neck, jointed arms and legs

5"	$400.00	$600.00
6"	$600.00	$775.00

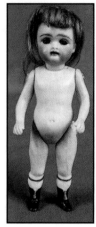

5" all-bisque Kestner, marks: "3/0" on back of head and below neck, bisque swivel head, blue sleep eyes, feathered brows, painted upper and lower lashes, accented nostrils, open mouth with two square upper teeth, original mohair wig and all-bisque body jointed at shoulders and hips, black boots with blue tassels, off-white simple dress with embroidered decoration, $1,300.00. Courtesy McMasters Harris Doll Acutions.

Immobiles, one-piece, in various poses

3"	$175.00	$350.00

Mildred (The Prize Baby), mold 880, ca. 1914+

Made for Borgfeldt; molded, short painted hair; glass eyes; closed mouth; jointed at neck, shoulders, and hips; round paper label on chest; molded and painted footwear

5"	$950.00	$1,250.00
7"	$900.00	$1,800.00

Tynie Baby, made for E.I. Horsman

Glass eyes

5"	$525.00	$725.00
8"	$950.00	$1,250.00

Painted eyes

5"	$350.00	$475.00

Pink Bisque Candy Baby, ca. 1920+

May be German or Japanese, lesser quality paint finish, given away with purchase of candy

3½"	$25.00	$35.00
6"	$35.00	$45.00

Mold 231 (A.M.), toddler, swivel neck, with glass eyes

9"	$1,025.00	$1,400.00

Mold 369, 372

7"	$545.00	$725.00
9"	$875.00	$1,100.00
11"	$1,050.00	$1,400.00+

CHILDREN

Rigid neck, glass eyes, 1890+

Head molded to torso, sometimes legs also, excellent bisque, open/closed mouth, sleep or set eyes, good wig, nicely dressed, molded one-strap shoes. Allow more for unusual footwear such as yellow multi-strap boots.

3"	$165.00	$275.00
5"	$165.00	$285.00
7"	$250.00	$400.00
9"	$550.00	$700.00

Bent knees

6"	$145.00	$285.00

Mold 100, 125, 150, 225 (preceded by 83/)

Rigid neck, fat tummy, jointed shoulders and hips, glass sleep eyes, open/closed mouth, molded black one-strap shoes with tan soles, white molded stockings with blue band. Similarly molded dolls, imported in 1950s by Kimport, have synthetic hair, lesser quality bisque. Add more for original clothing.

Mold number appears as a fraction, with the following size numbers under 83; Mold "83/100," "83/125," "83/150," or "83/225." One marked "83/100" has a green label on torso reading, "Princess//Made in Germany."

8¾" all-bisque Kestner, mold 150, marks: "150//3" on back of head, bisque head with stiff neck, blue sleep eyes, feathered brows, painted upper and lower lashes, accented nostrils, open mouth with four upper teeth, original mohair wig on plaster pate, jointed at shoulders and hips, molded and painted blue knee-high shirred stockings, black one-strap shoes, faded blue plaid dress, antique lace-trimmed underclothing, $450.00. Courtesy McMasters Harris Doll Auctions.

100	5¾"	$225.00	$325.00
125	6¾"	$275.00	$350.00
150	7½"	$325.00	$425.00
225	8¼"	$350.00	$475.00

Mold 130, 150, 168, 184, 257, 602, 790, 791, 792 (Bonn or Kestner)

Painted blue or pink stockings, one-strap black shoes

4"	$150.00	$295.00
6"	$200.00	$385.00
7"	$215.00	$425.00
8"	$250.00	$500.00
9"	$300.00	$675.00
10"	$375.00	$750.00
11"	$450.00	$900.00

Mold 155, 156 (smile)

6"	$225.00	$450.00

Swivel neck

5½"	$300.00	$600.00
7"	$165.00	$325.00

Swivel neck, glass eyes, ca. 1880+

Pegged or wired joints, open or closed mouth, molded-on shoes or boots and stockings. Allow more for unusual footwear such as yellow or multi-strap boots.

3"	$175.00	$300.00
4"	$200.00	$350.00
5½"	$350.00	$525.00
7"	$375.00	$675.00
8"	$600.00	$800.00
9"	$675.00	$900.00
10"	$975.00	$1,300.00

Mold 130, 150, 160, 208, 602 (Kestner)

4"	$250.00	$500.00
6"	$300.00	$600.00
8"	$450.00	$900.00
10"	$650.00	$1,300.00

Mold 184 (Kestner)

4 – 5"	$350.00	$700.00
8"	$800.00	$1,600.00

Simon & Halbig or Kestner types

Closed mouth, excellent quality

5"	$400.00	$775.00
6"	$600.00	$1,150.00
8"	$975.00	$1,900.00

Jointed knees

6"	$1,500.00	$3,000.00

Original factory box with clothes/accessories

5"	$1,750.00	$3,500.00

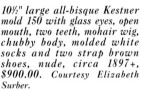

10½" large all-bisque Kestner mold 150 with glass eyes, open mouth, two teeth, mohair wig, chubby body, molded white socks and two strap brown shoes, nude, circa 1897+, $900.00. Courtesy Elizabeth Surber.

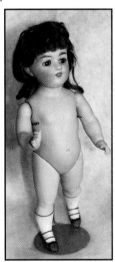

10½" large all-bisque Kestner mold 150 with glass eyes, open mouth, two teeth, mohair wig, chubby body, molded white socks and two-strap brown shoes, nude, circa 1897+, $900.00. Courtesy Elizabeth Surber.

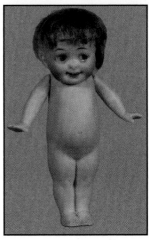

4¾" all-bisque Our Fairy, marks: "222/12" on back of head, bisque head with stiff neck, blue glass eyes set to side, single stroke brows, painted upper and lower lashes, tiny accents on nostrils, open-closed mouth with two painted upper teeth, original thin mohair wig, jointed at shoulders only, arms held at side, $190.00. Courtesy McMasters Harris Doll Auctions.

4½" all-bisque Amberg Mibs, painted blue eyes, closed mouth, molded and painted hair, pink bisque body, jointed at shoulders, molded and painted socks and shoes, original green dress, circa 1921, $300.00. Courtesy McMasters Harris Doll Auctions.

Bare feet

5"	$1,350.00	$1,800.00
7½"	$1,950.00	$2,600.00

Early round face

6"	$525.00	$900.00
8"	$900.00	$1,300.00

Mold 881, 886, 890 (Simon & Halbig)

Painted high-top boots with four or five straps

4½"	$600.00	$800.00
7½"	$1,200.00	$1,600.00
9½"	$1,500.00	$2,100.00

Long stockings, above knees

4½"	$325.00	$650.00
6"	$450.00	$900.00

Mold 102, Wrestler (so called)

Fat thighs, arm bent at elbow, open mouth (can have two rows of teeth) or closed mouth, stocky body, glass eyes, socket head, individual fingers or molded fist

6"	$900.00	$1,250.00
8"	$1,250.00	$1,650.00
9"	$1,600.00	$2,150.00

Painted eyes, ca. 1880+

Head molded to torso, molded hair or wig, open or closed mouth, painted-on shoes and socks, dressed or undressed, all in good condition. Allow more for unusual footwear such as yellow boots.

2"	$45.00	$85.00
4½"	$105.00	$190.00
6½"	$125.00	$250.00
8"	$175.00	$350.00

Black stockings, tan slippers

6"	$275.00	$400.00

Ribbed hose

4½"	$150.00	$200.00
6"	$275.00	$375.00
8"	$425.00	$575.00

Molded hair

4½"	$90.00	$175.00
6"	$175.00	$350.00

Early very round face

7"	$1,200.00	$2,300.00

Characters, ca. 1910+

Campbells Kids, molded clothes, Dutch bob

5"	$125.00	$245.00

Chin-chin, Gebruder Heubach, ca. 1919, jointed arms only, triangular label on chest

4"	$225.00	$300.00

Happifats, designed by Kate Jordan for Borgfeldt, ca. 1913 – 1921

4"	$200.00	$275.00

Jeanne Orsini, ca. 1919+, designed by Orsini for Borgfelt, produced by Alt, Beck & Gottschalck; Chi Chi, Didi, Fifi, Mimi, Vivi

Glass eyes

5"	$2,300.00*

Painted eyes

5"	$675.00	$925.00

Max, Moritz, Kestner, ca. 1914, jointed at the neck, shoulders, and hips, many companies produced these characters from the Wilhelm Busch children's story

4½"	$2,000.00	$2,300.00 pair

Mibs, Amberg, ca. 1921, molded blond hair, molded and painted socks and shoes, pink bisque, jointed at shoulders, legs molded to body, marked "C.//L.A.&S.192//GERMANY"

3"	$200.00	$275.00
5"	$375.00	$425.00

Our Fairy, mold 222, ca. 1914 (see Googly under Hertel & Schwab)

Peterkin, ca. 1912, one-piece baby, side-glancing googly eyes, molded and painted hair, molded blue pajamas on chubby torso, arms molded to body with hands clasping stomach

6"	$250.00	$350.00

September Morn, ca. 1913, jointed at shoulders and hips, Grace Drayton design, George Borgfeldt

5"	$2,500.00	$3,500.00
7"	$4,400.00*	

Molded Clothes, ca. 1890+

Jointed at shoulders only or at shoulders and hips, painted eyes, molded hair, molded shoes or bare feet, excellent workmanship, no breaks, chips, or rubs

3½"	$85.00	$115.00
5"	$200.00	$275.00

Lesser quality

3"	$45.00	$85.00
4"	$50.00	$100.00
6"	$70.00	$140.00

Molded on hat or bonnet

In perfect condition

5 – 6½"	$190.00	$365.00+
8 – 9"	$250.00	$500.00+

8½" all-bisque Gebruder Kuhnlenz with closed mouth, glass eyes, orange boots, black tassels, kid-lined joints, marked "Gk, 13-19" on back of head, "12-19" on back, circa 1890+, $600.00+. Courtesy McMasters Harris Doll Auctions.

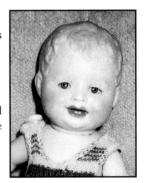

5½" all-bisque Bonnie Babe, open mouth with two bottom teeth, molded and painted blond hair, blue one-strap molded and painted shoes, original swim wear, $750.00. Courtesy Connie Lee Martin.

Stone (porous) Bisque

4 – 5"	$70.00	$135.00
6 – 7"	$85.00	$165.00

Slender Bodies, ca. 1900+

Slender dolls with head molded to torso, usual wire or peg-jointed shoulders and hips. Allow much more for original clothes. May be in regional costumes. Add more for unusual color boots, such as gold, yellow, or orange, all in good condition.

Glass eyes, open or closed mouth

3"	$145.00	$200.00
5 – 6"	$250.00	$350.00

Swivel neck, closed mouth

4"	$225.00	$300.00
5 – 6"	$350.00	$500.00
8½"	$600.00	$900.00
10"	$900.00	$1,300.00

Bent at knees

6"	$100.00	$200.00

Jointed knees and/or elbows with swivel waist

6"	$1,000.00	$1,950.00
8"	$1,600.00	$3,200.00

Swivel waist only

6"	$1,000.00	$2,000.00

Painted eyes, swivel neck, open or closed mouth, painted one-strap shoes

4"	$100.00	$200.00
6"	$175.00	$350.00
8"	$250.00	$475.00
10"	$350.00	$675.00

Flapper Body, ca. 1920+

One-piece body and head with thin limbs, fired-in fine bisque, wig, painted eyes, painted-on long stockings, one-strap painted shoes

5"	$225.00	$300.00
7"	$325.00	$450.00

Molded hair

6"	$250.00	$350.00
8"	$325.00	$450.00

Pink Bisque Child

Wire joints, molded hair, painted eyes

4"	$40.00	$75.00

Molded hat

4"	$185.00	$250.00

Aviatrix

5"	$175.00	$250.00

Swivel waist

4½"	$300.00	$400.00

Molded cap with rabbit ears

4½"	$275.00	$400.00

3¾" all-bisque German bonnet-head flapper, molded and painted maroon cloche hat, wire jointed, stiff neck, painted black high-heels, dark brown leather dress, circa 1920s, $75.00. Courtesy Dorothy Bohlin.

IMMOBILES, figures with no joints
Child

3"	$25.00	$50.00

Adults

5"	$75.00	$165.00

Santa

4"	$70.00	$140.00

Child with animal on string

4"	$75.00	$165.00

NODDERS, CA. 1920

When their heads are touched, they "nod," molded clothes, made both in Germany and Japan, decoration not fired in so wears off easily, all in good condition.

Animals, cat, dog, rabbit

3 – 5"	$45.00	$100.00

Child/Adult, made in Germany

4 – 6"	$35.00	$150.00

Child/Adult with molded-on clothes

4"	$65.00	$135.00

Child/Adult comic characters

3 – 5"	$65.00	$250.00

Child/Adult, sitting position

5"	$70.00	$140.00

Santa Claus or Indian

6"	$150.00	$190.00

Teddy Bear

5"	$125.00	$200.00

Japan/Nippon

3½"	$10.00	$25.00
4½"	$20.00	$45.00

FIGURES, PAINTED

Top layer of paint not fired on and the color can be washed off, usually one-piece figurines with molded hair, painted features, including clothes, shoes, and socks. Some have molded hats.

First price indicates with paint chips, second price is good condition with no paint chips, can be German or Japanese.

Baby, German

3½"	$35.00	$50.00
5"	$40.00	$60.00

Baby, Japanese

3"	$9.00	$15.00
5"	$15.00	$25.00

Child, German

3"	$20.00	$30.00
5"	$45.00	$65.00

Child, Japanese

3"	$7.50	$15.00
5"	$15.00	$25.00

4" Japanese all-bisque Bride and Groom wedding topper from owner's parents' 1930 wedding cake, all-original groom wears silk top hat, painted features, molded hair, jointed arms only, $100.00 for pair. Courtesy Sue Ann Blott.

4" pair all-bisque girls marked "Japan" on back, painted features, molded and painted hair with molded and painted ribbons, molded and painted socks and shoes, all-original in box, circa 1930s, $75.00 pair. Private collection.

Made by various Japanese companies. Quality varies greatly. They are jointed at shoulders and may also be jointed at hips. Good quality bisque is well painted with no chips or breaks.

The first price indicates poorer quality, flaking paint, flaws; second price indicates good quality, nicely finished.

4" painted all-bisque Japanese squaw, circa 1920s, some paint rubs, $35.00. Courtesy Marguerite Long.

BABY, WITH BENT LIMBS

May or may not be jointed at hips and shoulders, very nice quality

3"	$20.00	$30.00
5"	$35.00	$70.00

Bye-Lo Baby-type, fine quality

3½"	$45.00	$85.00
5"	$70.00	$140.00

CHILDREN

Child with molded clothes

4½"	$23.00	$35.00
6"	$35.00	$50.00

Child, ca. 1920s – 1930s

Pink or painted bisque with painted features, jointed at shoulders and hips, has molded hair or wig, excellent condition

3"	$7.50	$15.00
4"	$15.00	$35.00

Betty Boop

Bobbed hair style, large eyes painted to side, head molded to torso

4"	$20.00	$40.00
6"	$35.00	$60.00

Bride & Groom, all original costume

4"	$75.00	$100.00

Indian

5"	$15.00	$25.00

Skippy

6"	$55.00	$135.00

Snow White

5"	$55.00	$110.00

Boxed with Dwarfs

	$325.00	$650.00

Three Bears/Goldilocks, boxed set

	$165.00	$325.00+

Nippon mark

5"	$40.00	$75.00

Occupied Japan mark

4"	$13.00	$35.00
7"	$25.00	$55.00

Alt, Beck & Gottschalck

Established as a porcelain factory in 1854 at Nauendorf, Thuringia, Germany, the Ciesliks report the company exported doll heads to the USA by 1882. They made heads in both china and bisque for other companies such as Bergmann, using Wagner and Zetzsche kid bodies. The Colemans report mold numbers from 639 to 1288.

Mark:

1352

First price indicates doll in good condition, with some flaws or nude; second price is for doll in excellent condition, original clothes or appropriately dressed.

BABIES, CA. 1920+

Open mouth, some have pierced nostrils, bent-leg baby body, wigs, more for toddler body or flirty eyes

11"	$275.00	$365.00
15"	$350.00	$475.00
20"	$575.00	$775.00
24"	$850.00	$1,150.00

Character Baby, ca. 1910+

Socket head on jointed composition body, glass or painted eyes, open mouth, nicely dressed with good wig or molded hair

Mold 1322, 1342, 1346, 1352, 1361

12"	$325.00	$425.00
16"	$425.00	$600.00
19"	$500.00	$675.00
24"	$700.00	$950.00

CHILD, ALL-BISQUE: See All-Bisque Section.

CHILD, BISQUE

Mold 630, glass eyes, closed mouth, ca. 1880

22"	$1,650.00	$2,200.00

Open mouth

9"	$575.00	$775.00

Mold 911, 916, swivel head, closed mouth, ca. 1890+; **Mold 915,** shoulder head, closed mouth, ca. 1890

22"	$1,975.00	$2,650.00

Mold 938, closed mouth

20"	$4,500.00*	

27" mold 1123, turned bisque shoulder head, brown sleep eyes, heavy feathered brows, painted upper and lower lashes, accented nostrils, open mouth with six upper teeth, human hair wig, kid body with bisque lower arms, gussets at elbows, hips, and knees, marked: "12" on back of head, "1123 1/2 Made in Germany No. 12" on shoulder plate, antique white dress with lace inserts and trim, antique underclothing, original socks and high lace books, $250.00. Courtesy McMasters Harris Doll Auctions.

25" bisque mold 1361 baby, marked "ABG (entwined//1361//62//Made in Germany//18" on back of head, human hair wig, brown flirty sleep eyes with tin lids, real lashes, painted lashes, feathered brows, pierced nostrils, open mouth, two upper teeth, wobble tongue, bent-limb composition baby body, working crier, antique baby dress with embroidery trim, antique baby bonnet, baby diaper cover, new socks, circa 1910+, $450.00. Courtesy McMasters Harris Doll Auctions.

Character Child, ca. 1910+

Mold 1357, ca. 1912, solid dome or wigged, painted eyes, open mouth; **Mold 1358, ca. 1910,** molded hair, ribbon, flowers, painted eyes, open mouth

15"	$750.00	$975.00
20"	$1,250.00	$1,700.00

Mold 1322, 1342, 1352, 1361, glass eyes

12"	$325.00	$425.00
14"	$375.00	$500.00
18"	$500.00	$650.00

Mold 1362, ca. 1912, Sweet Nell, more for flapper body

14"	$335.00	$450.00
20"	$400.00	$525.00
26"	$600.00	$800.00

Mold 1367, 1368, ca. 1914

15"	$355.00	$475.00

SHOULDER HEADS, BISQUE, CA. 1880+

Mold 639, 698, 784, 870, 890, 911, 912, 916, 990, 1000, 1008, 1028, 1032, 1044, 1046, 1064, 1123, 1127, 1142, 1210, 1234, 1235, 1254, 1304, cloth or kid body, bisque lower limbs, molded hair or wig, no damage and nicely dressed. Allow more for molded hat or fancy hairdo.

> Mark:
> 1000 # 10

Glass eyes, closed mouth

11"	$400.00	$550.00
15"	$500.00	$750.00
18"	$750.00	$1,000.00
21"	$925.00	$1,250.00

Painted eyes, closed mouth

14"	$300.00	$385.00
21"	$485.00	$650.00

Turned Bisque Shoulder Heads, 1885+

Bald head or plaster pate, kid body, bisque lower arms, all in good condition, nicely dressed. Dolls marked "DEP" or "Germany" after 1888. Some have Wagner & Zetzsche marked on head, paper label inside top of body. Allow more for molded bonnet or elaborate hairdo.

Closed mouth, glass eyes

18"	$600.00	$800.00
21"	$775.00	$1,050.00

Open mouth

15"	$300.00	$400.00
18"	$375.00	$500.00
22"	$490.00	$650.00

SHOULDER HEADS, CHINA, CA. 1880+

Mold 639, 698, 784, 870, 890, 912, 974, 990, 1000, 1008, 1028, 1032, 1044, 1046, 1064, 1112, 1123, 1127, 1142, 1210, 1222, 1234, 1235, 1254, 1304, cloth or kid body, bisque lower limbs, molded hair or wig, no damage and nicely dressed. Allow more for molded hat or fancy hairdo.

15"	$275.00	$365.00
19"	$318.00	$425.00
23"	$395.00	$525.00
28"	$475.00	$625.00

Amberg, Louis & Sons

Ca. 1878 – 1930, Cincinnati, Ohio; from 1898 on, New York City. Used other name before 1907. Imported dolls made by other firms. First company to manufacture all American-made composition dolls.

BISQUE

Baby Peggy, ca. 1924

Bisque socket head, sleep eyes, closed mouth, original wig with bangs, dimples, composition or kid body with bisque lower arms

Mold 972, solemn socket head; Mold 973, smiling socket head

Baby Peggy Mark:
"19 ©. 24//LA & S NY// GERMANY"

Newborn Babe Marks:
"L.A.&S. 1914/G45520 GER-MANY, L. AMBERG AND SON/7886" or
"COPYRIGHT By LOUIS AMBERG"

Body Twist Tag attached to clothes reads:
"AN AMBERG DOLL/ BODY TWIST/PAT. PEND. #32018."

17"	$1,725.00	$2,300.00
22"	$1,995.00	$2,650.00

Mold 982, solemn shoulder head; Mold 983, smiling shoulder head

17"	$1,800.00	$2,400.00
22"	$2,100.00	$2,800.00

BABY PEGGY, ALL-BISQUE, see All-Bisque section.
MIBS, ALL-BISQUE, 1921, see All-Bisque section.

Newborn Babe, ca. 1914, reissued 1924

Bisque head with cloth body; either celluloid, composition, or rubber hands; lightly painted hair; sleep eyes; closed mouth with protruding upper lip

8"	$275.00	$365.00
11"	$325.00	$425.00
14"	$400.00	$550.00
18"	$655.00	$825.00

Open mouth, marked "L.A.& S. 371"

10"	$300.00	$400.00
15"	$340.00	$450.00

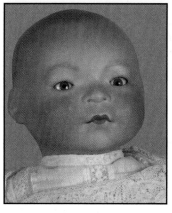

16" newborn babe, solid dome bisque flange head, blue sleep eyes, softly blushed brows, painted upper and lower lashes, accented nostrils, closed mouth, lightly molded and painted hair, cloth body with celluloid hands and curved legs, marked: "©LA & S 1914//#G 45520//Germany #4 on back of head, antique white lace-trimmed dress, slip, and diaper, $275.00. Courtesy McMasters Harris Doll Auctions.

Charlie Chaplin Mark: Black suit, white suit, cloth label on sleeve or inside seam of coat that reads: CHARLIE CHAPLIN DOLL// World's Greatest Comedian// Made exclusively by Louis Amberg//&Son, NY//by Special Arrangement with//Essanay Film Co.

Edwina Sue Mark: AMBERG PAT. PEN. L.A. & S.

Mibs Mark: Original dress has ribbon label that reads: "L.A.&S.//Amberg Dolls//The World Standard//Created by//Hazel Drukker//Please Love Me/I'm MIBS."

Sunny Orange Maid Mark on head: "A.//L.A. & S.//1924." Label on dress reads: "SUNNY ORANGE MAID."

Vanta Baby, ca. 1927 – 1930

Bisque head, sleep eyes, crier, bent-limb body, in sizes from 10" to 25", distributed by Sears with advertising promotion for Vanta baby garments

Glass eyes, open mouth

18"	$825.00	$1,100.00
21"	$950.00	$1,275.00

Closed mouth

18"	$1,050.00	$1,400.00
24"	$1,500.00	$2,000.00

COMPOSITION

First price is for doll in good condition, but with flaws, crazing, or nude; second price is for doll in excellent condition, may have light crazing, original or appropriate clothing.

Baby Peggy, ca. 1923

Portrait doll of child actress, Peggy Jean Montgomery; composition head, arms, and legs; cloth body; molded brown bobbed hair; painted eyes with molded lower eyelids; closed mouth. More for boxed, mint.

15"	$85.00	$365.00
18"	$125.00	$500.00
20"	$200.00	$775.00

Body Twists (Teenie Weenies, Tiny Tots), ca. 1929

All-composition with swivel waist made with ball attached to torso, boy or girl with molded hair and painted features

7½ – 8½"	$50.00	$200.00

Charlie Chaplin, ca. 1915

Composition portrait head, painted features, composition hands, cloth body and legs

14"	$175.00	$650.00

Edwina (Sue or It), ca. 1928

All-composition with painted features, molded hair with side part and swirl bang across forehead, body twist (waist swivels on ball attached to torso)

14"	$125.00	$475.00

Happinus, 1918+

Coquette-type, all-composition with head and body molded in one-piece, jointed shoulders and hips, molded and painted brown hair, molded ribbon, closed mouth, painted features, unmarked, well modeled torso, original clothes

10"	$75.00	$300.00

Mibs, ca. 1921

Composition turned shoulder head designed by Hazel Drukker, molded and painted hair, painted eyes, closed mouth. Two different body styles: cork-stuffed cloth, composition arms and legs with molded shoes, painted socks; and a barefoot, swing-leg, mama-type cloth body with crier.

16"	$225.00	$900.00

Sunny Orange Maid, 1924

For a photo of Sunny Orange Maid, see 1997 edition.

Composition shoulder plate, cloth body, composition arms and legs, molded orange cap

14½"	$400.00	$1,200.00

Vanta Baby, ca. 1927 – 1930

Composition head, sleep eyes, crier, bent-limb body, in sizes from 10" to 25", distributed by Sears with advertising promotion for Vanta baby garments

18"	$75.00	$275.00
23"	$100.00	$400.00

13" Charlie Chaplin, composition head and hands, painted features, cloth body stuffed with excelsior, cloth tag on coat sleeve reads "Charlie Chaplin Doll//World's Greatest Comedian//Made Exclusively By Louis Amberg & Son, NY//By Special Arrangement with Essanay Film Co." circa 1915, $450.00+. Courtesy Debbie Crume.

Arnold, Max Oscar

Ca. 1878 – 1925, Neustadt, Thuringia. Made jointed dressed dolls and mechanical dolls including phonograph dolls.

BABY, BISQUE HEAD

12"	$125.00	$165.00
16"	$215.00	$285.00
19"	$375.00	$500.00

CHILD, MOLD 150, 200, 201, 250, OR "M.O.A."

Excellent bisque

12"	$190.00	$250.00
15"	$265.00	$350.00
21"	$450.00	$600.00
32"	$1,150.00*	

Poor to medium quality bisque

15"	$125.00	$165.00
20"	$200.00	$300.00
24"	$340.00	$450.00

Mark:

21" bisque socket head by Max Oscar Arnold for Welsch, dolly face, jointed composition body, marked "MOA (in star)//200 Welsch//Made in Germany" circa 1920, $500.00. Courtesy Ellen Cummings.

10½" x 13", no marks, pale bisque head with straight neck on bisque shoulder plate, set pale blue eyes, multi-stroke brows, painted upper and lower lashes, accented nostrils, closed mouth, pierced-in ears, carton torso, composition legs, wire upper arms, bisque lower arms, white peasant blouse, red/white striped skirt, white apron, underclothing, black crocheted shawl, antique white bonnet, wooden shoes, key is missing, doll switches cow and cow and girl turn heads, $3,100.00. Courtesy McMasters Harris Doll Auctions.

Various manufacturers used many different mediums including bisque, wood, wax, cloth, and others to make dolls that performed some action. More complicated models performing more or complex actions bring higher prices. The unusual one-of-a-kind dolls in this category make it difficult to provide a good range. *All these auction prices are for mechanicals in good working order.

Autoperipatetikos, circa 1860 – 1870s
Bisque by American Enoch Rice Morrison, key wound mechanism
        12" $1,000.00*

Ballerina
Bisque Simon & Halbig mold 1159, key rotates head and arms lower, leg extends, keywound, Leopold Lambert, ca. 1900
        23" $4,250.00*

Bébé Automate Respirant
Bisque Bru Jne R socket head, fully jointed body, keywound mechanism in torso, eyelids open and close, bellows allow to breathe, by Paul Girard for Maison Bru, ca. 1892
        20" $9,000.00*

Bébé Cage
Bisque Jumeau mold 203, keywound, turns head, hand gives berry to bird, bird flies, one tune, Leopold Lambert, ca. 1890
        19" $13,500.00*

Bébé Eventail
Bisque Tete Jumeau, keywound, moves head, lifts flower and fan, plays "La Mascotte," blue silk costume, Leopold Lambert, ca. 1890
        19" $12,500.00*

Bébé Piano
Bisque Jumeau, socket head, carton body, plays piano with four tunes, keywound, Leopold Lambert, ca. 1886
        20" $31,000.00*

Bébé with Fan and Flowers
Bisque Tete Jumeau, keywound, moves hand, fans herself, sniffs flower, plays "Le Petit Bleu," Leopold Lambert, ca. 1892
        19" $16,500.00*

Garden Tea Party
Three bisque children, painted eyes, move head and arms at tea table on 9" x 9" base

12" $3,050.00*

Laughing Girl with Kitten
Bisque laughing Jumeau socket head, carton torso, keywound mechanism, turns head, smells flower, kitten pulls ribbon, Leopold Lambert, ca. 1890

20" $10,000.00*

Little Girl with Marionette Theater
French bisque socket head, keywound, head moves, lifts curtain, stage rotates, shows five different players, Renou, ca. 1900

16½" $16,500.00*

Waltzing Lady with Mandolin
Bisque socket head, carton body, rotates, turns head, strums mandolin, keywound, Alexandre Theroude, ca. 1865

15" $8,000.00*

Averill, Georgene

Ca. 1915+ New York City, New York. Georgene Averill made composition and cloth dolls operating as Madame Georgene Dolls, Averill Mfg. Co., Georgene Novelties, and Madame Hendren. The first line included dressed felt dolls, Lyf-Lyk, the patented Mama Doll in 1918, and the Wonder line. She designed dolls for Borgfeldt, including Bonnie Babe.

First price indicates doll in good condition, some flaws; second price doll in excellent condition, original clothes, or appropriately dressed.

> *Tag on original outfit reads:* "BONNIE BABE COPYRIGHTED BY GEORGENE AVERILL MADE BY K AND K TOY CO."
>
> *Mark:*
> COPR GEORGENE AVERILL
> 1005/3652 GERMANY

BISQUE

Bonnie Babe, ca. 1926 – 1930+
Designed by Georgene Averill, distributed by Borgfeldt. Bisque head, open mouth, two lower teeth, composition arms (sometimes celluloid) and legs on cloth body

Mold 1005, 1368, 1402

12"	$865.00	$1,150.00
14 – 15"	$1,075.00	$1,450.00
Celluloid head		
10"	$300.00	$500.00
16"	$350.00	$675.00

16" bisque Bonnie Babe, marked "Copr. By Georgene Averill//7005 13652//Germany" on back of head, "Bonnie Babe//Copyrighted//Georgene Averill//Made by K and K Toy Co." on tag on bib, solid dome bisque flange head, brown sleep eyes, softly blushed brows, painted lashes, open mouth, molded tongue, lightly molded and painted hair, cloth body, composition arms and legs, original blue romper, tagged lace-trimmed bib, matching bonnet, original socks and shoes, circa 1926 – 1930+, $400.00. Courtesy McMasters Harris Doll Auctions.

ALL-BISQUE BONNIE BABE, see All-Bisque section.

CLOTH, 1930+

Mask face with painted features, yarn hair, cloth body

12"	$40.00	$125.00
15"	$70.00	$150.00
22"	$85.00	$295.00
24"	$115.00	$335.00

Characters designed by Maud Tousey Fangel, ca. 1938, Peggy-Ann, Snooks, and Sweets

13"	$350.00	$675.00
17"	$450.00	$875.00
22"	$900.00	$1,150.00

Animals, ca. 1930s

B'rer Rabbit, Fuzzy Wuzzy, Nurse Jane, Uncle Wiggly, etc.

18"	$175.00	$650.00+

Krazy Kat, 1916, felt, not jointed

14"	$90.00	$350.00
18"	$125.00	$500.00

Brownies and Girl Scouts

14"	$85.00	$275.00

Comic Characters

Alvin, Little Lulu, Nancy, Sluggo, Tubby Tom, 1944 – 1961, with mask and painted features

13 – 14"	$500.00+

Little Lulu, in cowgirl outfit

16½"	$585.00

Becassine, 1950s, French cartoon character

13"	$500.00	$750.00

Dolly Dingle, 1923+, designed by Grace Drayton

12 – 14"	$115.00	$450.00

Tear Drop Baby, one tear painted on cheek

16"	$60.00	$335.00

COMPOSITION

First price is for doll in good condition but with flaws; second price is for doll in excellent condition with original clothes or appropriately dressed. Add more for boxed with tags or exceptional dolls.

Patsy-type, 1928+

All-composition, with jointed arms and legs, molded or wigged hair, painted or sleep eyes, open or closed mouth, all in good condition, original clothing

14"	$250.00	$300.00
17"	$325.00	$350.00

Baby Georgene or Baby Hendren

Composition head, arms, and lower legs; cloth body with crier; and marked with name on head

16"	$85.00	$275.00
20"	$95.00	$335.00
26"	$200.00	$600.00

Character or Ethnic
Composition head, cloth or composition body, character face, painted features, composition arms and legs. Whistlers, such as Whistling Dan, Sailor, Indian, Dutch Boy had bellows inside body. When pushed down on feet bellows created a whistling sound. Clothes often felt.

12"	$40.00	$150.00
16"	$75.00	$300.00

Black

14"	$125.00	$450.00

Dolly Reckord, 1922 – 1928
Composition head, arms, and legs; human hair wig; sleep eyes; open mouth and teeth; record player in torso

26"	$250.00	$650.00

Mama Doll, 1918+
Composition shoulder head and arms, cloth torso with crier, composition swing legs, molded hair or mohair wig, painted or sleep eyes, good condition, original clothes

15 – 18"	$200.00	$300.00
20 – 22"	$400.00	$500.00

Snookums, 1927
Child star of Universal-Stern Bros. movie comedies, has laughing mouth, two rows of teeth, pants attached to shirt with safety pin

14"	$100.00	$375.00

14" composition Snookums, child star of Universal-Stern Bros. movie comedies, "The Newlyweds and Their Baby" portrayed by Sunny McKeen, molded and painted blond hair with hole for missing tuft of real hair, painted blue eyes, open/closed laughing mouth with painted upper and lower teeth, cloth body and legs, marked "MADAME HENDREN/ /DOLL" on shoulder plate, green and white silk romper is melting, circa 1927, $325.00. Private collection.

Bähr & Pröschild

Ca. 1871 – 1930+, Ohrdruf, Thuringia, Germany. This porcelain factory made china, bisque, and celluloid dolls, as well as doll parts and Snow Babies. They made dolls for Kley & Hahn, Bruno Schmidt, Wiesenthal, Schindel & Kallenberg.

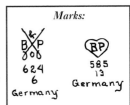

Marks:

BABY, CHARACTER FACE, 1909+
Bisque socket head, solid dome or wigged, bent leg, sleep eyes, open mouth

Mold 585, 586, 587, 602, 604, 619, 620, 624, 630, 641, 678

13"	$355.00	$475.00
17"	$500.00	$675.00
22"	$650.00	$875.00

Toddler body

18"	$750.00	$1,000.00
20"	$1,200.00	$1,600.00

Mold 526, other series 500, and 2023, 2072, or marked BP baby body, open closed mouth

14"	$2,100.00	$2,800.00
18"	$2,625.00	$3,500.00

15" mold #678 Baby, bisque socket head, blue sleep eyes, feathered brows, painted upper and lower lashes, accented nostrils, open mouth, two upper teeth, antique mohair wig, composition bent-limb baby body, marked "678//7//BP (in heart)//Made in//Germany" on back of head, "Made in Germany" stamped in red on lower back, pale pink baby dress, new underclothing, socks, and shoes, $275.00. Courtesy McMasters Harris Doll Auctions.

CHILD

Belton-type or Dome head
Mold 200 series, with small holes, socket head or shoulder plate, composition or kid body

12"	$1,300.00	$1,750.00
16"	$1,550.00	$1,900.00
24"	$2,350.00	$3,100.00

Child, open or closed mouth
Mold 200 and 300 series, full cheeks, jointed composition German body, French-type, or kid body

Mold Numbers 204, 224, 239, 246, 252, 273, 274, 275, 277, 286, 289, 293, 297, 309, 325, 332, 340, 379, 394

9"	$1,450.00* Mold 204	
14"	$510.00	$675.00
17"	$600.00	$800.00
23"	$825.00	$1,100.00

Mold 224, open mouth, dimpled cheeks

15"	$715.00	$950.00
23"	$1,050.00	$1,400.00

Child, kid body, open mouth

16"	$300.00	$400.00
24"	$510.00	$675.00

Mold 642, character, open mouth

17"	$2,700.00*

Mold 520, character, closed mouth

13"	$2,500.00*

Mold 247, character, open/closed mouth

26"	$2,100.00*

Ca. 1844 – 1877, Paris, France. Dolls marked "E.B." are attributed to this early manufacturing firm that used bisque and china heads with that mark. It is not known who made the heads for them. Bisque shoulder head with glass or painted eyes, closed mouth, kid body, may have wooden and bisque arms, good condition. China head has painted eyes and painted, molded hair. Exceptional dolls may be more.

Marks:			
E 3 B		12"	$1,500.00	$2,000.00
E. 8 DEPOSE **B.**		13"	$2,500.00	$3,000.00

12"	$1,500.00	$2,000.00
13"	$2,500.00	$3,000.00

Fashion Type
Pressed bisque head, glass eyes, cloth or kid body

15"	$2,500.00	$3,300.00
15"	$10,000.00* with trousseau	
21"	$3,500.00	$4,600.00

Bathing Beauties, ca. 1920. All-bisque figures, usually one piece, in various poses, were made by most porcelain factories in Germany and the U.S. in the 1920s. Beautifully detailed features, undressed or molded-on clothing or dressed in bathing costumes. All in excellent condition, no chips or damage.

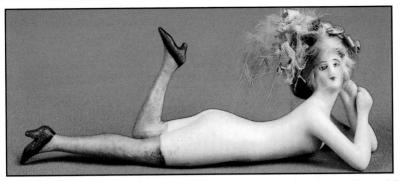

1¾" tall all-bisque Bathing Beauty, marked "1740 2/0 B" on bottom of right leg, 4½" long, delicate painted pale blue eyes with red accent line, single stroke brows, closed mouth, original mohair with ribbon-trimmed hat, unjointed body in lying position with hands coming up to face, left leg bent at knee, painted gray calf-high stockings, dark gray molded and painted high heels, circa 1920s, $400.00. Courtesy McMasters Harris Doll Auctions.

Painted eyes

3"	$150.00	$300.00
6"	$300.00	$500.00

Reclining woman

Lying on stomach, painted features, orange suit, marked "Germany," holding up fruit in one hand

4"	$325.00*

Wigged, painted features, silver mesh suit and hat, legs crossed

5"	$700.00*

Seated woman, nude, painted features, putting on slipper

4¾"	$550.00*

With animal

5½"	$1,125.00	$1,500.00

Two modeled together

4½ – 5½"	$1,600.00+

Action figures

5"	$340.00	$450.00+
7½"	$490.00	$650.00

Wigged action figure

7"	$450.00	$600.00

Marked Japan

3"	$50.00	$75.00
5 – 6"	$65.00	$100.00
9"	$125.00	$175.00

Belton Type

Marks: None, or may have Mold 100, 116, 117, 120, 125, 127, 137, 154, 183, 185, 190, or others.

Ca. 1870+. No dolls marked "Belton" found; only mold numbers. Belton-type refers to small holes found in tops of solid bisque head dolls; holes were used for stringing. Used by various German firms such as Bähr & Pröschild, Limbach, and Simon & Halbig. Socket head, paperweight eyes, wood and composition jointed French-type body with straight wrists, appropriately dressed in good condition.

* at auction

17½" Bahr & Proschild #204, bisque socket head with flat area with three holes on top, set brown eyes, heavy feathered brows, painted upper and lower lashes, accented nostrils, open-closed mouth, pierced ears, old mohair wig, jointed wood and composition body with straight wrists, wooden upper arms and upper legs, well-modeled torso, marked "204//11" on back of head, white factory chemise trimmed with blue lace, pants, new black socks and shoes, $1,400.00. Courtesy McMasters Harris Doll Auctions.

Bru-type face
14"	$1,800.00	$2,400.00
18"	$2,200.00	$2,925.00

French-type face, Mold 137, 183
9"	$900.00	$1,200.00
12"	$1,500.00	$2,000.00
16"	$1,775.00	$2,350.00
20"	$2,250.00	$3,050.00
24"	$2,800.00	$3,700.00

German-type face
9"	$800.00	$1,100.00
12"	$900.00	$1,250.00
18"	$1,450.00	$1,950.00
23"	$2,050.00	$2,750.00
25"	$2,250.00	$3,000.00

Bergmann, C.M.

29" bisque socket head, blue sleep eyes, molded and feathered brows, painted lashes, accented nostrils, open mouth, four upper teeth, pierced ears, original human hair wig, jointed wood and composition body, marked "C.M. Bergmann//Simon & Halbig//13 1/2" on back of head, pale green taffeta dress, lace bonnet, antique underclothing, socks, and center-snap leatherette shoes, $500.00. Courtesy McMasters Harris Doll Auctions.

Ca. 1889 – 1930+, Thuringia, Germany. Made dolls, but also used heads made by Alt, Beck & Gottschalck, Armand Marseille, and Simon & Halbig.

Mark:
C.M.B
SIMON & HALBIG
Eleonore

Baby
Mold 612, open/closed mouth
14"	$1,150.00	$1,600.00
15"	$2,200.00*	

Character Baby, open mouth, socket head, five-piece bent-leg body
14"	$245.00	$325.00
18"	$435.00	$575.00
21"	$525.00	$700.00

Child
Head by A.M., or unknown maker, open mouth, wig, jointed composition body
10"	$275.00	$375.00
15"	$300.00	$400.00
20"	$335.00	$450.00
23"	$425.00	$535.00

* at auction

30"	$900.00*	
34"	$1,000.00	$1,400.00
42"	$1,575.00	$2,100.00

Mold 1916 and other heads by Simon & Halbig

14"	$300.00	$400.00
19"	$375.00	$500.00
23"	$475.00	$650.00
28"	$675.00	$900.00
33"	$900.00	$1,200.00

Eleonore

| 18" | $490.00 | $650.00 |
| 25" | $640.00 | $850.00 |

Lady, flapper-style body with thin arms and legs

| 12" | $470.00 | $625.00 |
| 16" | $1,125.00 | $1,500.00 |

Bisque, Unknown or Little Known Maker

ENGLISH

Diamond Tile Co. Ltd., 1933 – 1943, Stoke-on-Trent, Staffordshire, England

| 12" | $200.00 |

Too few in database for reliable range.

FRENCH

Ca. 1870+. A number of French doll makers produced unmarked dolls with only a size number, Paris, or France. Many are also being attributed to German makers who produced for the French trade. Also included here are little known companies that produced wonderful rarely seen dolls. Unmarked, pressed bisque socket head, closed or open/closed mouth, paperweight eyes, pierced ears, excellent quality bisque and finely painted features, on French wood and composition body with straight wrists. No damage, appropriately dressed.

Unknown Maker

Early desirable very French-style face. Marks such as *"J.D."* (possible J. DuSerre) *"J.M. Paris,"* and *"H. G."* (possibly Henri & Granfe-Guimonneau).

17"	$12,750.00	$17,000.00+
21"	$15,750.00	$21,000.00+
27"	$20,250.00	$27,000.00+

Jumeau or Bru style face, may be marked *"W. D."* or *"R. R."*

14"	$1,900.00	$2,650.00
19"	$2,400.00	$3,175.00
24"	$3,775.00	$5,050.00
27"	$4,000.00	$5,350.00

Closed mouth, Marks: *"F.1," "F.2," "J," "137," "136,"* or others
Excellent quality, unusual face

| 10" | $1,250.00 | $1,700.00 |
| 15" | $3,000.00 | $4,000.00 |

8½" French bisque, marked "39.17//S" in old, possibly original, sailor outfit, possibly Edmond Hieuille, circa 1917, $750.00+. Private collection.

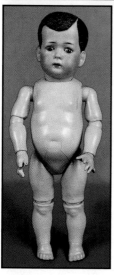

14" German character, solid dome bisque socket head, set blue eyes, feathered brows, painted upper and lower lashes, accented nostrils, closed mouth, original flocked hair, jointed wood and composition toddler body with diagonal hip joints, marked "Made in Germany," stamped in red on middle of back, lace-trimmed ecru shirt, brown corduroy jacket and pants trimmed with green braid, cotton striped socks, new black leather shoes, $800.00. Courtesy McMasters Harris Doll Auctions.

18"	$3,600.00	$4,750.00
23"	$4,500.00	$6,000.00
27"	$5,250.00	$7,000.00

Standard quality, excellent bisque

13"	$1,825.00	$2,450.00
18"	$2,600.00	$3,450.00
23"	$3,375.00	$4,500.00

Lesser quality, may have poor painting and/or blotches on cheeks

15"	$900.00	$1,200.00
21"	$1,350.00	$1,800.00
26"	$1,725.00	$2,300.00

Open mouth

Excellent quality, ca. 1890+, French body

15"	$1,125.00	$1,500.00
18"	$1,725.00	$2,300.00
21"	$1,800.00	$2,400.00
24"	$2,325.00	$3,100.00

High cheek color, ca. 1920s, may have five-piece papier-mâché body

15"	$475.00	$625.00
19"	$600.00	$800.00
23"	$725.00	$950.00

Known Makers

CSFJ, Chambre Syndicale des Fabricants de Jouets et Jeux et Engrins Sportif, 1886 – 1928+, Paris, France. Trade organization composed of French toy makers. Numbers refer to list of manufacturers. First price is for doll in good condition, but with flaws; second price indicates doll in excellent condition with original or appropriate clothing.

Child, closed mouth, excellent quality bisque

12"	$700.00	$925.00
16"	$975.00	$1,300.00

Danel & Cie, 1889 – 1895, Paris. Danel, once director of Jumeau factory, was sued by Jumeau for copying Bébés Jumeau.

Paris Bébé

Bisque socket head, appropriate wig, pierced ears, paperweight eyes, closed mouth, nicely dressed in good condition

> *Marks:*
> *E. (Size number)*
> *D. on head.*
> *Eiffel Tower*
> *"PARIS BEBE"*
> *on body; shoes with*
> *"PARIS BEBE"*
> *in star.*

First price is for doll in good condition, but with flaws; second price indicates doll in excellent condition with original or appropriate clothing.

19"	$4,500.00	$6,000.00
21"	$4,725.00	$6,500.00
29"	$16,500.00*	

* at auction

Delcrois, Henri, ca. 1865 – 1867

Bisque socket head, closed mouth, pierced ears, paperweight eyes, wig, marked *"PAN"* with size mark that varies with size of doll, wood and composition jointed French body

13"	$2,100.00	$3,000.00*

Too few in database for reliable range.

Halopeau, A, ca. 1880

Marked *"H,"* pressed bisque, open/closed or closed mouth, glass paperweight eyes, pierced ears, cork pate, French wood and composition body with straight wrists

21½"	$36,340.00*
22½"	$52,693.00*

Too few in database for reliable range.

J.M. marked Bébé, ca. 1880+

Socket head, closed mouth, pressed ears, French composition and wood body

13"	$5,000.00 – 7,000.00

Mascotte, 1882 – 1901

Trademark of May Freres Cie, using sizes similar to Bébés Jumeau. Became part of Jules Steiner in 1898. Bisque socket head, wig over cork pate, closed mouth, paperweight eyes, pierced ears, jointed composition French-style body.

> Marks:
> On head:
> MASCOTTE
> On body:
> Bébé Mascotte
> Paris
> Child marked:
> Mascotte on head

18"	$2,800.00	$3,750.00

Too few in database for reliable range.

18" K & K Toy Co. baby, bisque shoulder head, blue sleep eyes, feathered brows, painted upper and lower lashes, accented nostrils, open mouth with two upper teeth, original mohair wig, cloth body with composition lower arms and lower legs, organdy baby dress and lace-trimmed bonnet, underclothing, socks, and booties, marked "38" on back of head, "K & K//45//Made in Germany" on back of shoulder plate, $225.00. Courtesy McMasters Harris Doll Auctions.

Mothereau, ca. 1880 – 1895

Bébé Mothereau was made by Alexandre C. T. Mothereau patented a joint for doll bodies. Upper arms and legs of wood, lower arms and legs have rounded joint and metal bracket for stringing. Pressed bisque socket head, glass eyes, closed mouth, pierced ears, cork pate, jointed composition body, marked *B.M.*

Bébé

17½"	$23,000.00*

Too few in database for reliable range.

Pannier, ca. 1875

Marked *"C 8 P,"* pressed bisque head, closed mouth, glass paperweight eyes

20"	$57,986.00*

P.D., Frederic Petit & Andre Dumontier, 1878 – 1890, Paris

Made dolls with bisque heads from Francois Gaultier factory. Pressed bisque socket head, rounded face, glass eyes, closed mouth, pierced ears, wig over cork pate, French composition and wood jointed body

> Mark:
> P 3 D

19"	$10,000.00	$13,000.00
25"	$11,450.00	$15,250.00

15" closed-mouth German, bisque socket head, pale blue threaded paperweight eyes, feathered brows, painted upper and lower lashes, accented nostrils, closed mouth, pierced ears, replaced wig, early jointed composition body with separate balls at shoulders, elbows, hips, and knees, straight wrists and cupped hands, marked "3 1/2" on back of head, re-dressed in French-style outfit, new underclothing, socks, and lace boots, $750.00. Courtesy McMasters Harris Doll Auctions.

Radiguet & Cordonnier, ca. 1880

Marked *"R C Depose"* on breast plate, bisque head, shoulder plate with molded bosom, closed mouth, glass eyes, bent bisque arm, molded shoes

17" $9,993.00*

Too few in database for reliable range.

Rochard, Antoine Edmond, ca. 1868

Pressed bisque swivel head, open mouth, glass eyes, used multicolored Stanhope lenses with painted scenes as decorative jewelry

Head only

6¾" $24,530.00*

Too few in database for reliable range.

Rostal, Henri, 1914, Paris

Made a bisque socket head, open mouth, glass eyes, wood and composition jointed body. *Mark: "Mon Tresor"*

35" $2,500.00*

GERMAN, CA. 1860+

Unknown or little-known German factories

Marks: May be unmarked or only a mold or size number or Germany.

Baby – Newborn, ca. 1924+

Cloth body

Bisque head, molded/painted hair, composition or celluloid hands, glass eyes, good condition, appropriately dressed

11"	$225.00	$300.00
14"	$345.00	$450.00
17"	$450.00	$600.00

Baby

Composition body

Solid dome or wigged, five-piece baby body, open mouth, good condition, appropriately dressed

Glass eyes

10"	$200.00	$275.00
15"	$400.00	$550.00
20"	$525.00	$700.00

Painted eyes

11"	$150.00	$200.00
16"	$210.00	$315.00
18"	$340.00	$450.00

Allow more for closed, or open/closed mouth, unusual face, or toddler body.

Child

Character face, 1910+

Glass eyes, closed or open/closed mouth. Unidentified, may have wig or solid dome, excellent quality bisque, good condition, appropriately dressed

15"	$2,800.00	$3,800.00
19"	$3,400.00	$4,600.00

Mold 111, glass eyes
  22" $16,500.00 $22,000.00+
Too few in database for reliable range.

Mold 128
  18" $6,250.00 $8,950.00+
Too few in database for reliable range.

Mold 163, painted eyes, closed mouth
  16" $900.00 $1,200.00
Too few in database for realiable range.

Child, closed mouth

Excellent bisque, appropriately dressed, jointed composition body

13"	$575.00	$765.00
16"	$800.00	$1,075.00
20"	$1,115.00	$1,350.00
24"	$1,450.00	$1,950.00

Kid, or cloth body, may have turned head, bisque lower arms

13"	$475.00	$625.00
15"	$650.00	$850.00
19"	$875.00	$1,150.00
23"	$1,000.00	$1,350.00

Child, open mouth, ca. 1880+

Dolly face, excellent pale bisque, glass eyes, jointed composition body

12"	$140.00	$190.00
15"	$220.00	$290.00
20"	$345.00	$455.00
25"	$440.00	$580.00
28"	$480.00	$630.00

Kid body

12"	$110.00	$145.00
15"	$135.00	$180.00
18"	$165.00	$215.00
22"	$200.00	$265.00

22" bisque shoulder head, blue glass eyes, heavy feathered brows, painted upper and lower lashes, accented nostrils, closed mouth, molded blond hair, new cloth body with bisque lower arms and lower legs, marked "196-10" along bottom of rear shoulder plate, redressed in ecru wool dress with lace and ribbon trim, underclothing, $600.00. Courtesy McMasters Harris Doll Auctions.

Molded hair doll, ca. 1880+

Bisque shoulder head with well modeled hair, often blond, painted or glass eyes, closed mouth with kid or cloth body, bisque lower arms, good condition, appropriately dressed. Mold 890, 1000, 1008, 1028, 1064, 1142, 1256, 1288 may be made by Alt, Beck & Gottschalck.

American Schoolboy, 1880+

Side-parted painted hair swept across forehead, glass eyes, closed mouth
Jointed composition body

11"	$950.00* original	
15"	$485.00	$650.00

Kid or cloth body

13"	$375.00	$500.00
15"	$400.00	$575.00
20"	$525.00	$700.00

Child or lady, molded hair or wigged, closed mouth

Glass eyes

8"	$145.00	$195.00
15"	$375.00	$500.00
19"	$650.00	$875.00
23"	$1,075.00	$1,450.00

Painted eyes

8"	$85.00	$115.00
15"	$245.00	$325.00
19"	$350.00	$475.00
23"	$575.00	$775.00

Decorated shoulder plate, fancy hairdo

Glass eyes

20"	$2,075.00	$2,750.00+

Painted eyes

22"	$1,800.00*

Smaller unmarked doll

Head of good quality bisque, glass eyes, on five-piece papier-mâché or composition body, good condition, appropriately dressed

Open mouth

6"	$140.00	$185.00
8"	$165.00	$225.00
10"	$235.00	$325.00

Jointed body

6"	$170.00	$225.00
8"	$250.00	$335.00
10"	$345.00	$460.00

Poorly painted

6"	$65.00	$85.00
9"	$95.00	$125.00
12"	$135.00	$175.00

Closed mouth

Jointed body

6"	$245.00	$325.00
8"	$300.00	$400.00
11"	$425.00	$575.00

Five-piece body

6"	$170.00	$235.00
9"	$245.00	$335.00
12"	$300.00	$415.00

JAPANESE, CA. 1914 – 1921+

Various Japanese firms such as Morimura and Yamato (marked *"Nippon"* or *"J.W."* from 1914 to 1921, after that were marked *"Japan"*) made dolls for export when supplies were cut off from Germany during World War I. Quality varies greatly.

First price indicates doll in good condition, but with flaws; second price is for doll in excellent condition, appropriately dressed or original clothes. Add more for boxed, tagged, or labeled.

* at auction

Baby, character face, ca. 1910+

Good to excellent quality bisque, well painted, nice body, and appropriately dressed

9"	$120.00	$155.00
11"	$160.00	$215.00
15"	$225.00	$300.00
19"	$400.00	$525.00
23"	$575.00	$765.00

Poor quality bisque

11"	$85.00	$115.00
15"	$125.00	$165.00
19"	$185.00	$250.00
23"	$300.00	$400.00

Gold Medal, marked Nippon

12"	$175.00	$250.00

25" Morimura Brothers child, brown mohair wig, glass eyes, open mouth with teeth, all original with box, $355.00+. Courtesy McMasters Harris Doll Auctions.

Hilda-type

Excellent quality, glass eyes, open mouth with two upper teeth

14"	$525.00	$700.00
17"	$635.00	$850.00

Poor quality bisque

14"	$85.00	$115.00
18"	$160.00	$215.00

Mold 600, marked *"Fy"*

13"	$285.00	$395.00
17"	$400.00	$535.00

Mark:

RUSSIAN

Juravlev & Kocheshkova, before the Revolution, ca. 1915+. Bisque socket head, sleep eyes, wig, jointed wood and composition body

26"	$400.00* with repair to head

Too few in database for reliable range.

Black or brown dolls can have fired-in color or be painted bisque, composition, cloth, papier-mâché, or other materials. The color can be from very black to a light tan. They can have the typical open mouth dolly faces or ethnic features. The quality of this group of dolls varies greatly and the prices will fluctuate with the quality.

10" black bisque Ernst Heubach mold 399 ethnic socket head, marked "Heubach Koppelsdorf//399 13/0 D.R.G.M.//Germany" on back of head, dark brown sleep eyes, painted lashes, accented nostrils, closed mouth, pierced ears with hoop earrings, lightly molded and painted black hair, bent-limb composition baby body, original "grass" skirt of red, brown, and white, circa 1930, $360.00. Courtesy McMasters Harris Doll Auctions.

7¼" Gebruder Kuhnlenz, brown bisque socket head, set brown eyes, single stroke brows, accented nostrils, open mouth with four upper teeth, light brown mohair over original black mohair on original pate, fully jointed wood and composition brown body, possibly original white dress, original underclothing, crocheted hat, marked "34//16" on back of head, $700.00. Courtesy McMasters Harris Doll Auctions.

The first price indicates doll in good condition, but with flaws, perhaps nude; the second price indicates doll in excellent condition with original clothes or appropriately dressed. Add more for boxed, labeled, tagged, or exceptional quality.

ALL-BISQUE

Glass eyes, head molded to torso

4 – 5"	$200.00	$385.00+

Swivel neck

5 – 6"	$300.00	$500.00+

Painted eyes, head molded to torso

5"	$125.00	$245.00

Swivel head

5"	$250.00	$500.00

French-type

4"	$300.00	$500.00

Marked by known maker such as J.D. Kestner or Simon & Halbig

6 – 7"	$975.00	$1,300.00

Automaton

Bisque standing man, key-wound, smoker

29"	$3,630.00*

Belton-type

Closed mouth

12"	$1,350.00	$1,800.00
15"	$2,025.00	$2,700.00

22" black Heinrich Handwerck girl, brown bisque socket head, brown sleep eyes, molded and feathered brows, painted upper and lower lashes, accented nostrils, open mouth with four upper teeth, pierced ears, black mohair wig, jointed wood and composition body painted brown, re-dressed in new red calico dress, antique underclothing and white pinafore, marked "Germany//Heinrich Handwerch//Simon & Halbig//3 1/2" on back of head, $1,900.00. Courtesy McMasters Harris Doll Auctions.

BISQUE, FRENCH

Bru (circle dot or Breveté)

13"	$6,000.00*
19"	$50,000.00*

Too few in database for reliable range.

Bru-Jne

23"	$26,250.00	$35,000.00+

Too few in database for reliable range.

E.D., open mouth

16"	$1,725.00	$2,300.00
22"	$1,950.00	$2,600.00

Fashion-type unmarked

Bisque shoulder head, kid body, glass eyes

14"	$1,500.00	$2,000.00+

Swivel neck, articulated body, original

16"	$9,750.00	$12,750.00

Shoulder head, original

16"	$4,500.00	$6,000.00

* at auction

F.G., open/closed mouth

Kid body, swivel neck

14"	$1,800.00	$2,400.00
17"	$2,800.00	$3,800.00

French, unmarked or marked DEP

Closed mouth

11 – 12"	$1,350.00	$1,800.00+
15"	$2,250.00	$3,000.00
20"	$3,150.00	$4,200.00

Open mouth

10"	$450.00	$600.00
15"	$825.00	$1,100.00
22"	$1,650.00	$2,200.00

Jumeau-type

Closed mouth

12"	$1,950.00	$2,600.00
15"	$2,700.00	$3,600.00
19"	$3,600.00	$4,800.00

Open mouth

12"	$825.00	$1,100.00
15"	$1,575.00	$2,100.00
19"	$2,400.00	$3,200.00

Painted bisque

Closed mouth

15"	$735.00	$975.00
20"	$800.00	$1,200.00

Open mouth

15"	$375.00	$500.00
20"	$750.00	$1,000.00

With ethnic features

18"	$3,450.00	$4,600.00+

Jumeau

Tête Jumeau, closed mouth

15"	$3,525.00	$4,700.00
18"	$3,825.00	$5,100.00
23"	$4,575.00	$6,100.00

Open mouth

10"	$1,650.00	$2,200.00
15"	$2,025.00	$2,700.00
18"	$2,250.00	$3,000.00
23"	$2,625.00	$3,500.00

E. J., closed mouth

15"	$6,200.00	$8,200.00+
17"	$7,000.00	$9,300.00+
19"	$31,000.00*	

Paris Bébé

16"	$3,450.00	$4,600.00
19"	$4,125.00	$5,500.00

S.F.B.J.

Mold 226

16"	$2,175.00	$2,900.00

8¼" Jules Steiner bébé, brown bisque socket head, brown paperweight eyes, feathered brows, painted upper and lower lashes, accented nostrils, open mouth with four upper teeth, pierced ears, mohair wig, jointed wood and composition body, red/black striped antique dress, antique underclothing, socks, and shoes, red/black/white chapeau, marked, "Le Parisien//Bte S.G.D.G.//A 1" on back of head, "Bébé Le Parisien//Medaille d'Or//Paris" stamped on front of left hip, $950.00. Courtesy McMasters Harris Doll Auctions.

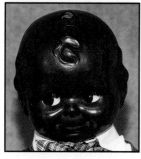

16" composition unmarked black boy, molded hair in tufts on top and sides, black side-glancing sleep eyes, real lashes, closed smiling mouth with red painted lips, jointed composition body, wearing white shirt, denim overalls, circa 1920s – 1930s, $2,300.00. Similar dolls such as this and the doll below, may sell for very different amounts in different areas of the country. Courtesy Anita Ladensack.

Mold 235, open/closed mouth

15"	$1,950.00	$2,600.00
17"	$2,212.50	$2,950.00

S & Q (Schuetzmeister & Quendt)

Mold 251

9"	$450.00	$600.00
15"	$1,500.00	$2,000.00

Mold 252, baby

20"	$1,250.00	$1,650.00

Child

20"	$1,350.00	$1,800.00

Jules Steiner

A series, closed mouth

18"	$4,425.00	$5,900.00
22"	$4,875.00	$6,500.00

Open mouth

13"	$3,225.00	$4,300.00
16"	$3,600.00	$4,800.00
21"	$5,750.00*	

C series

18"	$4,000.00	$6,000.00
21"	$4,650.00	$6,200.00

Unis France

Mold 301 or 60, open mouth

14"	$340.00	$450.00
17"	$600.00	$800.00

BISQUE, GERMAN

Unmarked

Closed mouth

10 – 11"	$225.00	$300.00
14"	$300.00	$400.00
17"	$395.00	$525.00
21"	$600.00	$800.00

Open mouth

10"	$375.00	$500.00
13"	$490.00	$650.00
15"	$640.00	$850.00

Painted bisque

Closed mouth

16"	$265.00	$350.00
19"	$375.00	$500.00

Open mouth

14"	$225.00	$300.00
18"	$375.00	$500.00

Ethnic features

15"	$2,250.00	$3,000.00
18"	$2,850.00	$3,800.00

Bähr & Pröschild, open mouth, mold 277, ca. 1891

10"	$525.00	$750.00
12"	$1,050.00*	

16" composition unmarked black girl, molded hair in tufts on top and sides, black side-glancing sleep eyes, real lashes, closed smiling mouth with red painted lips, jointed composition body, original white dress with flower print, circa 1920s – 1930s, $700.00. Courtesy Anita Ladensack.

* at auction

Bye-Lo Baby

16"	$2,250.00	$3,000.00

Cameo Doll Company

Kewpie (Hottentot) bisque

4"	$400.00
5"	$565.00
9"	$985.00

Composition

12"	$400.00
15"	$725.00

Papier-mâché

8"	$265.00

Scootles, composition, original outfit

13"	$750.00
13"	$1,050.00*

Handwerck, Heinrich, mold 79, 119

Open mouth

12"	$600.00	$800.00
18"	$1,200.00	$1,600.00
22"	$1,425.00	$1,900.00
29"	$1,950.00	$2,600.00

Heubach, Ernst (Koppelsdorf)

Mold 271, 1914, shoulder head, painted eyes, closed mouth

10"	$300.00	$475.00

Mold 320, 339, 350

10"	$325.00	$425.00
13"	$400.00	$535.00
18"	$525.00	$700.00

Mold 399, allow more for toddler

10"	$300.00	$400.00
14"	$415.00	$550.00
17"	$525.00	$700.00

Mold 414

9"	$340.00	$450.00
14"	$1,100.00*	
17"	$715.00	$950.00

Mold 418 (grin)

9"	$510.00	$675.00
14"	$650.00	$900.00

Mold 444, 451

9"	$300.00	$400.00
14"	$525.00	$700.00

Mold 452, brown

7½"	$285.00	$375.00
10"	$360.00	$475.00
15"	$510.00	$675.00

12" cloth Babyland Rag topsy-turvy, unmarked, white head, arms, and torso on one end, black head and arms on other end of torso, both faces are life-like with printed features, mitten hands, antique long white christening dress trimmed in lace, white chemise covers torso when white head shows; both heads wear new bonnets, circa 1912 – 1914, $405.00. Courtesy McMasters Harris Doll Auctions.

9" DeFuisseux mulatto, bisque socket head, painted brown eyes, single stroke brows, accented nostrils, closed mouth, mohair wig in coiled braids, five-piece composition body, factory ethnic-type red dress with black velvet bodice, panties, chemise, replaced socks, red leatherette tie shoes, marked "D.F.//B.//E. 4" on back of head, $350.00. Courtesy of McMasters Harris Doll Auctions.

Mold 458

10"	$350.00	$465.00
15"	$525.00	$700.00

Mold 463

12"	$475.00	$625.00
16"	$715.00	$950.00

Mold 1900

14"	$375.00	$500.00
17"	$450.00	$600.00

Heubach, Gebruder, Sunburst mark

Boy, eyes to side, open/closed mouth

12"	$1,875.00	$2,500.00

Mold 7657, 7658, 7668, 7671

9"	$950.00	$1,250.00
13"	$1,300.00	$1,800.00

Mold 7661, 7686

10"	$900.00	$1,200.00
14"	$1,950.00	$2,600.00
17"	$2,850.00	$3,800.00

Kammer & Reinhardt (K * R)

Child, no mold number

7½"	$340.00	$450.00
14"	$515.00	$675.00
17"	$660.00	$875.00
19"	$2,000.00*	

Mold 100

10"	$525.00	$700.00
14"	$825.00	$1,100.00
17"	$1,200.00	$1,600.00
20"	$1,785.00*	

Mold 101, painted eyes

15"	$3,300.00*	

Mold 101, glass eyes

17"	$3,700.75	$4,925.00

Mold 114

13"	$3,150.00	$4,200.00

Mold 116, 116a

15"	$2,250.00	$3,000.00
19"	$2,800.00	$3,725.00

Mold 122, 126, baby body

12"	$565.00	$750.00
18"	$845.00	$1,125.00

Mold 126, toddler

18"	$1,200.00	$1,600.00

Kestner, J. D.

Baby, no mold number, open mouth, teeth

10"	$1,500.00*	

Hilda, mold 245

12"	$2,100.00	$2,800.00
14"	$4,125.00	$5,500.00

Child, no mold number

Closed mouth

14"	$475.00	$625.00
17"	$715.00	$950.00

Open mouth

12"	$340.00	$450.00
16"	$490.00	$650.00

Five-piece body

9"	$215.00	$285.00
12"	$265.00	$350.00

Konig & Wernicke (KW/G)

14"	$900.00*	
18"	$565.00	$750.00

Ethnic features

17"	$750.00	$1,000.00

Kuhnlenz, Gebruder

Closed mouth

15"	$675.00	$900.00
18"	$1,350.00	$1,800.00

Open mouth, mold 34.14, 34.16, 34.24, etc.

3"	$725.00* boxed	
3½"	$450.00*	
6"	$700.00*	
12"	$415.00	$550.00

Ethnic features

16"	$3,000.00	$4,000.00

Marseille, Armand

No mold number, ebony

11"	$850.00*	

Mold 341, 351, 352, 362

10"	$300.00	$400.00
16"	$545.00	$825.00
20"	$925.00	$1,200.00

Mold 390, 390n

16"	$415.00	$550.00
19"	$585.00	$775.00
23"	$675.00	$895.00
25"	$2,200.00*	
28"	$825.00	$1,100.00

Mold 451, 458 (Indians)

9"	$265.00	$350.00
12"	$375.00	$500.00

27" handmade black rag doll, unmarked, made of dyed muslin, all soft-stuffed, unjointed neck, glass eyes, fur brows, applied nose, mouth, and ears, black hair attached with skin strips, original clothing of brown print plain dress, white slip and pants, black wool socks, $1,000.00. Courtesy McMasters Harris Doll Auctions.

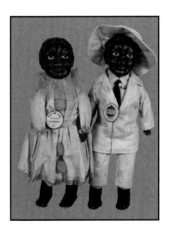

12½" and 13" pair composition ROL Ragtime Kids, papier-mâché brown heads with exaggerated ethnic features, painted brown eyes are slightly intaglio, accented nostrils, closed mouth, molded and painted black curly hair, cloth bodies with composition hands, black felt legs (boy has pink cloth legs) with long thin oilcloth feet, original clothing, marked "Ragtime Kids//(Name Registered)// 'Alexander'// Bavaria" on one side of round tag, "R.O.L.//Trade Mark" on other side of tag, $950.00. Courtesy McMasters Harris Doll Auctions.

15" cloth Playtime Indian doll with photographic face, yarn braids, white cloth torso, brown cloth arms and legs, wearing tagged "Playtime//Unbreakable" fringed brown Indian two-piece suit with faded felt moccasins, Rouech-Bowden Co., distributed by Louis Wolfe and Sons, 1906 – 1908, $500.00. Private collection.

Mold 966, 970, 971, 992, 995 (some in composition)

9"	$200.00	$265.00
14"	$415.00	$550.00
18"	$660.00	$875.00

Mold 1894, 1897, 1912, 1914

12"	$400.00	$525.00
14"	$550.00	$750.00
18"	$635.00	$850.00

Recknagel, *marked "R.A.," mold 126, 138*

16"	$545.00	$725.00
22"	$1,075.00	$1,430.00

Schoenau Hoffmeister (S PB H)

Hanna

8"	$285.00	$375.00
10 – 12"	$415.00	$550.00
15"	$525.00	$700.00
18"	$640.00	$850.00

Mold 1909

16"	$400.00	$525.00
19"	$525.00	$700.00

Simon & Halbig

Mold 639

14"	$5,100.00	$6,800.00
18"	$7,500.00	$10,000.00

Mold 739, open mouth

16"	$1,300.00	$1,800.00
22"	$2,250.00	$3,000.00

Closed mouth

13"	$1,500.00*	
17"	$1,950.00	$2,600.00

Mold 939, closed mouth

18"	$2,475.00	$3,300.00
21"	$3,375.00	$4,500.00

Open mouth

13"	$2,300.00* original outfit

Mold 949, closed mouth

18"	$2,550.00	$3,400.00
21"	$3,000.00	$3,950.00

Open mouth, fat cheeks

15"	$2,250.00	$3,000.00

Too few in database for reliable range.

Mold 1009, 1039, 1079, open mouth

11"	$1,600.00* mold 1009	
12"	$950.00	$1,250.00
16"	$1,250.00	$1,700.00
18"	$1,500.00	$2,000.00

9½" composition Effanbee Mammy has one-piece torso and head, wire spring upper arms, oversize molded boots attached to side of torso, hands fit metal carriage with rubber wheels (also comes with composition carriage), circa 1947+, $600.00. Courtesy Cornelia Ford.

Pull-string sleep eyes

19"	$1,725.00	$2,300.00

Mold 1248, open mouth

15"	$1,125.00	$1,500.00
16"	$4,100.00*	
18"	$1,350.00	$1,800.00

Mold 1272

20"	$1,600.00	$2,000.00

Mold 1302, closed mouth, glass eyes, character face

18"	$5,250.00	$7,000.00

Indian, sad expression, brown face

18"	$5,500.00	$7,400.00

Mold 1303, Indian, thin face, man or woman

16"	$4,574.00	$6,100.00
21"	$6,000.00	$8,000.00

Mold 1339, 1368

16"	$4,450.00	$5,900.00

Mold 1358, ca. 1910

23"	$1,900.00*

CELLULOID

The first price indicates doll in good condition, but with flaws, perhaps nude; the second price indicates doll in excellent condition with original clothes or appropriately dressed.

All-celluloid

10"	$150.00	$200.00
15"	$265.00	$350.00
18"	$400.00	$600.00

Celluloid shoulder head, kid body, add more for glass eyes

17"	$265.00	$350.00
21"	$340.00	$450.00

French-type, marked "SNF"

14"	$265.00	$350.00
18"	$400.00	$600.00

13" cloth Dean's Rag Golliwog, tagged "Dean's Gwentoy Group//Rye-Pontejpool" in mid back seam, sewn on black synthetic hair, red pants, yellow vest, black shoes with white spats form the body of the doll, removable blue felt jacket, with Robertson's Premium Golly Jar marked "50 GOLDEN YEARS//1930-1980//Robertson's Golly," jam jar marked "Golliberry Bramble Seedless," and Golly tokens, circa 1978, jar and Golly, $60.00; tokens, $6.00 each. Courtesy Ginger Reid.

Kammer & Reinhardt, mold 775, 778

11"	$150.00	$200.00
18"	$350.00	$475.00

CLOTH

The first price indicates doll in good condition, but with flaws, perhaps nude; the second price indicates doll in excellent condition with original clothes or appropriately dressed.

Alabama, see Cloth dolls section.

Bruckner, see Cloth dolls section.

1930s Mammy-type

14"	$85.00	$125.00
18"	$125.00	$275.00

Golliwog, 1895 to present

Character from 1895 book *The Adventures of Two Dutch Dolls and a Golliwogg*, all-cloth, various English makers. See also Cloth, Deans Rag.

1895 – 1920

13"	$375.00	$750.00

1930 – 1950

11"	$150.00	$300.00
15"	$250.00	$400.00

1950 – 1970s

13"	$150.00	$250.00
18"	$200.00	$400.00

Stockinette, oil-painted features

16"	$1,800.00	$2,400.00
22"	$2,475.00	$3,300.00

COMPOSITION

The first price indicates doll with heavy crazing, perhaps nude; the second price indicates doll in excellent condition, may have very fine crazing, with original clothes. More for boxed, labeled, or exceptional quality.

Unmarked, or unknown company

16"	$200.00	$600.00

Borgfeldt, Geo

Tony Sarg Mammy with baby

18"	$150.00	$600.00

Effanbee

Baby Grumpy

10"	$75.00	$300.00
16"	$115.00	$475.00

Bubbles

Light crazing, original clothing, very good condition

17"	$110.00	$450.00
22"	$165.00	$700.00

Candy Kid
With original shorts, robe, and gloves
| 12" | $75.00 | $300.00 |

Skippy, with original outfit
| 14" | $900.00* |

Horsman
| 12" | $475.00* |

Ideal
Marama, Shirley Temple body, from the movie, *Hurricane*
| 13" | $800.00* |

CHINA
Frozen Charlie/Charlotte
3"	$100.00	$135.00
6"	$190.00	$250.00
8 – 9"	$265.00	$350.00

Jointed at shoulder
| 3" | $150.00 | $200.00 |
| 6" | $265.00 | $350.00 |

HARD PLASTIC
Terri Lee, Patty-Jo
| 16" | $450.00 | $600.00 |
| 16" | $1,904.00* |

PAPIER-MÂCHÉ
Leo Moss, late 1880s – early 1900s
Papier-mâché or composition head and lower limbs, molded hair or wig, inset glass eyes, closed mouth, ethnic features with full lips, excelsior filled brown twill body, more with tear on check
| 17" | $3,700.00 | $5,500.00 |

Papier-mâché with ethnic features
| 8" | $210.00 | $275.00 |
| 17" | $625.00 | $825.00 |

Bonnet Head

1860 – 1940+. Heads of various materials with molded and painted bonnets, hats, or headgear.

ALL-BISQUE
German, one-piece body and head, painted or glass eyes
5"	$135.00	$175.00
7"	$175.00	$235.00
8"	$215.00	$285.00
10"	$285.00	$375.00

12" stone bisque Bonnet Head marked "Germany," painted blond hair with curls at the front and forehead ending in a fancy braided bun in back, unusual headdress with brown and coral colored accents, bisque lower arms with spoon hands, bisque lower legs with brown glazed boots, original cloth body, old clothes, bloomers, slip, circa 1880+, $80.00. Courtesy Travis Cannon.

* at auction

12" stone bisque Bonnet Head marked "Germany," pink bonnet with pink bows at the top brim, and neck, ruffles, blue painted eyes, blushed cheeks, original cloth slip-covered sawdust filled body, bisque lower arms with spoon hands, bisque lower legs with glazed brown heeled boots, re-dressed in old green dress, underwear, and bloomers, circa 1860+, $125.00. Courtesy Travis Cannon.

BISQUE

Painted eyes, bisque head, hat or bonnet
Five-piece papier-mâché, kid, or cloth body

7"	$75.00	$100.00
12"	$95.00	$125.00
20"	$225.00	$275.00

Glass eyss, bisque arms, jointed composition, kid or cloth body

7"	$150.00	$200.00
9"	$265.00	$350.00
12"	$365.00	$485.00
15"	$545.00	$725.00

Alt, Beck & Gottschalck
Glass eyes

18"	$2,907.00*

Painted eyes

18"	$1,430.00*

Handwerck, Max, WWI military figure, painted eyes, marked *"Elite"*

12"	$2,200.00*

Heubach, Gebruder, Baby Stuart, mold 7977

10"	$825.00	$1,100.00
15"	$1,125.00	$1,500.00

Japanese

8 – 9"	$55.00	$85.00
12"	$95.00	$135.00

Molded shirt or top

15"	$625.00	$825.00
21"	$1,015.00	$1,350.00

Recknagel, painted eyes

8"	$300.00	$450.00

Stone bisque

8 – 9"	$125.00	$165.00
12"	$170.00	$225.00
15"	$290.00	$385.00

Googly, see that section.

Borgfeldt & Co., George

Ca. 1881 – 1930+, New York. Assembled and distributed dolls. Used dolls from many companies and employed designers such as Rose O'Neill, Grace Corry, Grace Storey Putnam, Joseph L. Kallus, Georgene Averill, and others. Konig & Wernicke made dolls for Borgfeldt.

BISQUE BABY, 1910+
Five-piece bent-leg baby body, open mouth

10"	$225.00	$300.00
17"	$425.00	$575.00
27"	$675.00	$900.00+

Mold 251, 1915+

Made by Armand Marseille, character baby, closed mouth

17"	$3,100.00*

Baby BoKaye

Designed by Joseph Kallus, made by Alt, Beck & Gottschalk for Borgfelt, bisque molded hair, open mouth, glass eyes, cloth body, composition limbs, Mold 1394

11"	$1,700.00*	
15"	$1,725.00	$2,300.00
18"	$2,025.00	$2,700.00

Babykins, 1931

Made for Borgfeldt by Grace Storey Putnam, round face, glass eyes, pursed lips

14"	$735.00	$980.00
17"	$900.00	$1,190.00+

BISQUE CHILD, Mold 325, 327, 328, 329, or marked "G.B.," "My Girlie," "Pansy"

1910 – 1922, bisque head, fully jointed composition body, open mouth, good condition, and appropriately dressed

11"	$175.00	$250.00
14"	$200.00	$275.00
16"	$250.00	$375.00
19"	$350.00	$500.00
21"	$500.00	$650.00
24"	$425.00	$550.00

COMPOSITION

Hug Me, closed mouth, googly eyes

9"	$750.00*

23" bisque Pansy girl, set brown eyes, open mouth, four teeth, replaced human hair wig, jointed wood and composition body, redressed, marked "X// Pansy// IV// Germany" on back of head, circa 1921, $375.00. Courtesy McMasters Harris Doll Auctions.

```
251
G.B.
Germany
A 1 M
DRMR 2498
```

Boudoir Dolls

Ca. 1915 – 1940. Bed dolls, originally used as decorations to sit on the bed, usually French, with extra long arms and legs, heads of cloth, composition, ceramics, wax, and suede, mohair or silk floss wigs, painted features, some with real lashes, cloth or composition bodies, dressed in fancy period costumes. Other manufacturers were Italian, British, or American.

First price is for doll in good condition, but with minor flaws; second price indicates doll in excellent condition, original clothes. Add more for boxed, labeled, or exceptional quality. Less for nude, flaking, cracked.

Two 30" cloth Blossom Doll Co. dolls, mask face swivel heads, painted blue eyes, molded lids, long lashes, blond mohair wigs, cloth bodies with long limbs, jointed at shoulders and hips, high-heeled feet, original pink silk Pierrot outfits, one with skirt, one with pants, net ruffle around necks, pink cloth high heels with wooden heels, marked "Blossom Doll Co.//Inc.//New York City//NRA member//We Do Our Part" on label on underclothing, circa 1920s, $350.00. Courtesy McMasters Harris Doll Auctions.

Boudoir Dolls

Standard quality, dressed

16"	$95.00	$125.00
28"	$135.00	$175.00
32"	$175.00	$235.00

Excellent quality, with glass eyes

15"	$225.00	$300.00
28"	$365.00	$475.00
32"	$75.00	$500.00

Lenci

18 – 26"	$1,500.00	$2,250.00+

Smoker, cloth

16"	$215.00	$285.00
25"	$375.00	$525.00

Composition

25"	$185.00	$245.00
28"	$285.00	$375.00

Black

	$450.00	$600.00+

Bru

Bru Jne. & Cie, ca. 1867 – 1899. Paris and Montreuil-sous-Bous French factories, eventually succeeded by Société Francaise de Fabrication de Bébé & Jouets (S.F.B.J.) 1899 – 1953. Bébés Bru with kid bodies are one of the most collectible dolls, highly sought after because of the fine quality of bisque, delicate coloring, and fine workmanship.

Identifying characteristics: Brus are made of pressed bisque and have a metal spring stringing mechanism in the neck. Add more for original clothes and rare body styles.

Bébé Breveté, ca. 1879 – 1880

Pressed bisque swivel head, shoulder plate, mohair or human hair wig, cork pate, paperweight eyes, multi-stroke eyebrows, closed mouth with space between lips, full cheeks, pierced ears, kid or wooden articulated bodies.

First price is for doll in good condition, but with some flaws; second price is for doll in excellent condition, appropriately dressed, add more for original clothes and marked shoes.

14"	$10,000.00	$13,750.00
19"	$14,500.00	$18,500.00
20"	$20,000.00* original dress, labeled body	

Bru Jne, 1880 – 1891

Pressed bisque swivel head, deep shoulder molded breastplate, mohair or human hair wig, cork pate, paperweight eyes, multi-stroke eyebrows, open/closed mouth with molded and painted teeth, pierced ears, bisque lower arms, good condition, nicely dressed. Add more for original clothes and marked shoes.

12"	$8,750.00	$11,500.00
14"	$10,500.00	$14,000.00

Bru Jne Marks:
"BRE JNE," with size number on head, kid over wood body marked with rectangular paper label.

Bre Jne R. Marks:
"BRU. JNE R." with size number on head, body stamped in red, "Bébé Bru," and size number.

Bébé Breveté Marks:
"Bébé Breveté"
Head marked with size number only; kid body may have paper Bébé Breveté label.

* at auction

17"	$12,750.00	$17,000.00
21"	$17,500.00*	
23"	$23,500.00*	
27"	$19,250.00	$25,500.00

Bru Jne R, 1891 – 1899

Pressed bisque swivel head, mohair or human hair wig, cork pate, paperweight eyes, multi-stroke eyebrows, open mouth with four or six upper teeth or closed mouth, pierced ears, articulated wood and composition body, good condition, nicely dressed. Add more for original clothes.

Closed mouth

11"	$1,900.00	$2,500.00
14"	$2,900.00	$3,800.00
17"	$3,800.00	$5,000.00
19"	$4,300.00	$5,750.00
21"	$4,875.00	$6,500.00

Open mouth

12"	$1,100.00	$1,400.00
14"	$1,100.00	$1,500.00
16"	$1,600.00	$2,100.00
20"	$2,250.00	$3,000.00

Circle Dot Bébé, 1879 – 1883

Pressed bisque swivel head, deep shoulder molded breastplate, mohair or human hair wig, cork pate, paperweight eyes, multi-stroke eyebrows, open/closed mouth with molded and painted teeth, pierced ears, gusseted kid body, bisque lower arms, good condition, nicely dressed. Add more for original clothes.

11"	$9,000.00	$12,000.00
14"	$11,000.00	$14,000.00
16"	$14,500.00*	
18"	$13,500.00	$19,000.00
23"	$16,500.00	$22,000.00
26"	$18,750.00	$25,000.00

Fashion-type (poupee), 1867 – 1877+

Swivel head of pressed bisque, bisque shoulder plate, metal spring stringing mechanism in neck, kid body, painted or glass eyes, pierced ears, cork pate, mohair wig. Add more for original clothes.

| 12" | $2,300.00 | $3,050.00 |
| 15" | $2,500.00 | $3,300.00 |

Fashion-type (poupee), Smiler 1873+

Pressed bisque swivel head, shoulder plate, articulated wood with metal spring stringing mechanism in neck, wood and kid or kid gusseted lady body, cork pate, mohair or human hair wig, glass paperweight eyes, pierced ears, closed smiling mouth, nicely dressed. Add more for original clothes.

16" Bébé Têteur, bisque socket head on bisque shoulder plate, blue paperweight eyes, feathered brows, painted upper and lower lashes, accented nostrils, open nurser mouth, pierced ears, curly mohair wig, kid body with shaped bisque lower arms, gussets at hips and knees, marked "Bru. Jne//6" on back of head, "1/0" on left shoulder of shoulder, christening dress with lace inserts and lace trim, matching slip, diaper, knit booties, lacy bonnet, $3,000.00. Courtesy McMasters Harris Doll Auctions.

> *Circle Dot Bébé Mark:*
> *Head marked dot within a circle or half circle.*

> *Fashion-Type Mark:*
> *Marked "A" through "M," "11" to "28," indicating size numbers only*

Kid body, kid or bisque arms, allow more for wooden arms

13"	$2,250.00	$3,000.00
15"	$3,500.00*	
21"	$4,200.00	$5,600.00

Wood body

16"	$4,500.00	$6,000.00
18"	$5,500.00*	

Variants

Bébé Automate (breather, talker), 1892+

With key or lever in torso, activates talking and breathing mechanism

19"	$4,600.00*
24"	$17,000.00

Bébé Baiser (kiss thrower), 1892

With a simple pull-string mechanism, which allows doll's arm to raise and appear to throw kisses

11"	$4,100.00*

Bébé Gourmand (eater), 1880

Open mouth with tongue to take food, which fell into throat and out through bottom of feet, had shoes with specially designed hinged soles to take out food. Legs bisque from knees; used Breveté version

16"	$25,000.00+

Too few in database for reliable range.

Bébé Marchant (walker), 1892

Clockwork walking mechanism which allows head to move and talk, has articulated body with key in torso

17"	$6,800.00
21"	$7,400.00
25"	$9,500.00*

Bébé Modele, 1880+

Carved wooden body

19"	$19,000.00+

Too few in database for reliable range.

Bébé Têteur (nursing), 1879

Open mouth to insert bottle, usually with screw type key on back of head to allow the doll to drink

14"	$7,000.00
17"	$9,200.00
20"	$9,600.00

Accessories

Bru shoes (marked) $500.00 – 800.00+

Bye-Lo Baby

1922 – 1952. Designed by Grace Storey Putnam to represent a three-day-old baby, manufactured by various firms, such as Kestner; Alt, Beck & Gottschalck; Hertel & Schwab; and others; body made by K&K, a subsidiary of George Borgfeldt & Co., New York, the sole licensee. Composition Bye-Lo Babies made by Cameo Doll Company, and came in sizes 10", 12", 14", and 16½".

Mark:

© 1923 by
Grace S. Putnam
MADE INGERMANY
7372145

First price is for doll in good condition with some flaws; second price is for doll in excellent condition, nicely dressed, add more for tagged original clothes, labels, and pin-back button.

ALL-BISQUE

All-bisque versions made by J.D. Kestner were 4" to 8" and marked "G.S. Putnam" on back, with dark green sticker on chest that read "Bye-Lo Baby."

Painted eye

4"	$300.00	$400.00

Glass eye

5"	$400.00	$600.00

BISQUE HEAD

Bisque head, molded and painted hair, blue sleep eyes, closed mouth, flange neck, cloth baby-shaped ("frog") body, some stamped "Bye-Lo Baby," celluloid hands

Head circumference

8"	$350.00	$475.00
10"	$375.00	$500.00
12"	$400.00	$525.00
15"	$525.00	$650.00
17"	$975.00	$1,200.00

COMPOSITION HEAD

Molded and painted hair, sleep or painted eyes, closed mouth, cloth body. First price indicates doll with crazing, flaws; second price is for doll in excellent condition, with good color and original clothes, or appropriately dressed.

12"	$95.00	$375.00
16"	$150.00	$575.00

CELLULOID

All-celluloid

4"	$45.00	$165.00
6"	$100.00	$200.00

Celluloid head, cloth body

12"	$175.00	$350.00
15"	$245.00	$465.00

WAX

Poured, sold in a New York boutique, 1925

14½"	$2,100.00*

VARIATIONS

Fly-Lo Baby, 1926 – 1930+

Ceramic, bisque, or composition head, glass or metal sleep eyes, molded and painted hair, flange type neck, cloth body. Marked "Copr. by//Grace S. Putnam." Cloth bodies with celluloid hands, satin wings, in green, gold, or pink.

6", solid dome bisque head jointed at neck, blue sleep eyes, softly feathered brows, painted upper and lower lashes, lightly molded and painted hair, all-bisque body jointed at shoulders and hips, molded and painted white socks and blue shoes, re-dressed in white linen diaper, white baby dress with lace trim, marked "15" on front of neck flange, "6 15//Copr. by//Grace S. Putnam//Germany" on back, "20//15" inside upper arms, "894-15" inside upper legs, $185.00. Courtesy McMasters Harris Doll Auctions.

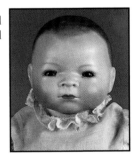

13", solid dome bisque flange head, blue sleep eyes, softly blushed brows, painted upper and lower lashes, accented nostrils, closed mouth, lightly molded and painted hair, cloth body with celluloid hands, lace-trimmed baby dress, underclothing, cotton socks, and booties, marks: "Copr. by//Grace S. Putnam//Made in Germany," on back of head, $140.00. Courtesy McMasters Harris Doll Auctions.

Bye-Lo Baby

Bisque, less for ceramic

11"	$2,100.00*	
13"	$3,750.00	$5,000.00

Composition

14"	$300.00	$900.00

VINYL, CA. 1950S

Vinyl head, cloth stuffed limbs, marked *"Grace Storey Putnam"* on head.

16"	$65.00	$225.00

Catterfelder Puppenfabrik

Mark:

1100

Catterfelder Puppenfabrik

2

25½" girl, bisque socket head, brown sleep eyes with real lashes, feathered brows, painted upper and lower lashes, accented nostrils, open mouth with four upper teeth, replaced synthetic wig, jointed wood and composition body with walking mechanism, white eyelet dress, underclothing, replaced socks and shoes, marked "13//K & Co//61//Germany//Made in//Germany," on back of head, $325.00. Courtesy McMasters Harris Doll Auctions.

1894 – 1930+, Catterfeld, Thüringia, Germany. Made dolls using Kestner bisque head on composition bodies.

BABY

1909 and after, wigged, or molded and painted hair, bent-leg body, glass or painted eyes. Add more for toddler body.

Mold 200 (similar to K*R #100), domed head, painted eyes, open/closed mouth, also black version

15"	$400.00	$500.00

Mold 201, domed head, painted eyes, closed mouth, more for toddler body

13"	$500.00	$750.00

Mold 207, character head, painted eyes, closed mouth

Mold 208, character baby or toddler with domed head or wigged, sleep eyes, open mouth, two teeth, movable tongue

Mold 209, character baby, movable tongue

Mold 218, character baby, domed head, sleep eyes, open mouth, movable tongue

Mold 262, character baby, sleep eyes, open mouth, movable tongue, only marked with mold number

Mold 263, character baby

14"	$485.00	$550.00

CHILD, DOLLY FACE

Open mouth, sleep eyes

18"	$550.00	$750.00

CHILD, CHARACTER FACE

Composition body, open or open/closed mouth

Mold 210, painted eyes, closed mouth

14"	$8,250.00*	

Mold 212, wide open/closed laughing mouth, painted teeth and eyes

Mold 215, 219, character face, wig, painted eyes

215	15"	$3,570.00*

Mold 220, character doll, sleeping eyes, open/closed mouth with two molded teeth

17"	$7,300.00	

Mold 264, character face, socket head, sleep eyes, open mouth

| | 27" | $550.00* |
| | 34" | $1,100.00* |

Mold 270, character face, socket head, open mouth, sleep eyes

Molds 1100, 1200, and 1357 were used for ball-jointed dolls.

Mark:

C. P.
208/34 S
Deponiert

Celluloid

1869+, celluloid became more durable after 1905 and in 1910, when better production methods were found. Dolls were made in England, France, Japan, Germany, Poland, and the United States. When short hair became faddish, the demand for celluloid hair ornaments decreased and companies produced more dolls.

American manufacturers:
Averill, Bo-Peep (H. J. Brown), Du Pont Viscoloid Co., Horsman, Irwin, Marks Bros., Parsons-Jackson Co. (stork mark), Celluloid Novelty Co.

English manufacturers:
Wilson Doll Co. and Cascelloid Ltd. (Palitoy)

French manufacturers:
Peticolin (profile head of an eagle mark), Widow Chalory, Convert Cie, Parisienne de Cellulosine, Neuman & Marx (Dragon), Société Industrielle de Celluloid (S.I.C.), Sicoine, Société Nobel Francaise (S N F in diamond)

German manufacturers:
Bähr & Pröschild, Buschow & Beck (helmet), Minerva, Catterfelder Puppenfabrik Co., Cuno & Otto Dressel, E. Maar & Sohn (3 M), Emasco, Kämmer & Reinhardt, Kestner, König & Wernicke, A. Hagedorn & Co., Hermsdorfer Celluloidwarenfabrik (lady bug), Dr. Paul Hunaeus, Kohn & Wengenroth, Rheinsche Gummi und Celluloid Fabrik Co. later known as Schildkrote (turtle mark), Max Rudolph, Bruno Schmidt, Franz Schmidt & Co., Schoberl & Becker (mermaid) who used *Cellba* for a tradename, Karl Standfuss, Albert Wacker

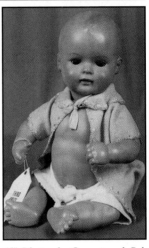

15" Rheinsche Gummi und Celluloid Fabrik Co. baby, socket head, brown eyes, closed mouth, painted hair original jacket, bent-limb baby body, turtle mark, circa 1920s – 1930s, $145.00. Courtesy McMasters Harris Doll Auctions.

Two 5" celluloid Rheinsche Gummi und Celluloid Fabrik Co. babies with turtle mark (in diamond), painted hair and eyes, jointed bent-leg baby bodies, one dressed in baby dress, other in green jacket, matching hat, white pajama bottoms, in wooden crib with red wheels, circa 1926+, $300.00 for pair in baby bed. Courtesy Marilyn Cross.

5" Irwin baby, marked "Made//Irwin (in banner)//in USA (all in a circle)" on back, molded and painted hair, painted side-glancing eyes, closed pouty mouth, bent-limb baby body, multicolored crocheted baby dress, circa 1930s, $40.00. Courtesy Barbara Hull.

20½" Buschow & Beck boy, marked "(helmet of Minerva)//No. 7//42//Germany," flange neck, molded and painted brown hair, blue intaglio eyes, closed mouth, cloth body is flesh-colored cotton with disc joints, missing hand, white shirt, blue print tie, brown suspenders, circa 1920s – 1930s, $400.00. Courtesy Inge Ramey.

Japanese manufacturers:
Various firms may be marked Japan
Polish manufacturers:
Zast ("A.S.K." in triangle)
First price is for doll with some flaws or nude; second price is for doll in excellent condition. More for boxed set, labeled, or tagged.

ALL CELLULOID

Baby

Painted eyes

4"	$15.00	$60.00
8"	$20.00	$80.00
12"	$45.00	$125.00
15"	$50.00	$180.00
19"	$70.00	$285.00

Glass eyes

13"	$45.00	$185.00
15"	$60.00	$250.00
19"	$100.00	$400.00

Child

Painted eyes, jointed shoulders, hips

5"	$10.00	$40.00
7"	$15.00	$60.00
11"	$30.00	$115.00
14"	$45.00	$185.00
19"	$100.00	$400.00

Jointed shoulders only

6"	$7.50	$30.00
8"	$13.00	$50.00
11"	$25.00	$95.00

Glass eyes

10"	$45.00	$125.00
14"	$60.00	$210.00
17"	$100.00	$400.00

Marked "France"

7"	$30.00	$130.00
9"	$45.00	$180.00
15"	$70.00	$280.00
18"	$140.00	$525.00

Molded-on clothes, jointed shoulders only

3"	$10.00	$40.00
5"	$15.00	$60.00
8"	$30.00	$110.00

Immobiles, no joints

3"	$4.00	$15.00
6"	$10.00	$45.00

Black, all-celluloid: see Black Dolls section.

Carnival Dolls
May have feathers glued to body/head, some have top hats

8"	$10.00	$40.00
12"	$20.00	$80.00
17"	$45.00	$175.00+

Shoulder head, 1900+
Germany, molded hair or wigged, open or closed mouth, kid or cloth bodies, may have arms of other materials
Painted eyes

13"	$85.00	$165.00
16"	$110.00	$215.00
18"	$180.00	$365.00

Glass eyes

15"	$110.00	$215.00
17"	$185.00	$375.00
20"	$240.00	$475.00

Averill, 1925
Bonnie Babe, cloth body, composition limbs

18"	$1,300.00*

Bye-Lo Baby: see that section.
Celluloid/Plush, 1910+
Teddy bear body, can have half or full celluloid body with hood half head.

12"	$325.00	$650.00
14"	$400.00	$785.00
17"	$475.00	$925.00

Hitler youth group

8"	$90.00	$175.00

Hermsdorfer Celluloidwarenfabrik, 1923 – 1926, ladybug mark

17"	$90.00* with neck repair

Heubach Köppelsdorf, Mold 399

11"	$18.00	$70.00

Jumeau, marked on head, jointed body

13"	$245.00	$485.00
16"	$295.00	$585.00

Kämmer & Reinhardt (K*R) shoulder head
Mold 225, 255, ca. 1920

14"	$185.00	$370.00
17"	$250.00	$485.00

Kämmer & Reinhardt (K*R) socket head
Mold 406, ca. 1910, glass eyes, open mouth
Mold 700, child or baby, ca. 1910, painted eyes, open/closed mouth

14"	$250.00	$400.00

Mold 701, ca. 1910, character, painted eyes, closed mouth

14"	$500.00	$975.00

14" Petitcollin ethnic girl, marked "(eagle head)// FRANCE//35," in Norman dress of red skirt with rick-rack trim, black vest, blue and white print apron, large brown plaid scarf in hair, white blouse trimmed with red ribbon and lace at cuffs, painted white socks and black one-strap shoes, circa 1909+, $125.00. Courtesy Carol Van Verst-Rugg.

14" German child, marked with crowned mermaid mark used by Schoberl & Becker (Celba), painted features, closed mouth, molded and painted hair, circa 1930s, $185.00. Courtesy Kate Treber.

Mold 715, ca. 1912, character, sleep eyes, closed mouth
     15" $300.00 $685.00
Mold 717, ca. 1920, character, sleep eyes, closed mouth
     15" $325.00 $650.00
     17" $700.00* flapper body, boxed
Mold 728, ca. 1928, character, sleep eyes, open mouth
     16" $250.00 $500.00
     20" $350.00 $700.00
All-celluloid toddler body
     18" $425.00*
Kestner
Mold 203, character baby
     12" $450.00*
Kewpie: see that section.
König & Wernicke (K&W)
Toddler
     15" $165.00 $325.00
     19" $250.00 $500.00
Max and Moritz, each
     7" $150.00 $300.00
Parsons-Jackson (stork mark)
Baby
     12" $100.00 $200.00
     14" $150.00 $285.00
Toddler
     15" $200.00 $385.00
Black
     14" $250.00 $485.00
Petitcolin
     18" $150.00 $250.00
Provencial costume
     15" $85.00 $165.00

Century Doll Co.

1909 – 1930, New York City. Founded by Max Scheuer and sons; used bisque heads on many later dolls. In about 1929, Century merged with Domec to become the Doll Corporation of America. Some heads were made by Kestner, Herm Steiner, and other firms for Century.

Mark:

CENTURY DOLL C°.
Kestner Germany

Chuckles Mark on back:
"CHUCKLES//A CENTURY DOLL"

First price is for doll in good condition, but with flaws; second price for doll in excellent condition, with original clothes or appropriately dressed. More for boxed, tagged, or labeled exceptional doll.

BISQUE
Baby, ca. 1926, by Kestner
Bisque head, molded and painted hair, sleep eyes, open/closed mouth, cloth body
     17" $550.00 $750.00

* at auction

Mold 275, solid dome, glass eyes, closed mouth, cloth body, composition limbs

14"	$715.00	$950.00

Child

Mold 285, by Kestner, bisque socket head, glass eyes, open mouth, wig, ball-jointed body

23"	$575.00	$750.00

COMPOSITION

Chuckles, 1927 – 1929

Composition shoulder head, arms, and legs, cloth body with crier, open mouth, molded short hair, painted or sleep eyes, two upper teeth, dimples in cheeks. Came as a bent-leg baby or toddler.

16"	$85.00	$325.00

Mama dolls, ca. 1922+

Composition head, tin sleep eyes, cloth body, with crier, swing legs and arms of composition

16"	$70.00	$250.00
23"	$120.00	$475.00

Chase: see Cloth dolls.

14" composition shoulder-head Pudgy Peggy with cloth body, molded loop in hair, marked "Pudgy Peggy/Century//Doll Co.//NY," circa 1928, $225.00. Courtesy Donna Nance.

China

Ca. 1840+. Most china shoulder head dolls were made in Germany by various firms. Prior to 1880, most china heads were pressed into the mold; later ones poured. Pre-1880, most china heads were sold separately with purchaser buying commercial body or making one at home. Original commercial costumes are rare; most clothing was homemade.

Early unusual features are glass eyes or eyes painted brown. After 1870, pierced ears and blond hair were found and, after 1880, more child chinas, with shorter hair and shorter necks were popular. Most common in this period were flat tops and low brows and the latter were made until the mid-1900s. Later innovations were china arms and legs with molded boots. Most heads are unmarked or with size or mold number only, usually on the back shoulder plate.

Identification tips: Hair styles, color, complexion tint, and body help date the doll.

First price indicates doll in good condition with some flaws; second price indicates doll in excellent condition with original or appropriate clothes. More for exceptional quality.

CHILD

Swivel neck, shoulder plate, may have china lower limbs

14"	$2,100.00	$2,850.00

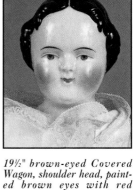

19½" brown-eyed Covered Wagon, shoulder head, painted brown eyes with red accent line and molded lids, single stroke brows, circular nostril accents, closed smiling mouth, molded and painted hair, cloth body with wooden arms, red socks and black oilcloth boots, unmarked, antique white dress with eyelet bodice and lace trim, antique underclothing, $475.00. Courtesy McMasters Harris Doll Auctions.

21" man, unmarked, shoulder head, painted blue eyes with molded lids, single stroke brows, circular nostril accents, closed mouth, molded and painted man's hairstyle with side part, new cloth body with china lower arms, re-dressed with antique fabric in white shirt, black pants, gold jacket with dark velvet collar, silk tie, $1,500.00. Courtesy McMasters Harris Doll Auctions.

18" Countess Dagmar, shoulder head, painted blue eyes, single stroke brows, accented nostrils, closed mouth, pierced ears, molded black hair with molded bow and curls in front, cloth body stitch jointed at shoulders, hips, and knees, leather lower arms with stitched fingers, striped lower legs and leather boots, re-dressed in two-piece gold silk taffeta outfit with black lace and tulle trim, antique underclothing, $775.00. Courtesy McMasters Harris Doll Auctions.

Child or boy

Short black or blond curly hairdo with exposed ears

13"	$195.00	$260.00
21"	$275.00	$365.00

French

Glass or painted eyes, open crown, cork pate, wig, kid body, china arms

14"	$2,350.00	$3,150.00
21"	$3,300.00*	

Japanese, ca. 1910 – 1920

Marked or unmarked, black or blond hair

10"	$110.00	$125.00
15"	$140.00	$190.00

K.P.M. (Königliche Porzellanmanufaktur Berlin), 1840s – 1850s+

Made china doll heads marked KPM inside shoulder plate.

Nymphenburg portrait, circa 1901

16"	$1,500.00*

Pink tint lady w/Latchmann 1874 body

19"	$5,100.00*

Brown hair man, 1869, marked

23"	$7,000.00*

Pink tint Morning Glory, 1860s

24"	$10,250.00*

Brown hair lady with bun, 1860s, marked

17"	$3,375.00	$4,500.00

Kling, marked with bell and number

13"	$265.00	$350.00
16"	$325.00	$435.00
22"	$400.00	$525.00

Man with curls

19"	$1,400.00	$1,850.00

Man or boy, glass eyes

17"	$1,975.00	$2,650.00

Pierced ears, various common hair styles

14"	$365.00	$485.00
18"	$475.00	$635.00

Pierced ears, with elaborate hair style

17"	$1,164.00	$1,550.00+

Queen Victoria, young

16"	$1,195.00	$1,600.00
23"	$1,875.00	$2,500.00

Sophia Smith

Straight sausage curls ending in a ridge around head, rather than curved to head shape

19"	$985.00	$1,325.00+

Spill Curls

With or without headband, a lot of single curls across forehead, around back to ringlets in back

13"	$325.00	$435.00
20"	$550.00	$750.00
26"	$650.00	$850.00

Swivel neck, flange type

10"	$1,550.00	$2,100.00
13"	$2,025.00	$2,700.00

1840 STYLES

China shoulder head with long neck, painted features, black or brown molded hair, may have exposed ears and pink complexion, with red-orange facial detail, may have bust modeling, cloth, leather, or wood body, nicely dressed, good condition.

Early marked china (Nuremberg, Rudolstadt)

14"	$1,700.00	$2,275.00+
17"	$2,125.00	$2,835.00

Brown hair, bun

16"	$2,650.00	$3,500.00

Boy, pressed china, smiling, side-parted brown hair

21"	$3,450.00	$4,600.00

Too few in database for reliable range.

Covered Wagon

Center part, combed back to form sausage curls

10"	$200.00	$275.00
14"	$300.00	$400.00
17"	$350.00	$475.00
20"	$425.00	$550.00
25"	$525.00	$700.00
31"	$650.00	$900.00+

Wood body

9"	$1,200.00	$1,575.00
13"	$1,600.00	$2,150.00
17"	$2,125.00	$2,850.00+

Pink tone, bun or coronet

15"	$2,100.00	$2,825.00

1850 STYLES

China shoulder head, painted features, bald with black spot or molded black hair, may have pink complexion, cloth, leather, or wood body, china arms and legs, nicely dressed, good condition.

Alice in Wonderland, snood, headband

12"	$225.00	$300.00
16"	$300.00	$400.00
20"	$375.00	$500.00

19½" Jenny Lind, shoulder head, painted blue eyes with red accent line, single stroke brows, accented nostrils, closed mouth, molded and painted black hair with full rolls on sides flowing back to bun, cloth body jointed at shoulders, hips, and knees, leather lower arms, antique two-piece outfit, antique underclothing, marked "6" on front edge of shoulder plate, $1,050.00. Courtesy McMasters Harris Doll Auctions.

22" Mary Todd Lincoln, shoulder head, painted blue eyes, single stroke brows, accented nostrils, closed mouth, molded and painted black hair with molded bows on side, snood on back of hair, deep shoulder plate with three sew holes, cloth body with red leather arms, individually stitched fingers, jointed at hips and knees, unmarked, antique red dress, and underclothing, knit socks, $1,200.00. Courtesy McMasters Harris Doll Auctions.

17" Currier & Ives, shoulder head, painted blue eyes, single stroke brows, accented nostrils, closed mouth, molded black hair wiht short wavy bangs, long curls on shoulders, exposed ears, pink cloth body with china lower arms and lower legs, molded black boots with blue tassels, old red/black plaid dress with white lace bodice, underclothing, marked "5" on back of shoulder plate, $500.00. Courtesy McMasters Harris Doll Auctions.

24" Dolly Madison, shoulder head, painted blue eyes, brown single stroke brows, accented nostrils, closed mouth, pierced ears, molded and painted blond hair with blue ribbon and bow, cloth body with leather lower arms, striped lower legs with leather boots, black velvet two-piece outfit with lace trim, antique underclothing, unmarked, $725.00. Courtesy McMasters Harris Doll Auctions.

Bald head, glazed china with black spot

Formerly called Biedermeir, human hair or mohair wig

12"	$475.00	$650.00
14"	$550.00	$750.00
21"	$800.00	$1,050.00

Bald head, with black spot, glass eyes, wig

14"	$1,250.00	$1,675.00
21"	$1,975.00	$2,650.00

Frozen Charlies or Charlottes: See that section.

Greiner-type with painted black eyelashes, various hairdos

Painted eyes

15"	$500.00	$750.00
18"	$900.00	$1,200.00

Glass eyes

13"	$1,850.00	$2,450.00
16"	$2,400.00	$3,200.00
21"	$2,975.00	$4,000.00

1860 STYLES

China shoulder head, center part, smooth black curls, painted features, seldom brushmarks or pink tones, all-cloth bodies or cloth with china arms and legs, may have leather arms. Decorated chinas with fancy hair styles embellished with flowers, ornaments, snoods, bands, ribbons, may have earrings.

Flat top Civil War

Black hair, center part, with flat top, curls on sides and back

7"	$75.00	$100.00
10"	$125.00	$165.00
14"	$180.00	$245.00
18"	$225.00	$300.00
22"	$280.00	$365.00
26"	$355.00	$475.00
34"	$465.00	$625.00

Swivel neck

15"	$750.00	$1,000.00

Molded necklace

21"	$525.00	$700.00+

Too few in database for reliable range.

Highbrow, curls, high forehead, round face

15"	$400.00	$535.00
19"	$525.00	$700.00
22"	$600.00	$800.00+

Grape Lady

With cluster of grape leaves and blue grapes

15"	$1,000.00	$1,325.00
18"	$1,500.00	$2,000.00

Mary Todd Lincoln
Black hair, gold snood, gold luster bows at ears

15"	$475.00	$625.00
21"	$650.00	$850.00

Blond with snood

21"	$1,300.00	$1,800.00

Too few in database for reliable range.

Morning Glory with flowers behind the ears

21"	$4,200.00	$5,600.00

Too few in database for reliable range.

1870 STYLES

China shoulder head, poured, finely painted, well molded, black or blond hair, cloth or cloth and leather bodies, now with pink facial details instead of earlier red-orange.

14"	$185.00	$275.00
18"	$225.00	$325.00
24"	$300.00	$400.00

14½", gold snood, shoulder head, painted blue eyes, single stroke brows, accented nostrils, closed mouth, molded black hair, cloth body, replaced legs with china lower legs, china lower arms, unmarked, antique three-piece outfit, antique underclothing, $950.00. Courtesy McMasters Harris Doll Auctions.

Adelina Patti

Hair pulled up and away, center part, brush-stroked at temples, partly exposed ears, ringlets across back of head

14"	$215.00	$325.00
20"	$400.00	$550.00
25"	$450.00	$600.00

Bangs, full cut across forehead, sometimes called Highland Mary
Black hair

14"	$225.00	$300.00
19"	$325.00	$425.00

Blond hair

14"	$265.00	$325.00

Jenny Lind, black hair pulled back into a bun or coronet

15"	$1,150.00	$1,550.00

1880 STYLES

Now may also have many blond as well as black hair examples, more curls, and overall curls, narrower shoulders, fatter cheeks, irises outlined with black paint, may have bangs. China legs have fat calves and molded boots.

15"	$225.00	$325.00
22"	$375.00	$475.00
27"	$550.00	$675.00

Dolley Madison

Black molded hair, two separate clusters of curls on forehead, molded ribbon and bow across top, ears partially exposed, painted blue eyes, irises and eyes outlined with black, black eyebrows

14"	$275.00	$375.00
18"	$350.00	$475.00
24"	$475.00	$635.00

1890 STYLES

Shorter fatter arms and legs, may have printed body with alphabet, emblems, flags

Common or low brow
Black or blond center part wavy hairdo that comes down low on forehead

10"	$85.00	$115.00
14"	$115.00	$155.00
19"	$150.00	$215.00
23"	$200.00	$300.00
27"	$250.00	$350.00
36"	$355.00	$475.00

With jewel necklace

14"	$175.00	$225.00
20"	$245.00	$325.00

PET NAMES, CA. 1899 – 1930+
Agness, Bertha, Daisy, Dorothy, Edith, Esther, Ethel, Florence, Helen, Mabel, Marion, Pauline, and Ruth

Made for Butler Brothers by various German firms. China head and limbs on cloth body. Molded blouse marked in front with name in gold lettering, molded blond or black allover curls.

9"	$80.00	$110.00
14"	$165.00	$225.00
17"	$185.00	$275.00
21"	$250.00	$325.00

Cloth

27" Art Fabric Mills girl with printed underwear, stitched fingers, stitch-jointed legs, red stockings, black shoes, printed on bottom "Art Fabric Mills//New York//Patented Feb. 13th, 1900," no tears, some wear, circa 1900s, $350.00. Courtesy Debbie Crume.

First price is for doll in good condition, but with some wear or soiled; second price is for doll in very good condition and clean with good color. Exceptional doll may be more.

ALABAMA INDESTRUCTIBLE DOLLS
Ca. 1900 – 1925, Roanoke, Alabama. Ella Gauntt Smith, made all-cloth dolls with painted features; jointed at shoulders and hips. Head construction may include round "monk's cap" on top of head. Painted feet varied, some with stitched toes, but most had one-button slippers or low boots. Shoes were painted black, brown, pink, or blue; came in seven heights, from 12" to 27".

Baby

12"	$750.00	$1,500.00
22"	$3,600.00*	

Black Baby

20"	$3,200.00	$6,200.00

Barefoot Baby, rare

23"	$1,500.00	$3,000.00

Child

15"	$800.00	$1,600.00
22"	$1,200.00	$2,400.00

> *Alabama Indestructible Dolls Marks:*
> "MRS. S.S. SMITH//MANUFACTURER AND
> DEALER IN// THE ALABAMA
> INDESTRUCTIBLE DOLL// ROANOKE, ALA.//
> PATENTED//SEPT. 26, 1905."

* at auction

Black Child

18"	$3,100.00	$6,200.00
23"	$3,400.00	$6,800.00

ART FABRIC MILLS

1899 – 1910+, New York, New Haven, and London. Lithographed in color, made cloth cut-out dolls

> Art Fabric Mills Marks: "ART FABRIC MILLS, NY, PAT. FEB. 13TH, 1900" on shoe or bottom of foot.

Improved Life Size Doll, with printed underwear

20"	$75.00	$275.00
30"	$100.00	$400.00

Punch and Judy, pair

27"	$200.00	$800.00

BABYLAND RAG

1893 – 1928. A. Bruckner made Babyland Rag Dolls, with oil-painted or lithographed faces for E.I. Horsman.

Lithographed

14½"	$175.00	$335.00
16½"	$200.00	$400.00
24"	$275.00	$550.00

Black

14½"	$240.00	$480.00
16½"	$275.00	$550.00
24"	$400.00	$800.00

Molded and painted faces

13"	$350.00	$700.00

Flat painted faces

16½"	$450.00	$900.00

Buster Brown

17"	$300.00	$550.00

Black

16½"	$490.00	$975.00
20"	$590.00	$1,180.00
30"	$885.00	$1,770.00

BEECHER, JULIA JONES

Ca. 1893 – 1910, Elmira, New York. Wife of Congregational Church pastor Thomas K., sister-in-law of Harriet Beecher Stowe. Made Missionary Ragbabies, of old silk jersey underwear, with flat hand-painted and needle sculpted features. All proceeds used for missionary work. Sizes 16" to 23" and larger.

Missionary Ragbabies

16"	$1,725.00	$3,450.00
23"	$2,500.00	$5,000.00

30" Babyland Rag, cloth head with flat face, hand-painted features, blushed cheeks, strip of human hair sewn across front of head for bangs, cloth body, stitched and jointed at shoulders, elbows, hips, and knees, stitched fingers, antique, possibly original faded blue dress with lace-trimmed bodice, matching bonnet, antique underclothing, unmarked, $1,850.00. Courtesy McMasters Harris Doll Auctions.

10½" Bing girl, painted cloth swivel head, painted blue eyes, closed mouth, original mohair wig, cloth body jointd at shoulders and hips, marked "Made in Germany," stamped in black on back, original felt dress with matching hat, teddy, cotton socks, and felt shoes, $300.00. Courtesy McMasters Harris Doll Auctions.

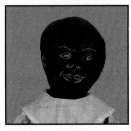

22" handmade black rag doll with unjointed neck, facial features embroidered with tan floss, hair indicated with black floss embroidery, cloth body stitch-jointed at shoulders, elbows, hips, and knees, unmarked, plaid dress with smocked bodice, large white collar and cuffs, matching pants, white apron, and eyelet trim, $400.00. Courtesy McMasters Harris Doll Auctions.

Black

16"	$1,750.00	$3,500.00
23"	$2,800.00	$5,600.00

Beecher-type

20"	$550.00	$2,200.00

BING ART

Bing Werke, Germany, 1921 – 1932. All-cloth, felt or composition head with cloth body, molded face, oil-painted features, wigged or painted hair, pin-jointed cloth body, seams down front of legs, mitt hands.

Painted hair, cloth or felt, unmarked or "Bing" on bottom of foot

13"	$275.00	$550.00
15"	$325.00	$650.00

Wigged

10"	$175.00	$350.00
10½"	$890.00* pair, all original	
16"	$325.00	$650.00

Composition head

12"	$45.00	$175.00
16"	$60.00	$225.00

BLACK, 1830+

Black cloth doll patterns in *American Girls Book*, describe how to make dolls of black silk or crepe, gingham or calico dress, apron, and cap. Beecher, Brückner, Chad Valley, Chase, and Lenci made black cloth dolls. Horsman advertised black cloth Topsy and Dinah cloth dolls, ca. 1912. Black cloth dolls were made ca. 1921 by Grace Cory for Century Doll Co. Many cloth dolls were homemade and one-of-a-kind. Patterns were available to make mammy doll toaster covers during the 1940s.

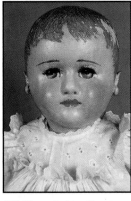

27" Chase baby, oil painted stockinet head, painted blue eyes with much shading, feathered brows, painted upper lashes, accent nostrils, closed mouth, applied ears, sateen covered cloth body with oil painted lower arms and lower legs, marked "The Chase Stockinet Doll//Made of Stockinet and Cloth//Stuffed with Cotton//Made by Hand//Painted by Hand//Made by Especially Trained Workers," on cloth tag on left side seam, antique eyelet-trimmed white baby dress, flannel slip, undershirt, pink leather booties, $450.00. Courtesy McMasters Harris Doll Auctions.

Mammy-style, with painted or embroidered features, 1910 – 1920s

12"	$65.00	$200.00
16"	$85.00	$285.00

1930s

15"	$55.00	$165.00+

Topsy-Turvy

Cloth dolls with two heads, some with black doll under one skirt, which when turned over reveals white doll under other skirt.

Oil-painted	$200.00	$650.00
Printed	$150.00	$425.00

Brückner Topsy Turvy

13"	$250.00	$875.00
13"	$950.00*	

19" Columbian Rag by Emma Marietta Adams, Oswego Center, NY, circa 1891 – 1910, oil painted features, body marked "Columbian Doll//Emma E. Adams//Oswego Center//NY." $7,500.00. Courtesy Sherryl Shirran.

Brownie Mark:
"Copyright 1892 by Palmer Cox" on right foot.

Brückner Mark:
On shoulder, "Pat'd July 8, 1901."

Chad Valley Marks:
Usually on sole of foot, "THE CHAD VALLEY CO. LTD//(BRITISH ROYAL COAT OF ARMS)//TOYMAKER TO//H.M." or "HYGIENIC TOYS//MADE IN ENGLAND BY//CHAD VALLEY CO. LTD."

BROWNIES BY PALMER COX

1892 – 1907. Printed cloth dolls based on copyrighted figures of Palmer Cox; 12 different figures, including Canadian, Chinaman, Dude, German, Highlander, Indian, Irishman, John Bull, Policeman, Sailor, Soldier, and Uncle Sam.

Single Doll

7½"	$100.00	

Set of three, uncut

7½"	$350.00	

Set of 12 with book $825.00*

BRÜCKNER, ALBERT

Ca. 1901 – 1930+, Jersey City. Obtained patent for cloth dolls using printed, molded mask face. Made dolls for Horsman.

14"	$165.00	$325.00

CHAD VALLEY

1917 – 1930+, Harbourne, England. Founded by Johnson Bros., made all types of cloth dolls, early ones had stockinette faces, later felt, with velvet body, jointed neck, shoulders, hips, glass or painted eyes, mohair wig. Mabel Lucie Atwell was an early designer.

Animals

Cat

12"	$75.00	$215.00+

Bonzo, cloth dog with painted eyes, almost closed and smile

4"	$65.00	$210.00
6"	$3,340.00* dressed, label, button	

Bonzo, eyes open

5½"	$80.00	$275.00
14"	$150.00	$575.00

Dog, plush

12"	$65.00	$260.00

Characters

Captain Blye, Fisherman, Long John Silver, Pirate, Policeman, Train Conductor, etc.

Glass eyes

18"	$325.00	$1,000.00
20"	$375.00	$1,300.00

24" cloth Salfield Publishing Co. Golden Locks Girl, marked on fabric tied around middle "Copyright//1908//by the Saalfield Pub. Co.//Akron, Ohio," lithographed cloth, painted blond hair, with red bow on side, painted smiling mouth, painted white ruffled blouse, red leather shoes, circa 1908, $165.00. Courtesy Elizabeth Fielding.

18" cloth Kamkins with wardrobe, oil painted swivel head, painted blue eyes, single stroke brows, accented nostrils, closed mouth, original mohair wig, cloth body with tab joints at shoulders, stitch-jointed hips, stitched fingers and separate thumb, original organdy dress with flower print trim along bottom, matching teddy with flower print trim, orange wool coat with matching hat, rayon socks, original brown leather shoes, comes with orange/gold/black/white striped dress, matching teddy and orange hat, white pique dress with matching print coat and hat, red mohair jacket and matching hat, extra pair of shoes; knit sweater, skirt, and matching hat, flannel pajamas, black felt buckle boots, $5,700.00. Courtesy McMasters Harris Doll Auctions.

15" Georgene Averill doll, mask face, brown yarn hair, painted side-glancing eyes, dressed in Saint Patrick's outfit with flower print skirt, green jacket, green felt hat with shamrock, white apron with green shamrock, circa 1930s – 1940s, $75.00. Courtesy Sandy Johnson Barts.

Painted eyes		
18"	$225.00	$775.00
20"	$250.00	$875.00
Ghandi/India		
13"	$175.00	$675.00
Rahmah-Jah		
26"	$225.00	$900.00

Child

Glass eyes

14"	$165.00	$625.00
16"	$200.00	$725.00
18"	$225.00	$775.00

Painted eyes

9 – 10"	$40.00	$150.00
12"	$65.00	$225.00
15"	$115.00	$425.00
18"	$160.00	$625.00

Royal Family, all with glass eyes, 16" – 18"

Princess Alexandra
	$400.00	$1,500.00

Prince Edward, Duke of Windsor
	$400.00	$1,500.00

Princess Elizabeth
	$425.00	$1,700.00

Princess Margaret Rose
	$400.00	$1,500.00

Story Book Dolls

Dong Dell
14"	$125.00	$475.00

My Elizabeth, My Friend
14"	$165.00	$675.00

Snow White & Dwarfs
12", 6½"	$4,500.00*	

Red Riding Hood
14"	$125.00	$500.00

* at auction

MARTHA CHASE

Ca. 1889 – 1930+, Paw-tucket, Rhode Island. Heads were made from stockinette covered masks reproduced from bisque dolls, heavily painted features including thick lashes, closed mouth, sometimes nostrils, painted textured hair, jointed shoulder, elbows, knees, and hips; later dolls only at shoulders and hips.

First price indicates doll in good condition with some flaws; second price indicates doll in excellent condition with original or appropriate clothes.

Martha Chase Marks: "CHASE STOCKINET DOLL" on left leg or under left arm. Paper label, if there, reads "CHASE//HOS-PITAL DOLL// TRADE MARK// PAWTUCKET, RI// MADE IN U.S.A."

7" ethnic Laplander dolls made by Ronnaug Petterssen made in Norway, $70.00 for pair. Courtesy Cherie Gervais.

Baby
16"	$425.00	$575.00
19"	$495.00	$700.00
24"	$625.00	$875.00

Hospital-type
20"	$500.00*	
29"	$450.00	$575.00

Child
Molded bobbed hair
12"	$900.00	$1,200.00
16"	$1,200.00	$1,600.00
22"	$1,650.00	$2,200.00

Solid dome, simple painted hair
15"	$365.00	$485.00
18"	$475.00	$625.00

Unusual hairdo, molded bun
15"	$2,200.00*

Characters

Alice in Wonderland, character, circa 1905, set of six dolls, including Alice, Duchess, Tweedledee and Tweedledum, Mad Hatter, and Frog Footman, 12" tall excluding hats, hard pressed muslin, with oil-painted features, stitch-jointed limbs, rare to find as a group
12"	$67,000.00* set of six

Benjamin Franklin
15"	$6,875.00*

Too few in database to give reliable range.

19" Poupee Raynal, pressed felt swivel head, marked "Paris," mohair wig in original set, painted blue eyes, single stroke brows, painted upper lashes, closed mouth, five-piece cloth body with stitched fingers, original light blue organdy dress with pink flower appliqué, matching hat, original teddy, blue organdy slip, socks, white leather shoes, circa 1922+, $725.00. Courtesy McMasters Harris Doll Auctions.

Later Dolls
Baby
14"	$150.00	$200.00
15"	$190.00	$250.00
19"	$300.00	$400.00

Child
15"	$215.00	$285.00
20"	$300.00	$400.00

* at auction

14" Marge comic character Nancy mask face, painted features, plush wig, white sleeves, black vest, orange skirt, circa 1944 – 1961, $500.00. Courtesy Debbie Crume.

21" Hol-le Toy Co. Eloise, a literary character, from book by Kay Thompson about little girl who lived at New York Plaza Hotel, tagged "Eloise©//© Eloise, Ltd.//Hol-le Toy Co.//NY/ /10//NY," painted features, rosy cheeks, yellow yarn hair, red bow on top of head, stuffed cloth body, original tagged blue skirt and white blouse, black oilcloth shoes, box says "ELOISE DOLL//Style 60/22E//Presented to Mfg. By Hol-Le Toy Co.//New York 10 NY," mint-in-box, circa 1955 – 1958+, $400.00. Courtesy Elizabeth Surber.

COLUMBIAN DOLL, 1891+, OSWEGO, NY

Emma E. Adams made rag dolls, distributed by Marshall Field & Co., and won awards at the 1893 Chicago World Fair. Succeeded by her sister, Marietta Adams Ruttan. Cloth dolls had hand-painted features, stitched fingers and toes.

> Columbian Doll Marks:
> "COLUMBIAN DOLL, EMMA E. ADAMS, OSWEGO, NY"

14"	$4,600.00*	
15"	$2,225.00	$4,500.00
19"	$2,850.00	$5,700.00

Columbian-type

16"	$650.00	$1,280.00
22"	$1,100.00	$2,200.00

COMIC CHARACTERS

15"	$150.00	$450.00

DEANS RAG BOOK CO.

1905+, London. Subsidiary of Dean & Son, Ltd., a printing and publishing firm, used "A1" to signify quality, made Knockabout Toys, Tru-to-life, Evripoze, and others. An early designer was Hilda Cowham.

Child

10"	$100.00	$285.00
16"	$185.00	$550.00
17"	$250.00	$750.00

Lithographed face

9"	$30.00	$85.00
15"	$55.00	$165.00
16"	$75.00	$225.00

Mask face, velvet, with cloth body and limbs

12"	$45.00	$125.00
18"	$90.00	$265.00
24"	$125.00	$385.00
30"	$155.00	$475.00
34"	$185.00	$565.00
40"	$225.00	$695.00

Golliwogs (English black character doll)

13"	$85.00	$250.00
15"	$150.00	$450.00

DRAYTON, GRACE

1909 – 1929, Philadelphia, Pennsylvania. An illustrator, her designs were used for cloth and other dolls. Made printed dolls with big eyes, flat faces.

Chocolate Drop, 1923, Averill Mfg. Corp., brown cloth, printed features, three tufts yarn hair

10"	$135.00	$400.00
14"	$185.00	$550.00

Dolly Dingle, 1923, Averill Mfg. Corp., cloth, printed features, marked on torso

11"	$115.00	$385.00
15"	$165.00	$550.00

Double face or topsy turvy

15"	$190.00	$625.00

Hug Me Tight, 1916, Colonial Toy Mfg. Co., printed cloth with boy standing behind girl, one-piece

12"	$75.00	$250.00
16"	$150.00	$435.00

Kitty Puss, all-cloth, cat face, wired posable limbs and tail

15"	$135.00	$400.00

Peek-A-Boo, Horsman, 1913 – 1915, printed features

9"	$55.00	$175.00
12"	$75.00	$225.00
15"	$90.00	$275.00

FANGEL, MAUD TOUSEY

1920 – 1930+. Designed cloth dolls, with flat printed faces, some with mitten hands. Some had three-piece heads and feet.

Baby

13"	$150.00	$425.00
17"	$200.00	$600.00

Child, Peggy Ann, Rosy, Snooks, Sweets

9"	$100.00	$300.00
12"	$165.00	$500.00
15"	$200.00	$625.00
21"	$250.00	$800.00

FARNELL, J.K. & CO. LTD. 1871 – 1968, LONDON

Baby

15"	$150.00	$475.00
18"	$200.00	$600.00

Child

10"	$85.00	$250.00
15"	$165.00	$500.00

King George VI, "H.M. The King"
Set of three

14"	$1,200.00*	

Palace Guard, "Beefeater"

15"	$225.00	$700.00

GUND

Circa 1898 on, CT & NY. Adolph Gund founded the company making stuffed toys. Later made teddy bears and dolls including Disney characters.

Gund Marks:
"A Gund Product, A Toy of Quality and Distinction."
From World War II on: Stylized "G" with rabbit ears and whiskers. Mid 1960s – 1987: Bear's head above the letter "U." From 1987 on: "GUND."

4" thread-wrapped Tiny Town Doll, red wig with yellow ribbon, painted features, yellow thread-wrapped arms, legs, and upper body, brown pantsuit, painted metal feet, circa 1940s, $25.00 – 75.00. Courtesy Barbara Hull.

14½" Chad Valley Bambina and 8" Bonzo, marked "Hygienic Toys//Made in England by Chad Valley, Co. Ltd." on label on left foot of Bambina and back foot of Bonzo. Bambina has pressed felt swivel head, set glass eyes, applied ears, mohair wig, velvet body jointed at shoulders and hips, original orange felt suit, teal jacket, matching shoes, Bonzo is unjointed velvet, swivel head, glass eyes, floss nose, floppy ears and tail trimmed with felt, circa 1920s, $550.00. Courtesy McMasters Harris Doll Auctions.

8" felt Norah Wellings sailor in original dark blue costume, with mask face, painted features, excellent condition, marked "Made in England by Norah Wellings" on foot, "Queen Elizabeth" on hat indicates it was sold as a souvenir aboard the Queen Elizabeth ocean liner, has matching plastic-type marked life preserver, 1930s+, $100.00. Courtesy Elizabeth Surber.

19" girl with original dress, bonnet, yarn hair, mask face, plastic eyes, original teddy bear hang tag reads "AT Playtoys//Atlanta Georgia," circa 1960s, $55.00. Courtesy Debbie Crume.

Character, cloth mask face, painted features

19"	$75.00	$300.00

KAMKINS

1919 – 1928. Cloth doll made by Louise R. Kampes Studio, made by cottage industry workers at home. All-cloth, molded mask face, painted features, swivel head, jointed shoulders and hips, mohair wig

> **Kamkins Marks:**
> Heart-shaped sticker:
> *"KAMKINS// A DOLLY MADE TO LOVE // PATENTED//FROM// L.R. KAMPES//STUDIOS// ATLANTIC CITY//N.J."*

19"	$600.00	$1,600.00

KRUSE, KÄTHE: See that section.

KRUEGER, RICHARD

1917+. Made many cloth dolls, some of oil-cloth or with oilcloth clothing, oil-painted mask face, yarn or mohair wig, label.

> **Kreuger Marks:**
> *"KRUEGER NY//REG. U.S. PAT. OFF/ /MADE IN U.S.A."*
> on body or clothing seam.

Child

12"	$40.00	$135.00
16"	$60.00	$195.00
20"	$80.00	$240.00

Walt Disney and other characters

Dwarf

12½"	$65.00	$200.00

Pinocchio

16"	$125.00	$425.00+

LENCI: See that section.

MOLLY-'ES

1929 – 1930+. Trademark used by Mollye Goldman of International Doll Co. of Philadelphia, PA. Made clothes for cloth dolls with masked faces (and composition dolls), dressed in international costumes.

Child

13"	$90.00	$130.00
17"	$45.00	$150.00
22"	$65.00	$200.00
27"	$85.00	$275.00

Lady, in long dresses or gowns

16"	$55.00	$175.00
21"	$75.00	$250.00

Internationals

13"	$30.00	$90.00
15"	$45.00	$135.00
27"	$100.00	$300.00

Princess, Thief of Bagdad
Blue painted Oriental-style eyes, harem outfit

14"	$100.00	$300.00

PETERSSEN, RONNAUG

1901 – 1980, Norway. Made cloth dolls, pressed felt head, usually painted side-glancing eyes, cloth bodies, intricate costumes, paper tags.

8"	$20.00	$40.00
14½"	$350.00	$700.00

PETZOLD, DORA

Germany, 1919 – 1930+. Made and dressed dolls, molded head, painted features, wig, stockinette body, sawdust filled, short torso, free-formed thumbs, stitched fingers, shaped legs.

18"	$200.00	$600.00
22"	$225.00	$775.00

PHILADELPHIA BABIES, J.B. SHEPPARD & CO.

Ca. 1860 – 1935. Shoulder head, stockinette rag doll with molded eyelids, stitched fingers and toes, painted features, sizes 18" – 22", also known as Sheppard Dolls.

18"	$1,200.00	$3,500.00
22"	$1,320.00	$4,000.00
21"	$4,730.00*	

PRINTED CLOTH

Ca. 1876+. Made by various firms such as Arnold Print Works, North Adams, MA (some marked Cocheco Manufacturing Co.), Art Fabric Mills (see previous listing), and other lesser or unknown firms who printed fabric for making cutout dolls, to be sewn together and stuffed.

> *Printed Cloth Marks:*
> *Cloth label usually on*
> *sole of the foot reads:*
> *"MADE IN ENG-*
> *LAND//BY//NORAH*
> *WELLINGS."*

Aunt Jemima
Set of four dolls $100.00 each

Black Child

16"	$150.00	$425.00

Cream of Wheat, Rastus

16"	$40.00	$125.00

Printed underwear, Dolly Dear, Flaked Rice, Merry Marie, etc.

Cut and sewn

7"	$35.00	$95.00
16"	$60.00	$175.00

Uncut

7"	$125.00	
19"	$275.00	

With printed clothing, ca. 1903

Cut and sewn

14"	$65.00	$200.00
19"	$115.00	$325.00

18" Izannah Walker, painted cloth head, painted brown eyes, single stroke brows, closed mouth, applied ears, painted brown hair, cloth body jointed at shoulders, elbows, hips, and knees, painted lower arms, painted lower legs, original black silk dress, $3,400.00. Courtesy McMasters Harris Doll Auctions.

19" Junel with blue painted side-glancing eyes, thickly painted brown lashes, red dots at nostrils, closed mouth, rosy cheeks, with blond yarn hair, original pink flower print dress and matching bonnet, mint condition in box, circa 1920s – 1930s, $275.00. Courtesy Kay Walimaa.

Uncut
Cocheco Darkey, 17" x 24"	$250.00*	
Our Soldier Boys, 17" x 24"	$175.00*	
Red Riding Hood, 18" x 24"	$300.00*	

Santa Claus/St. Nicholas
Cut and sewn
15" $100.00 $325.00
Uncut
15" $600.00

Santa Claus/St. Nicholas
Marks:
"Pat. Dec 18, 1886//Made by
E.S.Peck NY"

RALEIGH, JESSIE MCCUTCHEON
Shoebutton Sue, flat face, painted spit curls, mitten hands, sewn on red shoes, shown in 1921 Sears catalog
15" $1,900.00*

RAYNAL
1922 – 1930+, Paris. Edouard Raynal made dolls of felt, cloth, or with celluloid heads with widely spaced eyebrows. Dressed, some resemble Lenci, except fingers were together or their hands were of celluloid; marked *"Raynal"* on soles of shoes and/or pendant.
14½" $125.00 $450.00
17" $175.00 $600.00

ROLLINSON, GERTRUDE F.
Ca. 1916 – 1929 Holyoke, Massachusetts. Designed and made cloth dolls with molded faces treated to be washable, painted features. Dolls were produced by Utley Co., distributed by Borgfeldt, L. Wolf and Strobel, and Wilken.
molded and painted hair
20" $400.00 $1,150.00
Wigged, stamped body
26" $1,500.00 $2,000.00

RUSSIAN
Ca. 1920+. All-cloth, molded and painted stockinette head, hands, in regional costumes
7" $25.00 $70.00
15" $50.00 $150.00
18" $60.00 $180.00

Raynal Trademark:
POUPEES RAYNAL
Rollinson Marks:
Cloth torso has diamond
stamp, "ROLLINSON
DOLL//HOLYOKE,
MASS."
Russian Marks:
"MADE IN SOVIET
UNION"
Izannah Walker Marks:
Some marked "PATENT-
ED NOV. 4, 1873"

STEIFF: See that section.

WALKER, IZANNAH
Ca. late 1800s, Central Fall, Rhode Island. Made cloth stockinette dolls, with pressed mask face, oil-painted features, applied ears, brush-stroked or corkscrew curls, stitched hands and feet, some with painted boots.
First price indicates very worn; second price for good condition. More for unusual hair style.
20" $6,600.00*

WELLINGS, NORAH
Victoria Toy Works, 1926 – 1930+, Wellington, Shropshire, England. Chief designer for Chad Valley, she and brother, Leonard, started their own factory. Made cloth dolls of velvet, velveteen, plush, and felt, specializing in sailor souvenir dolls for steamship lines. The line included children, adults, blacks, ethnic, and fantasy dolls.

Baby

Molded face, oil-painted features, some papier-mâché covered by stock-inette, stitched hip and shoulder joints

15"	$200.00	$600.00
22"	$300.00	$900.00

Child, painted eyes

13"	$125.00	$400.00
18"	$200.00	$600.00
22"	$235.00	$700.00
28"	$300.00	$900.00

Glass eyes

15"	$175.00	$550.00
18"	$275.00	$850.00
22"	$425.00	$1,300.00

Characters in uniform, regional dress

Mounties, Policemen, others

13"	$125.00	$385.00
17"	$250.00	$750.00
24"	$350.00	$1,100.00

Black Islander or Scot

9"	$30.00	$90.00
13"	$61.00	$185.00
16"	$75.00	$225.00

Creche

Figures of various materials made especially for religious scenes such as the Christmas manger scene. Usually not jointed, some with elaborate costumes. Some early created figures were gesso over wood head and limbs, fabric covered bodies with wire frames, later figures made of terra-cotta or other materials. Some with inset eyes.

Man, wood shoulder head, glass eyes, wire body
8" $115.00

Lady, carved shoulder head, glass eyes, wire body
10½" $350.00

Lady, gesso over wood, glass eyes, wire frame
14½" $500.00

Too few in database for reliable range.

10½" glass-eyed composition Creche lady, $350.00. Courtesy McMasters Harris Doll Auctions.

DEP

The "DEP" mark on the back of bisque heads stands for the French "Depose" or the German "Deponirt," which means registered claim. Some dolls made by Simon & Halbig have the "S&H" mark hidden above the "DEP" under the wig. Bisque head, swivel neck, appropriate wig, paperweight eyes, open or closed

Mark:
DEP
(Size number)

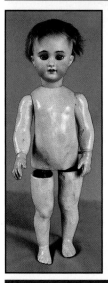

mouth, good condition, nicely dressed on French style wood and composition body.

First price is for doll in good condition, but with flaws; second price indicates doll in excellent condition with original or appropriate clothing.

Closed mouth

15"	$1,600.00	$2,150.00
19"	$1,900.00	$2,550.00
23"	$2,300.00	$3,150.00

Open mouth

13"	$625.00	$825.00
18"	$875.00	$1,200.00
23"	$1,300.00	$1,725.00
28"	$1,900.00	$2,550.00

16½" bisque boy walker, socket head, blue sleep eyes with real lashes, feathered brows, painted lower lashes, accented nostrils, open mouth with four upper teeth, antique mohair wig, pierced ears, composition body, key-wind mechanism in legs, marked "DEP//6" on back of head, $800.00. Courtesy McMasters Harris Doll Auctions.

Dollhouse Dolls

3½" china unknown German doll, painted eyes, molded and painted black hair, flat head, cloth body, china hands, arms, and feet, all-original lace over red dress, circa 1870s, $150.00. Courtesy Nelda Shelton.

Small dolls generally under 8" usually dressed as member of a family or in household-related occupations, often sold as a group. Made of any material, but usually bisque head by 1880.

First price is for doll in good condition, but with flaws; second price is for doll in excellent condition with original clothes.

BISQUE

Adult, man or woman, painted eyes, molded hair, wig

6"	$125.00	$225.00

Glass eyes, molded hair

6"	$300.00	$400.00

Glass eyes, wigged

6"	$400.00	$600.00

Black man or woman, molded hair, original clothes

6"	$360.00	$475.00

Chauffeur, molded cap

6"	$200.00	$285.00

Grandparents, or with molded on hats

6"	$200.00	$265.00

Military man, mustache, original clothes

6"	$435.00	$575.00+

With molded-on helmet

6"	$525.00	$700.00+

Children, all-bisque

4"	$40.00	$75.00

CHINA
With early hairdo

4"	$225.00	$300.00

With low brow or common hairdo, ca. 1900s+

4"	$115.00	$150.00

COMPOSITION, PAPIER-MÂCHÉ, PLASTER, ETC.

5"	$150.00	$225.00

Door of Hope

1901 – 1950, Shanghai, China. Cornelia Bonnell started the Door of Hope Mission in Shanghai, to help poor girls sold by families. As a means to learn sewing skills, the girls dressed carved pearwood heads from Ning-Po. The heads and hands were natural finish, stuffed cloth bodies were then dressed in correct representation for 26 different Chinese classes. Carved wooden head with cloth or wooden arms, original handmade costumes, in very good condition.

First price indicates doll with faded clothing or soiled; second price is for doll in excellent condition with clean, bright clothing. Exceptional dolls could be higher.

ADULT, MAN, WOMAN, OR CHILD

12"	$400.00	$600.00

Bride

11"	$1,050.00* elaborate dress	
12"	$350.00	$750.00

Groom

12"	$325.00	$650.00

Bridal couple in traditional dress

12"	$1,000.00*	

Amah with Baby

	$375.00	$750.00

Manchu Lady or Man

12"	$500.00	$1,000.00

Mourner

	$325.00	$750.00

Policeman

11½"	$2,025.00* with "Made in China" hang tag	

Schoolchild

8"	$200.00	$550.00

Left: 11½" Mourner, carved wood swivel head, carved and painted black eyes, closed smiling mouth, painted black hair, unjointed cloth body with wooden lower arms, marked "Made//in//China" on paper tag, original muslin leggings and robe, coarse sackcloth robe with frog closures and rop belt, hat, $1,800.00. Right: 11" Widow, carved wooden swivel head, carved and painted black eyes, closed mouth, painted black hair, unjointed cloth body with wooden lower arms, original muslin pants, skirt, and jacket, front fastened sackcloth jacket, rope belt, and muslin head covering, unmarked, $1,500.00. Courtesy McMasters Harris Doll Auctions.

Dressel, Cuno & Otto

Ca. 1873 – 1945, Sonnenberg, Thüringia, Germany. The Dressels made wood, wax, wax-over-composition, papier-mâché, composition, china, and bisque heads for their dolls which they produced, distributed, and exported. Their bisque heads were made by Simon & Halbig, Armand Marseille, Ernst Heubach, Schoenau & Hoffmeister, and others.

BISQUE

Baby, 1910+, character face
Marked "C.O.D.," more for toddler body

13"	$225.00	$325.00
15"	$375.00	$475.00
19"	$450.00	$600.00

Child, mold 1912, open mouth, jointed composition body

14"	$225.00	$300.00
18"	$400.00	$475.00
22"	$450.00	$550.00

Child, character face, closed mouth, jointed child or toddler body

Painted eyes

13"	$1,200.00	$1,625.00
14"	$1,850.00	$2,450.00
18"	$2,300.00	$3,000.00

Glass eyes

15"	$2,000.00	$2,500.00
18"	$2,400.00	$3,400.00
23"	$3,100.00*	

19½" bisque child, mold 1349, open mouth, four teeth, pierced ears, original human hair wig, jointed wood and composition body, circa 1910, $515.00. Courtesy McMasters Harris Doll Auctions.

Flapper
Closed mouth, five-piece composition body with thin legs and high heel feet, painted on hose up entire leg, mold 1469

12"	$2,500.00	$3,300.00
15"	$2,850.00	$3,800.00

Jutta
Baby open mouth, bent-leg body

16"	$400.00	$550.00
21"	$600.00	$800.00
24"	$1,000.00	$1,400.00

Child, 1906 – 1921, open mouth, marked with "Jutta" or "S&H" mold 1914, 1348, 1349, etc.

14"	$300.00	$425.00
17"	$450.00	$625.00
21"	$575.00	$775.00
25"	$800.00	$950.00
29"	$900.00	$1,300.00

Toddler

8"	$400.00	$550.00
15"	$500.00	$675.00
18"	$700.00	$950.00
23"	$975.00	$1,400.00
27"	$1,400.00	$1,900.00

Portrait dolls, 1896+
Bisque head, glass eyes, composition body
Admiral Dewey, Admiral Byrd

8"	$500.00	$700.00
12"	$1,150.00	$1,550.00

15½" bisque, Uncle Sam, $1,000.00. Courtesy McMasters Harris Doll Auctions.

Heubach•Köppelsdorf
Jutta-Baby
Dressel
Germany
1922
10

---

* at auction

Buffalo Bill

10"	$575.00	$765.00

Farmer, Old Rip, Witch

8"	$475.00	$650.00
12"	$600.00	$800.00

Father Christmas

12"	$1,125.00	$1,500.00+

Uncle Sam

13"	$750.00	$1,000.00
15½"	$900.00	$1,400.00

COMPOSITION

Holz-Masse, 1875+. Composition shoulder head, wigged or molded hair, painted or glass eyes, cloth body, composition limbs, molded on boots

Molded hair

13"	$65.00	$250.00
17"	$100.00	$400.00
24"	$150.00	$565.00

Wigged

16"	$80.00	$325.00
24"	$110.00	$425.00

20" bisque mold 1349 dolly face Jutta, marked "1/2//1349//Dressell," blue sleep eyes, real and painted lashes, open mouth with teeth, rosy cheeks, red wig, rust-colored checked dress over white long sleeve blouse, dark bonnet, circa 1910, $725.00. Courtesy JoAnn Threadgill.

E.D.

E.D. Bébés marked with *"E.D."* and a size number and the word *"Depose"* were made by Etienne Denamure, ca. 1890s, Paris. Other marked E.D. dolls with no Depose mark were made when Emile Douillet was director of Jumeau and should be priced as Jumeau Tête face dolls. Denamure had no relationship with the Jumeau firm and his dolls do not have the spiral spring used to attach heads used by Jumeau. Denamure bébés have straighter eyebrows, the eyes slightly more recessed, large lips, and lesser quality bisque. Smaller sizes of Denamure E.D. bébés may not have the Depose mark.

First price is for doll in good condition, but with some flaws; second price indicates doll in excellent condition, more for original costumes.

Closed mouth

11"	$2,800.00*	
18"	$2,200.00	$2,900.00
25"	$3,000.00	$4,000.00
27"	$3,100.00	$4,250.00

Open mouth

14"	$975.00	$1,300.00
16"	$1,200.00	$1,600.00
21"	$1,650.00	$2,200.00
27"	$2,100.00	$2,700.00

Eden Bébé

1890 – 1899, made by Fleischmann & Bloedel; 1899 – 1953, made by Société Francaise de Fabrication de Bébés & Jouet (S.F.B.J.). Dolls had bisque heads, jointed composition bodies.

Mark:
EDEN BEBE
PARIS

24" bisque socket head, paperweight eyes, closed mouth, pierced ears, and jointed French body, $3,000.00+. Courtesy McMasters Harris Doll Auctions.

First price indicates doll in good condition, but with some flaws; second price indicates doll in excellent condition, with original clothes or appropriately dressed.

Closed mouth, pale bisque

15"	$1,800.00	$2,375.00
18"	$2,200.00	$2,800.00
22"	$2,300.00	$3,100.00

High color, five-piece body

13"	$900.00	$1,200.00
19"	$1,200.00	$1,600.00
22"	$1,450.00	$1,950.00

Open mouth

15"	$1,125.00	$1,500.00
16"	$2,225.00*	
26"	$1,950.00	$2,600.00

Walking, Talking, Kissing

Jointed body, walker mechanism, head turns, arm throws a kiss, heads by Simon & Halbig using mold 1039 and others, bodies assembled by Fleischmann & Bloedel. Price for perfect working doll.

21"	$1,600.00

Too few in database for reliable range.

Fashion Type

14" bisque, socket head on bisque shoulder plate, pale blue threaded paperweight eyes, multi-stroke brows, painted upper and lower lashes, closed mouth, mohair wig, kid body, marked "1" on back of head and shoulders, re-dressed in grayish two-piece outfit trimmed with lace, $1,000.00. Courtesy McMasters Harris Doll Auctions.

COLLECTOR ALERT:
French fashion types are being reproduced, made to look old. Quality information is available to members and research is continuing by the United Federation of Doll Clubs (UFDC). See Collectors' Network at back of book.

French Poupee, 1869+. Glass eyes, doll modeled as an adult lady, with bisque shoulder head, stationary or swivel neck, closed mouth, earrings, kid or kid and cloth body, nicely dressed, good condition. Add more for original clothing, jointed body, black, or exceptional doll.

UNMARKED OR WITH SIZE NUMBER ONLY

12"	$1,250.00	$1,700.00
14"	$1,500.00	$2,000.00
16"	$1,600.00	$2,200.00
18"	$1,900.00	$2,500.00
21"	$2,600.00	$3,400.00
27"	$3,500.00	$4,600.00

Painted eyes, kid body

14"	$1,900.00

Wooden articulated body, glass eyes

13"	$2,300.00	$2,900.00
15"	$3,500.00	$4,500.00
18"	$4,000.00	$5,000.00

BARROIS (E.B.): See that category.
BLACK: See that section.
BRU: See that category.
F. G.: See Gaultier and Gesland categories.
FORTUNE TELLER DOLLS
Fashion-type head with swivel neck, glass or painted eyes, kid body, skirt made to hold many paper "fortunes." Exceptional doll may be more.

Closed mouth
15"	$3,450.00	$4,100.00+

Open mouth
18"	$2,150.00	$3,100.00+

China, glazed finish, 1870 – 1880 hairstyle
15"	$1,250.00	$1,700.00

Wood, German, with tuck comb
16"	$2,300.00	$3,100.00

GESLAND, marked F.G.: See that category.
HURET: See that category.
JUMEAU: See that category.
ROHMER: See that category.
ACCESSORIES

Dress	$500.00+
Shoes marked by maker	$500.00+
unmarked	$250.00
Trunk	$250.00+
Wig	$250.00+

22" male, solid dome bisque shoulder head, cobalt blue eyes, multistroke brows, painted lashes, closed mouth, human hair wig, cloth body with kid lower arms, black stockings and leather boots, unmarked, chemise-style shirt, white silk vest, black wool jacket, gray striped pants, $1,400.00. Courtesy McMasters Harris Doll Auctions.

Frozen Charlie or Charlotte

Ca. 1860 – 1940. Most porcelain factories made all-china dolls in one-piece molds with molded or painted black or blond hair, and usually undressed. Sometimes called Bathing Dolls, they were dubbed "Frozen Charlotte" from a song about a girl who went dancing dressed lightly and froze in the snow. Victorians found them immoral. They range in size from under 1" to over 19". Some were reproduced in Germany in the 1970s. Allow more for pink tint, extra decoration, or hairdo.

All china
2"	$50.00	$70.00
5"	$85.00	$135.00
7"	$150.00	$200.00
9"	$200.00	$275.00
15"	$350.00	$500.00

Black china
6"	$200.00	$275.00
8"	$275.00	$375.00

Blond hair, flesh tones head and neck
9"	$300.00	$400.00
12"	$400.00	$550.00

Frozen Charlie or Charlotte

15½" pink-tint china Frozen Charlie, stiff neck, molded and painted blond hair, painted blue eyes, heavy black shading on lids, two-tone brows, accented nostrils, closed mouth with accent line between lips, rosy cheeks, unjointed china body with arms held out, hands closed in fists, finger and toe nails outlined, dressed in knit one-piece underwear, circa 1880s – 1890s, $525.00. Courtesy McMasters Harris Doll Auc-

Jointed shoulders
5"	$110.00	$145.00
7"	$165.00	$225.00

Molded boots
4"	$150.00	$225.00
8"	$200.00	$275.00

Molded clothes or hats
3"	$185.00	$250.00
6"	$225.00	$300.00
8"	$325.00	$425.00

Pink tint, hairdo
3"	$200.00	$225.00
5"	$300.00	$375.00

Pink tint, bonnet-head
3"	$350.00	$400.00
5"	$425.00	$500.00

Stone bisque, molded hair, one piece
3"	$20.00	$25.00
6"	$30.00	$40.00

Parian-type, ca. 1860
5"	$150.00	$200.00
7"	$200.00	$250.00

Fulper Pottery Co.

14" bisque baby, blue sleep eyes, open mouth with two teeth, mohair wig, marked "Fulper (vertically) Made in U.S.A." at hairline, circa 1918 – 1921, $275.00. Courtesy McMasters Harris Doll Auctions.

1918 – 1921, Flemington, NJ. Made dolls with bisque heads and all-bisque dolls. Sold dolls to Amberg, Colonial Toy Mfg. Co., and Horsman. "M.S." monogram stood for Martin Stangl, in charge of production.

First price indicates doll in good condition, with flaws; second price indicates doll in excellent condition with original or appropriate clothes.

Baby, bisque socket head, glass eyes, open mouth, teeth, mohair wig, bent-leg body
15"	$300.00	$500.00
19"	$500.00	$700.00

Child, kid body
22"	$250.00	$350.00

Toddler, straight-leg body
16"	$700.00*	
17"	$200.00	$300.00

Mark:

Gans & Seyfarth

1908 – 1922, Waltershausen, Germany. Made bisque dolls; had a patent for flirty and googly eyes. Partners separated in 1922, Otto Gans opened his own factory.

Baby, bent-leg baby, original clothes or appropriately dressed

16"	$375.00	$525.00
20"	$465.00	$625.00
25"	$575.00	$775.00

Child, open mouth, composition body, original clothes, or appropriately dressed

15"	$375.00	$500.00
21"	$500.00	$675.00
28"	$675.00	$900.00

Gaultier, Francois

1860 – 1899. After 1899, became part of S.F.B.J., located near Paris, they made bisque doll heads and parts for lady dolls and for bébés and sold to many French makers of dolls. Also made all-bisque dolls marked "F.G."

BÉBÉ (CHILD), "F.G." IN BLOCK LETTERS, 1879 – 1887
Closed mouth, excellent quality bisque socket head, glass eyes, pierced ears, cork pate

Composition and wood body with straight wrists

11"	$2,975.00	$3,950.00
13"	$3,100.00	$4,100.00
15"	$3,200.00	$4,250.00
20"	$4,200.00	$5,600.00
28"	$5,000.00	$7,000.00

Kid body, may have bisque forearms

15"	$3,300.00	$4,450.00
17"	$3,800.00	$5,000.00

BÉBÉ (CHILD), "F.G." IN SCROLL LETTERS, 1887 – 1900
Composition body, closed mouth

12"	$1,000.00	$1,325.00
17"	$2,225.00	$2,975.00
23"	$2,825.00	$3,725.00
28"	$3,400.00	$4,500.00

With padded metal armature

40"	$26,000.00*

Composition body, open mouth

11"	$475.00	$650.00
16"	$1,350.00	$1,800.00
24"	$2,000.00	$2,700.00

FASHION-TYPE POUPÉE, 1860+
Marked one-piece shoulder head, glass eyes, kid body

13½"	$1,125.00	$1,500.00
17"	$1,800.00	$2,400.00
21"	$2,000.00	$2,750.00

14", bisque socket head on bisque shoulder plate, blue paperweight eyes, heavy feathered brows, painted upper and lower lashes, closed mouth, pierced ears, replaced mohair wig, kid body, marked "4." on back of head, "F.G." on left shoulder, re-dressed in pale green plaid two-piece outfit made with antique fabric, antique underclothing, new socks and lace boots, $1,400.00. Courtesy McMasters Harris Doll Auctions.

Painted eyes

11"	$600.00	$800.00
15"	$825.00	$1,100.00
18½"	$1,025.00	$1,350.00

F.G., marked swivel head on bisque shoulder plate, kid body
May have bisque lower arms, glass eyes

12"	$1,200.00	$1,600.00
15"	$1,700.00	$2,250.00
18½"	$2,100.00	$2,775.00
20½"	$2,300.00	$3,100.00

Wood body

16"	$3,000.00	$4,250.00
20"	$3,600.00	$4,750.00

Gesland

1860 – 1928, Paris. Made, repaired, exported, and distributed dolls, patented a doll body, used heads from Francois Gaultier with "F.G." block or scroll mark. Gesland's unusual body had metal articulated armature covered with padding and stockinette, with bisque or wood/composition hands and legs.

Bébé (child) on marked Gesland body
Closed mouth

12"	$2,900.00	$3,900.00
17"	$3,375.00	$4,500.00
20"	$3,750.00	$5,000.00

Poupee (fashion-type) Gesland
Stockinette covered metal articulated fashion-type body, bisque lower arms and legs

17"	$4,400.00	$5,800.00
23"	$4,950.00	$6,600.00

Mark:

E. GESLAND
Bᵀᴱ S. G. D. G.
PARIS

Gladdie

17" ceramic, designed by Helen W. Jensen, made by K & K for Borgfeldt, glass eyes, open/closed mouth with two upper teeth, molded and painted short blond bob, ruddy rose cheeks, red print dress, circa 1928 – 1930, $1,250.00. Courtesy Bette Yadon.

Mark:

Gladdie
Copyriht By
Helen W. Jensen
Germany

1928 – 1930+. Tradename of doll designed by Helen Webster Jensen, made in Germany, body made by K&K, for Borgfeldt. Flange heads made of bisque and biscaloid, an imitation bisque and composition that is like a terra-cotta ceramic, with molded hair, glass or painted eyes, open/closed mouth with two upper teeth and laughing expression, composition arms, lower legs, cloth torso, some with crier and upper legs. Mark *"copyriht"* (misspelled).

Biscaloid ceramic head

18"	$875.00	$1,150.00
20"	$1,050.00	$1,400.00

* at auction

Bisque head

14"	$2,000.00	$3,000.00
18"	$3,000.00	$4,000.00
21"	$4,000.00	$5,000.00

Goebel, Wm. and F. & W.

1871 – 1930 on, Oeslau, Bavaria. Made porcelain and glazed china dolls, as well as bathing dolls, Kewpie-types, and others. Earlier mark was triangle with half moon.

First price indicates doll in good condition, with flaws; second price indicates doll in excellent condition, appropriately dressed or original clothes. Exceptional dolls may be more.

Character Baby, after 1909

Open mouth, sleep eyes, five-piece bent-leg baby body

15"	$365.00	$485.00
18"	$450.00	$600.00

Toddler body

14"	$425.00	$550.00
16"	$750.00*	

Child, 1895

Socket head, open mouth, composition body, sleep or set eyes

12"	$200.00	$275.00
17"	$350.00	$475.00

Child, open/closed mouth, shoulder plate, wig, molded teeth, kid body, bisque hands

17"	$625.00	$850.00
20"	$850.00	$1,150.00

Character Child, after 1909

Mold 120, circa 1921 – 1932, sleep eyes, open mouth, wigged

12½"	$300.00	$400.00
18"	$550.00* all original	

Mold 521, circa 1921 – 1932, sleep eyes, open mouth, wigged

19"	$400.00	$525.00

Molded hair

May have flowers or ribbons, painted features, with five-piece papier-mâché body

6"	$200.00	$275.00
9"	$325.00	$425.00

Molded on bonnet or hat

Closed mouth, five-piece papier-mâché body, painted features

9"	$400.00	$525.00

9" vinyl Hummel boy, marked "M.I. Hummel//© W. Goebel," painted brown side-glancing eyes, open/closed mouth with painted teeth, heavily molded and painted hair, cotton clothes, felt hat, and large brown felt shoes, with tag, all original, circa 1975, $90.00. Courtesy Nelda Shelton.

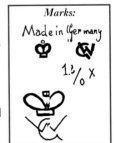

Marks:

Made in Germany

1³/₀ X

Googly

(Side-glancing eyes.) Sometimes round, painted, glass, tin, or celluloid, when they move to side they are called flirty eyes. Popular 1900 – 1925, most doll

Pair of 7" bisque Armand Marseille Googlies, mold 323, both have bisque socket heads, blue sleep side-glancing eyes, single stroke brows, painted upper and lower lashes, closed smiling mouths, blond mohair wigs, molded and painted socks and shoes, ethnic-type costumes, $1,800.00. Courtesy McMasters Harris Doll Auctions.

10½" bisque Armand Marseille Googly, mold #241, bisque socket head, side-glancing blue sleep eyes, single stroke brows, painted upper and lower lashes, closed smiling mouth, repalced human hair wig, five-piece toddler body, marked "241//0" on back of head, re-dressed in old red/white check dress, white dotted Swiss pinafore, underclothing, replaced socks and shoes, white bonnet, $2,500.00. Courtesy McMasters Harris Doll Auctions.

manufacturers made dolls with googly eyes. With painted eyes, they could be painted looking to side or straight ahead; with inserted eyes, the same head can be found with and without flirty eyes. May have closed smiling mouth, composition or papier-mâché body, molded hair or wigged.

First price is for doll in good condition with flaws; second price is for doll in excellent condition appropriately dressed or with original clothes. Exceptional dolls can be more.

ALL-BISQUE

Jointed shoulders, hips, molded shoes, socks

Rigid neck, glass eyes

3"	$200.00	$275.00
5"	$365.00	$465.00

Painted eyes

3"	$150.00	$200.00
5"	$275.00	$350.00

Swivel neck, glass eyes

5"	$425.00	$575.00
7"	$650.00	$875.00

With jointed elbows, knees

5"	$1,725.00	$2,300.00
7"	$2,100.00	$2,750.00

Too few in database for reliable range.

Marked by maker, Mold 189, 292

5"	$675.00	$900.00
7"	$1,050.00	$1,400.00

Mold 217, 330, 501

5"	$500.00	$650.00
7"	$600.00	$800.00

BÄHR & PRÖSCHILD

Marked "B.P."

Mold 686, ca. 1914, Baby

16"	$1,400.00	$1,800.00

Mold 686, Child

13"	$1,850.00	$2,500.00
15"	$2,250.00	$3,000.00

DEMACOL, MADE FOR DENNIS MALLEY & CO., LONDON

Bisque socket head, closed watermelon mouth, mohair wig, five-piece composition toddler body

13"	$900.00	$1,200.00

HANDWERCK, MAX

Marked "Elite," bisque socket head, molded helmet

14"	$1,350.00	$1,800.00

HERTEL SCHWAB & CO.

Mold 163, ca. 1914, solid dome, molded hair, closed smiling mouth

16"	$6,250.00*

Mold 165, ca. 1914, socket head, closed smiling mouth
    11" $4,100.00*

Mold 172, ca. 1914, solid dome, closed smiling mouth
    15" $4,875.00 $6,500.00

Mold 173, ca. 1914, solid dome, closed smiling mouth
    16" $4,350.00 $5,800.00

Mold 222, Our Fairy, all-bisque, wigged, glass eyes
    7" $800.00 $1,200.00
    11" $1,350.00 $1,800.00
Painted eyes, molded hair
    8" $650.00 $850.00
    12" $1,100.00 $1,500.00

HEUBACH, ERNST
Mold 262, ca. 1914, "EH" painted eyes, closed mouth

Mold 264, ca. 1914, character
    8" $300.00 $400.00
    11" $375.00 $500.00

Mold 291, ca. 1915, "EH" glass eyes, closed mouth
    9" $1,000.00 $1,350.00

Mold 318, ca. 1920, "EH" character, closed mouth
    11" $960.00 $1,285.00
    14" $1,500.00 $2,050.00

Mold 319, ca. 1920, "EH" character, tearful features
    8" $425.00 $575.00
    11" $850.00 $1,150.00

Mold 322, ca. 1915, character, closed smiling mouth
    10" $600.00 $750.00

Mold 417, Mold 419
    8" $400.00 $525.00
    13" $900.00 $1,200.00

HEUBACH, GEBRÜDER
    9" $600.00 $800.00
    13" $1,250.00 $1,700.00

Mold 8556
    15" $6,000.00 $8,000.00

Mold 8676
    9" $650.00 $850.00
    11" $775.00 $1,050.00

Mold 8723, 8995, glass eyes
    13" $2,200.00 $2,900.00

Mold 8764, Einco, shoulder head, closed mouth
For Eisenmann & Co.
    20" $11,500.00*
Too few in database for reliable range.

6½" Armand Marseille Googly, mold #324, bisque socket head, blue intaglio eyes to side, single stroke brows, closed smiling mouth, molded and painted hair, five-piece body with molded and painted socks and shoes, marked "324//A 11/0 M//Germany," on back of head, two-piece outfit with tunic top trimmed in red with white buttons, matching short pants, $400.00. Courtesy McMasters Harris Doll Auctions.

12½" bisque Kestner mold #221 googly, with large oversize brown eyes, closed smiling mouth, painted raised eyebrows, brown human hair wig, nicely dressed, $4,500.00 – 6,000.00+. Courtesy McMasters Harris Doll Auctions.

6½" Armand Marseille Googly, mold #322, bisque socket head, blue intaglio eyes to the side, single stroke brows, closed smiling mouth, molded and painted boy's hair, five-piece composition body, molded and painted socks and one-strap shoes, marked "322//1. 11/1 M.//Germany" on the back of head, one-piece romper with belt, $375.00. Courtesy McMasters Harris Doll Auctions.

Mold 9056, ca. 1914, square, painted eyes closed mouth

8"	$525.00	$700.00

Too few in database for reliable range.

Mold 9573

7"	$675.00	$900.00
11"	$1,050.00	$1,400.00

Mold 9578, Mold 11173, "Tiss Me," ca. 1914

10"	$1,050.00	$1,450.00
14"	$1,200.00	$1,600.00

Mold 9743

Sitting, open/closed mouth, top-knot, star shaped hands

7"	$450.00	$600.00

Winker, one eye painted closed

14"	$1,600.00	$2,200.00

Too few in database for reliable range.

KÄMMER & REINHARDT

Mold 131, ca. 1914, "S&H//K*R," closed mouth

8½"	$6,500.00* toddler	
13"	$4,150.00	$5,500.00
15"	$12,000.00*	

KESTNER

Mold 221, ca. 1913, "JDK ges. gesch"

Character, smiling closed mouth

12"	$4,500.00	$6,000.00
14"	$12,000.00*	

KLEY & HAHN

Mold 180, ca. 1915

"K&H" by Hertel Schwab & Co. for Kley & Hahn, character, laughing open/closed mouth

15"	$2,025.00	$2,700.00
17"	$2,550.00	$3,400.00

LENCI: See Lenci category.

LIMBACH

Marked with crown and cloverleaf, socket head, large round glass eyes, pug nose, closed smiling mouth

7"	$1,600.00*	
10"	$1,050.00	$1,400.00

ARMAND MARSEILLE

Mold 200, "AM 243," ca. 1911, closed mouth

8"	$950.00	$1,250.00
11"	$1,500.00	$2,000.00

Mold 210, "AM 243," ca. 1911, character, solid-dome head, painted eyes, closed mouth

8"	$1,400.00	$1,850.00
13"	$1,000.00*	

Mold 223, ca. 1913, character, closed mouth

7"	$550.00	$750.00
11"	$725.00	$950.00

Mold 240, ca. 1914, "AM" dome, painted, closed mouth

10"	$2,400.00*	
11"	$2,100.00	$2,600.00

Mold 252, "AM 248," ca. 1912

Solid dome, molded tuft, painted eyes, closed mouth

9"	$1,350.00	$1,800.00
12"	$1,800.00	$2,400.00

Mold 253, "AM Nobbikid Reg. U.S. Pat. 066 Germany," ca. 1925

6"	$750.00	$1,000.00
10"	$2,000.00	$2,500.00

Mold 254, ca. 1912, "AM" dome, painted eyes, closed mouth

10"	$500.00	$700.00

Mold 310, "AM//JUST ME" 1929, for Geo. Borgfeldt

9"	$1,200.00	$1,600.00
12"	$1,350.00	$1,800.00

Mold 310, painted bisque, "Just Me"

9"	$525.00	$700.00
12"	$825.00	$1,100.00

Mold 320, "AM 255," ca. 1913, dome, painted eyes

9"	$575.00	$775.00
12"	$700.00	$950.00

Mold 322, "AM," ca. 1914, dome, painted eyes

8"	$500.00	$675.00
11"	$650.00	$875.00

Mold 323, 1914 – 1925, glass eyes, also composition

7½"	$800.00	$1,100.00
11"	$1,200.00	$1,500.00
13"	$1,700.00	$2,200.00

Mold 323, baby body

13"	$800.00	$1,200.00

Mold 323, painted bisque baby

11"	$350.00	$475.00

Mold 325, ca. 1915, character, closed mouth

9"	$548.00	$725.00
14"	$750.00	$1,000.00

P.M. Porzellanfabrik Mengersgereuth, ca. 1926

"PM" character, closed mouth. Previously thought to be made by Otto Reinecke.

Mold 950

11"	$3,100.00*	
15"	$1,200.00	$1,600.00

* at auction

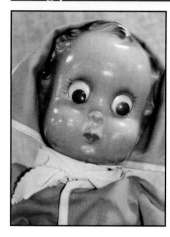

15" composition unmarked Freundlich GooGoo Eyes Dutch girl, unmarked, molded and painted curly hair, cloth body and hands, blue Dutch-style dress and hat, wooden shoes, circa 1937, $100.00. Courtesy Thelma Williams.

S.F.B.J.
   Mold 245
      8" $1,800.00*
      Fully jointed body
      10" $1,200.00 $1,600.00
STEINER, HERM
   Mold 133, ca. 1920, "HS" closed mouth, papier-mâché body
      8" $500.00 $700.00
STROBEL & WILKIN
   Mold 405
      7" $1,400.00*
WALTER & SOHN
   Mold 208, ca. 1920, "W&S" closed mouth
      Five-piece papier-mâché body, painted socks/shoes
      8" $525.00 $700.00
      9" $1,100.00*

Greiner, Ludwig

1840 – 1874. Succeeded by sons, 1890 – 1900, Philadelphia, PA. Papier-mâché shoulder head dolls, with molded hair, painted/glass eyes, usually made up to be large dolls, 13" – 38".

First price is for doll in good condition with flaws; second price is for doll in excellent condition appropriately dressed or with original clothes.

Mark:
GREINER'S
PATENT HEADS.
No. 0.
Pat. March 30th, '58.

30" papier-mâché shoulder head, painted blue eyes, painted upper lashes, closed mouth, molded and painted black hair, homemade cloth body, one hand missing. marked "Greiner's//(Pa)tent Heads//No. 11//Pat. March 30th, '58," on label on back of shoulder plate, original red jacket in poor condition, replaced antique child's dress, slip, pants, long wool socks, $750.00. Courtesy McMasters Harris Doll Auctions.

With "1858" label

17"	$400.00	$750.00
23"	$600.00	$1,100.00
25"	$2,500.00*	
30"	$750.00	$1,400.00
35"	$750.00	$1,500.00
38"	$1,000.00	$2,000.00
Glass eyes		
21"	$1,200.00	$1,600.00
26"	$1,725.00	$2,300.00

With "1872" label

18"	$225.00	$450.00
21"	$265.00	$525.00
26"	$425.00	$750.00
30"	$550.00	$1,075.00

Pre Greiner, unmarked, ca. 1850
Papier-mâché shoulder head, cloth body, leather, wood, or cloth limbs, painted hair, black glass eyes, no pupils

18"	$900.00	$1,200.00
26"	$1,200.00	$1,600.00
30"	$1,425.00	$1,900.00
Painted eyes		
18"	$335.00	$450.00
26"	$475.00	$650.00
30"	$600.00	$825.00

Handwerck, Heinrich

1876 – 1930, Gotha, Germany. Made composition doll bodies, sent Handwerck molds to Simon & Halbig to make bisque heads. Trademarks included an eight-point star with French or German wording, a shield, and "Bébé Cosmopolite," "Bébé de Reclame," and "Bébé Superior." Sold dolls through Gimbels, Macy's, Montgomery Wards, and others. Bodies marked *"Handwerk"* in red on lower back torso. Patented a straight wrist body.

First price is for doll in good condition with flaws; second price is for doll in excellent condition appropriately dressed or with original clothes. Exceptional dolls may be more.

CHILD WITH MOLDS 69, 89, 99, OR NO MOLD NUMBER
Open mouth, sleep or set eyes, ball-jointed body, bisque socket head, pierced ears, appropriate wig, nicely dressed

11"	$400.00	$500.00
15"	$450.00	$575.00
21"	$550.00	$700.00
24"	$575.00	$775.00
28"	$775.00	$1,050.00
30"	$825.00	$1,100.00
32"	$1,000.00	$1,400.00
36"	$1,500.00	$2,000.00
40"	$2,500.00	$3,100.00

CHILD WITH MOLD NUMBER, OPEN MOUTH
Molds 79, 109, 119, 139, 199

13"	$400.00	$500.00
15"	$475.00	$625.00
18"	$525.00	$725.00
22"	$625.00	$825.00
25"	$675.00	$900.00
29"	$750.00	$1,000.00
32"	$1,050.00	$1,350.00
36"	$1,550.00	$2,100.00
40"	$2,650.00	$3,400.00

Mark:

119 - 13
HANDWERCK
5
Germany

25", mold #119, bisque socket head, blue sleep eyes, painted lashes, open mouth, four upper teeth, pierced ears, original mohair wig, jointed wood and composition body, marked "119-123/4//Handwerck//Germany//43/4" on back of head, lavender organdy dress and bonnet, $450.00. Courtesy McMasters Harris Doll Auctions.

Handwerck, Heinrich

Kid body, shoulder head, open mouth

14"	$175.00	$235.00
17"	$250.00	$330.00
24"	$350.00	$475.00

Mold 79, 89 closed mouth

15"	$1,300.00	$1,800.00
18"	$1,700.00	$2,200.00

Too few in database for reliable range.

Mold 189, open mouth

15"	$600.00	$800.00
18"	$700.00	$950.00
22"	$900.00	$1,200.00

Bébé Cosmopolite

28"	$1,500.00* boxed

Handwerck, Max

Marks:

21", mold #421, bisque socket head, blue sleep eyes, painted lashes, open mouth, four upper teeth, pierced ears, mohair wig, jointed wood and composition body, marked "421//11 1/2//Germany//M.Handwerck//3 1/2" on back of head, pale green silk dress, slip, factory chemise, new socks and shoes, $700.00. Courtesy McMasters Harris Doll Auctions.

1899 – 1930, Walthershausen, Germany. Made dolls and doll bodies, registered trademark, "Bébé Elite." Used heads made by Goebel.

CHILD

Bisque socket head, open mouth, sleep or set eyes, jointed composition body

Mold 283, 286, 291, 297, 307, and others

23"	$400.00	$550.00

BÉBÉ ELITE, CA. 1900

Bisque socket head, mohair wig, glass sleep eyes, mohair lashes, open mouth, pierced ears, jointed composition/wood body

Marks: *"Max Handwerck Bébé Elite 286 12 Germany" on back of head.*

15"	$425.00	$575.00
20"	$600.00	$800.00
27"	$750.00	$975.00

Bébé Elite, flange neck, cloth body

15"	$350.00	$445.00
20"	$475.00	$650.00

GOOGLY: See Googly category.

Hartmann, Carl

1889 – 1930, Neustadt, Germany. Made and exported bisque and celluloid dolls, especially small dolls in regional costumes, called Globe Babies.

Kämmer & Reinhardt made heads for Hartmann.

CHILD

Bisque socket head, open mouth, jointed composition and wood body

| 22" | $225.00 | $375.00 |

GLOBE BABY

Bisque socket head, glass sleep eyes, open mouth, four teeth, mohair or human hair wig, five-piece papier-mâché or composition body with painted shoes and stockings

| 8" | $315.00 | $450.00 |
| 9" | $375.00 | $500.00 |

Mark:

Globe Baby
DEP
Germany
C 3 H

Hartmann, Karl

1911 – 1926, Stockheim, Germany. Doll factory, made and exported dolls. Advertised ball-jointed dolls, characters, and papier-mâché dolls.

Marks:

30

K
H
3

CHILD

Bisque socket head, open mouth, glass eyes, composition body

18"	$350.00	$500.00
22"	$400.00	$600.00
32"	$700.00	$875.00

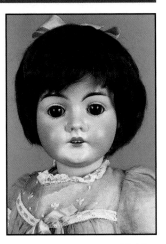

22½", bisque socket head, brown sleep eyes, painted lashes, open mouth, four upper teeth, mohair wig, jointed wood and composition body, marked "28.5//K//O" inside large "H" on back of head, blue lace-trimmed organdy dress, underclothing, socks, replaced shoes, $200.00. Courtesy McMasters Harris Doll Auctions.

Hertel Schwab & Co.

1910 – 1930+, Stutzhaus, Germany. Founded by August Hertel and Heinrich Schwab, both designed doll heads used by Borgfelt, Kley and Hahn, König & Wernicke, Louis Wolf, and others. Made china and bisque heads as well as all-porcelain; most with character faces. Molded hair or wig, painted blue or glass eyes (often blue-gray), open mouth with tongue or closed mouth, socket or shoulder heads. Usually marked with mold number and *"Made in Germany,"* or mark of company that owned the mold.

BABY

Bisque head, molded hair or wig, open or open/closed mouth, teeth, sleep or painted eyes, bent-leg baby composition body

Mold 130, 142, 150, 151, 152

9"	$250.00	$325.00
11"	$335.00	$450.00
16"	$475.00	$650.00
22"	$675.00	$900.00
24"	$700.00	$950.00

Mark:

Made
in
Germany
151/0

Hertel Schwab & Co.

17" bisque solid dome, mold #151 baby, socket head, brown sleep eyes, painted lashes, open mouth with two painted upper teeth, lightly molded and brush-stroked hair, composition bent-limb baby body, marked "151//10" on back of head, blue/white checked romper with with trim, $250.00. Courtesy McMasters Harris Doll Auctions.

Toddler body

14"	$400.00	$600.00
20"	$600.00	$800.00

CHILD

Mold 127, ca. 1915, character face, solid dome with molded hair, sleep eyes, open mouth, Patsy-type

15"	$1,000.00	$1,350.00
17"	$1,500.00	$2,000.00

Mold 131, ca. 1912, character face, solid dome, painted closed mouth

18"	$1,300.00*

Mold 134, ca. 1915, character face, sleep eyes, closed mouth

15"	$15,000.00*

Mold 136, ca. 1912, *"Made in Germany,"* character face, open mouth

24"	$700.00	$1,000.00

Mold 140, ca. 1912, character, glass eyes, open/closed laughing mouth

12"	$2,550.00	$3,400.00

Mold 141, ca. 1912, character, painted eyes, open/closed mouth

12"	$2,400.00	$3,200.00
18"	$10,200.00*	

Mold 149, ca. 1912, character, glass eyes, closed mouth, ball-jointed body

17"	$9,500.00*

Mold 154, ca. 1912, character, solid dome, molded hair, glass eyes, open mouth

20"	$1,900.00*

Mold 159, ca. 1911, two faces

10"	$850.00*

Mold 167, ca. 1912, "K&H" character, open/closed or closed mouth, made for Kley & Hahn

15"	$2,000.00*

GOOGLY: See Googly category.

Heubach, Ernst

1886 – 1930+, Köppelsdorf, Germany. In 1919, the son of Armand Marseille married the daughter of Ernst Heubach and merged the two factories. Mold numbers range from 250 to 452. They made porcelain heads for Dressel (Jutta), Revalo, and others.

BABY

Mark:

Open mouth, glass eyes, socket head, wig, five-piece bent-leg composition body, add more for toddler body, flirty eyes

Mold 267, 300, 320, 321, 342

11"	$190.00	$250.00
14"	$300.00	$400.00
20"	$400.00	$550.00
27"	$725.00	$975.00

Baby, Newborn, ca. 1925+

Solid dome, molded and painted hair, glass eyes, closed mouth, cloth body, composition or celluloid hands

Mold 338, 339, 340, 348, 349, 399

12"	$300.00	$425.00
14"	$425.00	$575.00
15"	$525.00	$700.00
17"	$600.00	$800.00

Black, mold 444

12"	$300.00	$400.00

CHILD, 1888+

Mold 1900 with Horseshoe Mark

Open mouth, glass eyes, kid or cloth body

12"	$115.00	$150.00
18"	$210.00	$275.00
22"	$310.00	$415.00
26"	$500.00	$650.00

Painted bisque

12"	$125.00	$175.00
16"	$175.00	$225.00

Mold 250, 251, 275 (shoulder head), 302,

open mouth, kid body

9"	$130.00	$200.00
13"	$150.00	$250.00
16"	$200.00	$300.00
19"	$325.00	$425.00
23"	$400.00	$525.00
27"	$500.00	$675.00
32"	$650.00	$900.00
36"	$900.00	$1,100.00

18" bisque, mold #320 character baby, marked "Heubach Koppelsdorf//320 6 //Germany" on back of socket head, human hair wig, blue sleep eyes, real and painted lashes, feathered brows, pierced nostrils, open mouth, two upper teeth, bent-limb composition baby body, antique christening dress, antique baby bonnet, slip, diaper, new socks and shoes, circa 1920, $275.00. Courtesy McMasters Harris Doll Auctions.

Heubach, Gebrüder

1820 – 1945, Lichte, Thüringia, Germany. Made bisque heads and all-bisque dolls, characters after 1910, either socket or shoulder head, molded hair or wigs, sleeping or intaglio eyes, in heights from 4" to 26". Mold numbers from 556 to 10633. Sunburst or square marks; more dolls with square marks.

MARKED *"HEUBACH,"* NO MOLD NUMBER

Open/closed mouth, dimples

18"	$3,300.00	$4,450.00
24"	$4,700.00	$6,300.00

Adult, open mouth, glass eyes

14"	$3,350.00	$4,500.00

Smile, painted eyes

15"	$2,700.00	$3,500.00

MARKED HEUBACH GOOGLY: See Googly category.

CHARACTER CHILD, SHOULDER HEAD

Mold 6688, ca. 1912, solid dome, molded hair, intaglio eyes, closed mouth

10"	$450.00	$625.00

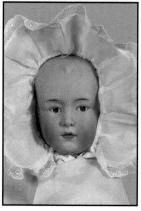

14½", mold #7603 baby, bisque socket head, blue intaglio eyes, closed mouth, lightly molded and painted hair, bent-limb composition baby body, marked "76 (sunburst//DEP) 03//6//Germany," on back of head, "87" on front of neck, long antique white baby dress, antique underclothing, baby bonnet, and pink silk cape, $600.00. Courtesy McMasters Harris Doll Auctions.

9", mold #8191 baby, bisque socket head, blue intaglio eyes, single stroke brows, open-closed mouth with molded tongue, four upper and six lower teeth, molded and painted hair, composition baby body, marked "2/0//81 Heubach (in square) 91//Germany, BL," in green all on back of head, "00" on left side of torso and on arm and leg joints, red/blue knit romper, $300.00. Courtesy McMasters Harris Doll Auctions.

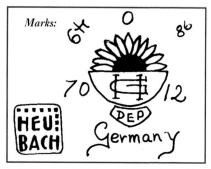

Marks:

Mold 6692, ca. 1912, sunburst, intaglio eyes, closed mouth

14"	$650.00	$875.00

Mold 6736, ca. 1912, square, painted eyes, laughing mouth

13"	$800.00	$1,100.00
16"	$1,400.00	$1,900.00

Mold 7345, ca. 1912, sunburst, pink-tinted closed mouth

17"	$1,150.00

Too few in database for reliable range.

Mold 7644, ca. 1910, sunburst or square mark, painted eyes, open/closed laughing mouth

14"	$650.00	$865.00
17"	$875.00	$1,200.00

Mold 7847, solid dome shoulder head, intaglio eyes, closed smiling mouth, teeth

20"	$2,100.00*

Too few in database for reliable range.

Mold 7850, ca. 1912, "Coquette," open/closed mouth

11"	$550.00	$750.00
15"	$800.00	$1,100.00

Mold 7925, ca. 1914, **Mold 7926,** ca. 1912, shoulder head, glass eyes, smiling open mouth, lady

15"	$1,500.00	$2,000.00
20"	$3,700.00, mold 7925*	

Too few in database for reliable range

Mold 7972, intaglio eyes, closed mouth

20"	$1,500.00	$2,000.00

Too few in database for reliable range.

Mold 8221, square mark, dome, intaglio eyes, open/closed mouth

14"	$500.00	$675.00

Too few in database for reliable range.

Mold 9355, ca. 1914, square mark, glass eyes, open mouth

13"	$650.00	$850.00
19"	$925.00	$1,250.00

* at auction

CHARACTER BABY OR CHILD, SOCKET HEAD

Mold 5636, ca. 1912, glass eyes, open/closed laughing mouth, teeth
13"	$1,500.00	$2,000.00
15"	$1,800.00	$2,400.00

Mold 5689, ca. 1912, sunburst mark, open mouth
14"	$1,350.00	$1,800.00
17"	$1,700.00	$2,250.00
22"	$2,200.00	$2,900.00

Mold 5730, "Santa," ca. 1912, sunburst mark, made for Hamburger & Co.
16"	$1,250.00	$1,700.00
19"	$1,900.00	$2,500.00
26"	$2,100.00	$2,800.00

Mold 5777, "Dolly Dimple," ca. 1913, open mouth, for Hamburger & Co.
14"	$1,725.00	$2,300.00
16"	$1,900.00	$2,500.00
24"	$2,600.00	$3,450.00

Mold 6894, 6897, 7759, all ca. 1912, sunburst or square mark, intaglio eyes, closed mouth, molded hair
7"	$275.00	$375.00
9"	$375.00	$500.00
12"	$525.00	$700.00

Mold 6969, ca. 1912, socket head, square mark, glass eyes, closed mouth
12"	$1,600.00	$2,000.00
16"	$2,500.00	$3,000.00

11" bisque twins, mold #7246, bisque socket heads, blue sleep eyes, painted lashes, closed pouty mouths, original mohair wigs, jointed wood and composition bodies with jointed wrists, marked "1//Germany//72 Heubach (in square) 46// 16" on back of heads, completely original factory outfits, boy wears two-piece wool outfit with felt cap, original socks and shoes, girl wears wool drop waist dress, straw hat, factory underclothing, socks, and shoes, $2,650.00. Courtesy McMasters Harris Doll Auctions.

Mold 6970, ca. 1912, sunburst, glass eyes, closed mouth
10"	$1,300.00	$1,800.00
13"	$1,700.00	$2,300.00
19"	$4,100.00*	

Mold 6971, ca. 1912, intaglio eyes, closed smiling mouth in original costume box
11"	$1,200.00*	

Mold 7246, 7248, ca. 1912, sunburst or square mark, closed mouth
16"	$975.00	$1,300.00

Mold 7247, ca. 1912, glass eyes, closed mouth
15"	$2,700.00	$3,500.00

Mold 7268, square, glass eyes, closed mouth
12"	$5,000.00*	

Mold 7407, character, glass eyes, open/closed mouth
18"	$2,500.00	$3,000.00

Mold 7602, 7603, ca. 1912, molded hair tufts, intaglio eyes
15"	$750.00	$1,000.00

Mold 7604, ca. 1912, open/closed mouth, intaglio eyes
12"	$550.00	$725.00

Baby
15"	$525.00	$700.00

27" Dainty Dorothy, mold #10633, boxed, bisque shoulder head, brown sleep eyes, painted lashes, kid body with composition lower arms and legs, open mouth, four teeth, original mohair wig, marked "10633//11" on back of head, "Gebr. Heubach//Germany//Heubach" in square on back of shoulder plate, "Dainty Dorothy//copyright 1910 by Sears Roebuck and Co.//Germany" on label, factory chemise, $675.00. Courtesy McMasters Harris Doll Auctions.

11½" bisque mold #10586 socket head, marked "10586//1//WZ//J" on back of head, blue sleep eyes, real lashes, feathered brows, painted lashes, open mouth with four upper teeth, original human hair wig, jointed wood and composition body, original ethnic costume from Turkey, circa 1920, $425.00. Courtesy McMasters Harris Doll Auctions.

Mold 7622, 7623, ca. 1912, intaglio eyes, closed or open/closed mouth

16"	$800.00	$1,200.00
18"	$1,000.00	$1,400.00

Mold 7681, dome, intaglio eyes, closed mouth

10"	$650.00*

Mold 7711, ca. 1912, glass eyes, open mouth, flapper body

10"	$525.00	$700.00

Mold 7759, ca. 1912, dome, painted eyes, closed mouth

12"	$900.00*

Mold 7911, ca. 1912, intaglio eyes, laughing open/closed mouth

9"	$525.00	$700.00
15"	$900.00	$1,200.00

Mold 7975, "Baby Stuart," ca. 1912, glass eyes, removable molded bisque bonnet

13"	$1,425.00	$1,900.00

Mold 7977, "Baby Stuart," ca. 1912, molded bonnet, closed mouth, painted eyes

8"	$600.00	$800.00
11"	$1,000.00	$1,400.00

Mold 8191, "Crooked Smile," ca. 1912, square mark, intaglio eyes, laughing mouth

11½"	$500.00*	
14"	$375.00	$500.00

Mold 8192, ca. 1914, sunburst or square mark, sleep eyes, open mouth

13"	$675.00	$900.00
20"	$1,250.00*	

Mold 8316, "Grinning Boy," ca. 1914, wig, open/closed mouth, eight teeth, glass eyes

16"	$2,500.00	$3,400.00
19"	$3,600.00	$4,800.00

Mold 8381, "Princess Juliana," molded hair, ribbon, painted eyes, closed mouth

14"	$5,000.00	$6,600.00+

Mold 8413, ca. 1914, wig, sleep eyes, open/closed mouth, molded tongue, upper teeth

8"	$550.00	$850.00

Too few in database for reliable range.

Mold 8420, ca. 1914, square mark, glass eyes, closed mouth

15"	$2,100.00	$2,800.00

Too few in database for reliable range.

Mold 8429, square mark, closed mouth

15"	$2,500.00*

Too few in database for reliable range.

Mold 8686, glass eyes, open/closed mouth
    14" $3,200.00*
Too few in database for reliable range.
    Mold 8774, "Whistling Jim," ca. 1914, smoker or whistler, square mark, flange neck, intaglio eyes, molded hair, cloth body, bellows
    14" $985.00*
Too few in database for reliable range.
    Mold 8819, square mark, intaglio eyes, open/closed mouth
    9" $1,050.00*
Too few in database for reliable range.
    Mold 8950, laughing girl, blue hairbow
    18" $7,000.00*
Mold 9027, dome, intaglio eyes, closed mouth
    13" $900.00 $1,200.00
Too few in database for reliable range.
    Mold 9055, intaglio eyes, closed mouth
    11" $275.00 $375.00
Too few in database for reliable range.
    Mold 9457, ca. 1914, square mark, dome, intaglio eyes, closed mouth, Eskimo

10½" bisque mold #7407 character girl, glass eyes, closed mouth, auburn human hair wig, print dress, straw hat, circa 1912, $1,800.00. Courtesy Elizabeth Surber.

    15" $1,875.00 $2,500.00
    18" $3,000.00 $4,000.00
    Mold 9746, square mark, painted eyes, closed mouth
    7½" $600.00 $800.00
Too few in database for reliable range.
    Mold 10532, ca. 1920, square mark, open mouth
    13½" $450.00 $600.00
    25" $1,125.00 $1,500.00
    Mold 11010, "Revalo," ca. 1922, sleep eyes, open mouth, for Gebr. Ohlhaver
    19" $525.00 $700.00
    24" $650.00 $850.00
    Mold 11173, "Tiss Me," socket head, wig
    8" $1,500.00 $2,000.00
Too few in database for reliable range.
FIGURINES
    Square or Sunburst mark, all at auction
    Seated Baby, dog 4½" $525.00
    Dutch pair   6" $750.00
    Coquette   16" $1,900.00
    Piano Baby, Mold 7287, 9693, and others
    5" $400.00 $525.00
    9" $525.00 $700.00
    13" $1,000.00*

Hulss, Adolph

    1915 – 1930+, Waltershausen, Germany. Made dolls with bisque heads, jointed composition bodies. *Trademark: "Nesthakchen,"* "h" in mold mark often resembles a "b." Made babies, toddlers, and child dolls with ball joints.

BABY

Bisque socket head, sleep eyes, open mouth, teeth, wig, bent-leg baby, composition body, add more for flirty eyes.

Mark:

Mold 156

14"	$425.00	$575.00
19"	$850.00	$1,125.00

Toddler

16"	$625.00	$800.00
20"	$775.00	$1,000.00

CHILD

Bisque socket head, wig, sleep eyes, open mouth, teeth, tongue, jointed composition body

Mold 176

15"	$575.00	$750.00
22"	$925.00	$1,250.00

Huret, Maison

1812 – 1930+, France. May have pressed, molded bisque, or china heads, painted or glass eyes, closed mouths, bodies of cloth, composition, gutta-percha, kid, or wood, sometimes metal hands. Used fur or mohair for wigs, had fashion-type body with defined waist.

What to look for: Dolls with beautiful painting on eyes and face; painted eyes are more common than glass, but the beauty of the painted features and/or wooden bodies increases the price.

Bisque shoulder head, kid body with bisque lower arms, glass eyes

15"	$4,500.00	$6,000.00
17"	$6,100.00	$8,000.00

Round face, painted blue eyes, cloth body

16"	$8,722.00*

Wood body

17"	$21,000.00*

Too few in database for reliable range.

China shoulder head, kid body, china lower arms

17"	$5,000.00	$7,000.00

Metal hands, swivel neck, glass eyes

15"	$10,550.00* (presumed Huret)

Too few in database for reliable range.

Pressed bisque shoulder head, wood body, painted eyes, labeled body

17"	$21,000.00*

Too few in database for reliable range.

Gutta-percha stamped body

17"	$17,500.00*

Pressed bisque, marked articulated body, with provenance

18"	$62,000.00*

Too few in database for reliable range.

Painted eyes, marked kid body

17"	$16,500.00*

Too few in database for reliable range.

Painted eyes, open/closed mouth, fashion body

* Only one reported, extremely rare

1827 – 1904, Paris, Conflans, St. Leonard. Had a porcelain factory, won some awards, purchased bisque heads from Francois Gaultier.

CHILD

Bisque socket head, wig, glass eyes, pierced ears, open mouth with teeth or closed mouth, on jointed composition body

Closed mouth

19"	$2,850.00	$3,800.00
24"	$3,175.00	$4,250.00

Open mouth

18"	$1,200.00	$1,600.00

1842 – 1899, Paris and Montreuil-sous-Bois; succeeded by S.F.B.J. through 1958. Founder Pierre Francois Jumeau made fashion dolls with kid or wood bodies; head marked with size number; bodies stamped *"JUMEAU//MEDAILLE D'OR//PARIS."* Early Jumeau heads were pressed pre-1890. By 1878, son Emile Jumeau was head of the company and made Bébé Jumeau, marked on back of head, on chemise, band on arm of dress. Tête Jumeaus have poured heads. Bébé Protige and Bébé Jumeau registered trademarks in 1886; Bee Mark in 1891; Bébé Marcheur in 1895, Bébé Francaise in 1896.

Mold numbers of marked EJs and Têtes approximate the following heights: 1 – 10", 2 – 11", 3 – 12", 4 – 13", 5 – 14", 6 – 16", 7 – 17", 8 – 18", 9 – 20", 10 – 21", 11 – 24", 12 – 26", 13 – 30".

First price is for doll in good condition, but with some flaws; second price is for doll in excellent condition, nicely wigged, and with appropriate clothing. Exceptional doll may be much more.

26" Tête Jumeau, bisque socket head, bulbous brown paperweight eyes, heavy feathered brows, painted lashes, closed mouth, pierced ears, human hair wig, jointed wood and composition body with jointed wrists, marked "Depose//Tête Jumeau//Bte S.G.D.G.//12" incised on back of head, "18" in red, black and red artists marks on back of head, "Jumeau//Medaille d'Or//Paris" stamped low on back, "12//(robed figure)" on bottom of shoes, $3,250.00. Courtesy McMasters Harris Doll Auctions

Fashion-type Jumeau

Marked with size number on swivel head, closed mouth, paperweight eyes, pierced ears, stamped kid body, add more for original clothes.

11"	$2,000.00	$2,600.00
17"	$3,050.00	$3,800.00
20"	$4,000.00	$4,600.00

Wood body, bisque lower arms

16"	$3,800.00	$5,100.00

Jumeau Portrait

21"	$4,850.00	$6,600.00

Wood body

20"	$6,300.00	$8,500.00

Almond eye

13½"	$8,500.00	$12,500.00
17"	$13,000.00	$17,500.00
20"	$20,000.00	$25,000.00

32", bisque socket head, deep blue paperweight eyes, painted lashes, open mouth, six upper teeth, replaced human har wig, jointed wood and composition body, marked "14" on back of head, "Jumeau//Medaille d'Or Paris" stamped in blue on lower back, antique white dress, antique underclothing, new socks and shoes, $2,700.00. Courtesy McMasters Harris Doll Auctions.

14" Tête Jumeau, bisque socket head, bulbous brown paperweight eyes, painted lashes, closed mouth, mohair wig, jointed wood and composition body, marked "Depose//Tête Jumeau//Bte. S.G.D.G.//5" and red and black artist marks on back of head, "Jumeau//Medaille d'Or//Paris" on lower back, low-waisted dress, factory underclothing, black antique net socks, new shoes and black bonnet, $3,300.00. Courtesy McMasters Harris Doll Auctions.

E.J. BÉBÉ, 1881 – 1886

Earliest "EJ" mark above with number over initials, pressed bisque socket head, wig, paperweight eyes, pierced ears, closed mouth, jointed body with straight wrists

Mark:
E.J. Bébé
1881 – 86
6
E.J.

17"	$7,200.00	$10,250.00
20"	$9,000.00	$12,000.00
26"	$15,000.00*	

EJ/A marked Bébé

17"	$20,000.00+

*Too few in database for reliable range.

Mid "EJ" mark has size number centered between E and J (E 8 J)

Mark:
Mid EJ mark has size number centered between E and J
(E 8 J)

15"	$4,700.00	$6,200.00
17"	$4,900.00	$6,600.00
20"	$5,400.00	$7,200.00
23"	$6,000.00	$8,000.00
26"	$6,750.00	$9,000.00

Later "EJ" mark is preceded by DEPOSE (DEPOSE/E 8 J)

15"	$3,800.00	$5,000.00
19"	$4,300.00	$5,850.00
23"	$5,025.00	$6,625.00
26"	$6,000.00	$8,000.00

DEPOSE JUMEAU, CA. 1886 – 1889

Poured bisque head marked, *"Depose Jumeau,"* and size number, pierced ears, closed mouth, paperweight eyes, composition and wood body with straight wrists marked *"Medaille d'Or Paris"*

14"	$3,750.00	$5,000.00
18"	$4,400.00	$5,900.00
23"	$5,200.00	$6,900.00

LONG FACE TRISTE BÉBÉ, 1879 – 1886

Head marked with number only, pierced applied ears, closed mouth, paperweight eyes, straight wrists on Jumeau marked body

27"	$15,000.00*

*Too few in database for reliable range.

TÊTE JUMEAU, CA. 1885+

Poured bisque socket head, red stamp on head, stamp or sticker on body, wig, glass eyes, pierced ears, closed mouth, jointed composition body with straight wrists. May also be marked E.D. with size number when Douillet ran factory, uses tête face.

The following sizes were used for Têtes: 1 – 10", 2 – 11", 3 – 12", 4 – 13", 5 – 14½", 6 – 16", 7 – 17", 8 – 19", 10–21½", 11 – 24", 12 – 26", 13 – 29", 14 – 31", 15 – 33", 16 – 34" – 35".

Bébé (Child), closed mouth

10"	$4,000.00	$5,500.00
12"	$2,700.00	$3,500.00
17"	$3,000.00	$4,100.00
19"	$3,500.00	$4,650.00
23"	$3,800.00	$5,000.00
26"	$4,000.00	$5,200.00
30"	$4,650.00	$6,200.00
32"	$6,000.00	$8,000.00

Trouseau/provenance

19"	$13,500.00*

Adult body, open mouth

15"	$1,875.00	$2,500.00
17"	$2,100.00	$2,800.00
21"	$2,400.00	$3,200.00
25"	$2,600.00	$3,500.00
28"	$2,700.00	$3,700.00
32"	$3,100.00	$4,200.00

Rare pressed brown bisque swivel head, "Madagascar"

24½"	$89,270.00*

"1907," CHILD, CA. 1907

Some with Tête Jumeau stamp, sleep or set eyes, open mouth, jointed French body

14"	$975.00	$1,850.00
17"	$1,800.00	$2,500.00
20"	$2,150.00	$2,900.00
23"	$2,350.00	$3,200.00
26"	$2,650.00	$3,600.00
29"	$2,950.00	$3,900.00
32"	$3,100.00	$4,150.00

B. L. BÉBÉ, CA. 1880S

Marked "*B. L.*" for the Louvre department store, socket head, wig, pierced ears, paperweight eyes, closed mouth, jointed composition body

20"	$3,800.00	$4,200.00

Too few in database for reliable range.

R.R. BÉBÉ, CA 1880S

Wig, pierced ears, paperweight eyes, closed mouth, jointed composition body with straight wrists

22"	$3,825.00	$5,100.00

Too few in database for reliable range.

CHARACTER CHILD

Mold 203, 208, and other 200 series
$50,000.00+

Too few in database for reliable range.

20" bisque Tête Jumeau, marked "Depose//Tête Jumeau//Bte S.G.D.G.//9" on back of head, "Jumeau// Medaille d'Or//Paris" on back, "9//Paris//(bee)// Depose" on shoes, human hair wig, blue paperweight eyes, painted lashes, closed mouth, pierced ears, jointed wood and composition body with jointed wrists, re-dressed in beige and red sailor-type dress, antique underclothing, socks, shoes, beige and red striped bow in hair, circa 1885+, $4,300.00. Courtesy McMasters Harris Doll Auctions.

20", bisque socket head, blue paperweight eyes, painted lashes, open mouth with six upper teeth, replaced human hair wig, jointed wood and composition French body, "Jumeau" stamped in red, "8" incised on back of head, re-dressed in pink satin French-style dress, antique underclothing, new socks, pink leatherette shoes, $950.00. Courtesy McMasters Harris Doll Auctions.

34", mold #1907, bisque socket head, brown paperweight eyes, painted lashes, open mouth with six upper teeth, replaced human hair wig, jointed wood and composition German body, marked "1907//14" on back of head, "Made in Germany" stamped on back of right hip, blue velvet drop waist dress, underclothing, socks, antique leather doll shoes, $1,100.00. Courtesy McMasters Harris Doll Auctions.

Mold 221, Great Ladies

10"	$400.00	$600.00

Mold 230, open mouth

16"	$1,100.00	$1,500.00
20"	$1,350.00	$1,800.00

Too few in database for reliable range.

Two-Faced Jumeau

18"	$14,500.00*

Too few in database for reliable range.

Phonograph Jumeau

Bisque head, open mouth, phonograph in torso, working condition

24"	$19,000.00*
25"	$7,800.00*

Too few in database for reliable range.

PRINCESS ELIZABETH

Made after Jumeau joined SFBJ and adopted Unis label, mark will be *"71 Unis//France 149//306//Jumeau//1938//Paris."* Bisque socket head with high color, closed mouth, flirty eyes, jointed composition body

Mold 306

18"	$1,600.00	$2,100.00
30"	$2,900.00	$3,500.00

Too few in database for reliable range.

ACCESSORIES

Marked shoes

5 – 6"	$225.00	$300.00
7 – 10"	$450.00	$600.00

Kämmer & Reinhardt

1886 – 1930+, Waltershausen, Germany. Registered trademark K*R, Majestic Doll, Mein Leibling, Die Kokette, Charakterpuppen (character dolls).

Designed doll heads, most bisque were made by Simon & Halbig; in 1918, Schuetzmeister & Quendt also supplied heads; Rheinische Gummi und Celluloid Fabrik Co. made celluloid heads for Kämmer & Reinhardt. Kämmer & Reinhardt dolls were distributed by Bing, Borgfeldt, B. Illfelder, L. Rees & Co., Strobel & Wilken, and Louis Wolf & Co. Also made heads of wood and composition, later cloth and rubber dolls.

*24½" girl, bisque socket head, blue sleep eyes with real lashes, molded and feathered brows, painted upper and lower lashes, accented nostrils, open mouth with four upper teeth, pierced ears, replaced synthetic wig, jointed wood and composition body, marked "Simon & Halbig//K*R//62" on back of head, "W" on front of forehead, antique drop waist dress, underclothing, new socks, replaced shoes, $450.00. Courtesy McMasters Harris Doll Auctions.*

Mold numbers identify heads starting with 1) bisque socket heads; 2) shoulder heads, as well as socket heads of black or mulatto babies; 3) bisque socket heads or celluloid shoulder heads; 4) heads having eyelashes; 5)

Marks:

K ✡ **R**

Germany

1126 - 21

googlies, black heads, pincushion heads; 6) mulatto heads; 7) celluloid heads, bisque head walking dolls; 8) rubber heads; 9) composition heads, some rubber heads. Other letters refer to style or material of wig or clothing.

First price indicates doll in good condition, but with some flaws. Second price indicates doll in excellent condition well dressed. Exceptional dolls may be more.

CHILD, DOLLY FACE

Mold 191, ca. 1900, open mouth, sleep eyes, jointed child body

17"	$650.00	$865.00
30"	$1,100.00	$1,500.00

Mold 192, ca. 1900, open mouth, sleep eyes, jointed child's body

9"	$750.00	$1,000.00
18"	$825.00	$1,100.00
22"	$975.00	$1,300.00

With trunk

9"	$1,800.00*

Closed mouth

18"	$2,100.00	$2,800.00

No mold numbers, or marked only "*K*R*" or size number in centimeters, or mold 401, 402, 403, socket head, glass eyes, open mouth

12"	$375.00	$500.00
19"	$550.00	$750.00
25"	$825.00	$1,100.00

Closed mouth, flapper body

14"	$2,400.00*

CHARACTERS

Mold 100, ca. 1909

Once called Kaiser Baby, but no connection has been found. Character baby, with dome head, jointed bent-leg body, intaglio eyes, open/closed mouth, appropriate dress, good condition

12"	$375.00	$575.00
15"	$575.00	$775.00
20"	$750.00	$1,100.00

24½" mold #126 baby, bisque socket head, blue sleep eyes, feathered brows, painted upper and lower lashes, accented nostrils, open mouth with two upper teeth and wobble tongue, original human hair wig, bent-limb composition baby body with working crier, marked "K*R//Simon & Halbig//Germany//126//62," on back of head, antique lace-trimmed organdy baby dress and slip, diaper, and antique bonnet, $425.00. Courtesy McMasters Harris Doll Auctions.

25" mold #121 baby, bisque socket head, blue flirty eyes with tin lids, feathered brows, painted upper and lower lashes, accented nostrils, open mouth with two upper teeth and wobble tongue, original mohair wig, composition body, marked "K*R//Simon & Halbig//121//62" on back of head, antique white baby coat, original white baby dress, original socks, cloth baby shoes, bonnet, $400.00. Courtesy McMasters Harris Doll Auctions.

10" mold #100 character baby, solid dome bisque socket head, painted blue eyes with molded lids, single stroke brows, accented nostrils, open-closed mouth, lightly molded and brush-stroked hair, composition bent-limb baby body, marked "28//K*R//100" on back of head, blue knit two-piece baby outfit, $375.00. Courtesy McMasters Harris Doll Auctions.

18" bisque mold #114, Hans character groom, painted eyes, closed mouth, mohair wig, original tuxedo, top hat, excellent condition, $4,700.00. Courtesy McMasters Harris Doll Auctions.

Mold 101, Peter or Marie, ca. 1909, painted eyes, closed mouth, jointed body

7 – 8"	$1,200.00	$1,700.00
12"	$2,125.00	$2,800.00
15"	$2,500.00	$3,200.00+
18"	$3,700.00	$4,900.00+
19"	$8,725.00*	

Glass eyes

18"	$8,000.00*

Too few in database for reliable range.

Mold 102, Elsa or Walter, ca. 1900, painted eyes, molded hair, closed mouth, very rare

14"	$32,000.00

Too few in database for reliable range.

Mold 103, ca. 1909, painted eyes, closed mouth

19"	$60,000.00+

Too few in database for reliable range.

Mold 104, ca. 1909, painted eyes, laughing closed mouth, very rare

18"	$65,000.00+

Too few in database for reliable range.

Mold 105, ca. 1909, painted eyes, open/closed mouth, very rare

21"	$170,956.00*

Too few in database to give reliable range.

Mold 106, ca. 1909, painted intaglio eyes to side, closed mouth, very rare

22"	$144,886.00* w/wrong body

Too few in database for reliable range.

Mold 107, Carl, ca. 1909, painted intaglio eyes, closed mouth

21"	$46,000.00*

Too few in database for reliable range.

Mold 108, ca. 1909, one example reported
$275,000.00+*

Mold 109, Elise, ca. 1909, painted eyes, closed mouth

14"	$5,500.00	$7,000.00
24"	$20,000.00*	

Too few in database for reliable range.

Mold 112, ca. 1909, painted open/closed mouth

13"	$8,000.00* with provenance

Mold 112X, flocked hair

17"	$16,500.00*

Too few in database for reliable range.

Mold 114, Hans or Gretchen, ca. 1909, painted eyes, closed mouth

9"	$1,350.00	$1,800.00
13"	$2,450.00	$3,275.00
18"	$4,200.00	$5,700.00
25"	$19,500.00*	

Glass eyes
9" $5,900.00*
15" $9,250.00*

Mold 115, ca. 1911, solid dome, painted hair, sleeping eyes, closed mouth, toddler
15" $4,250.00 $5,750.00

Mold 115A, ca. 1911, sleep eyes, closed mouth, wig

Baby, bent-leg body
13" $2,000.00 $3,000.00
19" $5,000.00*

Toddler, composition, jointed body
15 – 16" $3,750.00 $5,000.00
18" $4,200.00 $5,500.00

Mold 116, ca. 1911, dome head, sleep eyes, open/closed mouth, bent-leg baby body
17" $3,200.00*

Mold 116A, ca. 1911, sleep eyes, open/closed mouth or open mouth, wigged, bent-leg baby body
15" $2,250.00 $2,950.00

Toddler body
16" $2,600.00 $3,400.00

Mold 117 Mein Liebling (My Darling), ca. 1911, glass eyes, closed mouth
15" $3,325.00 $4,400.00
18" $4,100.00 $5,400.00
23" $5,100.00 $6,850.00

Mold 117A, ca. 1911, glass eyes, closed mouth
8" $1,800.00 $2,300.00
20" $3,500.00 $4,700.00
28" $6,500.00 $8,500.00

Flapper body
8" $3,500.00*

Mold 117N, Mein Neuer Liebling (My New Darling), ca. 1916, flirty eyes, open mouth
16" $1,100.00 $1,500.00
20" $1,450.00 $1,900.00
28" $2,400.00 $2,900.00

Mold 117X, ca. 1911, socket head, sleep eyes, open mouth
42" $4,800.00*

Mold 118, 118A, sleep eyes, open mouth, baby body
15" $1,125.00 $1,500.00
18" $1,700.00 $2,275.00

Mold 119, ca. 1913, sleep eyes, open/closed mouth, marked *"Baby,"* five-piece baby body
25" $16,000.00*

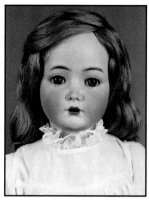

27" mold #117N, bisque socket head, blue sleep eyes with real lashes, feathered brows, painted upper and lower lashes, accented nostrils, open mouth with four upper teeth, replaced human hair wig, jointed wood and composition French-type body with jointed wrists, marked "K*R//Simon & Halbig/ /117n//65" on back of head, "12" impressed on back, redressed in antique white dress with pink velvet sash, new underclothing, white cotton socks, leatherette shoes, $1,100.00. Courtesy McMasters Harris Doll Auctions.

22½", bisque socket head, blue sleep eyes, painted upper and lower lashes, accented nostrils, open mouth with four upper teeth, pierced ears, original human hair wig, jointed wood and composition body, marked "S&H//K*R//58" on back of head, original white lace dress, underclothing, socks, and shoes, $650.00. Courtesy McMasters Harris Doll Auctions.

32", bisque socket head, large brown sleep eyes missing real lashes, molded and feathered brows, painted upper and lower lashes, accented nostrils, open mouth with accented lips and four upper teeth, pierced ears, original blond curly mohair wig, jointed wood and composition K*R body, marked "S&H//K*R//80" on back of head, original white cape dress, original underclothing and factory chemise, $1,100.00. Courtesy McMasters Harris Doll Auctions.

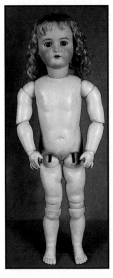

Same doll, this view nude to show German composition and wood ball-jointed body.

Mold 121, ca. 1912, sleep eyes, open mouth, baby body

10"	$450.00	$600.00
16"	$700.00	$900.00
24"	$950.00	$1,300.00

Toddler body

14"	$750.00	$1,100.00
18"	$1,850.00*	

Mold 122, ca. 1912, sleep eyes, bent-leg baby body

11"	$525.00	$700.00
16"	$635.00	$850.00
20"	$825.00	$1,100.00

Original wicker layette basket and accessories

22"	$2,800.00*	

Toddler body

13"	$825.00	$1,100.00
19"	$975.00	$1,300.00
22"	$1,025.00	$1,400.00

Mold 123 Max and Mold 124 Moritz, ca. 1913, flirty sleep eyes, laughing/closed mouth

16" each	$14,500.00*
16" pair	$37,400.00*

Mold 126 Mein Liebling Baby (My Darling Baby), ca. 1914

Sleep or flirty eyes, bent-leg baby, 1914 – 1930s

14"	$500.00	$700.00
18"	$700.00	$1,000.00
25"	$1,025.00	$1,400.00

Toddler body

6"	$400.00	$600.00
15"	$1,000.00	$1,450.00
17"	$750.00	$1,000.00
22"	$1,050.00	$1,400.00
24"	$1,375.00	$1,800.00

Mold 127, 127N, ca. 1914, domed head-like mold 126, bent-leg baby body, add more for flirty eyes

14"	$800.00	$1,200.00
18"	$1,200.00	$1,600.00

Toddler body

20"	$1,650.00	$2,200.00
26"	$1,950.00	$2,600.00

Mold 128, ca. 1914, sleep eyes, open mouth, baby body

13"	$925.00	$1,250.00

Original clothes, with layette in wicker basket

10"	$1,600.00*

Mold 131: See Googly category.

Mold 135, ca. 1923, sleep eyes, open mouth, baby body

| | 13" | $625.00 | $850.00 |

Toddler body

| | 18" | $1,150.00 | $1,550.00 |

Mold 171 Klein Mammi (Little Mammy), ca. 1925, dome, open mouth

| | 18" | $1,500.00* |

Too few in database for reliable range.

Mold 214, ca. 1909, shoulder head, painted eyes, closed mouth, similar to mold 114, muslin body

| | 12" | $2,600.00* |

Too few in database for reliable range.

Kestner, J.D.

1805 – 1930+, Waltershausen, Germany. Kestner was one of the first firms to make dressed dolls. Supplied bisque heads to Catterfelder Puppenfabrik. Borgfeldt, Butler Bros., Century Doll Co., Horsman, R.H. Macy, Sears, Siegel Cooper, F.A.O. Schwarz, and others were distributors for Kestner. Besides wooden dolls, papier-mâché, wax over composition, and Frozen Charlottes, Kestner made bisque dolls with leather or composition bodies, chinas, and all-bisque dolls. Early bisque heads with closed mouths marked X or XI, turned shoulder head, and swivel heads on shoulder plates are thought to be Kestners. After 1892, dolls were marked *"made in Germany"* with mold numbers.

Marks:

Bisque heads with early mold numbers are stamped *"Excelsior DRP No. 70 685"*; heads of 100 number series are marked *"dep."* Some early characters are unmarked or only marked with the mold number. After "211" on, it is believed all dolls were marked *"JDK"* or *"JDK, Jr."* Registered the "Crown Doll" (Kronen Puppe) in 1915, used crown on label on bodies and dolls.

The Kestner Alphabet is registered in 1897 as a design patent. It is possible to identify the sizes of doll heads by this key. Letter and number always go together: B/6, C/7, D/8, E/9, F/10, G/11, H/12, H¾/12¾, J/13, J¾/13¾, K/14, K½/14½, L/15, L½/15½, M/16, N/17. It is believed all dolls with plaster pates were made by Kestner.

First price is for doll in good condition with some flaws; second price is for doll in excellent condition with original clothes or appropriately dressed. Exceptional dolls may be more.

14" solid dome baby, bisque socket head, painted blue eyes with molded lips, single stroke brown brows, accented nostrils, open-closed mouth, lightly molded and brush-stroked hair, composition baby body, marked "11" on back of head, re-dressed in blue/white gingham romper, diaper, lace-edged socks, $325.00. Courtesy McMasters Harris Doll Auctions.

20" mold #257 baby, bisque socket head, brown sleep eyes, feathered brows, painted upper and lower lashes, accented nostrils, open mouth with outlined lips and two upper teeth, spring tongue, original pale blond caracul wig, composition baby body, marked "257//51" visible on back of head, "Made in Germany" stamped in red on upper back, antique christening dress, antique underclothing, booties, and bonnet, $900.00. Courtesy McMasters Harris Doll Auctions.

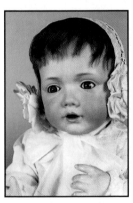

25" bisque mold #245 Hilda, original mohair wig, open mouth, two upper teeth and tongue, nicely dressed, marked "Q Made in Germany 20//245//JDK Jr. 1914C Hilda// GES gesch N. 1070," $3,900.00+. Courtesy McMasters Harris Doll Auctions.

EARLY BABY

Unmarked, or only "JDK," "made in Germany," or with size number, solid dome bisque socket head, glass sleep eyes, molded and/or painted hair, composition bent-leg baby body. Add more for body with crown label and/or original clothes.

16"	$700.00	$950.00
20"	$750.00	$1,000.00

Baby Jean, solid dome, fat cheeks

15"	$1,050.00	$1,400.00
23"	$1,500.00	$2,000.00

EARLY CHILD

Bisque shoulder head, ca. 1880s

Closed or open/closed mouth, plaster pate, may be marked with size numbers only, glass eyes, may sleep, kid body, bisque lower arms, appropriate wig and dress, in good condition, more for original clothes.

15"	$525.00	$700.00
17"	$600.00	$800.00
19"	$1,050.00*	

Open mouth, ca. 1892+, Mold 145, 147, 148, 154, 166, 195

17"	$300.00	$400.00
21"	$350.00	$500.00
24"	$500.00	$650.00

Mold 154, all original, unplayed-with condition

22"	$950.00*

Turned shoulder head, ca. 1880s, closed mouth, size number only

16"	$550.00	$750.00
18"	$650.00	$850.00
22"	$650.00	$900.00
25"	$750.00	$1,000.00
28"	$2,700.00*	

Bisque socket head

Open mouth, glass eyes, Kestner ball-jointed body, add more for square cut teeth on body marked only with number and letter.

Mold 142, 144, 146, 164, 167, 171

8"	$500.00	$700.00
18"	$700.00	$950.00
24"	$950.00	$1,000.00
42"	$4,100.00*	

Mold 171, 18" size only called "Daisy"

18"	$850.00	$1,150.00

A.T. type, closed mouth, glass eyes, mohair wig over plaster pate, early composition and wood ball-jointed body with straight wrists. Marked only with size number such as 15 for 24".

21"	$17,000.00*

Mold XI, 103 pouty closed mouth

16"	$3,500.00*	
20"	$1,950.00	$2,600.00
23"	$2,625.00	$3,500.00

Mold 128, 169, pouty closed mouth, glass eyes, composition and wood ball-jointed body, wigged

9"	$2,500.00* original costume	
15"	$900.00	$1,000.00
20"	$1,100.00	$1,400.00

Mold 129, 130, 149, 160, 161, 168, 173, 174, 196, 214, open mouth, glass eyes, composition wood jointed body, add more for fur eyebrows

12"	$450.00	$600.00
15"	$500.00	$675.00
19"	$700.00	$950.00
23"	$800.00	$1,100.00
28"	$1,100.00	$1,400.00
33"	$1,700.00*	

Mold 143, ca. 1897, open mouth, glass eyes, jointed body

8"	$475.00	$700.00
9"	$625.00	$850.00
13"	$750.00	$1,000.00
18"	$900.00	$1,250.00

Mold 155, ca. 1897, open mouth, glass eyes, five-piece or fully jointed body

7½"	$700.00	$925.00

CHARACTER BABY, 1910+

Socket head with wig or solid dome with painted hair, glass eyes, open mouth with bent-leg baby body. More for toddler body.

Mold 211, 226, 236, 260, 262, 263

8"	$650.00	$800.00
12"	$600.00	$775.00
16"	$675.00	$900.00
18"	$750.00	$1,000.00
24"	$1,050.00	$1,450.00+
26"	$1,250.00	$1,650.00

Mold 210, ca. 1912, Mold 234, 235, ca. 1914, shoulder head, solid dome, sleep eyes, open/closed mouth or open mouth

12"	$550.00	$700.00
14"	$1,300.00*	

Too few in database for reliable range.

Mold 220, sleep eyes, open/closed mouth

14"	$3,225.00	$4,300.00
Toddler		
19"	$4,650.00	$6,200.00
26½"	$10,000.00*	

13" Baby Jean, solid dome bisque socket head, blue sleep eyes, feathered brows, painted upper and lower lashes, accented nostrils, open mouth with two upper teeth, lightly molded and brush-stroked hair, composition baby body, marked "J.D.K.//made in 10 Germany" on back of head, lace-trimmed white baby dress, slip, diaper, blue crocheted booties, $300.00. Courtesy McMasters Harris Doll Auctions.

13" mold #143, bisque socket head, blue sleep eyes, painted upper and lower lashes, open mouth with two upper teeth, original mohair wig on original plaster pate, jointed wood and composition body, marked "C. made in//Germany7//143" on back of head, "Germany" stamped in red on body, original baby clothing, including long christening gown, original factory chemise, cotton half slip, flannel slip, diaper, and knit booties, $925.00. Courtesy McMasters Harris Doll Auctions.

25" mold #164, bisque socket head, large brown sleep eyes, molded and feathered brows, painted lower lashes, accented nostrils, open mouth with outlined lips and four upper teeth, original mohair wig in original ringlets, jointed wood and composition body, marked "K 1/2 made in Germany 14 1/2//164//u" on back of head, original print dress with yellow trim, underclothing, socks, and black leatherette shoes, $500.00. Courtesy McMasters Harris Doll Auctions.

30" mold #146, bisque socket head, brown sleep eyes, heavy feathered brows, painted upper and lower lashes, accented nostrils, open mouth with full accent lips, four upper teeth, mohair wig, jointed wood and compsition body, marked "Made in Germany 16//146" on back of head, antique white dress, bonnet, underclothing, new socks and shoes, $525.00. Courtesy McMasters Harris Doll Auctions.

Mold 237, 245 (Mold 1070, bald solid dome), **ca. 1914.** Hilda, sleep eyes, open mouth

13"	$1,800.00	$2,400.00
15"	$2,400.00	$3,200.00
17"	$2,500.00	$3,400.00
25"	$5,795.00*	

Mold 243, ca. 1914, Oriental baby, sleep eyes, open mouth

13"	$3,000.00	$4,000.00
15"	$3,900.00	$5,400.00
19"	$4,950.00	$6,600.00

Mold 247, ca. 1915, socket head, open mouth, sleep eyes

15"	$1,425.00	$1,900.00

Mold 249, ca. 1915, socket head, open mouth, sleep eyes

14"	$1,300.00*	

Too few in database for reliable range.

Mold 255, ca. 1916, marked *"O.I.C. made in Germany,"* solid dome flange neck, glass eyes, large open/closed screamer mouth, cloth body

10½"	$750.00	$1,000.00

Too few in database for reliable range.

Mold 257, ca. 1916, socket head, sleep eyes, open mouth

10"	$450.00	$650.00
14"	$675.00	$900.00
17"	$775.00	$1,025.00
23"	$1,050.00	$1,400.00
25"	$1,800.00	$2,400.00
Toddler body		
16"	$700.00	$950.00
24"	$1,350.00	$1,800.00

CHARACTER CHILD, CA. 1910+

Socket head, wig, closed mouth, glass eyes, composition and wood jointed body; add more for painted eyes.

Mold 175, 176, 177, 178, 179, 180, 181, 182, 184, 185, 187, 188, 189, 190

15"	$3,000.00	$4,000.00
20"	$3,750.00	$5,000.00

Mold 206, ca. 1910, fat cheeks, closed mouth, glass eyes child or toddler

15"	$6,700.00	$8,900.00

Too few in database for reliable range.

Mold 208, ca. 1910, glass eyes, for all-bisque, see that category

16"	$6,750.00	$9,000.00

Too few in database for reliable range.

Mold 208, painted eyes

12"	$2,500.00	$3,300.00
20"	$7,000.00	$9,300.00

Too few in database for reliable range.

Mold 239, ca. 1914, socket head, open mouth, sleep eyes

Toddler, also comes as baby

16"	$2,325.00	$3,100.00

Too few in database for reliable range.

Mold 241, ca. 1914, socket head, open mouth, sleep eyes

18"	$3,900.00	$5,200.00

Too few in database for reliable range.

ADULT

Mold 162, ca. 1898, bisque, open mouth, glass eyes, composition body, slender waists and molded breasts

18"	$1,150.00	$1,525.00
20"	$1,800.00*	

Mold 172, ca. 1900, Gibson Girl, shoulder head, closed mouth, glass eyes, kid body, bisque forearms

10"	$650.00	$850.00
18"	$2,000.00	$2,700.00
20"	$2,200.00	$3,000.00

WUNDERKIND

Set includes doll body with four interchangeable heads, some with extra apparel, one set includes heads with mold numbers 174, 178, 184, and 185.

11"	$7,500.00	$10,000.00
15"	$9,475.00	$12,600.00

15" mold #167, bisque socket head, blue sleep eyes, feathered brows, painted upper and lower lashes, accented nostrils, open mouth with accented lips and four upper teeth, original light brown mohair wig in original long curls, jointed wood and composition body, marked "B made in//Germany 6//167" on back of head, "Germany //0 1/2" on lower back, original white dress, original slip, pants, and undershirt, blue socks and blue cloth shoes, $850.00. Courtesy McMasters Harris Doll Auctions.

18½" mold #171, bisque socket head, blue sleep eyes with real lashes on bisque lids, feathered brows, painted lower lashes, accented nostrils, open mouth with outlined lips, four upper teeth, antique blond mohair wig, jointed wood and composition body, marked "c 1/2 made in //Germany 7 1/2//171//10" on back of head, "Germany//1 1/2" stamped in red on body, ecru lace-trimmed antique style dress, antique underclothing, socks, and black leatherette shoes, $850.00. Courtesy McMasters Harris Doll Auctions.

Kewpie

1912+, designed by Rose O'Neill. Manufactured by Borgfeldt, later Joseph Kallus, and then Jesco in 1984, and various companies with special license, as well as unlicensed companies. They were made of all-bisque, celluloid, cloth, composition, rubber, vinyl, zylonite, and other materials. Kewpie figurines (action Kewpies) have mold numbers 4843 through 4883. Kewpies were also marked with a round paper sticker on back, *"KEWPIES DES. PAT. III, R. 1913; Ger-*

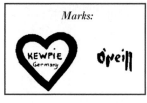

Marks:

KEWPIE Germany O'Neill

many; REG. US. PAT. OFF." On the front, was a heart-shaped sticker marked *"KEWPIE//REG. US.// PAT. OFF."* May also be incised on the soles of the feet, *"O'Neill."*

First price indicates doll in good condition, with some flaws; second price indicates doll in excellent condition with no chips. Add more for label, accessories, original box, or exceptional doll.

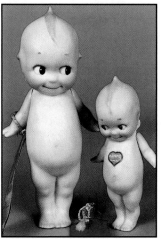

Left: 8" all-bisque, Rose O'Neill Kewpie, marked "O'Neill" on bottom of feet, right: 6" all-bisque Kewpie, marked "Germany" on paper heart label on chest, "O'Neill" on feet, $600.00+. Courtesy McMasters Harris Doll Auctions.

Left: 4" all-bisque, circa 1912+ Kewpie Traveler, $125.00; right: 3¾" bisque seated Kewpie with cat, $835.00. Courtesy McMasters Harris Doll Auctions.

ALL-BISQUE

Immobiles

Standing, legs together, immobile, no joints, blue wings, molded and painted hair, painted side-glancing eyes

2"	$55.00	$110.00
2½"	$70.00	$135.00
4½"	$75.00	$150.00
5"	$90.00	$175.00
6"	$150.00	$275.00

Jointed shoulders

2"	$50.00	$95.00
4½"	$65.00	$130.00
6"	$100.00	$195.00
8½"	$200.00	$400.00
10"	$350.00	$625.00

Carnival chalk Kewpie with jointed shoulders

13"	$50.00	$165.00

Jointed shoulders with any article of molded clothing

2½"	$100.00	$200.00
4½"	$2,600.00* pirate	
6"	$115.00	$330.00
8"	$190.00	$375.00

With Mary Jane shoes

6½"	$250.00	$500.00

Jointed hips and shoulders

5"	$815.00*	
7"	$375.00	$750.00
10"	$500.00	$1,000.00
12½"	$650.00	$1,300.00

BISQUE ACTION FIGURES

Arms folded

6"	$300.00	$600.00

Aviator

8½"	$425.00	$850.00

Back, laying down, kicking one foot

4"	$100.00	$200.00

Basket and ladybug, Kewpie seated

4"	$900.00	$1,800.00

Bear holding Kewpie
3½" $110.00 $220.00
"Blunderboo," Kewpie falling down
1¾" $240.00 $465.00
Bottle, green beverage, Kewpie standing, kicking out
2½" $330.00 $660.00
Bottle stopper
2" $75.00 $150.00
Box, heart shaped, with Kewpie kicker atop
4" $440.00 $880.00
Bride and Groom
3½" $175.00 $350.00
Boutonniére
1½" $55.00 $110.00
2" $70.00 $135.00
Candy container
4" $250.00 $500.00
Card holder
2" $250.00 $500.00
With label
2¼" $330.00 $660.00
Carpenter, wearing tool apron
8½" $550.00 $1,100.00
Cat, black with Kewpie
2¼" $150.00 $300.00
Cat, gray on lap of seated Kewpie
2¼" $850.00*
Cat, gray with Kewpie on back
3" $275.00 $525.00
Cat, tan with Kewpie
3" $150.00 $300.00
Cat, white with Kewpie
3" $220.00 $440.00
Chick with seated Kewpie
2" $300.00 $600.00
Cowboy
10" $400.00 $800.00
Dog, with Kewpie on stomach
3" $3,400.00*
Dog, with Red Cross Kewpie
4" $300.00
Doodle Dog alone
1½" $350.00 $700.00
3" $625.00 $1,350.00
Doodle Dog with Kewpie
2½" $125.00 $250.00
Drum on brown stool, with Kewpie
3½" $1,200.00 $2,400.00

10" Kestner Kewpie, solid dome bisque socket head with topknot, oversize brown glass eyes set to side, dash brows, painted upper and lower lashes, closed smiling mouth, five-piece chubby composition body with "starfish" hands, marked "Ges. gesch./O'Neill. J.D.K.//10" on back of head, old white underwear with crocheted trim, peach organdy dress with new blue silk ribbon trim, $4,600.00. Courtesy McMasters Harris Doll Auctions.

10" Kestner Kewpie, nude.

Farmer

6½"	$450.00	$900.00

Flowers, Kewpie with bouquet in right hand

5"	$475.00	$935.00

Fly on foot of Kewpie

3"	$300.00	$600.00

Governor

2½"	$150.00	$275.00
3¼"	$250.00	$500.00

Hottentot, black Kewpie

3½"	$225.00	$425.00
5"	$300.00	$575.00
9"	$450.00	$950.00
12"	$4,500.00+	

Huggers

2½"	$65.00	$125.00
3½"	$75.00	$150.00
4½"	$100.00	$200.00

Inkwell, with writer Kewpie

4½"	$250.00	$500.00

Jack-O-Lantern between legs of Kewpie

2"	$250.00	$500.00

Jester, with white hat on head

4½"	$300.00	$575.00

Kneeling

4"	$375.00	$750.00

Mandolin, green basket and seated Kewpie

2"	$150.00	$275.00

Mandolin held by Kewpie in blue chair

4"	$475.00	$925.00

Mandolin, with Kewpie on moon swing

2½"	$4,400.00*	

Mayor, seated Kewpie in green wicker chair

4½"	$475.00	$950.00

Minister

5"	$125.00	$250.00

Nursing bottle, with Kewpie

3½"	$300.00	$600.00

Reader Kewpie seated with book

2"	$125.00	$250.00
3½"	$165.00	$325.00
4"	$250.00	$500.00

Sack held by Kewpie with both hands

4½"	$1,430.00*	

Salt Shaker

2"	$165.00	

Seated in fancy chair

4"	$200.00	$400.00

Soldier bursting out of egg

4"	$6,900.00*	

* at auction

Soldier, Confederate
4"	$200.00	$400.00

Soldier in egg
3½"	$6,600.00*

Soldier taking aim with rifle
3½"	$500.00	$990.00

Soldier vase
6½"	$330.00	$660.00

Soldier with black hat, sword, and rifle
4½"	$200.00	$385.00

Soldier with helmet
2¾"	$300.00	$400.00
4½"	$300.00	$600.00

Soldier with red hat, sword, and rifle
3½"	$150.00	$300.00
5¼"	$415.00	$825.00

Stomach, Kewpie laying flat, arms and legs out
4"	$225.00	$450.00

Thinker
4 – 5"	$150.00	$275.00

Traveler with dog and umbrella
3½"	$1,300.00*

Traveler with umbrella and bag
4"	$175.00	$350.00
5"	$300.00	$600.00

Vase with card holder and Kewpie
2½"	$165.00	$330.00

Vase with Doodle Dog & Kewpie
4½"	$2,600.00*

Vase with huggers
3¾"	$325.00	$650.00

Writer, seated Kewpie with pen in hand
2"	$255.00	$475.00
4"	$265.00	$550.00

BISQUE SHOULDER HEAD

Cloth, or stockinette body
7"	$285.00	$565.00

Head only
3"	$165.00+

CELLULOID

Bride and Groom
4"	$15.00	$40.00

Jointed arms, heart label on chest
12"	$175.00	$325.00

CHINA

Perfume holder, one piece with opening at back of head
4½"	$550.00	$1,100.00

Salt Shaker
1¼"	$85.00	$165.00

12" cloth Richard Krueger Cuddle Kewpie, label reads "Richard Krueger//Kewpie//New York//Patent # 1785800//Copyright Rose O'Neill," mask face, painted side-glancing eyes, rosy cheeks, plush pale blue body, circa 1930s, $150.00. Private collection.

Kewpie

Dishes

Service for 4	$650.00	$900.00
Service for 6	$975.00	$1,200.00

CLOTH

Richard Krueger "Cuddle Kewpie," silk screened face, sateen body, tagged

13"	$350.00	$600.00

Plush, with stockinette face, tagged

8"	$115.00	$225.00

COMPOSITION

Hottentot, all-composition, heart decal to chest, jointed arms, red winks, ca. 1946

11"	$300.00	$575.00

All-composition, jointed body, blue wings

11"	$125.00	$375.00
13"	$200.00	$450.00

Composition head, cloth body, flange neck, composition forearms, tagged floral dress

11"	$250.00	$875.00

Talcum container

One-piece composition talcum shaker with heart label on chest

7"	$35.00	$65.00

HARD PLASTIC

Original box, ca. 1950, Kewpie design

8½"	$200.00	$385.00

Sleep eyes, five-piece body with starfish hands

14"	$150.00	$300.00

METAL

Figurine, cast steel on square base, excellent condition

5½"	$30.00	$55.00

SOAP

Kewpie soap figure with cotton batting

Colored label with rhyme, marked *"R.O. Wilson, 1917"*

4"	$55.00	$110.00

Kley & Hahn

1902 – 1930+, Ohrdruf, Thüringia, Germany. Bisque heads, jointed composition or leather bodies, exporter; bought heads from Kestner (Walkure) and Hertel Schwab & Co. Also made composition and celluloid head dolls.

First price indicates doll in good condition, but with some flaw; second price indicates doll in excellent condition, with original clothes, or appropriately dressed.

CHARACTER BABY

Mold 133, 135, 138, 158, 160, 161, 167, and 571

Mold 133 (made by Hertel Schwab & Co.), solid-dome, painted eyes, closed mouth

Mold 135 (made by Hertel Schwab & Co.), solid-dome, painted eyes, open/closed mouth

Mold 138 (made by Hertel Schwab & Co.), solid-dome, painted eyes, open/closed mouth

Mold 158 (made by Hertel Schwab & Co.), painted eyes, open mouth

Mold 160 (made by Hertel Schwab & Co.), sleep eyes, open/closed mouth

Mold 161 (made by Hertel Schwab & Co.), character face, sleep eyes, open/closed mouth

Mold 167 (made by Hertel Schwab & Co.), sleep eyes, open/closed or open mouth

Mold 571, "K&H" (made by Bähr & Pröschild) character, solid-dome, glass eyes, open/closed mouth, laughing, giant baby

13"	$450.00	$575.00
16"	$500.00	$675.00
19"	$600.00	$800.00
22"	$750.00	$1,025.00

Toddler body

21"	$1,050.00	$1,400.00
26"	$1,300.00	$1,750.00

Mold 567 (made by Bähr & Pröschild) character multi-face, laughing face, glass eyes, open mouth; crying face, painted eyes, open/closed mouth

15"	$1,475.00	$1,950.00
17"	$1,875.00	$2,500.00
19"	$2,550.00	$3,400.00

Mold 680, "K & CO K&H" with "266 K&H," ca. **1920,** made by Kestner, character, sleep eyes, open mouth

17"	$700.00	$925.00

Toddler

19"	$975.00	$1,300.00

CHILD

Mold 250, 282, or Walkure, circa 1920 (made by J.D. Kestner, Jr.), dolly face, sleep eyes, open mouth

21"	$475.00	$625.00
28"	$700.00	$925.00
33"	$900.00	$1,200.00

Mold 325, "Dollar Princess," open mouth

25"	$325.00	$525.00

CHARACTER CHILD

Mold numbers 154, 166, 169, ca. 1912

Mold 154, 166 (made by Hertel Schwab & Co.), solid-dome, glass eyes, closed mouth

Mold 169 (made by Hertel Schwab & Co.), sleep eyes, closed or open/closed mouth

17"	$2,000.00	$2,600.00
19"	$2,175.00	$2,900.00
27"	$2,600.00	$3,500.00

Baby body with bent legs

12"	$1,785.00*

Mold 162, ca. 1912 (made by Hertel Schwab & Co.), open mouth, voice cut out

17"	$1,100.00	$1,500.00

Too few in database for reliable range.

22" mold #548 toddler, bisque socket head, blue sleep eyes with real lashes, feathered brows, painted upper and lower lashes, open-closed laughing mouth, molded tongue and dimples, replaced curly mohair wigs with "tails," heavy jointed composition toddler body with diagonal hip joints, marked "K&H (in banner)//548//15//Germany" on back of head, antique white clothing, antique underclothing, and fabric boots, $3,800.00. Courtesy McMasters Harris Doll Auctions.

22" mold #548, nude.

31" Kley & Hahn Walkure, bisque socket head, blue sleep eyes with real lashes, molded and feathered brows, painted upper and lower lashes, accented nostrils, open mouth with outlined lips, four upper teeth, pierced ears, human hair wig, jointed wood and composition body, marked "5 1/2//Walkure//Germany//15" on back of head, "80" stamped in red on bottom of both feet, re-dressed in ecru and blue outfit with matching tam, underclothing, socks, and old leather shoes, $550.00. Courtesy McMasters Harris Doll Auctions.

Mold 178, ca. 1918 (made by Hertel Schwab & Co.), dome, molded hair, googly, open mouth

Mold 180, ca. 1915 (made by Hertel Schwab & Co.), googly, open/closed mouth

17"	$2,550.00	$3,400.00

Too few in database for reliable range.

Mold 292, 520, 525, 526, 531, character face

Mold 292 "KH 1930," ca. 1930 (made by J. D. Kestner, Jr.), character face

Mold 520 "K&H," ca. 1910 (made by Bähr & Pröschild), painted eyes, closed mouth

Mold 525 "K & H," ca. 1912 (by Bähr & Pröschild), dome, painted eyes, open/closed mouth

Mold 526 "K&H," ca. 1912 (made by Bähr & Pröschild), painted eyes, closed mouth (see photo in *Doll Values, 3rd Edition*)

Mold 531 "K&H," ca. 1912 (made by Bähr & Pröschild), solid dome, painted eyes, open/closed mouth

Baby bent-leg body

9½"	$250.00	$325.00

Child

14"	$3,700.00*	Mold 520
17"	$2,200.00*	Mold 531
21"	$2,250.00	$3,000.00

Mold 546, 549, ca. 1912, character face

Mold 546 "K&H" (made by Bähr & Pröschild), glass eyes, closed mouth, child body

Mold 549 "K&H" (made by Bähr & Pröschild), painted eyes, closed mouth, also in celluloid

16"	$3,150.00	$4,200.00
18"	$3,375.00	$4,500.00

Mold 554, 568, ca. 1912, character face

Mold 554 "K&H" (made by Bähr & Pröschild), glass eyes, open/closed mouth

Mold 568 (made by Bähr & Pröschild), solid dome, sleep eyes, smiling

21"	$1,400.00*

Too few in database for reliable range.

Marks:

525
6
Germany
)K & H(

Kling, C.F. & Co.

1836 – 1930+ Ohrdruf, Thüringia, Germany. Porcelain factory that made china, bisque, and all-bisque dolls, and snow babies. Often mold number marks are followed by size number.

First price indicates doll in good condition, but with some flaws; second price indicates doll in excellent condition, with original clothes, or appropriately dressed, more for exceptional doll with elaborate molded hair or bodice.

Mark:

BISQUE SHOULDER HEAD
  Painted eyes, wig or molded hair, cloth or kid body

15"	$300.00	$400.00
19"	$465.00	$575.00
21"	$475.00	$650.00

  Glass eyes

13"	$400.00	$525.00

  Mold 123, 124, ca. 1880, incised with bell mark, glass eyes, closed mouth, shoulder head

15"	$650.00	$850.00

  Mold 131, 167, 178, 182, 189, ca. 1885
  Mold 131, incised bell, shoulder head, glass eyes, closed mouth
  Mold 167, incised bell, solid dome, with wig, closed mouth
  Mold 178, shoulder head, molded hair, glass eyes, closed mouth
  Mold 182, shoulder head, molded hair, painted eyes, closed mouth
  Mold 189, shoulder head, molded hair, painted eyes, closed mouth

15"	$800.00	$1,075.00

  Mold 135, ca. 1885, molded bodice, flower in molded hair

21"	$825.00	$1,200.00

  Mold 370, 372, 373, 377, ca. 1900, sleep eyes, open mouth

15"	$375.00	$500.00
21"	$525.00	$700.00

  Bisque socket head, open mouth, jointed body

13"	$300.00	$400.00
17"	$425.00	$550.00
21"	$550.00	$725.00

CHINA SHOULDER HEAD
  Mold numbers 131, 188, 189, 202, ca. 1880s
  Cloth or kid body, china limbs, blond or black molded hair
  Mold 131, painted eyes, closed mouth
  Mold 188, molded hair, glass eyes, closed mouth
  Mold 189, molded hair, painted eyes, closed mouth
  Mold 202, molded hair, painted eyes, closed mouth

13"	$200.00	$275.00
18"	$335.00	$450.00
21"	$375.00	$500.00

Knoch, Gebrüder

1887 – 1918+, Neustad, Thüringia, Germany. Made bisque doll heads and doll joints, with cloth or kid body. Succeeded in 1918 by Max Oscar Arnold.

SHOULDER HEAD
  Mold 203, 205, ca. 1910
  Mold 203, character face, painted eyes, closed mouth, stuffed cloth body
  Mold 205, "GKN" character face, painted eyes, open/closed mouth, molded tongue

12"	$600.00	$800.00
14"	$750.00	$1,000.00

Too few in database for reliable range.

Mark:
GK
N
Made in Germany
Ges N. 216 Gesch
15/0

Mold 223, "GKN GES. NO. GESCH," ca. 1912

Character face, solid-dome or shoulder head, painted eyes, molded tears, closed mouth

Too few in database for reliable range.

SOCKET HEAD

Mold 179, 181, 190, 192, 193, 201, ca. 1900

(Mold 201 also came as black), dolly face, glass eyes, open mouth

13"	$185.00	$250.00
17"	$300.00	$425.00

Mold 204, 205, ca. 1910, character face

15"	$865.00	$1,150.00

Mold 206, ca. 1910, "DRGM" solid dome, intaglio eyes, open/closed mouth

11"	$750.00*

Mold 216, ca. 1912, "GKN" solid dome, intaglio eyes, laughing, open/closed mouth

12"	$315.00*

Too few in database for reliable range.

229: See All-Bisque category.

230, ca. 1912, molded bonnet, character shoulder head, painted eyes, open/closed mouth laughing

232, ca. 1912, molded bonnet, character shoulder head, laughing

13"	$675.00	$900.00
15"	$1,200.00	$1,600.00

König & Wernicke

Mark:
K&W
HARTGUMMI
555 o
GERMANY

1912 – 1930+, Waltershausen, Germany. Had doll factory, made bisque or celluloid dolls with composition bodies, later dolls with hard rubber heads.

BISQUE BABY

Mold 98, 99, ca. 1912, *"made in Germany"* (made by Hertel Schwab & Co.), character, socket head, sleep eyes, open mouth, teeth, tremble tongue, wigged, composition bent-leg baby body

9"	$275.00	$375.00
18"	$500.00	$675.00
22"	$600.00	$800.00

Mold 1070, ca. 1915, socket head, open mouth, bent-leg baby body

12"	$400.00	$550.00
16"	$500.00	$650.00

Toddler

17"	$1,000.00	$1,400.00
19"	$1,150.00	$1,575.00

COMPOSITION CHILD

Composition head on five-piece or fully-jointed body, open mouth, sleep eyes, add more for flirty eyes.

14"	$225.00	$300.00
16"	$350.00	$450.00

24" bisque socket head with toddler composition body, character face, open mouth, sleep eyes, human hair wig, nicely dressed, circa 1912, $2,000.00. Private collection.

1910 – 1980 on, Prussia, after W.W.II, Bavaria. Made dolls of waterproof muslin, wool, and stockinette with heads, hair, and hands oil painted. The skeleton frame was rigid with movable parts; early dolls are stuffed with deer hair. Early thumbs are part of the hand; after 1914 they are attached separately, later again, they're part of the hand. Marked on the bottom of the left foot with number and name *"Käthe Kruse,"* in black, red, or purple ink. After 1929, dolls had wigs, but some still had painted hair. Original doll modeled after Dutch bust sculpture "Fiammingo" by Francois Duquesnois.

CLOTH

Doll I Series, 1910 – 1929

All-cloth, jointed shoulders, wide hips, painted eyes and hair

Three vertical seams in back of head, marked on left foot

17"	$1,700.00	$4,800.00

Ball-jointed knees, 1911 variant produced by Kämmer & Reinhardt

17"	$5,500.00+

Too few in database for reliable range.

Doll I Series, later model, 1929+, now with slim hips

17"	$1,600.00	$3,100.00

Doll IH Series, wigged version, 1929+

17"	$1,600.00	$3,000.00

Bambino, a doll for a doll, circa 1915 – 1925

8"	$500.00+

Too few in database for reliable range.

Doll II Series, "Schlenkerchen," ca. 1922 – 1936

Smiling baby, open/closed mouth, stockinette covered body and limbs, one seam head

13"	$10,400.00*

Too few in database for reliable range.

Doll V, VI, Sandbabies Series, 1920s+

"Traumerchen" (closed eyes) and "Du Mein" (open eyes) were cloth dolls with painted hair, weighted with sand or unweighted, with or without belly buttons, in 19⅝" and 23⅝" sizes. One- or three-seam heads, or cloth over cardboard. Later heads were made in the 1930s from a heavy composition called magnesit.

19⅝"	$2,000.00	$3,900.00

Magnesit head, circa 1930s+

20"	$350.00	$1,500.00
40"	$2,650.00	$3,500.00

16" doll, oil-painted cloth head, painted blue eyes with radiating irises, accented nostrils, closed mouth, painted brown hair, cloth body with wide hips, tab-jointed shoulders, separately applied thumb, disk joints at hips, antique white dress, slip, crocheted bonnet, sweater, socks, original leather shoes, two stamp marks illegible, "Stroh Schneider" hand-printed down front of torso, $1,500.00. Courtesy McMasters Harris Doll Auctions.

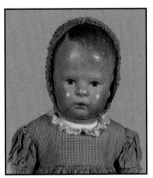

16" Baby Hampleschatz, molded and painted cloth head, painted brown eyes, single stroke brows, accented nostrils, closed mouth, painted hair, cloth body, original green dress, matching bonnet, slip, pants, socks, and white felt shoes, marked "(illegible stamp)//6 9195" in red on left foot, $1,300.00. Courtesy McMasters Harris Doll Auctions.

Mark:

Doll VII Series, circa 1927 – 1952

Two versions were offered.

A smaller 14" Du Mein open eye baby, painted hair or wigged, three-seam head, wide hips, sewn on thumbs, 1927 – 1930

14"	$1,500.00	$2,800.00

Too few in database for reliable range.

A smaller Doll I version, with wide hips, separately sewn on thumbs, painted hair or wigged, after 1930 – 1950s slimmer hips and with thumbs formed with hand

14"	$1,000.00	$2,000.00

Doll VIII Series, Deutsche Kind, the "German child," 1929+

Modeled after Kruse's son, Friedebald, hollow head, swivels, one verticle seam in back of head, wigged, disk-jointed legs, later made in plastic during the 1950s

20"	$1,300.00	$2,500.00

Doll IX Series, "The Little German Child," 1929+

Wigged, one seam head, a smaller version of Doll VIII

14"	$1,000.00	$1,800.00

Doll X Series, 1935+

Smaller Doll I with one-seam head that turns

14"	$1,200.00	$2,400.00

Doll XII Series, 1930s

Hampelchen with loose legs, three vertical seams on back of head, painted hair, button and band on back to make legs stand. The 14" variation has head of Doll I; the 16" variation also has the head of Doll I, and is known after 1940s as Hempelschatz, Doll XIIB.

14"	$800.00	$1,200.00
16"	$900.00	$1,500.00
18"	$1,100.00	$2,100.00

XIIH, wigged version

18"	$1,200.00	$2,200.00

XII/I, 1951+, legs have disc joints

18"	$300.00	$650.00

U.S. Zone, after World War II, circa 1946+

Cloth	14"	$300.00	$600.00

Magnesit (heavy composition)

14"	$400.00	$800.00

HARD PLASTIC, 1952 – 1975 (CELLULOID AND OTHER SYNTHETICS)

Turtle Dolls, 1955 – 1961, synthetic bodies

14"	$125.00	$325.00
16"	$150.00	$400.00
18"	$200.00	$500.00

Glued-on wigs, sleep or painted eyes, pink muslin body

18"	$200.00	$600.00
21"	$250.00	$750.00

1975 to date, marked with size number in centimeters, B for baby, H for hair, and G for painted hair

10"	$100.00	$200.00
13"	$175.00	

1884 – 1930, Kronach, Bavaria. Made dolls, doll heads, movable children, and swimmers. Butler Bros. and Marshall Field distributed their dolls.

Mark:

Mold 28, 31, 32, ca. 1890, bisque socket head, closed mouth, glass eyes, pierced ears, wig, wood and composition jointed body

19"	$1,800.00	$2,400.00
23"	$2,100.00	$2,800.00

Mold 34, Bru type, paperweight eyes, closed mouth, pierced ears, composition jointed body

12½"	$1,650.00	$2,200.00

Mold 38, solid dome turned shoulder head, closed mouth, pierced ears, kid body

20"	$900.00	$1,200.00

Mold 41, solid dome socket head, open mouth, glass eyes

16"	$900.00	$1,125.00

Mold 44, small dolls marked *"Gbr. K"* in sunburst, socket head, glass eyes, open mouth, five-piece composition body, molded and painted socks and shoes

7"	$250.00	$325.00
22½"	$800.00*	

Mold 165, ca. 1900, socket head, sleep eyes, open mouth, teeth

22"	$350.00	$450.00
33"	$525.00	$650.00

18" #38, bisque shoulder head, blue threaded paperweight eyes, feathered brows, painted upper and lower lashes, accented nostrils, closed mouth, pierced ears, old mohair wig, kid body with cloth torso and top of arms, gussets at elbows, hips, and knees, bisque lower arms, marked "G.K. 38-27" along edge of back of shoulder plate, antique white dress, underclothing, orignal black stockings and red leather high button boots, $425.00. Courtesy McMasters Harris Doll Auctions.

1915 – 1924, Limoges, France. Porcelain factory, made dolls and heads, including heads. Lady dolls were dressed in French provincial costumes, bodies by Ortyz; dolls were produced for Association to Aid War Widows.

ADULT, CA. 1915

Marked *"Caprice," "Cherie," "Favorite," "La Georgienne," "Lorraine,"* or *"Toto,"* bisque socket head, open/closed mouth with teeth, composition adult body

17"	$700.00	$1,000.00
22"	$1,000.00*	

Painted eyes

12½"	$1,975.00*

CHILD

Bisque socket head, open mouth with teeth, wig, composition jointed body

17"	$525.00	$725.00
23"	$700.00	$950.00

14" bisque probably Lanternier and Coiffe Limoges Boy, marked "L (anchor) C//O" on back of head, set brown eyes, open mouth, five upper teeth, auburn mohair wig, crude five-piece late French body, original factory chemise under handmade clothing with feather stitching, watch, velvet spats over shoes, wool beret, circa 1914+, $325.00. Courtesy McMasters Harris Doll Auctions.

Leather

Leather was an available resource for Native Americans to use for making doll heads, bodies, or entire dolls. Some examples of Gussie Decker's dolls were advertised as "impossible for child to hurt itself" and leather was fine for teething babies.

12"	$275.00

Too few in database for reliable range.

25"	$325.00

Too few in database for reliable range.

Lenci

16" 400/D girl, pressed felt swivel head, painted brown eyes to side, painted upper lashes, closed mouth, original long mohair wig, cloth torso with felt arms and legs, marked "Lenci Turin// (Italy)//Di E. Scavini// Made in Italy//400/D// Pat. Sept. 8-1921 - Pat. N. 142433//Bte S.G.D.G. X 87395 - Brevetto 501-178" on paper tag, light green felt dress, original underclothing, silk stockings to hips, black leather shoes, felt cap, coat, matching hat, $800.00. Courtesy McMasters Harris Doll Auctions.

1918 – 80+, Turine, Italy. Trademark and name of firm started by Enrico and Elenadi Scavini, that made felt dolls with pressed faces, also made composition head dolls, wooden dolls, and porcelain figurines and dolls. Early Lenci dolls have tiny metal button, hang tags with *"Lenci//Torino//Made in Italy."* Ribbon strips marked *"Lenci//Made in Italy"* were found in the clothes ca. 1925 – 1950. Some, but not all dolls have Lenci marked in purple or black ink on the sole of the foot. Some with original paper tags may be marked with a model number in pencil.

Dolls have felt swivel heads, oil-painted features, often side-glancing eyes, jointed shoulders and hips, sewn together third and fourth fingers, sewn-on double felt ears, often dressed in felt and organdy original clothes, excellent condition. May have scalloped socks.

The most sought after are the well constructed early dolls from the 1920s and 1930s, when Madame Lenci had control of the design and they were more elaborate with fanciful well made accessories. They carried animals of wood or felt, baskets, felt vegetables, purses, or bouquets of felt flowers. This era of dolls had eye shadow, dots in corner of eye, two-tone lips, with lower lip highlighted and, depending on condition, will command higher prices.

The later dolls of the 1940s and 1950s have hard cardboard-like felt faces, with less intricate details, like less elaborate appliqués, fewer accessories, and other types of fabrics such as taffeta, cotton, and rayon, all showing a decline in quality and should not be priced as earlier dolls. The later dolls may have fabric covered cardboard torsos. Model numbers changed over the years, so what was a certain model number early, later became another letter or number.

Identification Tips:

Lenci characteristics include double layer ears, scalloped cotton socks. Early dolls may have rooted mohair wig, 1930s dolls may have "frizzed" played-with wigs. Later dolls are less elaborate with hard cardboard-type felt faces.

Mark:

(Lenci)

First price indicates doll in poor condition, perhaps worn, soiled, or faded, price in this condition should reflect 25 percent value of doll in excellent condition; second price indicates doll in excellent condition, clean, with colors still bright. Deduct for dolls of the 1940s and 1950s or later. Add more for tags, boxes, or accessories. Exceptional dolls and rare examples may go much higher.

BABY

13"	$375.00	$1,500.00
16"	$1,700.00*	
22"	$2,000.00	$3,200.00

CHILD, 1920s – 1930s, softer face, more elaborate costume

13"	$500.00	$1,750.00
17"	$650.00	$2,500.00
21"	$750.00	$2,750.00

1940s – 1950s+, hard face, less intricate costume

13"	$75.00	$400.00
15"	$100.00	$500.00
17"	$125.00	$600.00

SMALL DOLLS

Miniatures, 9"

Child	$125.00	$400.00
Tyrol Boy	$100.00	$375.00
Young Flower Merchant		$1,300.00*
10 – 11"	$125.00	$500.00

Mascottes, 8½", have swing legs like Mama dolls, may have loop on neck

8½"	$80.00	$325.00

In rare outfit, carrying accessories

8½"	$115.00	$450.00

FADETTE

With adult face, flapper or boudoir body with long slim limbs

17"	$265.00	$1,050.00
32"	$650.00	$2,600.00
48"	$1,250.00	$5,000.00

CELEBRITIES

Bach

17"	$715.00	$2,850.00

Jack Dempsey

18"	$875.00	$3,500.00

Tom Mix

18"	$875.00	$3,500.00

Mendel

22"	$925.00	$3,700.00

Mozart

14"	$3,000.00*

Pastorelle

14"	$3,000.00*

14" Oriental, pressed felt swivel head, painted brown eyes, molded slanted brows, painted upper and lower lashes, closed two-tone mouth, original black mohair wig, cloth torso, felt arms and legs, original outfit, marked "Lenci//Made in Italy," on cloth tag, $1,200.00. Courtesy McMasters Harris Doll Auctions.

16" girl, pressed felt swivel head, painted brown eyes, painted upper and lower lashes, closed mouth, original mohair wig, cloth torso with felt arms and legs, original clothes, marked "Lenci" on feet, $600.00. Courtesy McMasters Harris Doll Auctions.

10½" ethnic girl, pressed felt swivel head with darkened skin tone, painted brown eyes to side, painted upper lashes, closed mouth, original mohair wig, jointed cloth body with felt arms, original colorful felt ethnic outfit, paper tags marked "Lenci//Torino//Made in Italy," "Scarlett/22," "Lenci//Made in Italy," "ACastrovillari," and "Kimport//dolls//Independence MO//This Doll/ /Was Made In//Italy" on skirt tag, $275.00. Courtesy McMasters Harris Doll Auctions.

CHARACTERS

Aladdin

14"	$1,925.00	$7,750.00

Athlete, Golfer, ca. 1930

17"	$2,700.00 *a few moth holes

Aviator, girl with felt helmet

18"	$800.00	$3,200.00

Benedetta

19"	$300.00	$1,100.00

Court Gentleman

18"	$400.00	$1,600.00

Cupid

17"	$1,300.00	$5,200.00

Devil

9"	$1,500.00*

Fascist Boy, rare

14"	$750.00	$1,500.00
17"	$1,250.00* missing ear

Flower Girl, ca. 1930

20"	$250.00	$1,000.00

Henriette

26"	$625.00	$2,500.00

Indian

17"	$900.00	$3,600.00

Squaw with papoose

17"	$1,050.00	$4,200.00

Laura

16"	$250.00	$950.00

Lucia 48, ca. 1930

14"	$200.00	$800.00

Pan, hooved feet

8"	$1,000.00*

Pierrot

21"	$1,500.00	$2,000.00

Pinocchio

11"	$1,100.00 MIB

Salome, ca. 1920, brown felt, ball at waist allows doll to swivel

17"	$850.00	$3,500.00

Series 300 Children

European boy

17"	$350.00	$1,400.00

Turkish boy

17"	$375.00	$1,500.00

19" Modello Depositato, pressed felt swivel head, painted brown eyes to side, single stroke brows, painted upper lashes, light blue shading under eyes, accented nostrils, closed mouth, applied felt ears, original mohair wig, cloth torso with felt at neckline for clothing style, felt arms and legs, marked "Modello Depositato//Lenci//Torino//Made in Italy," on paper tag on back of dress, "19/72//100/96 " handwritten on back of tag, "Vie//iemonte" on paper tag on wrist, original black felt dress, white organdy bonnet with silk bow around face, original underclothing, socks, and shoes, $300.00. Courtesy McMasters Harris Doll Auctions.

Smoker
Painted eyes
| 28" | $600.00 | $2,400.00 |
Glass eyes
| 24" | $975.00 | $3,900.00 |

Sport Series Boy
| 17" | $4,000.00* |

Val Gardena
| 19" | $225.00 | $900.00 |

Winking Bellhop with Love Letter
| 11" | $200.00 | $750.00 |

ETHNIC OR REGIONAL COSTUME
Bali dancer
| 15" | $375.00 | $1,500.00 |

Eugenia
| 25" | $275.00 | $1,100.00 |

Chinese Boy, ca. 1925
| 16" | $1,700.00* |

Madame Butterfly, ca. 1926
| 17" | $800.00 | $3,200.00 |
| 25" | $1,200.00 | $4,800.00 |

Marenka, Russian girl, ca. 1930
| 14" | $1,100.00* |

Scottish girl, ca. 1930
| 14" | $175.00 | $700.00 |

Spanish girl, ca. 1930
| 14" | $200.00 | $800.00 |
| 17" | $250.00 | $1,000.00 |

Tyrol boy or girl, ca. 1935
| 14" | $200.00 | $800.00 |

EYE VARIATIONS
Glass eyes
| 16" | $400.00 | $1,600.00 |
| 22" | $750.00 | $3,000.00 |

Flirty glass eyes
| 15" | $550.00 | $2,200.00 |
| 20" | $700.00 | $2,800.00 |

Surprise eye, Widow, "O" shaped eyes and mouth
| 19" | $1,500.00* |

MODERN, CA. 1979+
13"	$65.00	$125.00
21"	$100.00	$200.00
26"	$125.00	$250.00

ACCESSORIES
Lenci Catalogs	$900.00 – 1,200.00
Lenci Dog	$100.00 – 150.00
Purse	$175.00	$225.00

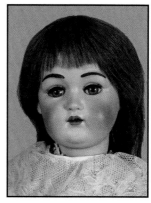

12" Orphant Annie, boxed, pressed felt swivel head, painted brown eyes to side, single stroke brows, painted upper lashes, accented nostrils, closed two-tone mouth, applied ears, original mohair wig, cloth torso with felt arms and legs, individual fingers with middle two together, original pink/white box plaid dress, apron, panties, socks, and pink felt shoes, holding original broom, marked "Modello Depositato//Lenci//Torino//Made in Italy" on tag on front of clothing, illegible mark bottom of feet, $500.00. Courtesy McMasters Harris Doll Auctions.

Lenci-Type

13" Alma boy and girl, pressed felt swivel heads, painted brown eyes to side, accented nostrils, closed mouths, applied felt ears on both, original mohair wigs, felt bodies jointed at shoulders and hips, mitten hands with stitched fingers, marked "12" on back of girl's head, "13" on boy's head, "Alma//Made in Italy," on bottom left foot of both, "Creazione Originale//Alma//Made In Italy" cloth tag on clothing of each, original colorful felt clothing with hats to match outfits, original underclothing, socks, and shoes on boy, just shoes on girl, $500.00 for pair. Courtesy McMasters Harris Doll Auctions.

1920 – 1950. These were made by many English, French, or Italian firms like Gre-Poir or Raynal from felt with painted features, mohair wig, original clothes. These must be in very good condition, tagged or unmarked. Usually Lenci-types have single felt ears or no ears.

CHILD

15"	$35.00	$145.00
Regional costume		
8"	$15.00	$45.00
Smoker		
16"	$100.00	$400.00

Gre Poir, France, New York City, ca. 1927 – 1930s; Eugenie Poir made felt or cloth mask dolls, unmarked on body, no ears, white socks with three stripes, hang tag

Cloth

17 – 18"	$150.00	$525.00
Felt		
19½"	$150.00	$500.00

Limbach

Mark:

Rita
3/0

1772 – 1927+, Alsbach, Thüringia, Germany. This porcelain factory made bisque head dolls, china dolls, bathing dolls, and all-bisque dolls. Usually marked with three leaf clover.

ALL-BISQUE

Child, small doll, molded hair or wigged, painted eyes, molded and painted shoes and socks, may have mark *"8661,"* and cloverleaf. More for exceptional dolls.

6"	$100.00	$175.00
8"	$185.00	$275.00
Glass eyes		
6"	$200.00	$275.00

BABY

Mold 8682, character face, bisque socket head, glass eyes, clover mark, bent-leg baby body, wig, open/closed mouth

8½"	$450.00*

CHILD

May have name above mold mark, such as Norma or Rita, bisque socket head, glass eyes, clover mark, wig, open mouth

20"	$700.00	$950.00

Ca. 1860 on and earlier. Doll's head on wooden or ivory stick, sometimes with whistle; when twirled some play music. Bisque head on stick made by various French and German companies. Add more for marked head.

Bisque, open mouth

| 14" | $625.00 | $1,025.00 |

Marseille, Armand, Mold 3200, open mouth

| 13" | $1,000.00 | $1,300.00 |

Mold 600, closed mouth, squeaker mechanism

| 13" | $900.00 | $1,200.00 |

Schoenau & Hoffmeister, mold 4700, circa 1905

| 15" | $800.00* pristine |

Celluloid

| 11" | $190.00 | $250.00 |

1885 – 1930+, Sonneberg, Köppelsdorf, Thüringia, Germany. One of the largest suppliers of bisque doll heads, ca. 1900 – 1930, to such companies as Amberg, Arranbee, Bergmann, Borgfeldt, Butler Bros., Dressel, Montgomery Ward, Sears, Steiner, Wiegand, Louis Wolf, and others. Made some doll heads with no mold numbers, but names, such as Alma, Baby Betty, Baby Gloria, Baby Florence, Baby Phyllis, Beauty, Columbia, Duchess, Ellar, Florodora, Jubilee, Mabel, Majestic, Melitta, My Playmate, Nobbi Kid, Our Pet, Princess, Queen Louise, Rosebud, Superb, Sunshine, and Tiny Tot. Some Indian dolls had no mold numbers. Often used Superb kid bodies, with bisque hands.

First price indicates doll in good condition with flaws; second price indicates doll in excellent condition, appropriately dressed. Add $50.00 more for composition body; add $100.00 more for toddler body; more for original clothes or exceptional doll.

Marks:

Armand Marseille
Germany
390
A. 4. M.

Made in Germany
Florodora
A 5 M

Queen Louise
Germany
7.

NEWBORN BABY

Newborn, bisque solid-dome socket head or flange neck, may have wig, glass eyes, closed mouth, cloth body with celluloid or composition hands

Mold 341, My Dream Baby, 351, ca. 1926, Rock-A-Bye Baby, marked *"AM"* in original basket with layette; head circumference:

10"	$185.00	$250.00
12"	$225.00	$325.00
15"	$350.00	$475.00

Mold 345, Kiddiejoy, ca. 1926, 352, bisque solid-dome socket head or flange neck, may have wig, glass eyes, closed mouth, cloth body with celluloid or composition hands, head circumference:

8"	$150.00	$225.00
11"	$200.00	$275.00
16"	$350.00	$525.00

With toddler body

| 28" | $900.00 | $1,200.00 |

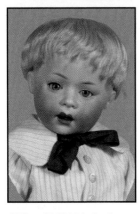

14½" mold #233 baby, bisque socket head, blue sleep eyes, feathered brows, painted upper and lower lashes, accented nostrils, open mouth with two upper teeth, blond mohair wig, composition baby body, marked "233//5" on back of head, "D.R.G.M.//575 144" on label inside head, redressed in white shirt with blue stripes, faded blue shorts buttoned to shirt, new socks and shoes, $425.00. Courtesy McMasters Harris Doll Auctions.

15" bisque baby, mold #971, blue sleep eyes, open mouth, two teeth, original wig, five-piece composition baby body, white dress, lace inserts, bonnet, booties, circa 1913, $265.00. Courtesy McMasters Harris Doll Auctions.

Mold 372 Kiddiejoy, ca. 1925, shoulder head, molded hair, painted eyes, open/closed mouth, two upper teeth, kid body

12"	$300.00	$400.00
18"	$500.00	$650.00
21"	$775.00	$1,025.00

CHARACTER BABY

Baby Betty, usually found on child composition body, some on bent-leg baby body

16"	$500.00*

Baby Gloria, solid dome, open mouth, painted hair

15"	$500.00	$675.00

Baby Phyllis, head circumference:

9"	$275.00	$450.00
13"	$300.00	$500.00

Fany, mold 230, 231, ca. 1912, can be child, toddler, or baby, more for molded hair

#231

16"	$6,300.00*	
17"	$3,150.00	$4,200.00

Mold 256, 259, 326, 327, 328, 329, 360a, 750, 790, 900, 927, 970, 971, 975, 980, 984, 985, 990, 991, 992 Our Pet, 995, 996, bisque solid-dome or wigged socket head, open mouth, glass eyes, composition bent-leg baby body, add more for toddler body or flirty eyes or exceptional doll

12"	$225.00	$300.00
15"	$300.00	$425.00
17"	$400.00	$550.00
21"	$525.00	$750.00
24"	$600.00	$800.00

CHILD

No mold number, or just marked *"A.M.,"* bisque socket head, open mouth, glass eyes, wig, composition jointed body

17"	$300.00	$400.00
32"	$700.00	$925.00
42"	$1,500.00	$2,000.00

Mold 1890, 1892, 1893 (made for Cuno & Otto Dressel), 1894, 1897, 1898 (made for Cuno & Otto Dressel), 1899, 1900, 1901, 1902, 1903, 1909, and 3200, kid body, bisque shoulder or socket head, glass eyes, open mouth with teeth, wig. Add more for original clothes, labels.

12"	$125.00	$150.00
16"	$135.00	$225.00
19"	$210.00	$280.00
22"	$255.00	$350.00
26"	$330.00	$450.00

Composition body

8"	$245.00	$325.00
10"	$200.00	$275.00
16"	$550.00* original	
18"	$350.00	$450.00
21"	$375.00	$500.00
24"	$465.00	$624.00

Mold 370, 390, ca. 1900, Duchess, Florodora, Lilly, Mabel, My Playmate, open mouth, glass eyes

Kid body

12"	$125.00	$165.00
15"	$190.00	$255.00
18"	$245.00	$325.00
22"	$525.00	$700.00

Composition body

10"	$375.00* original costume	
13"	$200.00	$270.00
18"	$285.00	$375.00
21"	$375.00	$450.00
24"	$425.00	$525.00
27"	$550.00	$700.00
33"	$750.00	$1,025.00

8½" bisque baby, mold #590, brown sleep eyes, open/closed mouth, original mohair wig, five-piece composition bent-limb baby body, crocheted romper and hat, circa 1926, $275.00. Courtesy McMasters Harris Doll Auctions.

Alma, Beauty, Columbia, Melitta, My Companion, Princess, Queen Louise, Rosebud

Kid body

15"	$150.00	$200.00
23"	$375.00	$450.00

Composition body

13"	$225.00	$325.00
17"	$285.00	$375.00
22"	$425.00	$565.00
28"	$475.00	$650.00
31"	$775.00	$1,075.00

CHARACTER CHILD

Mold 225, ca. 1920, bisque socket head, glass eyes, open mouth, two rows of teeth, composition jointed body

14"	$2,700.00	$3,600.00
19"	$3,500.00	$4,650.00

Mold 250, ca. 1912, domed

9"	$400.00*	
15"	$450.00	$600.00
18"	$750.00	$1,000.00

Mold 251, ca. 1912, socket head, open/closed mouth

13"	$1,100.00	$1,450.00
17"	$1,500.00	$2,000.00

Open mouth

14"	$600.00	$800.00

16" bisque Kiddiejoy Baby, set blue eyes, open mouth, molded and painted hair, cloth body, celluloid hands, antique white baby dress, socks, and booties, circa 1926, $325.00. Two 9" composition Effanbee Patsy Babyette Twins, blue sleep eyes, closed mouths, molded and painted hair, five-piece composition baby bodies, blue/white rompers, all original, circa 1932, $300.00. Courtesy McMasters Harris Doll Auctions.

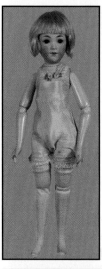

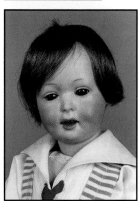

14½" #401 lady, bisque socket head, brown sleep eyes with real lashes, feathered brows, painted upper and lower lashes, accented nostrils, closed mouth, original mohair wig, jointed composition lady body with high-heeled feet, original pale green silk teddy, silk stockings, marked "Armand Marseille//Germany//401.//A.5/0. M." on back of head, $2,300.00. Courtesy McMasters Harris Doll Auctions.

Mold 253: See Googly.

Mold 310, Just Me, ca. 1929, bisque socket head, wig, flirty eyes, closed mouth, composition body

7½"	$800.00	$1,100.00
9"	$1,000.00	$1,400.00
11"	$1,300.00	$1,700.00
13"	$1,600.00	$2,100.00

Painted bisque, with Vogue labeled outfits

8"	$625.00	$850.00
10"	$750.00	$1,000.00

Mold 350, ca. 1926, glass eyes, closed mouth

16"	$1,650.00	$2,250.00
20"	$2,100.00	$2,850.00

Mold 360a, ca. 1913, open mouth

12"	$300.00	$400.00

Too few in database for reliable range.

Mold 400, 401, ca. 1926, glass eyes, closed mouth

13"	$1,100.00	$1,400.00

Flapper body, thin limbs

16"	$1,800.00	$2,300.00

Mold 449, ca. 1930, painted eyes, closed mouth

13"	$475.00	$635.00
18"	$900.00	$1,200.00

Painted bisque

11"	$250.00	$350.00
15"	$575.00	$765.00

Mold 450, glass eyes, closed mouth

14"	$550.00	$725.00

Mold 500, 620, 630, ca. 1910, domed shoulder head, molded/painted hair, painted intaglio eyes, closed mouth

17"	$750.00	$1,000.00

Mold 520, ca. 1910, domed head, glass eyes, open mouth

Composition body

12"	$575.00	$775.00
19"	$1,625.00	$2,175.00

Kid body

16"	$700.00	$1,000.00
20"	$1,125.00	$1,500.00

Mold 550, ca. 1926, domed, glass eyes, closed mouth

14"	$1,400.00*	

Too few in database for reliable range.

15" #590 child, bisque socket head, blue sleep eyes, single stroke brows, painted upper and lower lashes, accented nostrils, open mouth with two upper teeth, human hair wig, jointed wood and composition body, marked "590//A.3 M.//Germany//D.R.G.M. on back of head, white sailor shirt, blue/white striped pants, socks, black leatherette shoes, $255.00. Courtesy McMasters Harris Doll Auctions.

11" Just Me, mold #310, bisque socket head, blue sleep eyes to side, single stroke brows, painted upper and lower lashes, accented nostrils, closed mouth, blond mohair wig, five-piece composition body with bent right arm, marked "Just Me//Registered//Germany/ /A. 310/3/0.M," factory original organdy dress with red organdy collar and trim, original underclothing, orignal cotton socks, and black leatherette shoes, $2,600.00. Courtesy McMasters Harris Doll Auctions.

Mold 560, ca. 1910, character, domed, painted eyes, open/closed mouth or **560A**, ca. 1926, wigged, glass eyes, open mouth

14"	$600.00	$850.00

Mold 570, ca. 1910, domed, closed mouth

12"	$1,400.00	$1,850.00

Mold 590, ca. 1926, sleep eyes, open/closed mouth

9"	$375.00	$500.00
16"	$1,050.00*	

Mold 600 (dome), #640, ca. 1910, character, painted eyes, closed mouth

10"	$625.00	$850.00
17"	$1,350.00	$1,800.00

Mold 700, ca. 1920, closed mouth
Painted eyes

12½"	$1,500.00	$1,870.00

Glass eyes

14"	$4,200.00*	

Too few in database for reliable range.

Mold 701, 711, ca. 1920, socket or shoulder head, sleep eyes, closed mouth

16"	$1,835.00	$2,450.00

Too few in database to give reliable range.

Mold 800, ca. 1910, socket head, 840 shoulder head

18"	$1,800.00	$2,400.00

Too few in database for reliable range.

Metal Heads

Ca. 1850 – 1930+. Often called Minerva, because of a style of metal shoulder head widely distributed in the United States. Dolls with metal heads were made by various manufactures, including Buschow & Beck, Alfred Heller, who made Diana metal heads, and Karl Standfuss who made Juno metal heads. In the United States, Art Metal Works made metal head dolls. Various metals used were aluminum, brass, and others, and they might be marked with just a size and country of origin or unmarked.

Metal shoulder head, cloth or kid body, molded and painted hair, glass eyes, more for wigged.

16"	$100.00	$175.00
18"	$150.00	$250.00
21"	$175.00	$300.00

15" metal Minerva shoulder head, marked on front, painted features, molded and painted hair, $175.00. Courtesy Martha Cramer.

Painted eyes

14"	$65.00	$125.00
20"	$125.00	$225.00

Child, all metal or with composition body, metal limbs

15"	$250.00	$400.00
20"	$350.00	$500.00

Swiss: See Bucherer in Modern Section.

Multi-Face, Multi-Head Dolls

Three-face bisque doll by Carl Bergner, bisque socket head with three faces. Smiling face has set blue eyes, feathered brows, painted upper and lower lashes, accented nostrils, open/closed mouth. Crying face has set blue eyes, feathered "knit" brows, painted upper and lower lashes, accented nostrils, open-closed mouth with molded tongue. Sleeping face has closed eyes with lashes, feathered brows, accented nostrils, closed mouth. Bisque head turns inside molded papier mâché hood fringed with mohair in front for hair. Doll has carton torso, jointed wood and composition arms, cloth upper legs, wood and composition lower legs, re-dressed in white antique-style dress, underclothing, socks, high button boots, marked "Dep." at crown of sleeping face, "450" on crying face, "2/1" on smiling face, "C.B." in oval on back of shoulder plate, $1,100.00. Courtesy McMasters Harris Doll Auctions.

1866 – 1930+. Various firms made dolls with two or more faces, or more than one head.

BISQUE

French

Bru, Surprise poupee, awake/asleep faces

12"	$9,500.00

Too few in database for reliable range.

Jumeau, crying, laughing faces, cap hides knob

18"	$15,950.00*

Too few in database for reliable range.

German

Bergner, Carl, bisque socket head, three faces, sleeping, laughing, crying, molded tears, glass eyes, on composition jointed body may have molded bonnet or hood, marked *"C.B."* or *"Designed by Carl Bergner"*

12"	$900.00	$1,200.00
15"	$1,050.00	$1,400.00

Kestner, J. D., ca. 1900+, Wunderkind, bisque doll with set of several different mold number heads that could be attached to body, set of one doll and body with additional three heads and wardrobe

With heads 174, 178, 184 & 185

11"	$10,000.00*

With heads, 171, 179, 182 & 183

        14½" $12,650.00*

Kley & Hahn, solid-dome bisque socket head, painted hair, smiling baby and frowning baby, closed mouth, tongue, glass eyes, baby body

        13" $1,100.00*

Simon & Halbig, smiling, sleeping, crying, turn ring at top of head to change faces, glass/painted eyes, closed mouth

        14½" $935.00*

CLOTH

Topsy-Turvy: one black, one white head. See Cloth section.

COMPOSITION

Berwick Doll Co., Famlee Dolls, ca. 1926+, composition head and limbs, cloth body with crier, neck with screw joint, allowing different heads to be screwed into the body, painted features, mohair wigs and/or molded and painted hair. Came in sets of two to 12 heads, with different costumes for each head.

Seven-head set including baby, girl in fancy dress, girl in sports dress, Indian, and clown

        16" $600.00 $800.00+

Effanbee, Johnny Tu Face

        16" $275.00

Too few in database for reliable range.

Ideal, 1923, Soozie Smiles, composition, sleep or painted eyes on happy face, two faces, smiling, crying, cloth body, composition hands, cloth legs, original romper and hat

        15½" $300.00 $400.00

Three-in-One Doll Corp., 1946+, Trudy, composition head with turning knob on top, cloth body and limbs, three faces, "Sleepy, Weepy, Smiley," dressed in felt or fleece snowsuit, or sheer dresses, more for exceptional doll

        15½" $85.00 $300.00

PAPIER MÂCHÉ

Smiling/crying faces, glass eyes, cloth body, composition lower limbs

        19" $550.00 $700.00

WAX

Smiling/crying faces, glass eyes, carton body, crier

        15" $400.00 $600.00

Munich Art Dolls

1908 – 1920s. Marion Kaulitz hand painted heads designed by Marc-Schnur, Vogelsanger, and Wackerle, dressed in German or French regional costumes. Usually composition heads and bodies distributed by Cuno & Otto Dressell and Arnoldt Doll Co.

Composition, painted features, wig, composition body, unmarked

        17" $5,750.00*

Ohlhaver, Gebrüder

1913 – 1930, Sonneberg, Germany. Had Revalo (Ohlhaver spelled backwards omitting the two H's) line; made bisque socket and shoulder head and composition dolls. Ernst Heubach supplied some heads to Ohlhaver.

> *Mark:*
>
> ₒRevaₗₒ.
> Germany

Baby or Toddler, character face, bisque socket head, glass eyes, open mouth, teeth, wig, composition and wood ball-jointed body (bent-leg for baby)

Baby

16"	$425.00	$575.00

Toddler

14"	$750.00	$975.00

Child, Mold 150, ca. 1920
Bisque socket head, open mouth, sleep eyes, composition body

16"	$175.00	$250.00
17"	$500.00	$675.00
18"	$325.00*	

Coquette-type
Bisque solid dome with molded and painted hair, ribbon, eyes, composition and wood body

13"	$550.00	$800.00+

Oriental Dolls

15" Simon & Halbig 1329 Oriental, bisque solcket head with olive complexion, brown sleep eyes with real lashes, feathered brows, painted upper and lower lashes, feathered brows, painted upper and lower lashes, accented nostrils, open mouth with four upper teeth, pierced ears, original black mohair wig in upswept hair style, jointed wood and composition body with olive finish, marked "1329//Germany//Simon & Halbig//S&H//4" on back of head, original kimono, underclothing, socks, and brown sandals, also with original hair decorations and turquoise necklace and earrings, $3,100.00. Courtesy McMasters Harris Doll Auctions.

ALL-BISQUE
Heubach, Gebrüder, Chin-Chin

4"	$250.00	$350.00

Kestner

6"	$1,050.00	$1,400.00
8"	$1,200.00	$1,600.00

Simon & Halbig

5"	$550.00	$750.00
7"	$750.00	$1,000.00

Unmarked or unknown maker, presumed German or French

6"	$400.00	$550.00

EUROPEAN BISQUE
Bisque head, jointed body
Amusco, mold 1006

17"	$900.00	$1,200.00

Belton-type, mold 193, 206

10"	$1,550.00	$2,075.00
14"	$2,000.00	$2,700.00

Bru, pressed bisque swivel head, glass eyes, closed mouth

20"	$26,000,00*

Too few in database for reliable range.

Kestner, J. D., 1899 – 1930+, mold 243, bisque socket head, open mouth, wig, bent-leg baby body, add more for original clothing

14"	$3,600.00	$4,700.00
16"	$4,600.00	$6,100.00

Solid dome, painted hair

15"	$3,750.00	$5,000.00

Armand Marseille, ca. 1925
   Mold 353, solid-dome bisque socket head, glass eyes, closed mouth
     Baby body

7½"	$900.00	$1,200.00
14"	$925.00	$1,225.00
16"	$1,050.00	$1,400.00

     Toddler

16"	$975.00	$1,300.00

     Painted bisque

7"	$350.00*

Schmidt, Bruno, marked "BSW"
   Mold 500, ca. 1905, glass eyes, open mouth

14"	$1,600.00	$2,100.00
18"	$2,200.00*	

Schoenau & Hoffmeister
   Mold 4900, bisque socket head, glass eyes, open mouth, tinted composition wood jointed body

10"	$375.00	$500.00

Simon & Halbig
   Mold 1199, ca. 1898, bisque socket head, glass eyes, open mouth, pierced ears

16"	$9,000.00*

   Mold 1079, 1129, 1159, 1329, bisque socket head, glass eyes, open mouth, pierced ears, composition wood jointed body

13"	$1,350.00	$1,800.00
18"	$2,100.00	$2,600.00

Unknown maker, socket head, jointed body, closed mouth

14"	$975.00	$1,300.00
20"	$2,200.00	$2,800.00

JAPANESE BISQUE
   Various makers including Morimura, Yamato, marked "FY," and others marked "Nippon" or "J.W." made dolls when doll production was halted in Europe during World War I.
   Baby, marked "Japan" or "Nippon" or by other maker

11"	$135.00	$180.00
15"	$225.00	$300.00
19"	$400.00	$525.00

   Child, marked "Nippon" or "Japan" or other maker

14"	$195.00	$250.00
17"	$250.00	$330.00
22"	$415.00	$550.00

11" carved wooden Chinese woman, tagged "OTA Shanghai," painted carved features, long wooden fingers, heavily embroidered dress, matching headdress, cloth body, circa early 1930s, $250.00+. Courtesy Mary Alice Scheflow.

17" gofun (crushed oyster shell over papier mâché) Japanese Ischimatsu (play doll), black wig, brown glass eyes, multistroke black eyebrows, closed mouth, traditional patterned Japanese kimono, circa 1920s, $500.00. Courtesy Valerie McArdle.

13½" gofun Japanese squeaker doll, black inset glass eyes, black stiff wig, composition feet and arms, cloth legs, all wire upper arms, composition lower arms, original red kimono, long sleeves of little girl, white collar underneath kimono, circa 1950s, $125.00. Courtesy Jean Thompson.

17" gofun (crushed oyster shell over papier mâché) unmarked Japanese boy, black wig, brown glass eyes, multi-stroke black eyebrows, closed mouth, squeaker in body, composition hands and feet, traditional patterned kimono clothing, brought home with five other dolls on sailing ship by Bette Eppinger's grand-dad for her sister and aunt, circa 1933, $250.00. Courtesy Betty Eppinger.

COMPOSITION

Child, unmarked, original outfit

16"	$65.00	$200.00

Effanbee

Butin-nose, in basket with wardrobe, painted Oriental features including black bobbed hair, bangs, side-glancing eyes, excellent color and condition

8"	$125.00	$500.00

Patsy, painted Oriental features, including black bangs, straight across the forehead, brown side-glancing eyes, dressed in silk Chinese pajamas and matching shoes, excellent condition

14"	$250.00	$800.00

Horsman

Baby Butterfly, ca. 1911 – 1913, composition head, hands, cloth body, painted hair, features

13"	$175.00	$650.00

Quan-Quan Co., California

Ming Ming Baby, all-composition jointed baby, painted features, original costume, yarn que, painted shoes

11"	$75.00	$250.00

TRADITIONAL CHINESE

Man or woman, composition type head, cloth-wound bodies, may have carved arms and feet, in traditional costume

11"	$115.00	$350.00
14"	$175.00	$525.00

TRADITIONAL JAPANESE

Ichimatsu, 1870s on, a play doll made of papier-mâché-type material with gofun finish of crushed oyster shells, swivel head, shoulder plate, cloth midsection, upper arms, and legs. Limbs and torso are papier mâché, glass eyes, pierced nostrils. Early dolls may have jointed wrists and ankles, in original dress. Later 1950s+ dolls imported by Kimport.

Traditional, Meiji era, ca. 1870s – 1912

10"	$300.00	$600.00+
16"	$475.00	$950.00+
22"	$675.00	$1,400.00+

Traditional child, painted hair, 1920s

12"	$225.00	$450.00
18"	$350.00	$675.00
24"	$475.00	$900.00

Traditional child, 1930s

14"	$80.00	$155.00
19"	$150.00	$300.00

Traditional child, 1940s on

15"	$50.00	$100.00

* at auction

Traditional Lady, 1920s – 1930s

14"	$135.00	$270.00
16"	$165.00	$325.00

Traditional Lady, 1940s – 1950s

14"	$50.00	$95.00
16"	$70.00	$135.00

Emperor or Empress, seated, ca. 1890s

8"	$285.00	$575.00

Ca. 1920s

6"	$90.00	$180.00
8"	$115.00	$225.00

Warrior, 1880 – 1890s

16"	$500.00	$650.00

Too few in database for reliable range.

On horse

15"	$1,100.00+

Too few in database for reliable range.

Warrior, 1920s

15"	$400.00

Too few in database for reliable range.

On horse

13"	$850.00+

Japanese baby, ca. 1920s, bisque head, sleep eyes, closed mouth, papier mâché body

8"	$50.00	$70.00
14"	$65.00	$90.00

Glass eyes

8"	$95.00	$125.00
14"	$200.00	$265.00

Japanese baby, gofun finish of crushed oyster-shell head, painted flesh color, papier mâché body, glass eyes and original clothes

8"	$25.00	$50.00
14"	$45.00	$95.00
18"	$95.00	$185.00

WOOD

Door of Hope: See that section.
Schoenhut: See that section.

Papier-Mâché

Pre-1600 on. Varying types of composition made from paper or paper pulp could be mass produced in molds for heads after 1810. It reached heights of popularity by mid-1850s and was also used for bodies. Papier-mâché shoulder head, glass or painted eyes, molded and painted hair, sometimes in fancy hairdos. Usually no marks.

First price indicates doll in good condition with flaws, less if poorly repainted; second price is for doll in excellent condition, nicely dressed. More for exceptional examples.

EARLY TYPE SHOULDER HEAD, CA. 1840s – 1860s

Cloth body; wooden limbs; with topknots, buns, puff curls, or braids; dressed in original clothing or excellent copy; may have some wear; more for painted pate.

19½" French shoulder head, pupilless eyes, open mouth, teeth, mohair wig, kid gusseted body, original costume, excellent condition, $1,000.00. Courtesy McMasters Harris Doll Auctions.

Painted eyes

9"	$225.00	$450.00
12"	$340.00	$675.00
18"	$525.00	$1,050.00
21"	$575.00	$1,150.00
26"	$1,500.00	$1,750.00
32"	$1,000.00	$2,000.00

Glass eyes

18"	$1,000.00	$1,700.00
24"	$1,100.00	$2,200.00

Long curls

14"	$375.00	$750.00
16"	$775.00	$1,550.00

MILLINER'S MODELS TYPE, CA. 1820 – 1860s

Many collectors may use this term "milliner's models" to describe dolls with molded hair, a shapely waist, kid body, and wooden limbs.

Apollo top knot (beehive), side curls

10"	$425.00	$850.00
14"	$2,200.00*	
16"	$1,050.00	$2,125.00

Braided bun, side curls

9"	$400.00	$800.00
15"	$800.00	$1,600.00

Center part, molded bun

9"	$325.00	$650.00
13"	$550.00	$1,100.00

Center part, sausage curls

14"	$275.00	$575.00
21"	$450.00	$950.00

Coiled braids over ears, braided bun

11"	$550.00	$1,000.00
21"	$1,150.00	$2,300.00

Covered Wagon or Flat Top hair style

10"	$175.00	$325.00
14"	$250.00	$500.00
16"	$300.00	$600.00

Molded bonnet, kid body, wood limbs, bonnet painted to tie under chin, very rare

15"	$1,700.00

Too few in database for reliable range.

Molded comb, side curls, braided coronet

16"	$1,650.00	$3,300.00

Too few in database for reliable range.

FRENCH TYPE, CA. 1835 – 1850

Painted black hair, brush marks, solid-dome, shoulder head, some have nailed on wigs, open mouth, bamboo teeth, kid or leather body, appropriately dressed

29", shoulder head with painted features, molded and painted black hair, cloth body, leather lower arms, circa 1870s – 1880s, $550.00. Courtesy McMasters Harris Doll Auctions.

Glass eyes

13"	$750.00	$1,000.00
18"	$1,500.00	$1,750.00
28"	$4,200.00*	

Painted eyes

12"	$375.00	$750.00
16"	$500.00	$1,000.00

Wooden jointed body

8"	$385.00	$765.00

GERMAN TYPE

1844 – 1892

"M & S Superior," Muller & Strasburger, Sonneberg, Germany, shoulder head, with blond or molded hair, painted blue or brown eyes, cloth body, with kid or leather arms and boots. Mold numbers on stickers reported are

17½" German unmarked shoulder head, set blue glass eyes, closed mouth, blond mohair wig, pink cloth body with composition lower arms, stitch jointed hips and knees, antique white print dress with embroidery trim, socks, and shoes, circa 1879 – 1900s, $275.00. Courtesy McMasters Harris Doll Auctions.

Mold 1020, 2020, 2015, and 4515

17"	$225.00	$425.00
22"	$365.00	$675.00
27"	$425.00	$850.00

Glass eyes

12"	$300.00	$500.00
16"	$500.00	$700.00

Wigged

13"	$675.00	$900.00

1879 – 1900s

Patent washable shoulder head with mohair wig, open or closed mouth, glass eyes, cloth body, composition limbs

Better quality

15"	$275.00	$550.00
18"	$400.00	$700.00
22"	$550.00	$900.00

Lesser quality

10"	$75.00	$150.00
16"	$125.00	$250.00

Turned shoulder head, solid dome, glass eyes, closed mouth, cloth body, composition forearms

16"	$350.00	$700.00
22"	$465.00	$925.00

M & S Superior or unmarked, ca. 1880 – 1910, Germany, shoulder head

15"	$150.00	$300.00
18"	$200.00	$400.00

16" milliner's model, kid body, leather lower limbs, $775.00+. Courtesy McMasters Harris Doll Auctions.

1920+

Head has brighter coloring, wigged, child often in ethnic costume, stuffed cloth body and limbs, or papier mâché arms

* at auction

Three 6" unmarked candy containers, character heads, painted eyes, large nose with pink wash on left and center, closed mouth with protruding lower lip on left and center, molded and painted sideburns and hair, papier mâché body hollow inside for candy, molded and painted clothes and hats, circa 1900, left: $210.00; center: $210.00; right: $265.00. Courtesy McMasters Harris Doll Auctions.

French

9"	$65.00	$125.00
13"	$100.00	$200.00
15"	$150.00	$300.00

German

10"	$40.00	$80.00
15"	$90.00	$165.00

Unknown maker

8"	$30.00	$60.00
12"	$60.00	$115.00
16"	$90.00	$175.00

Clowns, papier mâché head, with painted clown features, open or closed mouth, molded hair or wigged, cloth body, composition or papier mâché arms, or five-piece jointed body

8"	$120.00	$235.00
14"	$245.00	$485.00
20"	$395.00	$785.00
26"	$460.00	$925.00

Eden Clown, socket head, open mouth, blue glass eyes, blond mohair wig, five-piece jointed body, all original with labeled box

16"	$4,000.00*

Parian-Type Untinted Bisque

Ca. 1850 – 1900+, Germany. Refers to very white color of untinted bisque dolls, often with molded blond hair, some with fancy hair arrangements and ornaments or bonnets; can have glass or painted eyes, pierced ears, may have molded jewelry or clothing. Occasionally solid dome with wig. Cloth body, nicely dressed in good condition.

First price indicates doll in good condition, but with flaws; second price indicates doll in excellent condition, appropriately dressed. Exceptional examples may be much higher.

LADY

Common hair style
Undecorated, simple molded hair

10"	$125.00	$175.00
15"	$225.00	$300.00
21"	$325.00	$425.00
25"	$400.00	$525.00

18½" glass eyes, untinted bisque cup-and-saucer-type swivel head on bisque shoulder plate, set blue glass eyes, multi-stroke brows, painted upper and lower lashes, accented nostrils, closed mouth, molded and painted blond hair, cloth body jointed at shoulders, elbows, hips, and knees, kid arms with stitched fingers and applied thumbs, antique two-piece ecru water silk dress, antique underclothing, no socks or shoes, $700.00. Courtesy McMasters Harris Doll Auctions.

28" unmarked, bisque shoulder head, painted blue eyes with red accent line, single stroke brown brows, closed mouth, pierced ears, molded blond hair with elaborate style, molded black ribbon necklace, molded blouse top, white dress, pantalettes, corset, and slip, $2,300.00. Courtesy McMasters Harris Doll Auctions.

Fancy hair style

With molded combs, ribbons, flowers, bands, or snoods, cloth body, untinted bisque limbs, more for very elaborate hairstyle

Painted eyes, pierced ears

16"	$685.00	$900.00
22"	$1,300.00	$1,700.00

Painted eyes, ears not pierced

13"	$550.00	$700.00

Glass eyes, pierced ears

15"	$1,200.00	$1,600.00
20"	$2,100.00	$2,700.00

Swivel neck, glass eyes

15"	$2,000.00	$2,700.00

Alice in Wonderland, molded headband or comb

16"	$475.00	$625.00
19"	$550.00	$750.00

Countess Dagmar, no mark, head band, cluster curls on forehead

21"	$750.00	$950.00

Dolly Madison

22"	$1,000.00	$1,600.00

Empress Eugenie, headpiece snood

25"	$500.00	$750.00

Irish Queen, Limbach, clover mark, #8552

14"	$350.00	$575.00

Mary Todd Lincoln, headband, snood

25"	$400.00	$700.00

Molded bodice, fancy trim

17"	$600.00	$800.00

Molded hat, blond or black painted hair

Painted eyes

16"	$1,700.00	$2,300.00
19"	$2,150.00	$2,900.00

13½", unmarked, untinted bisque shoulder head, painted blue eyes with red accent line, single stroke brows, accented nostrils, closed mouth, cafe au lait hair, molded blouse with collar and striped tie, cloth body with kid arms, stitched fingers, two-piece red outfit, cotton socks, and leather boots, $600.00. Courtesy McMasters Harris Doll Auctions.

Mark:
Seldom any mark; may have number inside shoulder plate.

Glass eyes

14"	$1,850.00	$2,400.00
17"	$2,250.00	$3,000.00

Necklace, jewels, or standing ruffles

17"	$9,700.00+

Too few in database for reliable range.

MEN OR BOYS

Center or side-part hair style, cloth body, decorated shirt and tie
Painted eyes

13"	$575.00	$775.00
17"	$750.00	$1,000.00

Glass eyes

16"	$2,100.00	$2,825.00

Piano Babies

Ca. 1880 – 1930+, Germany. These all-bisque figurines were made by Gebrüder Heubach, Kestner, Dressel, Limbach, and others. May have molded on clothes; came in a variety of poses. Some were reproduced during the 1960s and 1970s and the skin tones are paler than the others.

First price indicates figurine in good condition with flaws; second price indicates figurine in excellent condition.

9" unmarked Gebrüder Heubach, unjointed bisque figure, blue intaglio eyes with molded lids, single-stroke brows, accented nostrils, open-closed mouth with outline on top lip, molded and painted hair; $300.00. *Courtesy McMasters Harris Doll Auctions.*

Excellent quality or marked "Heubach," fine details

4"	$235.00	$300.00
6"	$350.00	$475.00
7½"	$600.00* with sunburst mark	
9"	$525.00	$700.00
16"	$850.00	$1,125.00

Black

5"	$300.00	$425.00
9"	$375.00	$500.00
14"	$675.00	$900.00

With animal, pot, flowers, chair, or other items

5"	$195.00	$260.00
8"	$315.00	$425.00
10"	$400.00	$525.00
15"	$750.00	$1,000.00

Medium quality, unmarked, may not have painted finish on back

4"	$75.00	$100.00
8"	$150.00	$200.00
12"	$225.00	$300.00

Ca. 1900 – 1930s, Germany, Japan. Half dolls can be made of bisque, china, composition, or papier mâché, and were used not only for pincushions but on top of jewelry or cosmetic boxes, brushes, and lamps. The hardest to find have arms molded away from the body as they were easier to break with the limbs in this position and thus fewer survived.

First price is for doll in good condition, with flaws; second price is for doll in excellent condition; add more for extra attributes. Rare examples may bring more.

6½" half doll, jointed arms, marked "(heart)//3538," bisque figure had painted blue eys with light red accent line, single-stroke brows, accented nostrils, closed mouth, molded and painted gray hair in elaborate style with curls on neck, molded bosom, jointed at shoulder, delicately shaped hands, $200.00. Courtesy McMasters Harris Doll Auctions.

ARMS AWAY

China or bisque figure, bald head with wig

4"	$105.00	$140.00
6"	$155.00	$210.00

Goebel mark, dome head, wig

5"	$195.00*

Holding items, such as letter, flower

4"	$135.00	$185.00
6"	$200.00	$275.00

Marked by maker or mold number

4"	$150.00	$200.00
6"	$225.00	$300.00
8"	$300.00	$400.00
12"	$675.00	$900.00

Pincushion

6"	$430.00* Flamenco Dancer

ARMS IN

Close to figure, bald head with wig

4"	$55.00	$80.00
6"	$80.00	$115.00

Hands attached

3"	$20.00	$35.00
5"	$30.00	$45.00
7"	$45.00	$70.00

Decorated bodice, necklace, fancy hair or holding article

3"	$85.00	$125.00
4¾"	$305.00* holding tray, cups	

Marked by maker or mold number

5"	$80.00	$135.00
6"	$110.00	$155.00

With legs, dressed, fancy decorations

5"	$225.00	$300.00
7"	$300.00	$400.00

Papier mâché or composition

4"	$25.00	$35.00
6"	$60.00	$80.00

4" china Gypsy lady half doll, marked "14393//Germany," orange scarf on head, one hand close to body, the other away, circa 1930s, $425.00+. Courtesy Patricia Wright.

14" bisque unmarked half doll lamp, painted side-glancing eyes, closed mouth, rosy cheeks, bald head with original blond mohair wig, arms away from body, all original, circa 1920s, $650.00. Courtesy Sheryl Schmidt.

JOINTED SHOULDERS

China or bisque, molded hair

5"	$110.00	$145.00
7"	$150.00	$200.00

Solid dome, mohair wig

4"	$165.00	$220.00
5¾"	$685.00*	
6"	$330.00	$400.00

MAN OR CHILD

4"	$90.00	$120.00
6"	$120.00	$160.00

MARKED GERMANY

4"	$150.00	$200.00
6"	$375.00	$500.00

MARKED JAPAN

3"	$10.00	$15.00
6"	$38.00	$50.00

OTHER ITEMS

Brush, with porcelain figurine for handle, molded hair, may be holding something

9"	$55.00	$75.00

Dresser box, unmarked, with figurine on lid

7"	$265.00	$350.00
9"	$345.00	$450.00

Dresser box, marked with mold number, country, or manufacturer

5"	$210.00	$285.00
6"	$275.00	$350.00

Perfume bottle, stopper is half-doll, skirt is bottle

6½"	$165.00*

3¾" china 14596 half doll flapper, molded and painted features, molded gold luster outfit with green hat and purse, white gloves, ermine wrap, marked "14596 Made in Germany," circa 1920s+, $275.00. Courtesy Elizabeth Surber.

Rabery & Delphieu

Mark: R.3. D

1856 – 1930 and later, Paris. Became S.F.B.J. in 1899. Some heads pressed (pre-1890) and some poured, purchased heads from Francois Gaultier.

First price indicates doll in good condition, but with some flaws; second price indicates doll in excellent condition, appropriately dressed. Exceptional dolls may be more.

25" bébé, bisque socket head, blue paperweight eyes, heavy feathered brows, painted upper and lower lashes, closed mouth, pierced ears, human hair wig, jointed wood and composition French body, antique striped silk dress, underclothing, socks, and leather shoes, marked "R.2.D." on back of head, $1,100.00. Courtesy McMasters Harris Doll Auctions.

CHILD

Closed mouth, bisque socket head, paperweight eyes, pierced ears, mohair wig, cork pate, French composition and wood jointed body

11"	$3,000.00	$4,500.00
12½"	$7,000.00* with presentation box	
17"	$3,800.00*	
23"	$4,200.00	$5,600.00

Open mouth, row of upper teeth

18"	$1,075.00	$1,400.00
24"	$1,250.00	$1,650.00
26"	$1,700.00	$2,300.00

Recknagel

1886 – 1930+, Thüringia, Germany. Made bisque heads of varying quality, incised or raised mark, wigged or molded hair, glass or painted eyes, open or closed mouth, flange neck or socket head.

BABY

Mold 23, 121, 126, 1924, bent-limb baby body, painted or glass eyes

6½"	$225.00	$300.00
8"	$250.00	$375.00

Bonnet head baby, painted eyes, open/closed mouth, teeth
Mold 22, 28, 44, molded white boy's cap, bent-leg baby body

8"	$425.00*	
11"	$600.00	$800.00

Oriental baby, solid-dome bisque socket head
Sleep eyes, closed mouth five-piece yellow tinted body

11"	$2,300.00*

Mold 137, Newborn, ca. 1925, flange neck, sleep eyes, closed mouth, cloth body, boxed

13"	$545.00*

CHILD

Dolly face, 1890s – 1914

Mold 1907, 1909, 1914, open mouth, glass eyes

Mark:

7"	$85.00	$110.00
12"	$150.00	$200.00
15"	$250.00	$325.00
29"	$650.00* Mold 1909	

Character face, ca. 1910+, may have crossed hammer mark

7"	$300.00	$400.00
12"	$550.00	$750.00

Mold 31, 32, Max and Moritz

8"	$500.00	$650.00

Rohmer

1857 – 1880, Paris. Mme. Rohmer held patents for doll bodies, made dolls of various materials.

First price is for doll in good condition, but with flaws; second price is for doll in excellent condition, appropriately dressed; may be much more for exceptional dolls.

Mark:

Rohmer

FASHION-TYPE
Bisque or china glazed shoulder or swivel head on shoulder plate, closed mouth, kid body with green oval stamp, bisque or wood lower arms

Glass eyes

14"	$3,400.00*	
17"	$7,200.00	$9,500.00

Painted eyes

14"	$4,200.00	$5,600.00
18"	$5,400.00* pink tint	

Untinted bisque swivel head, lined shoulder plate, cobalt glass eyes, kid over wood arms, kid gusseted body, original costume

16"	$7,400.00*

China head, painted eyes

17"	$2,800.00	$3,700.00

Schmidt, Bruno

1900 – 1930+, Waltershausen, Germany. Made bisque, composition, and wooden head dolls, after 1913 also celluloid. Acquired Bähr & Pröschild in 1918. Often used a heart-shaped tag.

CHARACTER BABY
Bisque socket head, glass eyes, composition bent leg body
Mold 2092, ca. 1920, **Mold 2097,** ca. 1911

13"	$375.00	$475.00
15"	$450.00	$600.00
21"	$675.00	$900.00

Mold 2097, toddler

15"	$500.00	$700.00
21"	$750.00	$1,000.00

CHILD
BSW, no mold numbers
Bisque socket head, jointed body, sleep eyes, open mouth, add $50.00 more for flirty eyes.

14"	$335.00	$450.00
18"	$475.00	$625.00
23"	$625.00	$850.00

CHARACTER
Oriental, mold 500, ca. 1905, yellow tint bisque socket head, glass eyes, open mouth, teeth, pierced ears, wig, yellow tint composition jointed body

11"	$1,100.00	$1,450.00
18"	$1,450.00	$1,900.00

Mold 529, "2052," ca. 1912, painted eyes, closed mouth

20"	$2,800.00	$4,000.00

Mold 539, "2023," ca. 1912, solid dome or with wig, painted eyes, closed mouth

24"	$2,250.00	$3,500.00

13½" bisque Wendy mold #2033, bisque socket head, closed mouth, human hair wig, made by Bähr & Pröschild for Bruno Schmidt, circa 1912, $14,000.00. Courtesy McMasters Harris Doll Auctions.

Mold 537, "2033," ca. 1912, sleep eyes, closed mouth
    13½" $14,000.00*
Too few in database for reliable range.

Mold 2048, ca. 1912, **Tommy Tucker, 2094, 2096,** ca. 1920, solid dome, molded and painted hair or wig, sleep eyes, open or closed mouth, composition jointed body

Open mouth

12"	$650.00	$900.00
18"	$950.00	$1,250.00
28"	$1,400.00	$2,000.00

Closed mouth

16"	$1,560.00	$2,050.00

Mold 2072, ca. 1920, sleep eyes

Closed mouth

16"	$2,550.00*	

Too few in database for reliable range.

Schmidt, Franz

1890 – 1930+, Georgenthal, Germany. Made, produced, and exported dolls with bisque, composition, wood, and celluloid heads. Used some heads made by Simon & Halbig.

Heads marked "*S & C,*" mold 269, 293, 927, 1180, 1310

Heads marked "*F.S. & C,*" mold 1250, 1253, 1259, 1262, 1263, 1266, 1267, 1270, 1271, 1272, 1274, 1293, 1295, 1296, 1297, 1298, 1310

Walkers: mold 1071, 1310

BABY

Bisque head, solid dome or cut out for wig, bent-leg body, sleep or set eyes, open mouth, some pierced nostrils. Add more for flirty eyes.

Marks:

1310

F.S.&C

or

S & C
ANVIL MARK

Mold 1271, 1272, 1295, 1296, 1297, 1310

10"	$325.00	$400.00
13"	$375.00	$500.00
18"	$500.00	$650.00
24"	$850.00	$1,100.00

Toddler

10"	$750.00	$1,000.00
18"	$975.00	$1,300.00
23"	$1,100.00	$1,475.00
25"	$1,325.00	$1,800.00

CHARACTER FACE

Mold 1266, 1267, ca. 1912, *marked "F.S. & Co.,"* solid dome, painted eyes, closed mouth

14"	$2,150.00	$2,850.00
19"	$2,900.00	$3,900.00

23" mold #1295 baby, bisque socket head, blue sleep eyes, painted upper and lower lashes, open nostrils, open mouth with protruding spring tongue, original mohair wig, bent-limb composition body, antique clothing, marked "1295//F.S. & Co.//60," $475.00. Courtesy McMasters Harris Doll Auctions.

Mold 1270, ca. 1910, solid dome, painted eyes, open/closed mouth

9"	$475.00	$650.00
13"	$1,350.00	$1,800.00

With two faces

16"	$1,075.00	$1,450.00

CHILD

Dolly face, Mold 269, ca. 1890s, **Mold 293**, ca. 1900, *marked "S & C,"* open mouth, glass eyes

7"	$200.00	$300.00
19"	$500.00	$650.00
23"	$625.00	$800.00
27"	$800.00	$1,050.00

Mold 1259, ca. 1912, *marked "F.S. & Co."* character, sleep eyes, pierced nostrils, open mouth

15"	$300.00	$500.00

Mold 1262, 1263, ca. 1910, *marked "F.S. & Co.,"* painted eyes, closed mouth

14"	$4,350.00	$5,800.00

Too few in database for reliable range.

Mold 1272, ca. 1910, *marked "F.S. & Co.,"* solid dome or wig, sleep eyes, pierced nostrils, open mouth

9½"	$700.00	$950.00

Too few in database for a reliable range.

Schmitt & Fils

1854 – 1891, Paris. Made bisque and wax-over-bisque or wax-over-composition dolls. Heads were pressed. Used neck socket like on later composition Patsy dolls.

First price is for doll in good condition, but with flaws; second price is for doll in excellent condition, appropriately dressed; more for exceptional doll with wardrobe or other attributes.

CHILD

Pressed bisque head, closed mouth, glass eyes, pierced ears, mohair or human hair wig, French composition and wood eight ball-jointed body with straight wrists.

Mark:

Shield on head, "SCH" in shield on bottom of flat cut derriere.

Early round face

12"	$7,875.00	$10,500.00
13"	$12,000.00*	trousseau, box
18"	$16,000.00*	
24"	$12,850.00	$17,125.00

Long face modeling

19"	$9,000.00	$13,000.00
24"	$12,500.00	$16,500.00

Wax over papier mâché, swivel head, cup and saucer type neck, glass eyes, closed mouth, eight ball-jointed body

16"	$1,125.00	$1,500.00
22"	$1,300.00	$1,700.00

* at auction

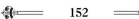

Schmitt body only, eight ball joints, straight wrists, separated fingers, marked "*SCH*" in shield

     15" $1,400.00*

Schoenau & Hoffmeister

1901 – 1953, Sonneberg, and Burggrub, Bavaria. Had a porcelain factory, produced bisque heads for dolls, also supplied other manufacturers, including Brückner, Dressel, E. Knoch, and others.

First price is for doll in good condition with flaws; second price is for doll in excellent condition, appropriately dressed. More for exceptional dolls.

Mark:

BABY

Bisque solid-dome or wigged socket head, sleep eyes, teeth, composition bent-leg body, closed mouth, newborn, solid dome, painted hair, cloth body, may have celluloid hands, add more for original outfit.

9" pair	$950.00* pair	
13"	$625.00	$825.00
15"	$700.00	$950.00
Toddler		
15"	$600.00	$800.00
21"	$1,100.00	$1,500.00

Mold 169, ca. 1930, open mouth, composition bent-leg body, wigged

23"	$385.00	$500.00
25"	$425.00	$575.00

Mold 170, ca. 1930, open mouth, composition five-piece toddler body

19"	$350.00	$475.00

Hanna, sleep eyes, open/closed mouth, bent-leg baby body, $100.00 more for toddler

13"	$375.00	$500.00
18"	$600.00	$800.00
24"	$1,000.00	$1,350.00

Princess Elizabeth, ca. 1929, socket head, sleep eyes, smiling open mouth, chubby leg toddler body

16"	$1,450.00	$1,950.00
22"	$1,925.00	$2,550.00

CHILD

Dolly face, bisque socket head, open mouth with teeth, sleep eyes, composition ball-jointed body

34½" mold #1906, bisque socket head, large brown sleep eyes with real lashes, molded and feathered brows, painted upper and lower lashes, accented nostrils, open mouth with outlined lips and four upper teeth, repaced wig, jointed wood and composition body, marked "Germany//S PB (in star) H//1906//No. 15" on back of head, antique white child's dress with ribbon insert, antique undercloth-ing, replaced socks and shoes, $300.00. Courtesy McMasters Harris Doll Auctions.

Mold 1906, 1909, 2500, 4000, 4600, 4700, 5500, 5700, 5800

14"	$250.00	$325.00
18"	$350.00	$450.00
26"	$650.00	$850.00

Mold 914, ca. 1925, character

30"	$625.00*

Mold 4900, ca. 1905, Oriental, dolly-face

10"	$350.00	$475.00

Schoenhut, A. & Co.

16" with carved bonnet, #16/106, wooden socket head, blue intaglio eyes with molded lids, feathered brows, accented nsotrils, closed pouty mouth, molded and painted brown hair showing from under white bonnet with red and yellow painted flowers, gold trim, spring jointed wooden body with joints at shouders, elbows, wrists, hips, knees, and ankles, white dress with red trim and cross stitch, slip, replaced knit underwear, old socks, and white three-button boots, marked "Schoenhut Doll//Pat. Jan. 17th 1911//U.S.A." on label on back, $3,700.00. Courtesy McMasters Harris Doll Auctions.

1872 – 1930+, Philadelphia, PA. Made all-wood dolls, using spring joints, had holes in bottoms of feet to fit into stands. Later made elastic strung with cloth bodies. Carved or molded and painted hair or wigged, intaglio or sleep eyes, open or closed mouth. Later made composition dolls.

First price is for doll in good condition, but with some flaws, perhaps touch-up; second price is for doll in excellent condition, appropriately dressed; more for exceptional doll.

INFANT

Graziano Infants, circa May 1911 – 1912

Schnickel – Fritz, carved hair, open/closed grinning mouth, four teeth, large ears, toddler

15"	$2,250.00	$3,000.00

Tootsie Wootsie, carved hair, open/closed mouth, two upper teeth, large ears on child body

15"	$2,600.00	$3,400.00

Too few in database for reliable range.

Model 107, 107W (walker)

Baby, nature (bent) limb, 1913 – 1926

13"	$375.00	$550.00

Toddler, 1917 – 1926

11"	$550.00	$700.00

Toddler, 1913 – 1926

14"	$575.00	$750.00

Toddler, elastic strung, 1924 – 1926

14"	$575.00	$750.00

Toddler, cloth body with crier

14"	$475.00	$600.00

Model 108, 108W (walker)

Baby, nature (bent) limb, 1913 – 1926

15"	$450.00	$600.00

Toddler, 1917 – 1926

17"	$650.00	$850.00

Toddler, elastic strung, 1924 – 1926

17"	$475.00	$725.00

Toddler, cloth body, crier, 1924 – 1928

17"	$425.00	$550.00

* at auction

Left: 16" 16/303, wooden character head, blue intaglio eyes with molded lids, feathered brows, open-closed mouth with six painted teeth, original mohair wig, spring-jointed wooden body, dressed in original clothing, marked "Schoenhut Doll//Pat. Jan. 17, '11, U.S.A.//& Foreign Countries" incised on back, "Made in U.S.A.//Strong, Durable and Unbreakable//Schoenhut//All Wood//Perfection//Art Doll," on original button, $3,300.00. Courtesy McMasters Harris Doll Auctions.

Right: 22" girl, marked "Schoenhut Doll//Pat. Jan. 17th 1911//U.S.A." on oval label on back, wooden socket head, blue intaglio eyes, feathered brows, accented nostrils, closed mouth, original mohair wig, spring-jointed wooden body, dressed in original knit union suit, replaced brown cotton socks, brown leather tie shoes, $1,400.00. Courtesy McMasters Harris Doll Auctions.

Model 109W, 1921 – 1923

Baby, nature (bent) limb, sleep eye, open mouth

13"	$350.00	$500.00

Toddler, sleep eye

14"	$575.00	$800.00

Too few in database for reliable range.

Model 110W, 1921 – 1923

Baby, nature (bent) limb, sleep eye, open mouth

15"	$475.00	$625.00

Toddler

17"	$675.00	$900.00

Too few in database for reliable range.

Bye-Lo Baby, *"Grace S. Putnam"* stamp, cloth body, closed mouth, sleep eyes

13"	$2,400.00*

CHILD

Graziano Period, 1911 – 1912, dolls may have heavily carved hair or wigs, painted intaglio eyes, outlined iris. All with wooden spring-jointed bodies and are 16" tall, designated with 16 before the model number, like "16/100."

Model 100, girl, carved hair, solemn face

Model 101, girl, carved hair, grinning, squinting eyes

Model 102, girl, carved hair, bun on top

Model 103, girl, carved hair, loose ringlets

Model 200, boy, carved hair, short curls

Model 201, boy, carved hair, based on K*R 114

Model 202, boy, carved hair, forelock

Model 203, boy, carved hair, grinning, some with comb marks

Carved hair dolls of this early period; add more if excellent condition, original clothes

16"	$2,200.00	$3,000.00+

Too few in database for reliable range.

* at auction

16" model #102, unmarked, wooden socket head, blue intaglio eyes, closed mouth, carved hair in braids, wooden spring-jointed body, re-dressed in copy of original sailor dress, knit union suit, cotton socks, cloth shoes, $850.00. Courtesy McMasters Harris Doll Auctions.

16" model #312, wooden socket head, closed mouth, brown intaglio eyes with molded lids, feathered brows, original mohair wig, spring-jointed wooden body, re-dressed in sailor dress, slip, knit union suit, cotton stockings, and black shoes, marked "Schoenhut Doll//Pat. Jan. 17, '11 U.S.A.//& Foreign Countries," on back, $850.00. Courtesy McMasters Harris Doll Auctions.

Model 300, girl, long curl wig, face of 102

Model 301, girl, bobbed wig with bangs, face of 300

Model 302, girl, wig, bases on K*R 101

Model 303, girl, short bob, no bangs, grinning, squinting eyes

Model 304, girl, wig in braids, ears stick out

Model 305, girl, snail braids, grinning, face of 303

Model 306, girl, wig, long curls, face of 304

Model 307, girl, short bob, no bangs, "dolly-type" smooth eye

Model 400, boy, short bob, K*R 101 face

Model 401, boy, side part bob, face of 300/301

Model 402, boy, side part bob, grin of 303

Model 403, boy, dimple in chin

Wigged dolls, with intaglio eyes, outlined iris of this period, more if original costume and paint

16" $750.00 $1,500.00

Transition Period, 1911 – 1912, designs by Graziano and Leslie, dolls may no longer have outlined iris, some models have changed, still measure 16", now have a groove above knee for stockings

Model 100, girl, same, no iris outline

Model 101, girl, short carved hair, bob/bow, round eyes/smile

Model 102, girl, braids carved around head

Model 103, girl, heavy carved hair in front/fine braids in back

Model 104, girl, fine carved hair in front/fine braids in back

Model 200, boy, carved hair, same, no iris outline

Model 201, boy, carved hair, same, iris outline, stocking groove

Model 202, boy, carved hair, same, smoother

Model 203, boy, smiling boy, round eyes, no iris outline

Model 204, boy, carved hair brushed forward, serious face

Carved hair is smoother, may no longer have outlined iris, some with stocking groove; more for excellent condition and original costume

16"   1,800.00 $2,400.00

Model 300, girl, long curl wig, dimple in chin

Model 301, girl, bob wig, face of 102

Model 302, girl, wig, same like K*R 101

Right: 16" Miss Dolly, #16/317, wooden socket head, blue sleep eyes, feathered brows, painted upper and lower lashes, open-closed mouth with painted teeth, original mohair wig, spring-jointed wooden body, dressed in original knit union suit, original socks, and original leatherette Schoenhut shoes, marked "Schoenhut Doll//Pat. Jan. 17, 1911//U.S.A." on label on back, $1,700.00. Courtesy McMasters Harris Doll Auctions.

Left: 8¾" Lady Rider, unmarked, bisque socket head, painted blue eyes, single stroke brows, accented nostrils, molded and painted blond hair, wooden body jointed at shoulders and hips, large oversize wooden feet, original green felt body suit with gold decoration, pink skirt with gold decoration, underwear, $275.00. Courtesy McMasters Harris Doll Auctions.

Model 303, girl, wig, similar to 303G, smiling, short bob, no bangs

Model 304, girl, wig, braids, based on K*R

Model 305, girl, wig, braids, face of 303

Model 306, girl, long curl wig, same face as 304

Model 307, girl, smooth eyeball

Model 400, boy, same (like K*R 101)

Model 401, boy, like K*R 114 (304)

Model 402, boy, smiling, round eyes

Model 403, boy, same as 300 with side part bob

Model 404, boy, same as 301, side part bob

Wigged boy or girl, similar to earlier models with some refinements; more for excellent condition, original costume.

	16"	$1,000.00	$1,500.00

Classic Period, 1912 – 1923

Some models discontinued, some sizes added, those marked with * were reissued in 1930

Model 101, girl, short carved hair bob, no iris outline

1912 – 1923*

	14"	$1,600.00	$2,200.00

1911 – 1916

	16"	$1,800.00	$2,400.00

Model 102, girl, heavy carved hair in front, fine braids in back

1912 – 1923*

	14"	$1,300.00	$1,900.00

1911 – 1923*

	16"	$1,400.00	$2,000.00

1912 – 1916

	19 – 21"	$1,500.00	$2,100.00

Model 105, girl, short carved hair bob, carved ribbon around head

1912 – 1923*

	14 – 16"	$1,100.00	$1,900.00

1912 – 1916
  19 – 21" $1,300.00 $2,100.00

Model 106, girl, carved molded bonnet on short hair, 1912 – 1916
  14" $1,500.00 $2,200.00
  16" $1,950.00 $2,600.00
  19" $2,100.00 $2,800.00

Model 203, 16" boy, same as transition
Model 204, 16" boy, same as transition*
Model 205, carved hair boy, covered ears
1912 – 1923
  14" – 16" $1,800.00 $2,400.00
1912 – 1916
  19 – 21" $2,000.00 $2,600.00

Model 206, carved hair boy, covered ears, 1912 – 1916
  19" $2,000.00 $2,600.00

Model 207, carved short curly hair boy, 1912 – 1916
  14" $1,800.00 $2,400.00

Model 300, 16" wigged girl, same as transition period, 1911 – 1923
Model 301, 16" wigged girl, same as transition, 1911 – 1924
Model 303, 16" wigged girl, same as transition 305, 1911 – 1916
Model 307, long curl wigged girl, smooth eye, 1911 – 1916
  16" $625.00 $850.00

Model 308, girl, braided wig, 1912 – 1916
  14" $575.00 $800.00
Bobbed hair, 1912 – 1924
  19" $650.00 $900.00
Bob or curls, 1917 – 1924
  19 – 21" $650.00 $900.00

Model 309, wigged girl, two teeth, long curls, bobbed hair, 1912 – 1913
  16" $650.00 $825.00
1912 – 1916
  19 – 21" $675.00 $875.00

Model 310, wigged girl, same as 105 face, long curls, 1912 – 1916
  14 – 16" $625.00 $775.00
  19 – 21" $675.00 $825.00

Model 311, wigged girl, heart shape 106 face, bobbed wig, no bangs, 1912 – 1916
  14 – 16" $650.00 $825.00
1912 – 1913
  19" $675.00 $850.00

Model 312, wigged girl, bobbed, 1912 – 1924; bobbed wig or curls, 1917 – 1924
  14" $625.00 $775.00

Model 313, wigged girl, long curls, smooth eyeball, receding chin, 1912 – 1916
  14 – 16" $650.00 $800.00
  19 – 21" $675.00 $825.00

Model 314, wigged girl, long curls, wide face, smooth eyeball, 1912 – 1916
  19" $575.00 $725.00

Model 315, wigged girl, long curls, four teeth, triangular mouth, 1912 – 1916
  21" $675.00 $825.00

Model 403, 16" wigged boy, same as transition, bobbed hair, bangs, 1911 – 1924

Model 404, 16" wigged boy, same as transition, 1911 – 1916
Model 405, boy, face of 308, bobbed wig, 1912 – 1924

14"	$450.00	$650.00
19"	$850.00*	

Model 407, wigged boy, face of 310 girl, 1912 – 1916

19 – 21"	$625.00	$825.00

MISS DOLLY

Model 316, open mouth, teeth, wigged girl, curls or bobbed wig, painted or decal eyes, all four sizes, circa 1915 – 1925

15 – 21"	$500.00	$675.00

Model 317, sleep eyes, open mouth, teeth, wigged girl, long curls or bob, sleep eyes, four sizes, 1921 – 1928

15 – 21"	$525.00	$700.00

Manikin

Model 175, man with slim body, ball-jointed waist, circa 1914 – 1918

19"	$2,400.00*

VARIATIONS

Circus performers, rare figures may be much higher
Bisque head, Bareback Lady Rider or Ringmaster

9"	$650.00* all original

Clowns

8"	$150.00 – $300.00
32"	$4,500.00* store display

Lion Tamer

8½"	$300.00 – $450.00

Ringmaster

8"	$225.00 – $325.00

Animals *some rare animals may be much higher

Gorilla

8"	$2,185.00*

Kangaroo

	$1,250.00*

Quacky Doodles, Daddy and children

	$1,239.00*

Bandwagon

	$7,000.00*

Seven Bandsmen

	$14,000.00*

Cartoon Characters

Maggie and Jiggs, from cartoon strip "Bringing up Father"

7 – 9"	$525.00 each

Max and Moritz, carved figures, painted hair, carved shoes

8"	$625.00 each
14"	$8,500.00*

Pinn Family, all wood, egg-shaped head, original costumes
Mother, and four children

	$667.00*

Baby

5"	$133.00*

* at auction   159

Schoenhut, A. & Co.

Rolly-Dolly figures
9 – 12"	$350.00	$850.00

Teddy Roosevelt
8"	$800.00	$1,600.00

Schuetzmeister & Quendt

1889 – 1930+, Boilstadt, Gotha, Thüringia. A porcelain factory that made and exported bisque doll heads, all-bisque dolls, and Nankeen dolls. Used initials "S & Q," mold 301 was sometimes incised *"Jeannette."*

BABY

Character face, bisque socket head, sleep eyes, open mouth, bent-leg body

Mold 201, 204, 300, 301, ca. 1920
14"	$335.00	$450.00
19"	$450.00	$600.00

Mold 252, ca. 1920, character face, black baby
15"	$575.00

Too few in database for reliable range.

CHILD

Mold 101, 102, ca. 1900, dolly face
17"	$350.00	$400.00
22"	$375.00	$500.00

Mold 1376, ca. 1900, character face
19"	$550.00

Too few in database for reliable range.

Mark:

201

S&Q

Germany

S.F.B.J.

Société Francaise de Fabrication de Bebes & Jouets, 1899 – 1930+, Paris and Montreuil-sous-Bois. Competition with German manufacturers forced many French companies to join together including Bouchet, Fleischmann & Bloedel, Gaultier, Rabery & Delphieu, Bru, Jumeau, Pintel & Godchaux, Remignard and Wertheimer, and others. This alliance lasted until the 1950s. Fleischman owned controlling interest.

First price indicates doll in good condition, but may have flaws; second price indicates doll in excellent condition, appropriately dressed; more for exceptional dolls.

Mark:

23
S.F.B.J.
236
PARIS
4

CHILD

Bisque head, glass eyes, open mouth, pierced ears, wig, composition jointed French body

Bluette, circa 1905 – 1960

This premium doll was first made in bisque and later in composition for a weekly children's periodical, *La Semanine De Suzette* (The Week of Suzette), that also produced patterns for Bleuette. **Premiere Bleuette** was a bisque socket head, Tete Jumeau, *marked only with a "1" superimposed on a "2,"* and 10⅝" tall. She had set blue or brown glass eyes, open mouth with four teeth, wig, and pierced ears. The composition jointed body was marked "2" on back and "1" on the sole of each foot. This mold was made only in 1905. **S.F.B.J.,** a bisque socket head, began production in 1905, using a Fleischmann and

Bloedel mold marked *"6/0,"* blue or brown glass eyes, wig, open mouth, and teeth. S.F.B.J. mold *marked "SFBJ 60" or "SFBJ 301 1"* bisque socket head, open mouth with teeth, wig, and blue or brown glass eyes. All Bleuettes were 10⅝" tall prior to 1933, after, all Bleuettes were 11⅜".

Bleuette, mold 60, 301, and 71
Unis/France 149//301

10⅝"	$650.00	$1,000.00+
11⅜"	$725.00	$975.00

Mold 301

6"	$225.00	$300.00
10⅝"	$1,835.00* Bleuette	
24"	$850.00	$1,150.00

Mold 301, Kiss Thrower

24"	$1,650.00*	

Lady body

22"	$1,250.00	$1,700.00

Jumeau type, no mold number, open mouth

13"	$675.00	$900.00
20"	$1,250.00	$1,650.00
24"	$1,500.00	$2,050.00
28"	$1,875.00	$2,700.00

CHARACTER FACES

Bisque socket head, wigged or molded hair, set or sleep eyes, composition body, some with bent baby limb, toddler or child body. Mold number 227, 235, and 236 may have flocked hair. Add $100.00 for toddler body.

Mold 226, glass eyes, closed mouth

20"	$1,800.00	$2,400.00

Mold 227, open mouth, teeth, glass eyes

14"	$1,125.00	$1,500.00
17"	$1,425.00	$1,900.00
21"	$1,750.00	$2,350.00

Mold 230, glass eyes, open mouth, teeth

12"	$850.00	$1,100.00
22"	$1,500.00	$2,000.00

Mold 233, ca. 1912, crying mouth, glass eyes

14"	$7,400.00*	

Mold 234

18"	$2,400.00	$3,250.00

Too few in database for reliable range.

Mold 235, glass eyes, open/closed mouth

18"	$1,350.00	$1,800.00
21"	$2,300.00*	

Mold 236, glass eyes, toddler

13"	$875.00	$1,150.00
15"	$1,000.00	$1,350.00

15" mold #236 baby, bisque socket head, blue sleep eyes, feathered brows, painted upper and lower lashes, open-closed mouth with two upper teeth, original blond human hair wig, five-piece composition baby body, marked "S.F. B. J.//236//Paris//-6-" on back of head, "S.F.B.J.//Fabrication Francaise//Paris" on back label, flannel baby dress, matching booties, lace bonnet and buttoned diaper, $675.00. Courtesy McMasters Harris Doll Auctions.

28½" mold #301, bisque socket head, blue sleep eyes, molded and feathered brows, painted lower lashes, open mouth with six upper teeth, pierced ears, replaced wig, jointed wood and composition French body, re-dressed in green taffeta French-style dress, bonnet, matching underclothing, silk stockings, antique shoes, marked "1926//France//S.F.B.J.//301//Par is//13; on back of head, "13" on neck, $800.00. Courtesy McMasters Harris Doll Auctions.

19" mold #226 character boy, solid dome bisque socket head, blue eyes, painted lashes, accented nostrils, open-closed mouth, molded hair, jointed wood and composition French body, marked "S.F.B.J. //226//Paris//6" on back of head, re-dressed in light blue velvet lace-trimmed outfit, matching hat, socks, shoes, $1,500.00. Courtesy McMasters Harris Doll Auctions.

Mold 237, glass eyes, open/closed mouth

16"	$1,300.00	$1,700.00

Mold 238, small open mouth

18"	$1,800.00	$2,400.00

Mold 239, ca. 1913, designed by Poulbot

14"	$4,000.00	$6,000.00

Mold 242, ca. 1910, nursing baby

15"	$3,000.00

Too few in database for reliable range.

Mold 247, glass eyes, open/closed mouth

13"	$1,050.00	$1,400.00
16"	$1,300.00	$1,800.00

Mold 248, ca. 1912, glass eyes, lowered eyebrows, very pouty closed mouth

12"	$7,500.00*

Mold 250, open mouth with teeth

12"	$3,300.00* trousseau box

Mold 251, open/closed mouth, teeth, tongue

15"	$1,125.00	$1,500.00

Mold 252, closed pouty mouth, glass eyes

15"	$3,000.00	$4,000.00
26"	$10,750.00*	

Simon & Halbig

21½" mold #540, bisque socket head, brown sleep eyes, painted lashes, open mouth with four upper teeth, antique red mohair wig, jointed wood and composition body, marked "540//Germany//Simon & Halbig//S & H" on back of head, "Heinrich Handwerck//Germany" stamped on back, two-piece velvet outfit, bonnet, underclothing, leather boots, $575.00. Courtesy McMasters Harris Doll Auctions.

1869 – 1930+, Hildburghausen and Grafenhain, Germany. Porcelain factory, made heads for Jumeau (200 series); bathing dolls (300 series); porcelain figures (400 series); perhaps doll house or small dolls (500 – 600 series); bisque head dolls (700 series); bathing and small dolls (800 series); more bisque head dolls (900 – 1000 series). The earliest models of a series had the last digit of their model number ending with an 8; socket heads ended with 9; shoulder heads ended with 0; and models using a shoulder plate for swivel heads ended in 1.

First price indicates doll in good condition, with flaws; second price indicates doll in excellent condition, appropriately dressed. Original or exceptional dolls may be more.

BABY, CHARACTER FACE, 1910+

Molded hair or wig, painted or glass eyes, open or

> **Marks:**
> 1079
> HALBIG
> S&H
> Germany
>
> SₓH. 1249
> DEP
> Germany
> SANTA
>
> Germany
> SH 13-1010 DEP.

closed mouth, bent-leg baby body. Add more for flirty eyes or toddler body.

Mold 1294, ca. 1912, glass eyes, open mouth

16"	$550.00	$750.00
19"	$800.00	$1,100.00

Mold 1294, clockwork mechanism moves eyes

26"	$1,575.00*

Mold 1428, ca. 1914, glass eyes, open/closed mouth

13"	$1,200.00	$1,600.00

Toddler

16"	$1,725.00	$2,300.00

Mold 1488, ca. 1920, glass eyes, open/closed or open mouth

20"	$3,375.00	$4,500.00+

Mold 1489, "Baby Erika," ca. 1925, glass eyes, open mouth, tongue

20"	$4,200.00*

Mold 1498, ca. 1920, solid dome, painted or sleep eyes, open/closed mouth

24"	$3,700.00*

23" bisque mold #570, marked "570//Germany//Halbig//S&H," sleep eyes, open mouth, four teeth, original blond mohair wig, jointed wood and composition body, antique maroon two-piece outfit, hat, circa 1890+, $500.00. Courtesy McMasters Harris Doll Auctions.

CHILD

Shoulder head, 1870s

Molded hair, marked "S&H," no mold number

19"	$1,275.00	$1,700.00

Mold 530, 540, 550, 570, ca. 1910, **927,** ca. 1913, **Baby Blanche**

19"	$500.00	$685.00
22"	$600.00	$800.00

Oily bisque

22"	$1,100.00*

Mold 719, ca. 1886, sleep eyes, closed mouth, pierced ears, composition/wood jointed body

18"	$2,800.00	$3,700.00

Open mouth

18"	$1,400.00	$1,850.00

Edison phonograph mechanism in torso

23"	$4,800.00*

Mold 739, ca. 1888, open or closed mouth, glass eyes, pierced ears, composition/wood jointed body, add more for closed mouth

15"	$1,575.00	$2,100.00

Mold 758, 759, 769, ca. 1888, **979,** ca. 1887

20"	$1,575.00	$2,100.00
36"	$3,300.00*	

Mold 905, ca. 1888, closed mouth; **908,** ca. 1888, open or closed mouth

Closed mouth

17"	$1,800.00*

8" bisque ethnic girl, marked "SH 2/0" on back of shoulder head, dark brown set pupiless eyes, single stroke brows, painted lashes, closed mouth, original mohair wig, cloth body, bisque lower arms, original ethnic-type clothing, paper shoes, circa 1880+, $250.00. Courtesy McMasters Harris Doll Auctions.

* at auction

Left: 10½" bisque mold #1078 ethnic doll, marked "1078//Simon & Halbig//S & H//2" on head, original mohair wig, blue sleep eyes, feathered brows, painted lashes, open mouth, four upper teeth, jointed wood and composition body, original ethnic type outfit, underclothing, replaced socks and shoes, circa 1892+, $315.00. Courtesy McMasters Harris Doll Auctions.

Right: 24", mold #1079 lady, bisque socket head, brown sleep eyes, molded and feathered brows, painted upper and lower lashes, open mouth with four upper teeth, pierced ears, original mohair wig, wood and composition lady body, marked "S&H1079//DEP//Germany//8 1/2" on back of head, "Heinrich Handwerck//Germany//3" stamepd on back of hip, original clothing, $700.00. Courtesy McMasters Harris Doll Auctions.

Open mouth

18"	$1,350.00	$1,800.00
22"	$1,025.00	$2,200.00

Mold 1009, ca. 1889, sleep eyes, open mouth, teeth, pierced ears, wig, add more for closed mouth

Kid body

19"	$350.00	$525.00

Jointed body

15"	$575.00	$750.00
25"	$1,125.00	$1,500.00

Mold 1010, 1040, 1170, 1080 (shoulder heads), 1029 (socket head)

18"	$425.00	$575.00
25"	$600.00	$800.00
28"	$675.00	$900.00

Mold 1039, 1049, 1059, 1069, 1078, 1079, 1099 (Oriental), bisque socket or swivel head with bisque shoulder plate, pierced ears, open mouth, glass eyes, composition/wood or papier mâché body; less for shoulder plate with kid or cloth body, more for walkers or original outfit

9"	$375.00	$500.00
17"	$550.00	$725.00
23"	$750.00	$1,000.00
34"	$1,400.00	$1,800.00
44"	$4,200.00*	

Pull-string eyes

18"	$1,000.00+

Mold 1079, Asian child, yellow tint bisque

8"	$1,900.00*

Mold 1079, Ondine, swimming doll

16"	$1,600.00*

Mold 1109, ca. 1893, open mouth, glass eyes, dolly face

13"	$500.00	$750.00
18"	$800.00	$1,050.00

Mold 1159, circa 1894, glass eyes, open mouth, Gibson Girl

20"	$2,200.00	$2,950.00

Mold 1248, 1249 "Santa," ca. 1898, open mouth, glass eyes

6"	$500.00	$650.00
10½"	$525.00	$700.00
18"	$900.00	$1,200.00
24"	$1,200.00	$1,600.00

Mold 1250, 1260, open mouth, glass eyes, shoulder head, kid body

16"	$500.00	$625.00
19"	$600.00	$800.00
23"	$800.00	$1,075.00

Mold 1269, 1279, sleep eyes, open mouth

14"	$1,100.00	$1,500.00
16"	$3,500.00* MIB	
25"	$2,550.00	

CHARACTER FACE, 1910+

Mold 150, ca. 1912, intaglio eyes, closed mouth

21"	$15,500.00*

Too few in database for reliable range.

Mold 151, ca. 1912, painted eyes, closed laughing mouth

15"	$3,750.00	$5,000.00

Too few in database for reliable range.

Mold 153, ca. 1912, molded hair, painted eyes, closed mouth

17"	$27,000.00

Too few in database for reliable range.

Mold 600, ca. 1912, sleep eyes, open mouth

17"	$900.00*

Too few in database for reliable range.

Mold 720, ca. 1887, dome shoulder head, glass eyes, closed mouth, wig, bisque lower arms, kid body

17"	$1,000.00*

Mold 729, ca. 1888, laughing face, glass eyes, open/closed mouth

16"	$1,900.00	$2,550.00

Mold 740, ca. 1888, dome shoulder head, glass eyes, closed mouth, cloth or kid body

11"	$1,700.00*	
18"	$1,200.00	$1,600.00

Mold 749, ca. 1888, socket head, glass eyes, pierced ears

Closed mouth

21"	$2,325.00	$3,100.00

Open mouth

13"	$825.00	$1,100.00

42" mold #1079, very large bisque socket head, brown sleep eyes, molded and feathered brows, painted lashes, open mouth with four upper teeth, original human hair wig, jointed wood and composition body, child's dress, underclothing, ecru coat, crocheted hat, no socks or shoes, marked "10079//S & H//DEP//18" on back of head, "Made in Germany," stamped on back, $3,900.00. Courtesy McMasters Harris Doll Auctions.

31" mold #1249, bisque socket head, brown sleep eyes, molded and feathered brows, painted lashes, open mouth, replaced synthetic wig, jointed wood and composition body, marked "1249//Germany//Halbig//S& H//14" on back of head, antique drop waist dress with lace overlay, antique underclothing, socks, and embroidered cloth shoes, $600.00. Courtesy McMasters Harris Doll Auctions.

27" mold #1249, Santa, bisque socket head, blue sleep eyes, feathered brows, painted lashes, open mouth, original human hair wig, jointed wood and composition body, original eyelet pantalettes, two half slips, ecru silk dress, navy blue velvet matching coat and hat, cotton socks, leatherette shoes, marked "S&H 1249//DEP//Germany//Santa//13" on back of head, "72" stamped on both feet, excellent condition, $1,300.00. Mold #1249, Santa, without navy coat and hat, good condition, $450.00. Courtesy McMasters Harris Doll Auctions.

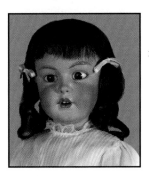

30" mold #1279, bisque socket head, blue sleep eyes, molded and feathered brows, painted lashes, open mouth, two upper teeth, antique human hair wig, jointed wood and composition body, low-waisted dress, underclothing, pink socks, lace-up boots, marked "S&H 1279//DEP/ /Germany//15" on back of head, $2,800.00. Courtesy McMasters Harris Doll Auctions.

Mold 759, ca. 1888, open mouth
17"	$900.00*	

Mold 919, ca. 1888, glass eyes, closed mouth
15"	$5,700.00	$7,600.00
19"	$6,400.00	$8,550.00

Too few in database for reliable range.

Mold 929, ca. 1888, glass eyes, open/closed or closed mouth
14"	$1,725.00	$2,300.00
23"	$2,850.00	$3,800.00
25"	$6,600.00*	

Mold 939, ca. 1888, bisque socket head, pierced ears, glass eyes

Open mouth
11"	$700.00	$925.00
16"	$1,300.00	$1,800.00

Closed mouth
16"	$1,600.00	$2,100.00
18"	$2,400.00	$3,000.00
20"	$3,400.00*	

Mold 940, 950, ca. 1888, socket or shoulder head, open or closed mouth, glass eyes

Kid body
14"	$485.00	$650.00
18"	$1,200.00	$1,575.00

Jointed body
8"	$415.00	$550.00
15"	$985.00	$1,300.00
21"	$1,700.00	$2,300.00

Mold 949, ca. 1888, glass eyes, open or closed mouth

Closed mouth
10"	$2,000.00*	
16"	$1,750.00	$2,350.00
21"	$2,000.00	$2,700.00
31"	$3,200.00	$4,250.00

Open mouth
15"	$1,050.00	$1,350.00
19"	$1,400.00	$1,800.00
24"	$1,700.00	$2,250.00

Mold 969, ca. 1887, open smiling mouth
19"	$5,700.00	$7,600.00

Too few in database for reliable range.

Mold 1019, ca. 1890, laughing, open mouth
14"	$4,275.00	$5,700.00

Too few in database for reliable range.

Mold 1246, ca. 1898, bisque socket head, sleep eyes, open mouth
18"	$2,400.00*	

Mold 1250, ca. 1898, dolly face, shoulder head
15"	$425.00	$550.00
23"	$600.00	$800.00

Mold 1299, ca. 1912, marked *"S&H"*
13"	$1,200.00	$1,600.00

Mold 1304, ca. 1902, closed mouth
14"	$4,500.00	$6,000.00

Too few in database for reliable range.

Mold 1448, ca. 1914, bisque socket head, sleep eyes, closed mouth, pierced ears, composition/wood ball-jointed body
16"	$17,500.00*

Too few in database for reliable range.

Mold 1478, ca. 1920, closed mouth
15"	$6,750.00	$9,000.00

Too few in database for reliable range.

ADULTS

Mold 1303, ca. 1902, lady face, glass eyes, closed mouth
14"	$5,815.00*

Too few in database for reliable range.

Mold 1305, ca. 1902, old woman, glass eyes, open/closed laughing mouth
18"	$10,035.00*

Too few in database for reliable range.

Mold 1308, ca. 1902, old man, molded mustache/dirty face, may be solid dome
18"	$4,200.00	$5,600.00

Too few in database for reliable range.

Mold 1388, ca. 1910, glass eyes, closed smiling mouth, teeth, wig
20"	$24,000.00*

Mold 1469, ca. 1920, flapper, glass eyes, closed mouth
15"	$2,625.00	$3,500.00

Portrait, Mary Pickford
40"	$34,000.00*

MECHANICALS

Walker, mold #1039, bisque, glass eyes, open mouth, wig, composition walking body
13"	$1,500.00	$2,000.00+

Walker, mold #1078, glass eyes, open mouth, pierced ears, clockwork mechanism in torso
23"	$2,200.00	$2,900.00

SMALL DOLLS — UNDER 9" TALL

Mold 749, ca. 1888, glass sleep eyes, open mouth, teeth, pierced ears, wig, composition/wood jointed body
5½"	$375.00	$550.00
9"	$700.00	$950.00

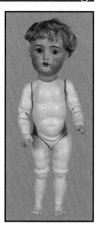

20" mold #1299 Toddler, bisque socket head, blue sleep eyes, molded and feathered brows, painted lower lashes, open mouth, original mohair wig, jointed composition toddler body, marked "1299//Simon & Halbig//S&H//11" on back of head, $1,300.00. Courtesy McMasters Harris Doll Auctions.

Mold 852, ca. 1880, all-bisque, Oriental, swivel head, yellow tint bisque, glass eyes, closed mouth, wig, painted shoes and socks

5½"	$825.00	$1,100.00

Mold 886, ca. 1880, all-bisque swivel head, glass eyes, open mouth, square cut teeth, wig, peg jointed, painted shoes and socks

7"	$1,600.00* in presentation box	
8"	$600.00	$800.00

Mold 950, ca. **1888,** shoulder head, closed mouth

8"	$375.00	$500.00

Mold 1078, ca. **1892,** glass eyes, open mouth, teeth, mohair wig, five-piece body, painted shoes and socks

8"	$400.00	$550.00

Mold 1078, pair Marquis and Marquise, original costume

8½"	$650.00 each*	

Flapper body

9"	$400.00	$600.00

Mold 1079, ca. **1892,** open mouth, glass eyes, five-piece body

8"	$400.00	$600.00

Yellow-tinted bisque, glass eyes, open mouth, teeth, five-piece papier mâché body

8"	$1,900.00*

Mold 1160, Little Women, ca. **1894,** shoulder head, glass eyes, closed mouth

7"	$265.00	$350.00

1¾" bisque German snow clown, marked "Germany," black eyes, round red nose, red open/closed mouth, arms outstretched, full suit with red painted cap with yellow painted pompon, in sitting position, circa 1901 – 1930s, $125.00 to $175.00. Courtesy Debra Ruberto.

1901 – 1930+. All-bisque dolls covered with ground porcelain slip to resemble snow, made by Bähr & Pröschild, Hertwig, C.F. Kling, Kley & Hahn, and others, Germany. Mostly unjointed, some jointed at shoulders and hips. The Eskimos named Peary's daughter Marie, born in 1893, Snow Baby, and her mother published a book in which she called her daughter Snow Baby and showed a picture of a little girl in white snowsuit. These little figures have painted features, various poses.

First price indicates figure in good condition, but with flaws or lessor quality; second price is for figure in excellent condition. More for exceptional figures.

SINGLE SNOW BABY

1½"	$40.00	$55.00
3"	$130.00	$175.00

On bear
| | $225.00 | $300.00 |

On sled
| 2" | $150.00 | $200.00 |

Pulled by dogs
| 3" | $275.00 | $375.00 |

With reindeer
| 2½" | $225.00 | $300.00 |

Jointed hips, shoulders
| 4" | $215.00 | $290.00 |
| 5" | $275.00 | $375.00 |

With Broom
| 4½" | $400.00 | $550.00 |

TWO SNOW BABIES, molded together
| 1½" | $100.00 | $125.00 |
| 3" | $185.00 | $250.00 |

On sled
| 2½" | $200.00 | $275.00 |

Mold 3200, Armand Marseille, candy container, two Snow Babies on sled
| 11" | $3,100.00* | |

THREE SNOW BABIES, molded together
| 3" | $190.00 | $350.00 |

On sled
| 2½" | $190.00 | $350.00 |

SIX SNOW BABIES, band with instruments
| 2" | $275.00* | |

NEW SNOW BABIES

Today's commercial reproductions are by Dept. 56 and are larger and the coloring is more like cream. Dept. 56 Snow Babies and their Village Collections are collectible on the secondary market. Individual craftsmen are also making and painting reproductions that look more like the old ones. As with all newer collectibles, items must be mint to command higher prices.

First price for Dept 56 Snow Babies is issue price; second price will be upper market price. Secondary market prices are extremely volatile; some markets may not bring upper prices. Usually offered in limited production, prices may rise when production is closed.

Dept 56	Issue Price	Current Price
1986		
Snowbaby Winged clip ornament	$61.00	
Climbing on Snowball, w/candle	$14.00	$118.00
Snowbaby on Brass Ribbon		$153.00*
1987		
Snowbaby Adrift		$125.00*
Winter Surprise		$27.00*
1988		
Snowbaby on Votive		$65.00*
Pony Express	$22.00	$90.00
1989		
All Fall Down, set 4	$36.00	$85.00

* at auction

Snow Babies

Finding Falling Star	$32.50	$200.00
Penquin Parade	$25.00	$70.00
1990		
A Special Delivery	$15.00	$50.00
Twinkle Twinkle Little Star, set 2	$37.50	$65.00
Who Are You?	$32.50	$140.00

Reproduction crafted Snow Babies, set of ten in various poses
1 – 1½" $25.00

Sonnenberg, Taufling

(Motschmann-type) 1851 – 1900+, Sonneberg, Germany. Various companies made an infant doll with special separated body with bellows and voice mechanism. Motschmann is erroneously credited with the body style; but he did patent the voice mechanism. Some bodies *stamped "Motschmann"* refer to the voice mechanism. The Sonneberg Taufling is a wax over papier-mâché head with wood body with twill cloth covered bellows, "floating" twill covered upper joints with lower joints of wood or china.

They have glass eyes, closed mouth, painted hair, or wigged. Other variations include papier mâché or wax over composition. The body may be stamped.

Bisque: See also Steiner, Jules.

China

China solid dome, shoulder plate, lower torso, arms, feet, padded twill body separates china portion, bellows crier
9½" $2,750.00*
Too few in database for reliable range.

Papier-mâché

Brown swivel head, flock-painted hair, black glass eyes, closed mouth, papier mâché shoulder plate, muslin body, working squeak crier, original outfit
5½" $2,600.00*
Too few in database for reliable range.

Wax Over Papier-mâché

Solid dome wax over papier-mâché, closed mouth, papier-mâché torso, wood arms and legs, original outfit
12" $750.00 $1,000.00

Wood

Carved wooden socket head, closed mouth, twill and wood torso, nude
17" $1,000.00*

Steiff, Margarete

Mark:

Button in ear

1877 – 1930+, Giengen, Wurtembur, Germany. Known today for their plush stuffed animals, Steiff made clothes for children, dolls with mask heads in 1889, clown dolls by 1898. Most Steiff dolls of felt, velvet, or plush have seam down the center of the face, but not all. Registered trademark button in ear in 1905. Button type eyes, painted features, sewn-on ears, big feet/shoes enable them to stand alone, all in excellent condition.

28" unmarked Steiff-type man and woman, felt faces with center seams, brown glass paperweight eyes, closed applied felt mouths, black felt hair, felt bodies with clothing as part of the body, jointed at shoulders and hips, individually stitched fingers, stitched toes, dressed in Spanish-type clothing with large brimmed felt hats, circa 1920 – 1940, $225.00. Courtesy McMasters Harris Doll Auctions.

Prices are for older dolls, newer dolls are much less. First price is for doll in good condition, but with some flaws (for soiled, ragged, or worn dolls, use 25% or less of this price); second price is for doll in excellent condition.

ADULTS

14½"	$1,400.00	$2,000.00
18"	$1,875.00	$2,500.00

CHARACTERS

Man with pipe, some moth holes, some soil
17"	$1,300.00*

Alphonse & Garton (Mutt & Jeff), circa 1915
13 – 18"	$4,700.00* pair

Happy Hooligan, moth holes
15"	$2,500.00*

CHILDREN

14"	$1,000.00	$1,300.00

MILITARY

Men in uniform and conductors, firemen, etc.
10½"	$1,275.00	$1,700.00
18"	$3,200.00	$4,275.00

MADE IN U.S. ZONE GERMANY, 1947 – 1953, glass eyes
12"	$575.00	$750.00

Steiner, Hermann

1909 – 1930+, near Coburg, Germany. Porcelain and doll factory. First made plush animals, then made bisque, composition, and celluloid head dolls. Patented the Steiner eye with moving pupils.

BABY

No mold number, entertwined HS mark
12"	$1,050.00* pair of toddlers

Mold 240, circa 1925, newborn, solid dome, closed mouth, sleep eyes
16"	$450.00	$600.00

Mold 246, circa 1926, character, solid dome, glass eyes, open/closed mouth, laughing baby, teeth, cloth or composition body
15"	$475.00	$625.00

Too few in database for reliable range.

Mary Ann & Her Baby Walker
6¾"	$200.00*

Mark:
Made in
Germany
HermSteiner
18
0

CHILD

Mold 128, character bisque socket head, sleep eyes, open mouth, teeth, wig, composition/wood jointed body

9" $700.00*

Too few in database for reliable range.

Mold 401, shoulder head, solid dome, painted eyes, open/closed laughing mouth, teeth, molded tongue

15" $350.00 $475.00

Steiner, Jules

16" Figure A, bisque socket head, blue paperweight eyes, feathered brows, painted upper and lower lashes, closed mouth, replaced human hair wig, composition body, marked "J S t e i n e r / / B t e S.G.D.G.//Paris//Fire A 9" on back of head, "Magasin des Enfants//Jouets//et//Jeux//Passage de l'Opera • Paris" on label on back, "Le Petit Parisien//Bébé J. Steiner//Marque//Deposee//Medaille d'Or Paris" on paper label, $3,100.00. Courtesy McMasters Harris Doll Auctions.

1855 – 1891+, Paris. Made dolls with pressed heads, wigs, glass eyes, pierced ears on jointed composition bodies. Advertised talking, mechanical jointed dolls and bébés. Some sleep eyes were operated by a wire behind the ear, *marked "J. Steiner."* May also carry the Bourgoin mark.

First price is for doll in good condition, but with flaws; second price is for doll in excellent condition, appropriately dressed. Add more for original clothes, rare mold numbers.

Bébé with Taufling (Motschmann) type body

Solid dome bisque head, shoulders, hips, lower arms and legs, with twill body in-between, closed mouth, glass eyes, wig

14" $3,600.00 $4,800.00
19" $3,000.00*

Gigoteur, "Kicker"

Crying bébé, key-wound mechanism, solid dome head, glass eyes, open mouth, two rows tiny teeth, pierced ears, mohair wig, papier-mâché torso

18" $1,650.00 $2,200.00

Early unmarked Bébé

Round face, ca. 1870s, pale pressed bisque socket head, rounded face, pierced ears, bulgy paperweight eyes, open mouth, two rows teeth, pierced ears, wig, composition/wood jointed body

18" $4,500.00 $6,000.00

Closed mouth, round face, dimples in chin

18" $8,250.00 $11,000.00

Bébé with series marks, ca. 1880s

Bourgoin red ink, Caduceus stamp on body, pressed bisque socket head, cardboard pate, wig, pierced ears, closed mouth, glass paperweight eyes, French composition/wood jointed body with straight wrists. Series C and A more common. Marked with series mark: Sie and letter and number; rare Series E and G models may be valued much higher.

Mark:

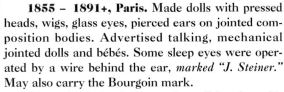

BÉBÉ "LE PARISIEN"
Médaille d'Or
PARIS

18½" Le Parisien, bisque socket head, blue paperweight eyes, heavy feathered brows, painted upper and lower lashes, closed mouth, replaced human hair wig, jointed composition body, redressed in ecru French style dress with matching bonnet, antique underclothing, mesh stockings, leather lace boots, marked "11//Paris" incised, "Le Parisien" stamped on back of head, "Bébé Le Parisien," stamped on hip, $3,250.00. Courtesy McMasters Harris Doll Auctions.

Series A, C, E, G

8"	$4,200.00* presentation case	
14"	$4,500.00	$6,000.00
22"	$6,400.00	$8,500.00
27"	$7,125.00	$9,500.00

Series C

14"	$3,500.00* round face	
34 – 38"	$9,750.00	$13,000.00+

Series E

24"	$22,000.00*

Series G

19"	$17,000.00*

Bébé with figure marks, ca. 1887+

Bisque socket head, pierced ears, closed mouth, glass eyes, wig, composition/wood jointed French body. May use body marked *"Le Petit Parisien."* Marked figure: *"FIre"* and letter and number, usually "A" or "C."

Closed mouth

13"	$2,625.00	$3,500.00
16"	$3,700.00	$4,900.00
23"	$4,400.00	$5,900.00
23"	$7,750.00* Figure C with stamped body	
34"	$8,000.00	$12,000.00

Open/closed mouth, dimple in chin

16"	$2,500.00	$3,500.00
27"	$3,275.00	$4,500.00

Bébé le Parisien, ca. 1895+

Bisque socket head, cardboard pate, wig, paperweight eyes, closed or open mouth, pierced ears, wig, composition jointed body. Head marked with letter, number, and Paris; body stamped in red, *"Le Parisien."*

10"	$2,700.00	$3,600.00
21"	$3,075.00	$4,100.00
27"	$4,000.00	$5,250.00

10¼" Series A, bisque socket head, set blue threaded eyes, multi-stroke brows, painted upper and lower lashes, closed mouth, replaced human hair wig, jointed composition body with straight wrists and short stubby fingers, marked "Sie A 3/0" on back of head, "Medaille d'Or//Paris" stamped on hip, white pique dress, new underclothing, socks, and antique white shoes, bonnet, $7,500.00. Courtesy McMasters Harris Doll Auctions.

Swaine & Co.

1910 – 1927, Huttensteinach, Thüringia, Germany. Made porcelain doll heads. Marked *"S & Co.,"* with green stamp. May also be incised *"DIP"* or *"Lori."*

BABY

Baby Lori, marked *"Lori,"* solid dome, open/closed mouth molded hair, sleep eyes

18"	$1,200.00	$1,600.00
23"	$1,870.00	$2,500.00

Mold 232, Lori variation, open mouth

12"	$750.00	$1,000.00
21"	$1,300.00	$1,750.00

DI, solid dome, intaglio eyes, closed mouth

11"	$600.00	$800.00
16"	$2,100.00* toddler	

DV, solid dome, sleep eyes, closed mouth

15"	$1,125.00	$1,500.00

FP, S&C, socket head, sleep eyes, closed mouth

8"	$750.00*

Too few in database for reliable range.

CHILD

AP, socket head, intaglio eyes, closed mouth

15"	$5,200.00*

BP, socket head, open/closed smiling mouth, teeth, painted eyes

14½"	$3,400.00*

Too few in database for reliable range.

DIP, S&C, socket head, sleep eyes, closed mouth

14"	$1,400.00	$1,700.00

Thuiller, A.

1875 – 1893, Paris. Made bisque head dolls with composition, kid, or wooden bodies. Some of the heads were reported made by Francoise Gaultier. Bisque socket head or swivel on shoulder plate, glass eyes, closed mouth with white space, pierced ears, cork pate, wig, nicely dressed, in good condition. First price is for doll in good condition, but with flaws; second price is for doll in excellent condition, appropriately dressed. Exceptionally beautiful dolls may run more.

CHILD

Closed mouth

13"	$23,250.00	$31,000.00
17"	$24,000.00*	
26 – 28"	$30,000.00	$40,000.00+

**See *Doll Values, First Edition, 1994,* for photo of an A. Thuiller doll.

1916 – 1930+. Mark used by S.F.B.J. (Société Francaise de Fabrication de Bebes & Jouets) is Union Nationale Inter-Syndicale.

CHILD

Mold 60, 301, bisque head, jointed composition/wood body, wig, sleep eyes, open mouth

9"	$350.00	$475.00
11½"	$1,050.00*	trunk, wardrobe
16"	$400.00	$600.00
21"	$600.00	$800.00

Mold 247, 251, toddler body

15"	$1,050.00	$1,400.00
27"	$1,650.00	$2,200.00

22" mold #301, bisque socket head, brown sleep eyes with real lashes, painted lower lashes, accented nostrils, open mouth with four upper teeth, original human hair wig, jointed wood and composition Jumeau body, marked "Unis//France//301 149//10" on back of head, "Tete Jumeau" decal on back of head, "Bébé Jumeau//Diplome D'Honneur" on lower back label, "10" on front of neck, $600.00. Courtesy McMasters Harris Doll Auctions.

1875 – 1930+, Ilmenau, Thüringia. Made dolls, doll parts, and doll clothes and shoes; used heads by Gebrüder Heubach, Armand Marseille, and Simon & Halbig.

CHILD

Bisque head, kid body, bisque lower arms, cloth lower legs

Closed mouth

21"	$675.00	$900.00

Open mouth

14"	$265.00	$350.00

Mark:

W.u.Z
y.
Germany

Too few in database for reliable range.

Inge, character, bisque solid dome, closed mouth, kid body

14½" $1,300.00*

Composition-type swivel head, painted eyes, closed mouth, kid body

16" $525.00*

Too few in database for reliable range.

Ca. 1850 – 1930. Made by English, German, French, and other firms, reaching heights of popularity ca. 1875. Seldom marked, wax dolls were poured, some reinforced with plaster, and less expensive, but more durable with wax over papier-mâché or composition. English makers included Montanari, Pierotti, and Peck. German makers included Heinrich Stier.

First price indicates doll in good condition, but with flaws; second price is for doll in excellent condition, original clothes, or appropriately dressed. More for exceptional dolls; much less for dolls in poor condition.

18" unmarked poured wax shoulder head, set blue eyes, few fine hairs for brows and lashes, original human hair inserted in wax, cloth body with poured wax lower limbs, nonworking voice box in tummy, antique clothing, print blouse, pleated skirt, underclothing, French-style chapeau, $650.00. Courtesy McMasters Harris Doll Auctions.

POURED WAX

Baby, shoulder head, painted features, glass eyes, English Montanari type, closed mouth, cloth body, wig, or hair inserted into wax

17"	$1,125.00	$1,500.00
25"	$1,700.00	$2,250.00

Infant nurser, slightly turned shoulder head, set glass eyes, open mouth, inserted hair wig, cloth body, wax limbs, nicely dressed

26"	$1,320.00*

Child, shoulder head, inserted hair, glass eyes, wax limbs, cloth body

13"	$825.00	$1,100.00
27"	$1,100.00	$1,400.00
24"	$2,600.00* by Lucy Peck	

Lady

8"	$575.00	$770.00
15"	$825.00	$1,100.00

Bride, rose wax shoulder head, blue glass eyes, closed mouth, wig, kid jointed fashion body

15"	$1,650.00*

WAX OVER COMPOSITION OR REINFORCED

Child, ca. 1860 – 1890, early poured wax reinforced with plastic, inserted hair, glass eyes, cloth body

14"	$750.00	$1,000.00

Child, wax over socket head, glass eyes

16"	$1,500.00*

Child, later wax over composition shoulder head, open or closed mouth, glass eyes, cloth body

11"	$165.00	$225.00
17"	$250.00	$350.00
23"	$425.00	$575.00

Molded hair, wax over composition, shoulder head, glass eyes, cloth body, wooden limbs, molded shoes

15"	$225.00	$300.00
23"	$350.00	$475.00

16" Soldier, poured wax or reinforced wax shoulder head, set brown glass eyes, closed mouth, hair insered into wax, cloth body with wax lower arms, wax lower legs missing, original military uniform, unmarked, $375.00. Courtesy McMasters Harris Doll Auctions.

Alice in Wonderland style, with molded headband

16"	$400.00	$525.00
19"	$475.00	$625.00

Slit-head wax, English, ca. 1830 – 1860s, wax over composition shoulder head, glass eyes may use wire closure

14"	$750.00	$1,000.00
18"	$900.00	$1,300.00
25"	$1,700.00	$2,300.00

Too few in database for reliable range.

17½" reinforced poured wax shoulder head, blue sleep eyes, feathered brows, painted upper and lower lashes, cloth body, stitch joints at hips and knees, ecru dress with ribbon, tucks, and silk ruffle trim, antique underclothing, black socks, no shoes, $350.00. Courtesy McMasters Harris Doll Auctions.

Mechanical Baby, dome over papier-mâché, painted hair, glass eyes, open mouth, papier-mâché torso with bellows mechanism

    18" $2,000.00*

Two-faced doll, ca. 1880 – 1890s, one laughing, one crying, body stamped *"Bartenstein"*

    15" $675.00 $900.00

BONNETHEAD

Child, 1860 – 1880, with molded cap

    16" $250.00 $325.00

Lady with poke bonnet

    25" $3,000.00*

Too few in database for reliable range.

Man, turned shoulder head, molded top hat, set eyes, cloth body, wooden arms

    17" $1,000.00*

Too few in database for reliable range.

Wislizenus, Adolf

1850 – 1930+, Walterhausen, Thüringia, Germany. Doll and toy factory that specialized in ball-jointed bodies and used Bähr & Pröschild, Simon & Halbig, and Ernst Heubach bisque heads for dolls they made.

CHILD

AW, bisque socket head, sleep eyes, open mouth, jointed body, original regional costume

    23" $950.00*

AW Special, 101 My Sweetheart, open mouth, sleep eyes

    22 – 23" $375.00 $500.00

Mold #110, socket head, glass eyes, open/closed mouth with teeth

    16" $2,400.00*

Mold #115, solid dome, open/closed mouth, painted eyes

    12" $1,200.00* toddler

Mark:

A W
W
DR 6 M
421481

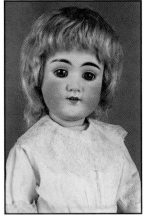

22½" bisque My Sweetheart, marked "01//11//My Sweetheart//B.J. & Co." on back of head, "58" stamped in red on bottom of feet, antique mohair wig, blue sleep eyes, painted lashes, feathered brows, open mouth, four upper teeth, jointed wood and composition body, antique silk doll dress with lace collar and cuffs, underclothing, new socks, antique shoes, circa 1910, $210.00. Courtesy McMasters Harris Doll Auctions.

* at auction

Wolf, Louis & Co.

Mark:	
152 L. W. & C? 12	**1870 – 1930+, Sonneberg, Germany, Boston, and New York City.** They made and distributed dolls, also distributed dolls made for them by other companies such as Hertel Schwab & Co. and Armand Marseille. They made composition as well as bisque dolls and specialized in babies and Red Cross nurses before World War I. May be marked *"L.W. & C."*

Baby, open or closed mouth, sleep eyes
12"	$360.00	$475.00

Sunshine Baby, solid dome, cloth body, glass eyes, closed mouth
15"	$1,000.00*

Wooden

1600s – 1700s+, England, Germany, Switzerland, Russia, United States, and other countries.

ENGLISH

William & Mary Period, 1690s – 1700

Carved wooden head, tiny multi-stroke eyebrow and eyelashes, colored cheeks, human hair or flax wig, wooden body, fork-like carved wooden hands, jointed wooden legs, cloth upper arms, medium to fair condition
19¾"	$36,350.00*
21¾"	$45,500.00*

Too few in database for reliable range.

Queen Anne Period, early 1700s

Dotted eyebrows, eyelashes, painted or glass eyes, no pupils, carved oval-shaped head, flat wooden back and hips, nicely dressed, good condition
14"	$7,500.00	$10,000.00
18"	$11,000.00	$14,900.00
24"	$18,000.00	$24,000.00

Too few in database for reliable range.

Georgian Period, 1750s – 1800

Round wooden head, gesso coated, inset glass eyes, dotted eyelashes and eyebrows, human hair or flax wig, jointed wooden body, pointed torso, medium to fair condition
13"	$2,300.00	$3,000.00
15¾"	$2,750.00	$3,650.00
24"	$3,100.00	$4,200.00

1800 – 1840

Gesso-coated wooden head, painted eyes, human hair or flax wig, original clothing comes down below wooden legs
12 – 13"	$900.00	$1,200.00
15"	$1,400.00	$1,875.00
20"	$2,100.00	$2,800.00

GERMAN

1810 – 1850s

Delicately carved painted hair style, spit curls, some with hair decorations, all wooden head and body, pegged or ball-jointed limbs
7"	$475.00	$650.00
12 – 13"	$1,050.00	$1,400.00
28¼"	$16,000.00* peg, disk jointed	

1850s – 1900

All wood with painted plain hair style; may have spit curls

5"	$95.00	$125.00
8"	$150.00	$200.00
14"	$300.00	$400.00

Wooden shoulder head, fancy carved hair style, wood limbs, cloth body

12"	$375.00	$500.00
16"	$1,000.00* man, carved hair	
23"	$650.00	$875.00

1900+

Turned wooden head, carved nose, painted hair, lower legs with black shoes, peg jointed

11"	$60.00	$80.00

Child, all-wood, fully jointed body, glass eyes, open mouth

15"	$335.00	$450.00
18"	$450.00	$625.00
23"	$600.00	$825.00

GRODNER TAL

1700s – 1930s, originally Austrian town, later Italian

Wooden dolls have been carved in this town for years. The Colemans report 2,000 carvers in the 1870s, plus painters making wooden dolls, jointed and unjointed, in sizes from ½" to 24".

Carved one-piece head and torso, dowel jointed limbs, dressed

5"	$165.00	$220.00
17"	$725.00	$975.00

Carved hair in bun

8½"	$1,050.00*

Character

24"	$5,250.00*

Ca. 1810

Molded bosom, painted chemise, dowel pin, eight ball-jointed body

14½"	$2,750.00*

Ca. 1820

Small (up to 5") peg-jointed dolls, period costumes

Set of 7	$4,361.00*

MATRYOSKIA — RUSSIAN NESTING DOLLS, 1900+

Set of wooden canisters that separate in the middle, brightly painted with a glossy finish to represent adults, children, storybook or fairytale characters, and animals. These come in sets usually of five or more related characters, the larger doll opening to reveal a smaller doll nesting inside, and so on.

Set pre 1930s

4"	$70.00	$100.00
7"	$115.00	$150.00
9"	$175.00	$230.00

Set new

5"	$20.00
7"	$30.00

Political set: Gorbachev, Yeltsin
5"	$35.00	
7"	$60.00	

SWISS, 1900+

Carved wooden dolls with dowel jointed bodies, joined at elbow, hips, knees, some with elaborate hair
12"	$315.00	$425.00
16"	$475.00	$635.00

ELLIS, JOEL

Cooperative Manufacturing Co., 1873 – 74, Springfield, VT. Manufactured wooden dolls patented by Joel Ellis. The head was cut into a cube, steamed until it softened, then compressed in hydraulic press to form features. Metal hands and feet painted black or blue, painted black molded hair sometimes blond. Similar type Springville wooden dolls were made by Joint Doll Co. and D. M. Smith & Co. have cut out hip joints.
12"	$700.00	$950.00
15"	$975.00	$1,300.00

FORTUNE TELLERS

Wooden half or full doll with folded papers with fortunes printed on them making up the skirt
18"	$2,600.00	$3,500.00

Too few in database for reliable range.

HITTY: See Artist Dolls.

SCHOENHUT: See that section.

Modern Dolls

14" hard plastic Effanbee Tintair, a Honey doll with white hair that could be tinted "glossy chestnut" or "carrot top" with her own safe coloring kit, color applicator, plastic dish, curlers, circa 1951, $400.00+. Courtesy McMasters Harris Doll Auctions. ▶

▲

16" hard plastic Terri Lee, brunette wig, painted brown eyes, closed mouth, in red dotted dress tagged "Swiss Heart Fund Costume #3530," marked on back of head "Terri Lee," circa 1950s, $375.00. Courtesy McMasters Harris Doll Auctions.

▲

17" composition Alexander Sonja Henie doll, blond human hair wig, brown sleep eyes with real lashes and eye shadow, open mouth, in original dress, marked on back of head "Madame Alexander//Sonja//Henie," on hang tag "Genuine Sonja//Henie//A Madame Alexander Product//All Rights Reserved," circa 1939 – 1942, $600.00. Courtesy McMasters Harris Doll Auctions.

14" vinyl head, hard plastic body ballerina by Valentine, blond rooted hair wig, sleep eyes with lashes, walker, original net tutu with gold bodice and vinyl toe shoes, doll unmarked, original box marked "Ballerina/Capezio," circa 1958, $100.00. Courtesy Carol Stover.

Aunt Jemima, cloth, stained
16"	$95.00 *	

Bell Telephone "Pioneers of America" Bell
| 15" | $30.00 | $75.00 |

Buster Brown Shoes
Composition head, cloth body, tag reads *"Buster Brown Shoes"*
| 15" | $256.00* | |

Capezio Shoes
"Aida, Toe Dancing Ballerina Dolls"
| | $40.00 | $150.00 |

Colgate Fab Soap Princess Doll, ca. 1951
| 5½" | $5.00 | $15.00 |

Gerber Baby, 1936+
An advertising and trademark doll for Gerber Products, a baby food manufacturer located in Fremont, Michigan. First price is for doll flawed, nude, or redressed, second price is for all original with package. More for black or special sets with accessories.

1936, cloth one-piece doll, printed, holds can
| 8" | $400.00 | $500.00 |

Sun Rubber Company, 1955 – 1958, designed by Bernard Lipfert, vinyl
| 12" | $50.00 | $150.00 |
| 18" | $35.00 | $100.00 |

Arrow Rubber & Plastic Co., 1965, vinyl
| 14" | $40.00 | $150.00 |

Amsco, Milton Bradley, 1972 – 1973, vinyl
| 10" | $60.00 | $100.00 |
| 14", 16", 18" | $35.00 | $50.00 |

Atlanta Novelty, 1979 – 1985, vinyl, flirty eyes, cloth body
| 17" | $25.00 | $90.00 |

Talker
| 17" | $25.00 | $100.00 |

Collector Doll, christening gown, basket
| 12" | $25.00 | $100.00 |

Porcelain, limited edition
| 17" | $75.00 | $350.00 |

Lucky Ltd. 1989 – 1992, vinyl
6"	$5.00	$15.00
11"	$10.00	$40.00
14 – 16"	$10.00	$40.00

Toy Biz, Inc. 1994 – 1996, vinyl
| 8" | $4.00 | $15.00 |
| 15" | $7.50 | $25.00 |

Battery operated
| 12 – 13" | $10.00 | $25.00 |

5½" hard plastic Colgate Princess doll, with jointed head and arms, fixed legs, brunette wig, sleep eyes, painted lashes and brows, stapled on striped taffeta gown, unmarked doll, mailed in folding box printed "Colgate Palmolive," circa 1951, $25.00. Courtesy Carol Stover.

8" hard plastic Lustre Crème Starlet Doll, blond synthetic wig, sleep eyes with molded lashes, strung, undressed in mailing carton with taffeta gown, panties, and pattern for clothing, doll unmarked, brochure in box printed "Luster Crème//"Startet Doll"/by//Inez Holland House," circa 1953, $100.00. Courtesy Carol Stover.

Talker		
14"	$10.00	$40.00
17"	$10.00	$50.00
Green Giant, Sprout, 1973		
10½"	$7.50	$25.00
Jolly Joan, Portland, Oregon, restaurant		
11"	$35.00	$125.00
Kellogg's cereals		
Corn Flakes & Pep Red Riding Hood, cloth		
13½"	$40.00	$150.00
Goldilocks & Three Bears, set of four		
12 – 15"	$80.00	$225.00
Korn Krisp cereal		
Miss Korn-Krisp, ca. 1900, cloth marked body		
24"	$60.00	$225.00
Lustre Créme, original dress, patterns		
7½"	$50.00	$100.00
Mr. Peanut, ca. 1970s		
19"	$10.00	$20.00
Pangburn Chocolates		
Hard plastic, gold foil label		
7"	$7.50	$15.00

Madame Alexander

In 1912, Beatrice and Rose Alexander, known for making doll costumes, began the Alexander Doll Co. They began using the "Madame Alexander" trademark in 1928. Beatrice Alexander Behrman became a legend in the doll world with her long reign as head of the Alexander Doll Company. Alexander made cloth, composition, and wooden dolls, and eventually made the transition to hard plastic and vinyl. Dolls are listed by subcategories of the material of which the head is made.

First price is for doll in good condition with flaws, may have soiled or worn clothing; second price is for complete beautiful doll in mint condition with original clothes, tag, labels, etc. Unusual dolls with presentation cases or rare costumes may be much more.

17" cloth Dionne Quintuplet doll with hand-painted pressed face and yarn ringlets, original pink organdy bonnet and dress tagged Madame Alexander, circa 1935 – 1939, $800.00. Courtesy Shirley's Doll House, Wheeling, IL.

7" composition Tiny Betty with fixed legs, jointed head and arms, molded and painted shoes and socks, painted features and side-glancing eyes, blond human hair wig, blue cotton dress with red and white hooded cape, marked on back "Alexander," original box, circa 1930s, $350.00. Courtesy Marge Meisinger.

CLOTH, CA. 1930 – 1950+

All-cloth head and body, mohair wig, flat or molded mask face, painted side-glancing eyes

Alice in Wonderland, ca. 1930

Flat face		$200.00	$875.00
Mask face			
	16"	$200.00	$675.00
Animals		$70.00	$275.00
Dogs		$75.00	$290.00
Baby			
	13"	$75.00	$300.00
	17"	$125.00	$475.00

Clarabell, the Clown, 1951 – 1953

	19"	$100.00	$350.00

Dionne Quintuplets, ca. 1935 – 1936

	16"	$250.00	$900.00
	24"	$450.00	$1,200.00

David Copperfield or other boys, ca. 1930s

	16"	$200.00	$800.00+

Funny, 1963 – 1977

	18"	$10.00	$70.00

Little Shaver, 1940 – 1944, yarn hair

	15"	$150.00	$600.00
	22"	$175.00	$650.00

Little Women, ca. 1930 – 1936

	16"	$125.00	$700.00+

Muffin, ca. 1965

	14"	$25.00	$95.00

So Lite Baby or Toddler, ca. 1930s – 1940s

	20"	$100.00	$375.00+

Suzie Q, 1940 – 1942

		$175.00	$650.00

Teeny Twinkle, 1946, disc floating eyes

		$150.00	$525.00

Tiny Tim, ca. 1930s

		$230.00	$725.00

COMPOSITION, CA. 1930 – 1950

Baby

Baby Genius, cloth body, sleep eyes, marked "Alexander"

	22"	$550.00* wrist tag, yellow taffeta tagged gown

Baby Jane, 1935

	16"	$325.00	$950.00+

Pinky, 1937 – 1939, composition

	23"	$100.00	$300.00

Princess Alexandria, 1937 only

	24"	$95.00	$300.00

7½" composition Dionne Quintuplets with strung bodies, molded hair, painted features and side-glancing brown eyes, closed mouths, wearing white flannel diapers and untagged white cotton dresses, marked on the heads "Dionne//Alexander" and "Alexander" on backs, circa 1930s, $850.00. Courtesy McMasters Harris Doll Auctions.

16" composition Baby Jane doll, brunette mohair wig, sleep eyes with real lashes, feathered brows, open smiling mouth with six upper teeth, in original white dress with red accents (remnants of dress tag), red bonnet, marked on head "Baby-Jane//Reg//Mme Alexander," circa 1930s, $900.00. Courtesy McMasters Harris Doll Auctions.

Child

Alice in Wonderland, 1930s, swivel waist

13"	$125.00	$425.00

Babs Skater, 1948, marked *"ALEX"* on head, clover tag

18"	$400.00	$1,250.00+

Bride and Bridesmaids, Wendy Ann, 1935 – 1943

15"	$100.00	$350.00
18"	$125.00	$450.00

Butch, 1942 – 1946, cloth body

12"	$40.00	$150.00

1950, vinyl, cloth body

14"	$45.00	$175.00

1965 – 1966, vinyl, cloth body

12"	$35.00	$125.00*

Carmen Miranda-type

7"	$350.00* near mint	
14"	$125.00	$450.00

Dionne Quintuplets, ca. 1935 – 1945, all-composition, swivel head, jointed toddler or baby body, molded and painted hair or wigged, sleep or painted eyes. Outfit colors: Annette, yellow; Cecile, green; Emilie, lavender; Marie, blue; Yvonne, pink. Add more for extra accessories or in layette.

Baby	8"	$75.00	$300.00
Set of five			
Toddler	8"	$275.00	$1,300.00
	11"	$400.00	$2,200.00
	14"	$500.00	$2,500.00
	20"	$700.00	$4,200.00

Set of five with wooden nursery furniture

8"	$1,750.00*	

Set of five in basket with extra dresses

8"	$3,800.00*	
11"	$560.00	$2,300.00

16" composition Jane Withers, brunette mohair wig, sleep eyes, open mouth with teeth, original green dress, may have had a hat, marked on head "Jane Withers/Alexander Doll," circa 1937 – 1939, $1,000.00. Courtesy Marge Meisinger.

15" composition Princess Elizabeth, human hair wig, brown glassene sleep eyes, open mouth, yellow organdy gown, silver shoes, and metal tiara set with stones, marked on head "Princess Elizabeth/ Alexander Doll Co.," circa 1937 – 1941, $750.00. Courtesy Marge Meisinger.

Dr. Dafoe, 1937 – 1939

14"	$525.00	$1,600.00+

Nurse

13"	$250.00	$900.00+

Fairy Queen, ca. 1940 – 1946, clover wrist tag, tagged gown

14"	$200.00	$700.00
18"	$225.00	$800.00

Flora McFlimsey, 1938, freckles, marked *"Princess Elizabeth"*

16"	$135.00	$550.00+
22"	$250.00	$800.00

Flower Girl, 1939 – 1947, marked *"Princess Elizabeth"*

20"	$175.00	$650.00+

Happy Birthday, set of 12, side-glancing eyes

7"	$2,700.00* all original

Jane Withers, 1937 – 1939, green sleep eyes, open mouth, brown mohair wig

15"	$425.00	$1,300.00
20"	$800.00	$1,600.00

Jeannie Walker, tagged dress, closed mouth, mohair wig

13"	$175.00	$675.00+

Judy, original box, wrist tag, Wendy-Ann face, eyeshadow

21"	$3,200.00+

Karen Ballerina, blue sleep eyes, closed mouth, *"Alexander"* on head

15"	$275.00	$900.00+
18"	$325.00	$1,200.00+

Kate Greenaway, yellow wig, marked *"Princess Elizabeth"*

13"	$200.00	$750.00
24"	$275.00	$900.00

Little Betty, 1939 – 1943, side-glancing painted eyes

9"	$85.00	$325.00
9"	$550.00*	Alice in Wonderland

Little Colonel

17"	$200.00	$750.00

Little Genius, blue sleep eyes, cloth body, closed mouth, clover tag

12"	$75.00	$200.00
16"	$100.00	$250.00

Little Women, Meg, Jo, Amy, Beth
Set of four

7"	$325.00	$1,200.00
9"	$300.00	$1,100.00

* at auction

Madelaine DuBain, 1937 – 1944

14"	$185.00	$550.00
17"	$250.00	$675.00

Marcella, ca. 1936, open mouth, wig, sleep eyes

24"	$200.00	$900.00+

Margaret O'Brien, 1946 – 1948

21"	$300.00	$1,250.00+

McGuffey Ana, 1935 – 1937, sleep eyes, open mouth, tagged dress

13"	$175.00	$675.00
15"	$200.00	$650.00
23"	$2,100.00* original	

Marionettes by Tony Sarg

12"	$125.00	$475.00

Princess Elizabeth, ca. 1937 – 1941

Closed mouth

13"	$185.00	$625.00+

Open mouth

15"	$200.00	$750.00+
28"	$275.00	$1,000.00+

Scarlett, ca. 1937 – 1946, add more for rare costume

14"	$200.00	$750.00
18"	$400.00	$1,200.00

Snow White, 1939 – 1942, marked *"Princess Elizabeth"*

14"	$150.00	$475.00
18"	$200.00	$750.00

Sonja Henie, 1939 – 1942, open mouth, sleep eyes

13"	$1,000.00* twist waist, MIB	
15"	$200.00	$750.00
21"	$350.00	$1,200.00

Tiny Betty, 1934 – 1943, side-glancing painted eyes

7"	$75.00	$275.00

W.A.A.C. (Army), W.A.A.F. (Air Force), W.A.V.E. (Navy), ca. 1943 – 1944

14"	$200.00	$750.00

Wendy-Ann, 1935 – 1948, more for special outfit

11"	$150.00	$575.00
14"	$100.00	$400.00
18"	$150.00	$600.00

HARD PLASTIC, 1948+, AND VINYL

Alexander-kins, 1953+

1953, 7½" – 8", straight leg nonwalker

Nude	$60.00	$225.00
Jumper, one-piece bodysuit	$375.00	
Garden Party long gown	$1,300.00+	

14" composition Sonja Henie, blond human hair wig, brown glassene sleep eyes, open mouth, yellow taffeta costume with gold skates (pin sold separately), marked on head "Mme Alexander/Sonja Henie," circa 1939 – 1942, $750.00. Courtesy Marge Meisinger.

11" composition Scarlett O'Hara using Wendy-Ann face mold, black human hair wig, green sleep eyes, shadow, real lashes, closed mouth, original cotton print gown and straw bonnet, pantalets, snap shoes, doll unmarked, circa 1939, $950.00. Courtesy Carol Stover.

18" composition Margaret O'Brien, brunette braided mohair wig, sleep eyes, closed mouth, original yellow bodice rayon dress with check skirt and suspenders, marked "Alexander" on head and body, circa 1946 – 1948, $1000.00. Courtesy Marge Meisinger.

8" hard plastic Wendy-kins, honey-blond wig, sleep eyes, molded lashes painted under, straight leg walker, original blue net ballet gown #554 with taffeta bodice trimmed with faux stones, marked on back "ALEX," circa 1954, $450.00. Courtesy Carol Stover.

1954 – 1955, straight leg walker

Basic	$35.00	$200.00
Cotton school dress		$425.00
Day in Country	$875.00	
Maypole Dance	$550.00	
Riding habit	$375.00+	
Sailor dress	$875.00+	

1956 – 1965, bent-knee walker, after 1963 marked *"Alex"*

Nude	$45.00	$125.00
Carcoat set	$850.00	
Flowergirl	$850.00	
Skater		$575.00
Swim suit	$85.00	$325.00

1965 – 1972, bent-knee non-walker

Nude	$40.00	$125.00
Party dress, long	$200.00	$800.00

1973 – 1975

Ballerina, straight leg	$80.00
Bride, straight leg	$100.00

1976 – 1994, straight leg non-walker, marked *"Alexander"*

Ballerina	$25.00	$85.00
Bride	$30.00	$100.00

BABIES

Baby Angel, #480, tagged tulle gown

	8"	$950.00*

Baby Brother or Sister, 1977 – 1982, vinyl

	14"	$20.00	$85.00

Baby Clown, #464, seven-piece walker, leashed dog, Huggy

	8"	$300.00	$1,200.00+

Baby Ellen, 1965 – 1972, vinyl, rigid vinyl body, marked *"Alexander 1965"*

	14"	$75.00	$125.00

Baby Precious, 1975, vinyl, cloth body

	14"	$25.00	$100.00

Bonnie Toddler, 1954 – 1955, vinyl

	19"	$35.00	$125.00

Happy, 1970 only, vinyl

	20"	$60.00	$225.00

Hello Baby, 1962 only

	22"	$40.00	$175.00

Honeybun, 1951, vinyl

	19"	$55.00	$200.00

Huggums, Big, 1963 – 1979

	25"	$25.00	$100.00

Huggums, Lively, 1963

	25"	$35.00	$150.00

Little Bitsey, 1967 – 1968, all-vinyl
    9" $35.00 $150.00
Little Genius, ca. 1956 – 1962, hard
plastic, varies with outfit, nude
    8" $25.00 $100.00
Littlest Kitten, vinyl, nude
    8" $30.00 $125.00
Mary Cassatt, 1969 – 1970, vinyl
    14" $50.00 $175.00
    20" $80.00 $250.00
Pussy Cat, ca. 1965 – 1985, vinyl
    14" $20.00 $65.00
Pussy Cat, black
    14" $35.00 $75.00
Rusty, 1967 – 1968 only, vinyl
    20" $80.00 $300.00
Sweet Tears, 1965 – 1974
    9" $20.00 $100.00
With layette, 1965 – 1973
           $50.00 $175.00
Victoria, 1967 – 1989
    20" $20.00 $100.00
Bible Character Dolls, 1954 only
Hard plastic, original box made like Bible
    8" $1,500.00 $7,000.00+

Cissette, 1957 – 1963
    10", hard plastic head, synthetic wig, pierced ears, closed mouth, seven-piece adult body, jointed elbows and knees, high-heeled feet, mold later used for other dolls. Marks: None on body, clothes tagged *"Cissette."*

Ballgown	$125.00	$500.00+
Ballerina	$100.00	$375.00
Beauty Queen	$100.00	$325.00
Bride	$100.00	$375.00
Doll only	$40.00	$125.00
Day dress	$85.00	$275.00
Formal	$150.00	$475.00
Gibson Girl	$250.00	$800.00+
Jacqueline	$160.00	$650.00+
Margot	$135.00	$475.00+
Portrette	$125.00	$450.00
Renoir	$135.00	$450.00
Scarlett	$135.00	$475.00
Sleeping Beauty (1959 only)		
	$100.00	$375.00
Tinkerbell	$125.00	$475.00+

8" all vinyl Littlest Kitten with rooted blond hair, sleep eyes, molded lashes, closed mouth, jointed with bent baby legs, original organdy gown yellowed with age, original hair bow, hang tag reads "Littlest Kitten Created by Madame Alexander," marked on head "Alex. Doll. Co.," circa 1963, $125.00. Courtesy Carol Stover.

10" hard plastic head Cissette with synthetic auburn wig, pierced ears, closed mouth, jointed arms, head, legs, and knees, high-heeled feet, basic lace lingerie outfit with high heels, original box and wrist tag reads "Cissette created by Madame Alexander," doll unmarked, circa 1959, $150.00. Courtesy Carol Stover.

17" hard plastic Wendy Bride with original wig, blue sleep eyes with real lashes, single stroke brows, closed mouth, white satin gown with rhinestones, original box with comb and curler set, gown tag "Madame Alexander//All rights reserves// New York USA, doll marked on head "Alexander," circa 1950s, $550.00. Courtesy McMasters Harris Doll Auctions.

8" hard plastic Wendy-kins Little Madeline from Ludwig Bemelmans stories, sleep eyes with molded lashes, synthetic auburn wig, strung non walker, dotted pink cotton dress and bonnet, marked "ALEX" on back, circa 1953, $775.00. Courtesy Marge Meisinger.

Cissy, 1955 – 1959

20", hard plastic, vinyl arms, jointed elbows and knees, high-heeled feet. Clothes are tagged "Cissy."

Ballgown	$225.00	$900.00+
Bride	$200.00	$650.00
Bridesmaid	$350.00	$650.00

Miss Flora McFlimsey, 1953 only (Cissy), vinyl head, inset eyes

15"	$150.00	$600.00
Formal	$400.00	$1,400.00
Southern Belle, #2244		$2,835.00*

Secret Armoire Trunk Set

	$450.00	$735.00
Princess	$275.00	$1,000.00
Queen	$400.00	$1,200.00

Scarlett, rare white organdy dress

	$500.00	$2,000.00+
Street dress	$125.00	$400.00
Pantsuits	$250.00	$375.00*

Others

Alice in Wonderland, 1949 – 1952, Margaret and/or Maggie

15"	$120.00	$450.00
23"	$200.00	$800.00

American Girl, 1962 – 1963, #388, seven-piece walker body, became McGuffey Ana in 1964 – 1965

8"	$100.00	$375.00

Annabelle, ca. 1952, Maggie head

20"	$250.00	$875.00+

Aunt Pitty-Pat, ca. 1957, #435, seven-piece body

8"	$1,700.00+	

Babs Skater, 1948 – 1950, hard plastic, Margaret

15"	$250.00	$1,000.00+
18"	$350.00	$1,250.00+

Bill/Billy, ca. 1960, seven-piece walker body

8"	$150.00	$475.00+

Binnie Walker, 1954 – 1955, Cissy

15"	$175.00	$325.00
Skater		$650.00*

Only in formals, 1955

25"	$125.00	$500.00+

Bitsey, ca. 1950, cloth body, molded hair, more for wigged version

11"	$75.00	$275.00

Brenda Starr, 1964 only, 12" hard plastic, vinyl arms, red wig

Ballgown	$75.00	$375.00
Bride	$75.00	$300.00
Raincoat/hat/dress	$65.00	$225.00
Street dress	$50.00	$225.00

Caroline, ca. 1961, #131, vinyl

15"	$90.00	$375.00

Cinderella, 1950, Margaret face, 14", hard plastic
Ballgown

14"	$225.00	$850.00+

Poor Cinderella, gray dress, original broom

14"	$300.00	$600.00

Ballgown

18"		$750.00*

Lissy, 1966

12"	$250.00	$950.00

1970 – 1986, vinyl body, ballgown (pink and blue)

14"	$40.00	$125.00

Cynthia, 1952 only, hard plastic

15"	$300.00	$850.00+
18"	$200.00	$850.00+
23"	$400.00	$1,200.00

Davy Crockett, ca. 1955, hard plastic, straight leg walker, coonskin cap

8"	$225.00	$700.00+

Edith, The Lonely Doll, 1958 – 1959, vinyl head, hard plastic body

8"	$250.00	$750.00+
16"	$175.00	$375.00

Elise, 1957 – 1964, 16", hard plastic body, vinyl arms, jointed ankles and knees

Ballerina	$200.00	$375.00+
Ballgown	$350.00	$700.00+
Street dress, MIB		$2,730.00*

Elise, 1963 only, 18", hard plastic, vinyl arms, jointed ankles and knees

Riding Habit	$175.00	$350.00
Bouffant hairstyle	$200.00	$425.00

Elise, 1966 – 1972, 17", hard plastic, vinyl arms, jointed ankles and knees

Street dress	$75.00	$275.00
Trousseau/Trunk	$175.00	$650.00+
Bride, 1966 – 1987	$40.00	$175.00

Estrella, 1953, Maggie face, walker body, tagged lilac gown, hard plastic body

18"	$600.00	$1,200.00+

8" vinyl head, hard plastic body Edith, The Lonely Doll #850, blond wig in special pulled back style like Dare Wright book character, sleep eyes with molded lashes, brass circle earrings, bent knee walker, pink check dress, white apron, circa 1958, $800.00. Courtesy Marge Meisinger.

8" hard plastic Wendy-kins, blond synthetic wig, sleep eyes, molded lashes, straight leg walker, Wendy Helps Mommy Serve Luncheon #428 navy taffeta dress with red striped cotton apron, circa 1956, $475.00. Courtesy Marge Meisinger.

18" vinyl head, hard plastic body Madeline, body jointed at shoulders, elbows, wrists, hips, and knees, original rooted wig with bangs, blue eyes with real lashes, red check dress, marked "Alexander" on back of head, circa 1961, $600.00. Courtesy Vicki Johnson.

Fairy Queen, 1948 – 1950, Margaret face
14" $225.00 $750.00
Fashions of a Century, 1954 – 1955, 14" – 18", Margaret face, hard plastic
          $900.00 $1,800.00+
First Ladies, 1976 – 1990
Set 1, 1976 – 1978
          $150.00 ea. $1,000.00 set
Set 2, 1979 – 1981
          $125.00 ea. $800.00 set
Set 3, 1982 – 1984
          $125.00 ea. $800.00 set
Set 4, 1985 – 1987
          $125.00 ea. $700.00 set
Set 5, 1988
          $125.00 ea. $700.00 set
Set 6, 1989 – 1990
          $125.00 ea. $700.00 set
Fischer Quints, 1964 only, vinyl, hard plastic body (Little Genius), 1 boy, 4 girls
7" $25.00 $75.00
Set of five $550.00
Flower Girl, ca. 1954, hard plastic, Margaret
15" $275.00 $550.00
Glamour Girl Series, 1953 only, hard plastic, Margaret head, auburn wig, straight leg walker
18" $800.00 $1,000.00+
Godey Bride, 1950 – 1951, Margaret, hard plastic
1950
14" $500.00 $1,000.00+
1950 – 1951
18" $700.00 $1,400.00
Godey Groom, 1950 – 1951, Margaret, hard plastic
1950, curls over ears
14" $475.00 $975.00
1950 – 1951
18" $600.00 $1,200.00
Godey Lady, 1950 – 1951, Margaret, clover wrist tag, hard plastic
1950
14" $500.00 $1,000.00
1950 – 1951
18" $750.00 $1,500.00
Gold Rush, 1963 only, hard plastic, Cissette
10" $400.00 $1,600.00

18" hard plastic Sweet Violet, brunette synthetic wig, blue sleep eyes with real lashes and painted lower lashes, closed mouth, walker, jointed at shoulders, elbows, wrists, hips, and knees, original tagged blue cotton dress and bonnet, carrying original pink hatbox, circa 1950s, $1,700.00 Courtesy McMasters Harris Doll Auctions.

Grandma Jane, 1970 – 1972, #1420, Mary Ann, vinyl body

14"	$125.00	$250.00

Groom, 1949 – 1951, Margaret, hard plastic

14" – 16"	$375.00	$750.00+

Groom, 1953 – 1955, Wendy-Ann, hard plastic

7½"	$225.00	$450.00+

Jacqueline, 1961 – 1962, 21", hard plastic, vinyl arms

Street dress	$325.00	$650.00+
Ballgown	$425.00	$850.00+

Janie, 1964 – 1966, #1156, toddler, vinyl head, hard plastic body, rooted hair

12"	$75.00	$275.00

Jenny Lind, 1969 – 1970, hard plastic head

14"	$100.00	$375.00
21"	$450.00	$1,400.00

John Robert Powers Model, ca. 1952, with oval beauty box, hard plastic

14"	$800.00	$1,650.00

Kathy, 1949 – 1951, Maggie, has braids

15" – 18"	$350.00	$700.00

Kelly, 1959 only, hard plastic, Lissy

12"	$250.00	$475.00

Kelly, 1958 – 1959, hard plastic, Marybel

15" – 16"	$150.00	$325.00

Leslie (black Polly), 1965 – 1971, 17", vinyl head, hard plastic body, vinyl limbs, rooted hair

Ballerina	$200.00	$375.00
Bride	$190.00	$375.00

Lissy, 1956 – 1958, 12", jointed knees and elbows, hard plastic

Ballerina	$215.00	$425.00
Bridesmaid	$325.00	$650.00
Street dress	$175.00	$350.00
Formal	$250.00	$500.00

Little Shaver, 1963 – 1965, painted eyes, vinyl body

12"	$75.00	$250.00

Little Women, 1947 – 1956, Meg, Jo, Amy, Beth, plus Marme, Margaret and Maggie faces

14" – 15"	$225.00	$450.00
Set of five	$1,100.00	$2,200.00
Set of five	$5,900.00* original box, tags	

14" hard plastic Maggie, blond nylon wig, sleep eyes with real lashes, five-piece body, pink pique dress, hair net case and wrist tag printed, "Maggie//by Madame Alexander," original box, unplayed with condition, doll unmarked, circa 1950s, $2,250.00. Courtesy McMasters Harris Doll Auctions.

21" vinyl head and body Jacqueline #2135, rooted brunette side-part wig, brown sleep eyes with real lashes, painted upper and lower lashes, closed mouth, high-heeled feet, silver lame gown with pink satin overskirt, marked on head "Alexander//19©61," circa 1962, $457.00. Courtesy McMasters Harris Doll Auctions.

14" hard plastic Little Women, original wigs, blue sleep eyes with real lashes, closed mouths, five-piece bodies, jointed at head, shoulders, and hips, original tagged dresses, Beth in original box, marked on dress tags "Louisa M. Alcott's//Little Women//(individual name)//by Madame Alexander, NY, USA//All Rights Reserved," dolls unmarked, circa 1950s, $525.00. Courtesy McMasters Harris Doll Auctions.

15" rigid vinyl Pollyana, rooted braided hair, sleep eyes with real lashes, painted lower lashes, open-closed mouth, jointed at shoulders, waist, hips, original pinafore dress, white tights, side two-snap shoes, marked on head "Mme//© 1958," Pollyanna//© Madame Alexander//Reg. US Pat Off N.Y. USA" on dress tag, original box and wrist tag, circa 1960, $275.00. Courtesy McMasters Harris Doll Auctions.

1955, Meg, Jo, Amy, Beth, plus Marme, Wendy-Ann, straight-leg walker

8"	$200.00	$375.00
Set of five	$900.00	$1,800.00

1956 – 1959, Wendy-Ann, bent-knee walker

8"	$225.00	$250.00
Set of five	$600.00	$1,300.00

1974 – 1992, straight leg, #411 – #415

8"	$40.00	$75.00
Set of five	$200.00	$375.00

1957 – 1958, Lissy, jointed elbows and knees

12"	$200.00	$375.00
Set	$850.00	$1,900.00

1959 – 1968, Lissy, one-piece arms and legs

12"	$125.00	$250.00
Set	$300.00	$1,500.00

Lovey-Dove Ringbearer, 1951, hard plastic, five-piece toddler body, mohair wig, satin top, shorts

12"	$325.00	$650.00+

Maggie Mixup, 1960 – 1961, 8", hard plastic, freckles

Angel	$325.00	$750.00
Overalls	$325.00	$750.00
Riding Habit	$225.00	$550.00
Roller Skates	$325.00	$750.00

Maggie Teenager, 1951 – 1953, hard plastic

15" – 18"	$300.00	$600.00

Margaret O'Brien, 1949 – 1951, hard plastic

14"	$250.00	$475.00

Margot Ballerina, 1953 – 1955, Margaret and Maggie, dressed in various colored outfits

15" – 18"	$325.00	$750.00

Mary Ellen, 1954 only, rigid vinyl walker

31"	$300.00	$600.00+

Mary Ellen Playmate, 1965 only, bendable vinyl body

17"	$175.00	$325.00

Mary Martin, 1948 – 1952, South Pacific character Nell, two-piece sailor outfit, hard plastic

14" – 17"	$475.00	$975.00

8" hard plastic American Girl, synthetic wig, blue sleep eyes, molded and painted lower lashes, walker jointed at shoulders hips, knees, and head, red and white gingham dress with eyelet pinafore, and straw hat, original box, marked on back "ALEX," circa 1962, $285.00. Courtesy McMasters Harris Doll Auctions.

Marybel, "The Doll That Gets Well," 1959 – 1965, rigid vinyl, in case

16"	$175.00	$350.00

McGuffey Ana, 1948 – 1950, hard plastic, Margaret

21"	$700.00	$1,400.00

1956 only, hard plastic, #616, Wendy Ann face

8"	$325.00	$750.00

1963 only, hard plastic, rare doll, Lissy face

12"	$1,000.00	$2,000.00+

Melanie, 1955 – 1956, #633, hard plastic, Wendy Ann Scarlett Series, lavender lace

8"	$25.00	$100.00+

1966, "Coco," #2050, blue gown

21"	$1,100.00	$2,200.00+

Melinda, 1962 – 1963, plastic/vinyl, cotton dress

14" – 22"	$185.00	$375.00+

Nancy Drew, 1967 only, vinyl body, Literature Series

12"	$165.00	$325.00

Nina Ballerina, 1949 – 1951, Margaret head, clover wrist tag

14"	$2,200.00* MIB	
19"	$425.00	$850.00+
23"	$400.00	$800.00

Peter Pan, 1953 – 1954, Wendy Ann Quiz-kin

8"	$400.00	$850.00+

1969, 14" Wendy (Mary Ann head), 12" Peter, Michael (Jamie head), 10" Tinker Bell (Cissette head)

Set of four	$1,000.00	

Pink Champagne/Arlene Dahl, hard plastic, red hair, pink lace, rhinestone bodice gown

18"	$2,750.00	$5,500.00+

Polly, 1965 only, 17"

Street dress	$150.00	$275.00

Polly Pigtails, 1949 – 1951, Maggie, hard plastic

14"	$250.00	$500.00
17"	$300.00	$625.00

Portraits, 1960+

Marked *"1961,"* Jacqueline, 21", early dolls have jointed elbows, later one-piece.

17" hard plastic Princess Margaret, original mohair wig, blue sleep eyes, real lashes, shadow, painted lower lashes, closed mouth, original yellow nylon dress with lace and ribbon trim, tagged "Margaret Rose//Madame Alexander, New York, USA/All Rights Reserved," marked on head "Alexander," circa 1950s, $375.00. Courtesy McMasters Harris Doll Auctions.*

Agatha	1967 – 1980	#2171	$675.00
Cornelia	1972	#2191	$450.00
Gainsborough	1968 – 1978	#2184	$650.00
Godey, Coco	1966	#2063	$2,300.00
Godey, Jacqueline	1969	#2195	$650.00
Goya	1968	#2183	$550.00
Jenny Lind	1969 – 1970	#2193	$1,400.00
Lady Hamilton	1968	#2182	$475.00
Madame	1966	#2060	$2,200.00
Madame Pompadour	1970	#2197	$1,200.00
Melanie (Coco)	1966	#2050	$2,200.00
Melanie	1970	#2196	$525.00
Magnolia	1977	#2297	$475.00
Queen	1965 – 1968	#2150	$750.00
Renoir	1965	#2154	$700.00
Scarlett	1965	#2152	$1,900.00+
Scarlett (Coco), white gown		#2061	$2,700.00+
Southern Belle	1965	#2155	$1,200.00
Southern Belle	1967	#2170	$625.00

Prince Charles, 1957 only, #397, hard plastic, blue jacket, cap, shorts

8"	$325.00	$750.00+

Prince Charming, 1948 – 1950, hard plastic, Margaret face, brocade jacket, white tights

14"	$350.00	$700.00

Princess Margaret Rose, 1949 – 1953, hard plastic, Margaret face

18"	$425.00	$975.00

1953 only, #2020B, hard plastic, Beaux Arts Series, pink taffeta gown with red ribbon, tiara, Margaret face

18"	$600.00	$1,700.00

Queen, 1953 only, #2025, hard plastic, Beaux Arts Series, white gown, long velvet cape trimmed with fur, Margaret

18"	$900.00	$1,800.00

Queen, Me and My Shadow Series, 1954 only, hard plastic

8"	$500.00	$1,000.00+
18"	$600.00	$1,200.00

Quiz-Kin, ca. 1953, hard plastic, back buttons, nods yes or no

8"	$250.00	$475.00

Renoir Girl, 1967 – 1968, vinyl body, Portrait Children Series

14"	$100.00	$195.00

Scarlett, 1950s, hard plastic, more for rare costumes, bent-knee walker

8"	$650.00	$1,300.00+
21"	$650.00	$1,300.00+

Shari Lewis, 1958 – 1959

14"	$325.00	$650.00
21"	$400.00	$850.00

Sleeping Beauty, ca. 1959, Disneyland Special

10"	$200.00	$355.00
16"	$325.00	$650.00
21"	$425.00	$850.00+

Smarty, 1962 – 1963, vinyl body

12"	$175.00	$325.00

Snow White, ca. 1952, gold vest, Walt Disney edition

15"	$325.00	$750.00
21"	$600.00	$1,200.00

Sound of Music, 1965 – 1970 (large), **1971 – 1973** (small), vinyl

Brigitta

10"	$95.00	$175.00
14"	$95.00	$195.00

Friedrich

8"	$115.00	$225.00
10"	$150.00	$275.00

Gretl

8"	$90.00	$175.00
10"	$100.00	$195.00

Liesl

10"	$125.00	$250.00
14"	$150.00	$275.00

Louisa

10"	$140.00	$275.00
14"	$140.00	$275.00

Maria

12"	$150.00	$300.00
17"	$150.00	$300.00

Marta

8"	$115.00	$225.00
10"	$95.00	$195.00

Set/seven small

	$625.00	$1,250.00

Set/seven large

	$700.00	$1,200.00

Southern Belle, hard plastic

1956 – 1963

8"	$375.00	$750.00

1968 – 1973

10"	$150.00	$450.00

1965 – 1981

21"	$400.00	$1,200.00

Timmy Toddler, 1960 – 1961, vinyl head, hard plastic body

23"	$50.00	$150.00

1960 only

30"	$85.00	$250.00

14" hard plastic head and body with vinyl arms Shari Lewis, auburn wig, sleep eyes with molded lashes, closed mouth, high-heel feet, original taffeta-skirted costume with straw hat, earrings, marked on neck "Alexander," circa 1959, $750.00. Courtesy Marge Meisinger.

Tommy Bangs, 1952 only, hard plastic, Little Men Series

11"	$450.00	$875.00

Wendy, Wendy-Ann, Wendy-kin, see Alexander-kins

Winnie Walker, 1953, Cissy, hard plastic

15"	$140.00	$275.00
18"	$175.00	$350.00
25"	$275.00	$550.00

SOUVENIR DOLLS, UFDC, LIMITED EDITION

Little Emperor, 1992, limit 400	8"	$500.00	
Miss Unity, 1991, limit 310	10"	$400.00	
Sailor Boy, limit 260	8"	$750.00	

Turn of Century Bathing Beauty, 1992, R9 Conference, limit 300

	10"	$275.00
Columbian 1893 Sailor, 1993	12"	$250.00
Gabrielle, 1998, limit 400	10"	$325.00

American Character Doll Co.

1919 – 1963, New York City. Made composition dolls; in 1923 began using Petite as a tradename for mama and character dolls; later made cloth, hard plastic, and vinyl dolls. In 1960 advertised as American Doll & Toy Co.

First price is for dolls in good condition, but with some flaws; second price is for dolls in excellent condition, in original clothes. Exceptional dolls may be more. All vinyl and hard plastic dolls should have original tagged clothes, wrist tags, etc.

CLOTH

12" hard plastic head, vinyl body Tiny Tears, blond rooted wig cap inserted in head, sleep eyes with lashes, holes for wetting and crying, five-piece baby body, originally in white sun suit or pink dress, marked on back of head "American Character Doll//Pat. # 2675644," circa 1950s, $180.00. Courtesy Carol Stover.

Eloise, ca. 1950s, cloth character, orange yarn hair, crooked smile

15"	$150.00	$260.00
Christmas dress		
	$90.00	$360.00
21"	$100.00	$425.00
Christmas dress		
	$135.00	$515.00

COMPOSITION

"A. C." or "Petite" marked baby

Composition head, limbs, cloth bodies, original clothes, good condition

14"	$50.00	$185.00
18"	$65.00	$225.00

"A. C." or "Petite" marked mama doll

Composition head, limbs, sleep eyes, mohair or human hair wig, cloth body with crier, swing legs, original clothes

16"	$75.00	$275.00
24"	$100.00	$385.00

Bottletot, 1926

Composition head, bent limbs, cloth body with crier, sleep eyes, painted hair, open mouth, composition arm formed to hold bottle, original outfit

13"	$75.00	$250.00
18"	$125.00	$325.00

1936 – 1938, rubber drink, wet doll with bottle, original diaper

11"	$35.00	$75.00
15"	$40.00	$95.00

Campbell Kids, 1928

All-composition, jointed neck, shoulders, hips, curl in middle of forehead. *Marks: "A Petite Doll"*

Allow more for original dress with label reading *"Campbell Kid."*

12"	$95.00	$350.00

Carol Ann Beery, 1935

All-composition Patsy-type, sleep eyes, closed mouth, braided cornet, celebrity doll, named for daughter of Hollywood actor, Wallace Beery. Originally came with two outfits such as a playsuit and matching dress. *Marks: "Petite Sally"* or *"Petite"*

13"	$100.00	$415.00
16½"	$150.00	$615.00
19½"	$200.00	$785.00

Chuckles, 1930s – 1940s

Composition head, open mouth, sleep eyes, cloth body. *Marks: "AM/Character"*

20"	$250.00	$350.00

Puggy, 1928

All-composition, jointed neck, shoulders, hip, pug nose, scowling expression, side-glancing painted eyes, molded and painted hair. Original costumes include Boy Scout, cowboy, baseball player, and newsboy. *Marks: "A //Petite// Doll"; tag on clothing: "Puggy// A Petite Doll"*

13"	$200.00	$500.00

Sally, 1930, a Patsy-look-alike

Composition head, arms, legs, cloth or composition body, crier, painted or sleep eyes

Marks: "Sally//A Petite Doll"

12½"	$60.00	$225.00
14"	$100.00	$400.00
16"	$115.00	$450.00
19"	$125.00	$500.00

Sally, 1934, Shirley Temple look-alike

Ringlet curls and bangs, composition shoulder plate, cloth body, sleep eyes, open mouth. Some dressed in Shirley Temple-type costumes.

24"	$100.00	$375.00

12" composition Pudgy, molded and painted hair, painted blue eyes and features, closed mouth, fully jointed with dimpled knees, original blue cotton pants with print top, matching blue cap, doll marked "A//Petite/ /Doll," circa 1930s, $525.00. Courtesy Marge Meisinger.

20" vinyl Ricky Jr. baby, molded hair, sleep eyes with lashes, hole for drinking and wetting, five-piece baby body with dimpled knees, original yellow romper monogrammed "Ricky Jr.," wrist tag "Ricky Junior," marked on head "Amer. Char.Doll," circa 1953, $225.00. Courtesy Hakes Americana.

17" hard plastic Baby Sue, short curly synthetic hair, blue sleep eyes, real lashes, closed mouth, baby body, pink and white checked romper, white shirt trimmed with lace, white shoes, hang tag reads "Baby Sue™//Baby Sue says 'Mama'//A baby doll for girls 3 – 8//American" circa 1953+, $200.00. Courtesy Joan Radke.

Sally Joy, 1934
Composition shoulder plate, cloth body, sleep eyes, open mouth, curly wig
Marks: "Petite; Amer Char. Doll Co."

24"	$100.00	$400.00

HARD PLASTIC AND VINYL
Baby
Hard plastic head, vinyl body, bottle, boxed

12"	$60.00	$250.00

Vinyl head, marked "American Character"

20"	$20.00	$80.00

Tiny Tears, 1950 – 1962, hard plastic and vinyl

8"	$17.50	$75.00
13"	$65.00	$225.00
16"	$100.00	$400.00

Mint-in-box, with accessories, ca. 1954

12"	$1,045.00*

1963, all-vinyl

9"	$20.00	$80.00
12"	$40.00	$150.00+
16"	$50.00	$200.00+

Toodles, ca. 1960, box, wardrobe, accessories

11"	$75.00	$285.00
29"	$150.00	$350.00

Toddler, with eight additional pieces of clothing, box #2503

24"	$150.00	$400.00

18" hard plastic Sweet Sue, blond synthetic wig, sleep eyes with lashes and painted lashes under, closed mouth, five-piece body, original pink taffeta gown with "Sweet Sue" acetate case and hang tag "American Character Doll Co.//New York 10, N.Y.," doll unmarked, circa 1950s, $275.00. Courtesy Marge Meisinger.

Child or Adult
Annie Oakley, hard plastic walker, embroidered on skirt

14"	$125.00	$400.00

Betsy McCall, 1957: See Betsy McCall category.
Cartwrights, Ben, Hoss, Little Joe, ca. 1966, TV show Bonanza

8"	$40.00	$140.00

Freckles, 1966, face changes

13"	$10.00	$40.00

Little Miss Echo, 1964, talker

30"	$65.00	$250.00

Miss America, 1963

	$15.00	$60.00+

Ricky Jr., 1954 – 1956, I Love Lucy TV show, starring Lucille Ball and Desi Arnez, vinyl, baby boy

12"	$300.00*	
20"	$50.00	$225.00

Sally Says, 1965, plastic and vinyl, talker

19"	$20.00	$70.00

Sweet Sue, 1953 – 1961, hard plastic

Some walkers, some with skull caps, some with extra joints at knees, elbows, and/or ankles, some hard plastic and vinyl, excellent condition, good cheek color, original clothes.

Marks: "A.C.," "Amer. Char. Doll," or "American Character" in circle

15"	$55.00	$225.00
22"	$65.00	$300.00

Sweet Sue Sophisticate, vinyl head, tag, earrings

19"	$55.00	$250.00
Bride	$65.00	$275.00
Sunday Best	$75.00	$350.00

Talking Marie, 1963, record player in body, battery operated

18"	$25.00	$50.00

Toni, vinyl head, ca. 1958, rooted hair

10½"	$50.00	$175.00
20",	$28.00* MIB	

Toodle-Loo, 1961, rooted blond hair, painted eyes, closed mouth, fully jointed, "Magic Foam" plastic body

18"	$50.00	$190.00

Tressy, her family and friends, 1963 – 1966, grow hair, 1963 – 1965

Tressy, all-vinyl high heel doll, marked *"American Doll & Toy Corp.//19C.63"* in circle on head

11"	$40.00	$115.00

Black Tressy

11"	$150.00	$300.00+

Pre-teen Tressy, 1963 only, vinyl, marked *"Am.Char.63"* on head

14"	$50.00	$250.00

Cricket, 1964 – 1966, all-vinyl pre-teen sister of Tressy, bendable legs, marked *"Amer Char//1964"* on head

9"	$75.00	$200.00

Magic Make Up, 1965 – 1966, vinyl, bendable legs, grow hair, not marked

11½"	$40.00	$75.00

Mary Make Up, 1965 – 1966, vinyl, Tressy's friend, high-heeled doll, no grow hair, not marked

11"	$40.00	$75.00

Whimette/Little People, ca. 1963, Pixie, Swinger, Granny, Jump'n, Go-Go

7½"	$6.00	$30.00

Whimsie, 1960, stuffed vinyl, painted on features, tag reads: *"Whimsie"* with name of doll, Bessie the Bashful Bride, Dixie the Pixie, Fanny (angel), Hedda-Get-Bedda, Hilda the Hillbilly, Lena the Cleaner, Miss Take, Monk, Polly the Lolly, Raggie, Simon, Strong Man, Suzie the Snoozie, Tillie the Talker, Wheeler the Dealer, Zack the Sack, and Zero the Hero (a football player)

10½" vinyl Toni doll, rooted auburn hair, sleep eyes with lashes (two lashes painted at side), fashion doll body with high-heel feet, original teal corduroy skirt with felt top and pocket trim, marked on back of head "Amer. Char. Doll Corp. 1958," marked lower back "American Character" in a circle, circa 1950s, $190.00. Courtesy Sandy Johnson Barts.

American Character Doll Co.

Bessie the Bashful Bride, box, tag	$100.00	$225.00
Devil, or Hilda the Hillbilly	$75.00	$150.00
Hedda Get Bedda	$65.00	$125.00
Trixie the Pixie	$100.00	$225.00
Zack, the Sack	$75.00	$140.00
Zero, the Hero	$100.00	$250.00

Annalee Mobilitee Doll Co.

10" felt Hula Hoop, blond hair, painted features, pink felt skirt with check top holding a yellow hula hoop, tagged "Annalee//Made Only In Meredith//New Hampshire//USA," circa late 1990s, $45.00. Courtesy Carol Stover.

1934+, Meredith, NH. Decorative cloth dolls, early labels were white with woven red lettering; then white rayon tags with red embroidered lettering. In about 1969, white satin tags with red lettering were used, after 1976 gauze type cloth was used. Until 1963, the dolls had yarn hair, ca. 1960 – 1963, it was orange or yellow chicken feathers, after 1963, hair was synthetic fur. Collector's Club started in 1983.

First price is issue price, if known; second price for doll in excellent condition on secondary market. Remember secondary market prices are volatile and fluctuate.

Celebrities, 10", all-cloth

Johnny Appleseed	1984	$80.00	$1,000.00
Annie Oakley	1985	$90.00	$700.00
Mark Twain	1986	$117.50	$500.00
Abraham Lincoln	1989	$119.50	$500.00
Christopher Columbus	1991	$119.50	$300.00

Logo Kids, all with collector's club logo

Christmas, with Cookie	1985	$675.00
Sweetheart	1986	$150.00
Naughty	1987	$300.00
Raincoat	1988	$150.00
Christmas Morning	1989	$125.00
Clown	1991	$125.00
Reading	1992	$100.00
Back to School	1993	$50.00
Ice Cream	1994	$50.00
Dress Up Santa	1994	$50.00
Goin' Fishing	1995	$25.00
Little Mae Flower, 7"	1996	$25.00

Clowns – A. Thorndike

Clown, 1956	10"	1987		$80.00
Clown	18"	1978		$225.00
Clown with Balloon	18"	1985		$150.00
Hot Air Balloon with 10" Clown		1985		$150.00

Halloween – A. Thorndike

Baby Witch with Diaper	3"	1987		$125.00
Scarecrow Kid, 3058	7"	1992		$55.00
Trick or Treat Mouse, 3005	7"	1977		$45.00
Bat, 2980	10"	1991		$80.00
Pumpkin (medium), 3027	10"	1987		$165.00
Witch Mouse on Broom, 3030	12"	1980		$95.00
Pumpkin (solid), 3025	14"	1986		$125.00
Trick or Treat Bunny Kid	18"	1990		$150.00
Witch (flying), 3008	18"	1989		$100.00

Others

8 Reindeer Sleigh	20"		$300.00*	
Betsy Ross		1990	$200.00*	
Bob Cratchet, w/ Tim, 7"	18"	1974	$11.95	$425.00
Elf Pixie		1964	$200.00*	
Girl Hiker with backpack			$1,111.00*	
Mr. & Mrs. Fireside Couple	18"	1970	$7.45	$300.00
Holly Hobby	22"	1973		$1,000.00
Bellhop	24"	1963	$13.95	$1,750.00
Woman Golfer			$356.00*	
Mr./Mrs. Santa, kids	30"	1990	$375.00*	
Mrs. Snow Woman, holder	29"	1972	$19.95	$700.00
Santa in chair, two 18" kids	30"	1984	$169.95	$1,200.00
Scarecrow	42"	1977	$61.95	$2,050.00
Santa	48"	1978	$600.00*	
Skier	10"	1956	$610.00*	

Arranbee Doll Co.

1922 – 1958, New York. Some of their bisque dolls were made by Armand Marseille and Simon & Halbig. Made composition baby, child, and mama dolls; early dolls have an eight-sided tag. Sold to Vogue Doll Co. which used molds until 1961.

> *Marks:*
> ARRANBEE//DOLL
> Co. or R & B

First price is for soiled, faded, or without complete costume dolls; second price is for perfect dolls, with good color, complete costume, more for MIB.

COMPOSITION

Baby, 1930s – 1940s

Cloth body, original clothes or appropriately dressed

16"	$50.00	$150.00

My Dream Baby, 1925

Bisque solid dome heads made by Armand Marseille, painted hair, sleep eyes, open or closed mouth, cloth body, composition hands

Marks: "A.M. 341," "351," or "ARRANBEE"

See Marseille, Armand for prices.

20" composition Nancy the Movie Queen, mohair wig, sleep eyes with lashes and painted lashes above, open mouth with teeth, rosy cheeks, original pink organdy dress with petal-shaped hem tied to wrists, marked on back of head "Nancy," circa 1939, $800.00. Courtesy Marge Meisinger.

18" hard plastic Nanette, synthetic blond wig in swept back style, sleep eyes with lashes and lashes painted under, closed mouth, strung body, blue organdy dress with eyelet collar possibly original, circa 1950s, $325.00. Courtesy Carol Stover.

Dream Baby, 1927+, composition, cloth body

17"	$250.00*	
19"	$125.00	$375.00+

Child, 1930s – 1940s, all-composition
Marks: "Arranbee" or "R & B"

9"	$45.00	$125.00
15"	$85.00	$300.00+

Debu' Teen, circa late 1930s, 1940
Usually all-composition, some cloth body, mohair or human hair wig, closed mouth, original costumes, unmarked or marked Arranbee. Hang tags or paper labels read *"Debu'Teen//R & B Quality Doll."*

14"	$75.00	$350.00
17"	$100.00	$400.00

Ice Skater, 1945, some with Debu' Teen tag

14"	$50.00	$250.00
17"	$75.00	$275.00
21"	$100.00	$375.00

Kewty, circa 1934 – 1936, all-composition with molded hair, several faces used form the marked Kewty body
Mark: "KEWTY"

14"	$100.00	$300.00

Nancy, 1930, a Patsy look-alike, molded hair, or wig, sleep eyes, open mouth
Marks: "ARRANBEE" or "NANCY"

12"	$75.00	$250.00
19"	$100.00	$500.00
21"	$135.00	$650.00

Nancy Lee, 1939+
Sleep eyes, mohair, or human hair wig, original clothes

12"	$75.00	$300.00
17"	$100.00	$400.00

Storybook Dolls, 1930s, Nursery Rhyme Characters

Little Bo-Peep, ca. 1935, with papier-mâché lamb

8½"	$100.00	$225.00

Little Boy Blue, ca. 1935, in decorated case, silver horn

8½"	$125.00	$500.00

HARD PLASTIC AND VINYL

Cinderella, ca. 1952, silver/pink dress, silver cords on both wrists

20"	$421.00* not mint	

Darling Daisy Bride, tagged

18"	$65.00	$325.00

Lil' Imp, 1960, hard plastic, red hair, freckles

10"	$20.00	$75.00

Littlest Angel, 1956+, hard plastic walker, "R&B" marked torso and seven-piece body

11"	$100.00	$275.00

Left: 20" hard plastic Nancy Lee, synthetic wig, sleep eyes with lashes and lashes painted under, original taffeta dress, leatherette skates, box label "R&B Quality Doll//Nancy Lee/4107," marked on head "R&B," circa 1950s, $600.00. Courtesy McMasters Harris Doll Auctions.

Right: 11" hard plastic Little Angel (per tag), saran wig, sleep eyes with lashes and painted lashes under, straight legs, walker, original pink dotted cotton gown, matching purse, straw hat, circa 1954, marked on torso "R&B," circa 1954, $250.00 with box. Courtesy Carol Stover.

Vinyl head, original dress, brochure
11½"	$15.00	$50.00

Red hair/freckles, 1960
10"	$20.00	$70.00

Miss Coty, ca. 1958, vinyl, "10½R" under right arm, high heels
10½"	$35.00	$175.00

My Angel, 1961, hard plastic and vinyl
17"	$10.00	$45.00
22"	$20.00	$70.00
36"	$45.00	$165.00

Walker, 1957 – 1959
30"	$40.00	$150.00

1959, vinyl head, oilcloth body
22"	$15.00	$60.00

Nancy, 1951 – 1952, vinyl head, arms, hard plastic torso, wigged
14"	$40.00	$150.00
18"	$50.00	$190.00

Walker
24"	$75.00	$285.00

Nancy Lee, 1950 – 1959, hard plastic
14"	$75.00	$450.00
17"	$100.00	$475.00
14"	$305.00* Evening Gown	

Nancy Lee Baby, 1952, painted eyes, crying look
15"	$70.00	$145.00

Nanette, 1949 – 1959, hard plastic, synthetic wig, sleep eyes, closed mouth, original clothes
14"	$75.00	$325.00
17"	$100.00	$350.00

Nannette Walker, 1957 – 1959
17"	$100.00	$400.00
20"	$115.00	$450.00

Taffy, 1956, looks like Alexander's Cissy
23"	$45.00	$165.00

18" cernit The Farmer's Daughter by Stephanie L. Cauley, one of a kind, auburn braided hair, brown eyes, closed mouth, white peasant shirt, flowered scarf tied around shoulders, standing barefoot with goat, circa 2000, $550.00. Courtesy Stephanie Cauley.

Original, one-of-a-kind, limited edition, or limited production dolls of any medium (cloth, porcelain, wax, wood, vinyl, or other material) made for sale to the public.

CLOTH

Barrie, Mirren
Historical children $95.00
Heiser, Dorothy, soft sculpture
Early dolls $400.00+
Queens $1,100.00+
Wright, R. John, cloth
7½" Elfin girl $800.00
Adult characters $1,500.00
Children $900.00 – $1,300.00
Christopher Robin, 8 animals
     $3,050.00*
Snow White, 7 Dwarfs, boxes
     $11,100.00*
Timothy & Rosemary $8,000.00*

OTHER MEDIA

Baker, Betsy, Sculpey
     $250.00 $500.00+
  Baron, Cynthia, resin plymer clay
     $100.00 $2,500.00+
  Blackeley, Halle, high-fired clay lady dolls
     $550.00 – $750.00
  Bollenbach, Cheryl, Cernit
     $600.00 $1,200.00+
    Cochran, Dewees, circa 1950s, latex composition
Peter Ponsett
     18" $2,500.00
Commissioned Portraits
     20" $2,500.00
Child
     15 – 16" $500.00 $900.00
    Florian, Gertrude, ceramic/composition
dressed ladies
     $300.00
Goodnow, June
Chocolate Delight, resin, cloth
     14" $920.00
Indian, Singer Drummer, one-of-a-kind, cernit
     14" $3,000.00
The Quilter, resin, cloth
     18" $500.00
  Hopkins, Lillian, Paperclay over gourd
     $500.00 $800.00+

14" porcelain Basketbabies Sonu (India), by Atelier Bets van Boxel, human hair wig, hand-crafted crystal eyes, closed pouty mouth, hand-knitted green sweater, cap, tan pants, made from natural fibers authentic from India, limited edition of 10, circa 2000, $1,500.00. Courtesy Atelier Bets van Boxel.

26" black vinyl marked on head, "Annette Himstedt Ayoka" glass eyes, vinyl and cloth body, vinyl limbs, dark wig with individual braids and colorful beads, original yellow and turquoise costume, bare feet, circa 1990, $1,100.00. Courtesy Cornelia Ford.

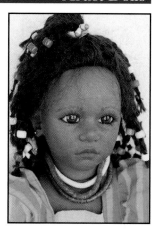

Huston, Marilynn, Sculpey
$300.00 $700.00+

Parker, Ann, historical character
$150.00 – $200.00

Poole, Daryl, Sculpey
$700.00 $1,000.00+

Russell, Sarah, wax over fimo
$1,800.00+

Simonds, Sandy, Creall-therm
$1,000.00 $1,500.00+

PORCELAIN AND CHINA

Armstrong-Hand, Martha, porcelain babies, children $1,200.00+

Brandon, Elizabeth, porcelain children
$300.00 – $500.00

Campbell, Astry, porcelain
Ricky & Becky, pair $850.00

Clear, Emma, porcelain, china, shoulder head dolls $350.00 – $500.00

Dunham, Susan, porcelain babies, children/adults $75.00 – $1,000.00+

Hoskins, Dorothy
Lilabeth Rose, one-of-a-kind porcelain
$6,000.00+

Kane, Maggie Head, porcelain
$400.00 – $450.00

Oldenburg, Maryanne, porcelain children
$200.00 – $250.00

Redmond, Kathy, porcelain ladies
$400.00 – $450.00

Roche, Lynn and Michael, porcelain
17" children $1,100.00 – $1,500.00

Sutton, Linda Lee
Babies, children $400.00 – $1,000.00

6" cloth R. John Wright Kewpie Flit souvenir doll from the 1999 UFDC Convention, marked "RJW" on gold button, "Flit//No. 053/250//Kewpie ® 1999. © Jesco, 1999. Under license from Jesco.//R.John Wright - Cambridge, NY" on tag, pressed felt swivel head, painted eyes to side, dash brows, closed smiling mouth, brown felt hair, green antennae, jointed body, green striped tummy, blue Kewpie wings, ladybug-type wings, holding flower, original marked box, circa 1999, $500.00. Courtesy McMasters Harris Doll Auctions.

13" cloth Feeling All Untied by Jane Darin, self portrait needle sculptured by hand and painted face made from 100% Swiss pima cotton knit, inspiration for this cloth figure was an ugly tie challenge, the tie fabric appears on the body, the collar, and cuffs, reflecting the mood of the artist after moving to a new home and unpacking her studio, oak base flooring, cardboard boxes, the hair is thread left over from fringing the shawls in the boxes, circa 1995, $6,000.00. Courtesy Jane Darin.

28" cernit Wine Stomper Folk-loric collectible by Lebba Kropp, from a folklore story about how mischevious elves were caught playing in a bobbin factory by the guardian of the fabric factories and he cast a spell making the bobbin part of them forever, circa 2000, $550.00 – $650.00 depending on costume. Courtesy Lebba Kropp.

30" stoneware clay Mountain Babies Kata by Denise Lemmon, one-of-a-kind, direct sculpt in high fire stoneware clay, her dark hair is made of hand-dyed silk, handmade outfit, the stand is buckeye burl, circa 2000, $3,600.00. Courtesy Denise Lemmon.

Thompson, Martha, porcelain
Betsy $900.00
Little Women, ea. $800.00 – $900.00
Queen Anne $2,300.00
Princess Caroline, Prince Charles, Princess Anne, ea.
    $900.00
Princess Margaret, Princess Grace
    ea. $1,500.00 – $2,000.00
Young Victoria $2,300.00
Thorpe, Ellery, porcelain children
    $300.00 – $500.00
Tuttle, Eunice, miniature porcelain children
    $700.00 – $800.00
Angel Baby $400.00 – $425.00
Walters, Beverly, porcelain miniature fashions
    $500.00+
Wick, Faith, porcelain, other materials
    $2,500.00+
Wyffels, Berdine, porcelain
Girl, glass eyes
    6" $195.00
Zeller, Fawn, porcelain
One-of-a-kind $2,000.00+
Angela $800.00 – $900.00
Polly Piedmont, 1965 $800.00 – $900.00
Holly, U.S. Historical Society
    $500.00 – $600.00
Polly II, U.S. Historical Society
    $200.00 – $225.00

VINYL

Good-Krueger, Julie, vinyl
    20" – 21" $150.00 $225.00
Hartman, Sonja, 1981+, vinyl and porcelain
Porcelain
    20" $300.00
Vinyl, Odette
    23" $375.00
Schrott, Rotrout, vinyl
Child $375.00
Spanos, FayZah, vinyl
Baby $250.00

WAX

Gunzel, Hildegard, wax over porcelain
    $1,500.00 – $2,000.00
Park, Irma, wax-over-porcelain miniatures
    $125.00+
Sorensen, Lewis
Father Christmas $1,200.00
Toymaker $800.00

Vargas family, wax ethnic figures
 10" – 11" $350.00 – $700.00
WOOD
Beckett, Bob and June, carved wood children
       $300.00 – $450.00
Bringloe, Frances, carved wood
American Pioneer Children
       $600.00
Bullard, Helen, carved wood
Holly $125.00
American Family Series (16 dolls)
       ea. $250.00
Hale, Patti, NIADA 1978, hand-carved character dolls, wooden heads, stuffed wired cloth bodies can pose; some all-wood jointed dolls
       $200.00+
JANCI, Nancy Elliott, Jill Sanders
       $400.00+
Sandreuter, Regina $550.00 – $650.00
Smith, Sherman, simple carved wood
 5 – 6" $65.00 $100.00
With finer details, souvenir dolls, etc.
 5 – 6" $235.00 $300.00
HITTY
Reproduced by modern artists to represent the small 6¼" – 6⅜" wooden doll from the literary character in Rachel Field's 1929 book, *Hitty, Her First 100 Years.* Original doll now resides in Stockbridge Library in Massachusetts.

Judy Brown	$195.00
Ruth Brown	$150.00
Helen Bullard	$350.00
DeAnn Cote	$400.00+
David Greene	$310.00
Patti Hale	$300.00
JANCI	$300.00
Lonnie Lindsay	$205.00
Jeff Scott	$175.00
Mary Lee Sundstrom/Sandy Reinke	$500.00+
Larry Tycksen, son-in-law of Sherman Smith	$65.00+

30" porcelain Linda Lee Sutton Snow White, black curly hair, blue intaglio eyes, closed mouth, holding a bird on her fingers, black beaded gown with white organdy sleeves, top, and collar, white petticoat, necklace, limited to 10 worldwide, circa 2001, $1,095.00; with the 13" porcelain Seven Dwarfs, intaglio eyes, in multicolored leather suede and velour outfits, circa 2001, $1,985.00. Courtesy Linda Lee Sutton.

Ashton Drake

Niles, IL. Markets via mail order and through distributors, has a stable of talented artists producing porcelain collector dolls. Many of these dolls are available on the volatile secondary market with prices fluctuating widely. See Gene category for Ashton Drake's hottest collectible.

Diana, The People's Princess

18"	$50.00	$200.00

Elvis: Legend of a Lifetime, 1991

68 Comeback Special	$75.00

Fairy Tale Heroines, designed by Diann Effner

Snow White	$65.00

Mother Goose Series, designed by Yolanda Bello

Mary, Mary, Diane Effner	$90.00
Miss Muffet, Yolanda Bello	$50.00

Picture Perfect Babies, designed by Yolanda Bello

Jason	$100.00	$475.00
Heather	$25.00	$50.00
Jennifer	$25.00	$50.00
Matthew	$25.00	$50.00
Jessica	$25.00	$50.00
Lisa	$25.00	$50.00
Emily	$25.00	$75.00
Danielle	$25.00	$50.00
Amanda	$25.00	$50.00
Michael	$55.00	$100.00
Sarah	$30.00	$60.00

Precious Memories of Motherhood, designed by Sandra Kuch

Loving Steps	$65.00

Barbie®

Mattel, Inc., 1959+, Hawthorne, CA.

First price indicates mint doll, no box; second price (or one price alone) is for mint never-removed-from-box doll. Doll alone, without box, would be less, and soiled or played-with dolls, much, much less. Even though Barbie is over 40 years old, she is still considered a newer doll by seasoned collectors.

In pricing newer dolls, the more perfect the doll has to be with mint color, condition, rare pristine outfit, complete with all accessories, retaining all tags, labels, and boxes to command the highest prices. This is not a complete listing of every Barbie doll, her friends, or accessories, but some of the more popular items.

Number One Barbie, 1959

11½", heavy vinyl solid body, faded white skin color, white irises, pointed eyebrows, soft ponytail, brunette or blond only, black and white striped bathing suit, holes with metal cylinders in balls of feet to fit round-pronged stand, gold hoop earrings

Marks:
1959 – 1962
BARBIE™
PATS. PEND.
©MCMLVIII
BY//MATTEL, INC.
1963 – 1968
MIDGE™©1962
Barbie®/©1958
BY//MATTEL, INC.
1964 – 1966
©1958//MATTEL, IN.
U.S. PATENTED
U.S. PAT. PEND.
1966 – 1969
©1966//MATTEL, INC.
U.S. PATENTED//
U.S. PAT. PEND//
MADE IN JAPAN

Ponytail
Blond

$3,500.00	$7,100.00

Brunette

$4,000.00	$7,500.00
#1 Barbie stand	$350.00
#1 Barbie shoes	$20.00
#1 Barbie earrings	$65.00

11½" #1 ponytail Barbie, brunette hair in replaced rubber band, red lips, nostril paint, white irises with blue eyeliner, green silk sheath, white nylon gloves, hoop earrings, circa 1959, $2,200.00. Courtesy McMasters Harris Doll Auctions.

11½" #2 Barbie, blond hair in ponytail with retied knot, red lips, nostril paint, eye shadow, blue eyeliner, black/white striped swim suit, hoop earrings, circa 1959, $3,500.00. Courtesy McMasters Harris Doll Auctions.

Number Two Barbie, 1959 – 1960

11½", heavy vinyl solid body, faded white skin color, white irises, pointed eyebrows, no holes in feet, some with pearl earrings, soft ponytail, brunette or blond only

Ponytail

Blond	$3,000.00	$6,500.00
Brunette	$3,500.00	$6,325.00

Number Three Barbie, 1960

11½", heavy vinyl solid body, some fading in skin color, blue irises, curved eyebrows, no holes in feet, soft ponytail, brunette or blond only

Ponytail

Blond	$600.00	$1,100.00+
Brunette	$650.00	$1,150.00+

Number Four Barbie, 1960

11½", same as Number Three, but solid body of skin-toned vinyl, soft ponytail, brunette or blond only

Ponytail	$250.00	$665.00+

Number Five Barbie, 1961

11½", vinyl head, now less heavy, hard plastic hollow body, firmer texture, saran ponytail, can now be redhead, has arm tag

Ponytail	$185.00	$560.00
Redhead	$320.00	$640.00+

Number Six Barbie, 1962

11½", same features and markings as Number Five Barbie except for a wider variety of hair and lip color, wears a different red jersey swimsuit, chubbier appearance to face

Ponytail	$250.00	$525.00

More Basic Barbie Dolls

Listed alphabetically, year of issue and value. First price indicates doll in excellent condition, no box; second price indicates mint-in-box doll. Never-removed-from-box (NRFB) dolls would be more; played-with dolls would be less.

Bendable Leg

American Girl, side part

1965	$1,900.00	$3,000.00

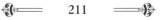

11½" #3 Barbie, brunette ponytail, red lips, hoop earrings, black and white stripe swim suit, original box, circa 1960, $950.00. Courtesy McMasters Harris Doll Auctions.

Left: 11½" #4 Barbie, brunette ponytail in original set, red lips, nostril paint, pearl earrings, white glasses with blue lenses, black and white swim suit, original box with cardboard neck insert, pedestal stand, booklet, circa 1960, $475.00. Courtesy McMasters Harris Doll Auctions.

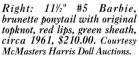

Right: 11½" #5 Barbie, brunette ponytail with original topknot, red lips, green sheath, circa 1961, $210.00. Courtesy McMasters Harris Doll Auctions.

11½" #6 Barbie, dark blond hair, coral lips, cheek blush, sweater outfit, circa 1962, $210.00. Courtesy McMasters Harris Doll Auctions.

American Girl, 1070		
1965	$500.00	$1,500.00
1966	$1,200.00	$2,500.00
Bubble Cut, 1961 – 1967		
Brown	$450.00	$1,000.00
White Ginger	$300.00	$875.00
Other	$150.00	$425.00
Color Magic		
Blond, cardboard box		
1966	$375.00	$2,500.00
Blond, plastic box		
1966	$375.00	$1,300.00
Midnight, plastic box		
1966	$1,450.00	$2,700.00
Fashion Queen		
1963 – 1964	$125.00	$320.00
Swirl Ponytail		
1964 – 1965	$200.00	$475.00
Swirl Platinum		
1964	$400.00	$1,000.00
Twist 'N Turn		
1967	$175.00	$475.00
Redhead		
1967	$475.00	$850.00

Other Barbie Dolls

First price is for doll only in excellent condition; second price is for mint in box.

Angel Face		
1983	$16.00	$45.00
Ballerina		
1976	$35.00	$95.00
Barbie Baby-sits		
1974	$20.00	$60.00
Beach Party		
1980	$25.00	$75.00

Beautiful Bride		
1976	$95.00	$240.00
Beauty Secrets		
1980	$20.00	$$55.00
Bicyclin'		
1994	$15.00	$40.00
Busy Barbie		
1972	$95.00	$260.00
Dance Club		
1989	$15.00	$40.00
Day-To-Night		
1985	$25.00	$75.00
Doctor		
1988	$22.50	$65.00
Dream Barbie		
1995	$20.00	$55.00
Fashion Jeans, black		
1982	$16.00	$45.00
Fashion Photo		
1978	$22.50	$65.00
Free Moving		
1975	$55.00	$150.00
Gold Medal Skater		
1975	$32.50	$90.00
Golden Dream w/coat		
1981	$32.50	$90.00
Growin' Pretty Hair		
1971	$125.00	$350.00
Hair Fair		
1967	$75.00	$200.00
Hair Happenin's		
1971	$375.00	$1,150.00
Happy Birthday		
1981	$17.50	$50.00
Ice Capades, 50th		
1990	$15.00	$40.00
Kellogg Quick Curl		
1974	$25.00	$65.00
Kissing		
1979	$15.00	$40.00
Live Action on Stage		
1971	$100.00	$270.00
Living Barbie		
1970	$110.00	$290.00
Loving You		
1983	$25.00	$65.00
Magic Curl		
1982	$17.50	$50.00
Magic Moves		
1986	$25.00	$65.00

11½" bubble cut Barbie, brunette hair, red lips, blue eyeshadow, black and white swim suit, original box brochure, all original, circa 1962, $375.00. Courtesy McMasters Harris Doll Auctions.

11½" swirl ponytail Barbie, platinum hair in original set with yellow ribbon tie, white lips, nostril paint, red nylon one-piece swim suit, pearl earrings, wrist tag, box with cardboard insert, booklet, gold wire stand, $2,025.00. Courtesy McMasters Harris Doll Auctions.

11½" bubble cut Barbie, white ginger colored hair, pink lips, black and white swim suit, faint green on earring holes, black wire stand, box, $490.00. Courtesy McMasters Harris Doll Auctions.

11½" Color Magic Barbie, lemon yellow hair, blue barrette, pink lips, nostril paint, diamond pattern nylon swim suit with belt and matching headband, purple plastic closet with gold sticker on front, packets, brush, sponge, $675.00. Courtesy McMasters Harris Doll Auctions.

Malibu (Sunset)		
1971	$25.00	$65.00
My First Barbie		
1981	$10.00	$30.00
My Size		
1993	$55.00	$150.00
Newport the Sport's Set		
1973	$62.50	$165.00
Peaches 'n Cream		
1985	$15.00	$40.00
Pink & Pretty		
1982	$15.00	$40.00
Rappin' Rockin'		
1992	$22.50	$60.00
Rocker		
1986	$20.00	$45.00
Roller Skating		
1980	$22.50	$60.00
Secret Hearts		
1993	$12.50	$35.00
Sensations		
1988	$25.00	$60.00
Sun Lovin' Malibu		
1979	$16.00	$45.00
Sun Valley – The Sport's Set		
1973	$32.50	$85.00
Super Fashion Fireworks		
1976	$45.00	$125.00
Super Size, 18"		
1977	$100.00	$265.00
Superstar Promotional		
1978	$32.50	$90.00
Talking		
1968	$130.00	$370.00
Talking Busy		
1972	$130.00	$365.00
Twinkle Lights		
1993	$25.00	$60.00
Walking Lively		
1972	$90.00	$245.00
Western (3 hairstyles)		
1981	$25.00	$55.00
Ward's Issue		
1972	$275.00	$700.00

Gift Sets

Mint-in-box prices; add more for NRFB (never removed from box), less for worn or faded.

Barbie Hostess	1966	$4,750.00
Beautiful Blues, Sears		
	1967	$3,300.00
Color Magic Gift Set, Sears		
	1965	$4,000.00
Fashion Queen Barbie & Friends		
	1963	$2,250.00
Fashion Queen & Ken Trousseau		
	1963	$2,600.00
Little Theatre Set	1964	$5,500.00
On Parade	1960	$2,350.00
Party Set	1960	$2,300.00
Pink Premier	1969	$1,600.00
Round the Clock	1964	$5,000.00
Sparkling Pink	1964	$2,500.00
Travel in Style, Sears		
	1964	$2,400.00
Trousseau Set	1960	$2,850.00
Wedding Party	1964	$3,000.00

Left: 11½" side-part American Girl Barbie, brown hair, coral lips, Dressed-UP! dress with gold/beige brocade top, belt and green satin skirt, $1,025.00. Courtesy McMasters Harris Doll Auctions.

Custom or Exclusive Barbie Dolls

Often the most sought after are the first editions of a series, or exclusive Barbie dolls such as those produced for Disney, FAO Schwarz, Wal-Mart, Target, and others. These types of Barbie dolls usually increase in price because the number made is less than others, so they are not as easily found.

Prices indicate mint-in-box.

Bob Macke Barbie Dolls

Gold	1990	$560.00
Starlight Splendor	1991	$670.00
Platinum	1991	$690.00
Neptune Fantasy	1992	$810.00
Empress Bride	1992	$830.00
Masquerade Ball	1993	$450.00
Queen of Hearts	1994	$300.00
Goddess of the Sun	1995	$205.00
Moon Goddess	1996	$110.00
Madame Du Barbie	1997	$250.00

Happy Holiday Series

Holiday, red gown	1988	$775.00
International Holiday	1988	$580.00
Holiday, white gown	1989	$240.00
Holiday, fuchsia gown		
	1990	$160.00
Holiday, green gown	1991	$185.00

11½" Talking Barbie, brunette hair, pink ribbon bows, pink lips, hot pink knit top bathing suit, some wear, $170.00. Courtesy McMasters Harris Doll Auctions

Holiday, silver gown	1992	$150.00
Holiday, red/gold gown	1993	$150.00
Holiday (black), fuchsia gown	1990	$105.00
Holiday (black), green gown	1991	$120.00
Holiday (black), silver gown	1992	$110.00
Holiday (black), red/gold	1993	$70.00
Classique Series		
Benefit Ball, Carol Spenser	1992	$165.00
City Styles, Janet Goldblatt	1993	$145.00
Opening Night, Janet Goldblatt	1994	$95.00
Evening Extravaganza, Perkins	1994	$85.00
Uptown Chic, Perkins	1994	$90.00
Midnight Gala, Abbe Littleton	1995	$110.00
Store Specials or Special Editions		
Avon, Winter Velvet	1996	$60.00
Ballroom Beauties, Starlight Waltz	1995	$75.00
Billy Boy, Feeling Groovy	1986	$290.00
Bloomingdales, Savvy Shopper	1994	$165.00
Disney		
Euro Disney	1992	$70.00
Disney Fun	1993	$55.00
FAO Schwarz		
Golden Greetings	1989	$225.00
Winter Fantasy	1990	$235.00
Night Sensation	1991	$200.00
Madison Avenue	1991	$245.00
Rockette	1993	$260.00
Silver Screen	1994	$275.00
Jeweled Splendor	1995	$335.00
Great Eras		
Gibson Girl	1993	$130.00
Flapper	1993	$200.00
Southern Belle	1994	$125.00
Hallmark		
Victorian Elegance	1994	$115.00
Sweet Valentine	1996	$75.00
Hills		
Party Lace	1989	$45.00
Evening Sparkle	1990	$45.00
Moonlight Rose	1991	$60.00
Blue Elegance	1991	$55.00
Hollywood Legends		
Scarlett O'Hara, red	1994	$70.00
Dorothy, Wizard of Oz	1995	$260.00
Glinda, Good Witch	1995	$105.00
Home Shopping Club		
Evening Flame	1991	$160.00
J.C. Penney		
Evening Elegance	1990	$105.00

Enchanted Evening	1991	$105.00
Golden Winter	1993	$70.00
Night Dazzle, blond	1994	$65.00
K-Mart		
Peach Pretty	1989	$40.00
Pretty in Purple	1992	$35.00
Mattel Festival		
35th Anniversary, brunette	1994	$520.00
Festival Banquet	1994	$225.00
Happy Holidays, brunette	1994	$1,120.00
Snow Princesss	1994	$830.00
Mervyns		
Ballerina	1983	$75.00
Fabulous Fur	1986	$70.00
Montogmery Ward		
#1 Replica, shipping box	1972	$710.00
#1 Replica, pink box	1972	$840.00
Prima Ballerina Music Box		
Swan Lake, music box	1991	$205.00
Nutcracker, music box	1992	$285.00
Sears		
Celebration, 100th Anniversary	1986	$90.00
Star Dream	1987	$70.00
Blossom Beautiful	1992	$315.00
Ribbons & Roses	1995	$60.00
Service Merchandise		
Blue Rhapsody	1991	$185.00
Satin Nights	1992	$80.00
City Sophisticate	1994	$110.00
Spiegel		
Sterling Wishes	1991	$140.00
Regal Reflections	1992	$250.00
Royal Invitation	1993	$120.00
Theatre Elegance	1994	$180.00
Target		
Gold 'n Lace	1989	$40.00
Party Pretty	1990	$30.00
Cute 'n Cool	1991	$30.00
Golden Evening	1991	$45.00
Toys R Us		
Dance Sensation	1985	$60.00
Pepsi Spirit	1989	$80.00
Vacation Sensation	1989	$80.00
Radiant in Red	1992	$70.00
Moonlight Magic	1993	$90.00
Harley-Davidson, #1	1997	$475.00
Firefighter	1995	$55.00
WalMart		
Pink Jubilee, 25th Anniversary	1987	$75.00

12" Ken, brunette hair, beige lips, blue jacket with red trim, cork sandals, red swim trunks, wrist tag, box, booklet, black wire stand, bag, $245.00. Courtesy McMasters Harris Doll Auctions.

11½" Twist 'N Turn Barbie, brunette hair, pink lips, cheek blush, #1804 knit hat, knit dress with blue lined bodice and pink skirt, $125.00. Courtesy McMasters Harris Doll Auctions

Frills & Fantasy	1988	$55.00
Dream Fantasy	1990	$50.00
Wholesale Clubs		
Party Sensation	1990	$65.00
Fantastica	1992	$70.00
Royal Romance	1992	$115.00
Very Violet	1992	$75.00
Season's Greetings	1994	$75.00
Winter Royale	1994	$75.00
After the Walk, Sam's Club		
	1997	$75.00
Country Rose, Sam's Club		
	1997	$100.00
Woolworths		
Special Expressions, white		
	1989	$30.00
Sweet Lavender	1992	$25.00

Barbie Related Dolls, Friends and Family

First price indicates doll in good condition, no box; second price indicates mint-in-box.

Allan, 1964 – 1967

Bendable legs	$175.00	$525.00
Straight legs	$60.00	$120.00

Bild Lilli, not Mattel

German doll made prior to Barbie, clear plastic cylinder case $500.00 $600.00

Casey, Twist 'N Turn

1967	$75.00	$150.00

Chris, brunette, bendable leg

1967	$90.00	$185.00

Francie

Bendable leg		
1966	$120.00	$300.00
Straight leg		
1966	$125.00	$320.00
Twist 'N Turn		
1967	$175.00	$385.00
Black		
1967	$900.00	$1,500.00
Malibu		
1971	$40.00	$50.00
Growin' Pretty Hair		
1971	$150.00	$250.00

Jamie, Walking

1970	$185.00	$385.00

Julia, Twist 'N Turn

1969	$125.00	$245.00
Talking		
1969	$120.00	$215.00

11½" *Francie Growin' Pretty Hair*, blond hair pulled back on top, long hair extension, pink lips, cheek plush, hot pink nylon short dress, $65.00. *Courtesy McMasters Harris Doll Auctions.*

11½" *Army Stars 'n Stripes Barbie*, special edition, blond hair, camouflage uniform, uniform, beret, original box, circa 1990s, $35.00. *Courtesy Carol Stover.*

Kelly

Quick Curl	1973	$65.00	$150.00
Yellowstone	1974	$150.00	$275.00

Ken, #1, straight leg, blue eyes, hard plastic hollow body, flocked hair, 12"

Mark: "Ken® MCMLX//by//Mattell//Inc."

	1961	$100.00	$185.00
Molded hair	1962	$55.00	$150.00
Bendable legs	1965	$125.00	$350.00
Midge			
Straight leg	1963	$90.00	$175.00
No freckles	1963	$225.00	$385.00
Bendable legs	1965	$275.00	$500.00
P.J.			
Talking	1970	$110.00	$225.00
Twist 'N Turn	1970	$60.00	$260.00
Live Action/Stage	1971	$90.00	$255.00
Ricky, straight legs	1965	$55.00	$160.00
Skipper			
Straight leg	1964	$65.00	$175.00
Bendable leg	1965	$70.00	$250.00
Twist 'N Turn	1968	$135.00	$195.00
Skooter			
Straight leg	1965	$65.00	$125.00
Bendable leg	1966	$100.00	$290.00
Stacey			
Talking	1968	$150.00	$300.00
Twist 'N Turn	1968	$160.00	$325.00
Todd, bendable, poseable			
	1966	$90.00	$180.00
Tutti, bendable, poseable			
	1967	$90.00	$145.00
Twiggy, Twist 'N Turn			
	1967	$165.00	$320.00

12" *Army Stars 'n Stripes Ken*, special edition, black hair, camouflage uniform, beret, original box, circa 1990s, $35.00. *Courtesy Carol Stover.*

Barbie Accessories

Animals

All American (horse)	1991	$35.00
Blinking Beauty (horse)	1988	$25.00
Champion (horse)	1991	$40.00
Dancer (horse)	1971	$100.00
Fluff (kitten)	1983	$20.00
Ginger (giraffe)	1988	$30.00
Prancer (horse)	1984	$35.00
Prince (poodle)	1985	$35.00
Snowball (dog)	1990	$35.00
Tahiti (bird w/cage)	1985	$20.00

Cases

Fashion Queen, black, zippered	1964	$150.00
Fashion Queen, round hatbox	1965	$250.00
Miss Barbie, zippered	1964	$160.00
Vanity, Barbie & Skipper	1964	$200.00

Clothing

Name of outfit, stock number; price for mint in package, much less for loose.

Aboard Ship	1631	$550.00
All That Jazz	1848	$350.00
Arabian Knights	874	$495.00
Barbie in Japan	821	$500.00
Beautiful Bride	1698	$2,100.00
Benefit Performance	1667	$1,400.00
Black Magic Ensemble	1609	$420.00
Bride's Dream	947	$350.00
Busy Gal	981	$450.00
Campus Sweetheart	1616	$1,750.00
Cinderella	872	$550.00
Commuter Set	916	$1,400.00
Country Club Dance	1627	$490.00
Dancing Doll	1626	$525.00
Debutante Ball	1666	$1,300.00
Dog 'n Duds	1613	$350.00
Drum Majorette	875	$265.00
Easter Parade	971	$4,500.00
Evening Enchantment	1695	$595.00
Fabulous Fashion	1676	$595.00
Formal Occasion	1697	$550.00
Fashion Editor	1635	$850.00
Formal Luncheon	1656	$1,400.00
Garden Wedding	1658	$575.00
Gay Parisienne	964	$4,500.00
Glimmer Glamour	1547	$5,000.00
Gold 'n Glamour	1647	$1,750.00
Golden Glory	1645	$495.00
Here Comes the Bride	1665	$1,200.00

Holiday Dance	1639	$625.00
International Fair	1653	$500.00
Intrigue	1470	$425.00
Invitation to Tea	1632	$600.00
Junior Prom	1614	$695.00
Knitting Pretty, pink	957	$450.00
Let's Have a Ball	1879	$325.00
Little Red Riding Hood	880	$625.00
Magnificence	1646	$625.00
Make Mine Midi	1861	$350.00
Masquerade	944	$250.00
Maxi 'n Midi	1799	$375.00
Midnight Blue	1617	$850.00
Miss Astronaut	1641	$700.00
On the Avenue	1644	$575.00
Open Road	985	$385.00
Pajama Pow	1806	$300.00
Pan American Stewardess	1678	$5,000.00
Patio Party	1692	$375.00
Picnic Set	967	$365.00
Plantation Belle	966	$600.00
Poodle Parade	1643	$985.00
Rainbow Wraps	1798	$350.00
Reception Line	1654	$600.00
Red Fantastic, Sears	1817	$850.00
Riding in the Park	1668	$625.00
Roman Holiday	968	$5,000.00
Romantic Ruffles	1871	$250.00
Satin 'n Rose	1611	$395.00
Saturday Matinee	1615	$950.00
Sears Pink Formal	1681	$2,450.00
Shimmering Magic	1664	$1,750.00
Sleeping Pretty	1636	$375.00
Smasheroo	1860	$275.00
Sorority Meeting	937	$300.00
Suburban Shopper	969	$350.00
Sunday Visit	1675	$595.00
Swirley-Cue	1822	$300.00
Trailblazers	1846	$250.00
Travel Togethers	1688	$300.00
Tunic 'n Tights	1859	$300.00
Under Fashions	1655	$695.00
Velveteens, Sears	1818	$850.00
Weekenders, Sears	1815	$950.00
Wedding Wonder	1849	$375.00
Wild 'n Wonderful	1856	$300.00
Furniture, Suzy Goose		
Canopy Bed, display box	1960s	$250.00
Chifferobe, cardboard box	1960s	$250.00

Queen Size Bed, pink	1960s	$600.00
Vanity, pink		$75.00
Vehicles		
Austin Healy, beige	1964	$3,300.00
Beach Bus	1974	$45.00
Mercedes, blue-green	1968	$450.00
Speedboat, blue-green	1964	$1,100.00
Sport Plane, blue	1964	$3,000.00
Sun 'n Fun Buggy	1971	$150.00
United Airlines	1973	$75.00

Betsy McCall

IDEAL DOLL COMPANY, 1952 – 1953

Based on May 1951 *McCall* magazine paper doll, designed by Bernard Lipfert, vinyl head, watermelon smile, strung hard plastic Toni body, rooted saran wig.

Mark: "McCall Corp.®" on head; "IDEAL DOLL//P 90" on back

14"	$65.00	$250.00

AMERICAN CHARACTER, 1957 – 1963

In 1957, American Character introduced an 8", hard plastic doll, with rigid vinyl arms, sleep eyes, single stroke eyebrows, molded eyelashes, metal barrettes in hair; first year dolls had mesh base wig, plastic peg-joined knees. Second year and later dolls had saran hair rooted in rubber-type skullcap, metal pin-jointed knees; the company advertised as American Doll & Toy Co. circa 1960. Marked in circle on back waist *"McCall © Corp."* One hundred

costumes available. First price for doll with flaws, perhaps nude, poor color. Second price for doll in basic chemise with great color. Double price for mint-in-box.

8"	$175.00	$350.00
Sunday Best, MIB		$985.00*

Accessories: complete costume, more for rare or NRFP

Town & Country	$75.00
Black vinyl shoes	$25.00
Red vinyl shoes	$85.00

1958, vinyl, four hair colors, rooted hair, flat feet, slim body, round sleep eyes, may have swivel waist or one-piece torso

Mark: "McCall 19©58 Corp." in circle

14"	$250.00	$500.00

1959, vinyl, rooted hair, slender limbs, some with flirty eyes, one-piece torso

Mark: "McCall 19©58 Corp." in a circle

19 – 20"	$250.00	$500.00
20"	$365.00*	

1959, vinyl, rooted hair (Patti Playpal style body)

Mark: "McCall Corp//1959" on head

36"	$60.00	$325.00

8", hard plastic with rigid vinyl arms American Character blond rooted saran hair in rubber skullcap, sleep eyes with molded lashes, closed mouth, jointed at shoulders and hips, pin-jointed knees, nylon chemise in original all pink mail-order box, marked in circle on back "McCall © Corp.," circa 1950s, $350.00. Courtesy Carol Stover.

14" vinyl, rooted brown hair, blue sleep eyes, jointed at waist, arms, hips, in black body suit, original box and trunk with extra outfits, printed on box "Betsy//McCall//American Character Doll Corp.," "Betsy McCall" on trunk, doll marked on head "McCall//19©58," circa 1958, $400.00. Courtesy McMasters Harris Doll Auctions.

1961, vinyl, five colors of rooted hair, jointed wrists, ankles, waist, blue or brown sleep eyes, four to six outfits available

Mark: "McCall 19©61 Corp." in a circle

22"	$30.00	$250.00
29"	$50.00	$300.00

Linda McCall (Betsy's cousin)

1959, vinyl, Betsy face, rooted hair

Mark: "McCall Corp//1959" on head

36"	$50.00	$350.00

Sandy McCall (Betsy's brother)

1959, vinyl, molded hair, sleep eyes, red blazer, navy shorts

Mark: "McCall 1959 Corp."; tag reads "I am Your Life Size Sandy McCall"

39"	$50.00	$350.00

22" vinyl, American Character, brown sleep eyes with real lashes, rooted hair, jointed at shoulders, wrists, waist, hips, upper legs, and ankles, plaid flannel dress #120, black tights, all original, doll unmarked, circa 1960s, $200.00. Courtesy McMasters Harris Doll Auctions.

UNEEDA

1964, vinyl, rooted hair, rigid vinyl body, brown or blue sleep eyes, slim preteen body, wore mod outfits, some mini-skirts, competitor of Ideal's Tammy

Mark: None

11½"	$35.00	$95.00+

HORSMAN

1974, vinyl with rigid plastic body, sleep eyes, came in Betsy McCall Beauty Box with extra hair piece, brush, bobby pins on card, eye pencil, blush, lipstick, two sponges, mirror, and other accessories

Mark: "Horsman Doll Inc.//19©67" on head; "Horsman Dolls Inc." on torso

12½"	$25.00	$50.00

1974, vinyl with rigid plastic teen type body, jointed wrists, sleep eyes, lashes, rooted hair with side part (some blond with ponytails), closed mouth, original clothing marked *"BMc"* in two-tone blue box marked *"©1974//Betsy McCall – she WALKS with you"*

Marks: "Horsman Dolls 1974"

29"	$75.00	$275.00

McCall Heirloom Tradition Figurines

Circa 1984, 12 one-piece procelain figurines in box, includes Back to School, Introducing Betsy McCall, Betsy McCall Gives a Tea Party, and Most Christmacy, match paper dolls published in *McCalls* magazine

4"	$5.00	$20.00

Rothchild

1986, 35th anniversary Betsy, hard plastic, sleep eyes, painted lashes below eyes, single stroke eyebrows, tied ribbon emblem on back

Marks: Hang tag reads "35th Anniversary//BetsyMcCall//by Rothschild (number) 'Betsy Goes to a Tea Party,' or 'Betsy Goes to the Fair.'" Box marked "Rothchild Doll Company//Southboro, MA 01722."

8"	$15.00	$35.00
12"	$20.00	$45.00

Robert Tonner

1996+, vinyl (some porcelain), rooted hair, rigid vinyl body, glass eyes, closed smiling mouth

Mark: "Betsy McCall//by//Robert Tonner//©Gruner & Jahr USA PUB."

14"	$69.00 retail	

Limited Editions	
Mouseketeer	$225.00*
Tonner Birthday	$145.00*
Kimono Betsy	$175.00
Roy Rogers Betsy	$225.00

Buddy Lee

Ca. 1920 – 1963. Trademark doll of H.D. Lee Co., Inc., who made uniforms and work clothes, first made of composition; ca. 1948 made in hard plastic, some marked *"Buddy Lee."* Engineer had Lee label on hat and overalls; cowboy hat band printed, *"Ride 'Em in Lee Rider Overalls."*

First price for played-with, incomplete outfit; second price for mint doll, more for rare uniform.

Composition		
Coca-Cola	$125.00	$625.00
Cowboy	$90.00	$400.00
Engineer	$95.00	$400.00
Engineer	$860.00*	
Gas station	$175.00	$650.00
Hard Plastic		
Coca-Cola	$275.00	$650.00
Cowboy	$200.00	$425.00
Engineer	$200.00	$425.00
Gas station	$300.00	$800.00+

12" hard plastic, molded face and brown painted hair, painted side-glance eyes, smiling watermelon mouth, lashes painted above eyes, closed mouth, jointed at shoulders only, molded and painted black boots, brown cotton Phillips 66 shirt and pants, belt, marked on back "Buddy Lee," pants label "Union Made//Lee//Sanforized," circa 1950s, $285.00. Courtesy McMasters Harris Doll Auctions.

Bucherer

1921 – 1930+, Armiswil, Switzerland. Made metal bodied dolls with composition head, hands, and feet, some with changeable heads — Charlie Chaplin, Mutt and Jeff, regional costumes, and others.

Regional, 6½" – 7½	$100.00	$285.00
Beccasine, 7¾"	$425.00*	

Cabbage Patch Kids

1978+, Babyland General Hospital, Cleveland, GA. Cloth, needle sculpture

"A" blue edition	1978	$1,500.00+
"B" red edition	1978	$1,200.00+
"C" burgundy edition	1979	$900.00+
"D" purple edition	1979	$800.00+
"X" Christmas edition	1979	$1,200.00+
"E" bronze edition	1980	$1,200.00+
Preemie edition	1980	$650.00+
Celebrity edition	1980	$600.00+
Christmas edition	1980	$600.00+
Grand edition	1980	$750.00+
New Ears edition	1981	$125.00+
Ears edition	1982	$150.00+
Green edition	1983	$400.00+
"KP" dark green edition	1983	$550.00+
"KPR" red edition	1983	$550.00+
"KPB" burgundy edition	1983	$200.00
Oriental edition, pair	1983	$260.00*
Indian edition	1983	$850.00
Hispanic edition	1983	$750.00
"KPZ" edition	1983 – 1984	$175.00
Champagne edition	1983 – 1984	$900.00
"KPP" purple edition	1984	$250.00
Sweetheart edition	1984	$250.00
Bavarian edition	1984	$250.00
World Class edition	1984	$175.00

"KPF," "KPG," "KPH," "KPI," "KPJ" editions

	1984 – 1985	$100.00 – 200.00+
Emerald edition	1985	$200.00 – 250.00

Coleco Cabbage Patch Kids

1983, have powder scent and black signature stamp

Boys and Girls	$95.00
Bald babies	$50.00 – $75.00
With freckles	$100.00
Black boys or girls	
With freckles	$175.00
Without freckles	$75.00
Red Hair boys, fuzzy hair	$175.00
Tsukuda	$300.00*

1984 – 1985, green signature stamp in 1984; blue signature stamp in 1985. Most dolls are only worth retail price, exceptions are

Single tooth, brunette with ponytail	$165.00+

Popcorn hairdos, rare	$200.00
Gray-eyed girls	$165.00
Freckled girl, gold hair	$95.00

Other

Baldies, popcorn curl with pacifier, red popcorn curls, single tooth, freckled girls, and gold braided hair are valued at retail to $65.00. Still easily obtainable for collectors are a host of other Cabbage Patch Kids, including ringmaster, clown, baseball player, astronaut, travelers, twins, babies, Splash Kid, Cornsilk Kid, valued at $30.00 – $50.00

1991 Convention Nurse Payne $199.00*

Cameo Doll Co.

1922 – 1930+, New York City, Port Allegheny, PA. Joseph L. Kallus's company made composition dolls, some with wood segmented bodies and cloth bodies. First price for played-with dolls; second price for mint dolls.

17" composition Annie Rooney, blond braided cotton yarn wig, painted features, black eyes, closed watermelon mouth, jointed at neck and shoulders only, cotton costume tagged on sleeve "Little//Annie Rooney//Trade-mark//Copyright 1925//Jack Collins//Pat. Applied For," doll unmarked, circa 1920s, $725.00. Courtesy Shirley's Doll House, Wheeling, IL.

BISQUE

Baby Bo Kaye, 1925

Bisque head, made in Germany, molded hair, open mouth, glass eyes, cloth body, composition limbs, good condition. *Mark: "J.L. Kallus: Copr. Germany// 1394/30"*

17"	$1,875.00	$2,500.00
20"	$2,100.00	$2,800.00

All-bisque, molded hair, glass sleep eyes, open mouth, two teeth, swivel neck, jointed arms and legs, molded pink or blue shoes, socks, unmarked, some may retain original round sticker on body

5"	$700.00	$1,500.00
6"	$900.00	$1,800.00

CELLULOID

Baby Bo Kaye

Celluloid head, made in Germany, molded hair, open mouth, glass eyes, cloth body

12"	$200.00	$400.00
15"	$350.00	$750.00

COMPOSITION

Annie Rooney, 1926

Jack Collins, designer, all-composition, yarn wig, legs painted black, molded shoes

12"	$125.00	$475.00+
17"	$175.00	$700.00+

Baby Blossom, 1927, *"DES, J.L.Kallus"*

Composition upper torso, cloth lower body and legs, molded hair, open mouth

19"	$300.00	$1,100.00

Baby Bo Kaye

Composition head, molded hair, open mouth, glass eyes, light crazing

14"	$350.00	$675.00

Bandy, 1929
Composition head, wood segmented body, marked on hat *"General Electric Radio,"* designed by J. Kallus

18½"	$600.00	$1,000.00

Betty Boop, 1932
Composition head character, wood segmented body, molded hair, painted features, label on torso

11"	$200.00	$650.00
13½"	$200.00	$850.00

Champ, 1942
Composition with freckles

16"	$175.00	$585.00

Giggles, 1946, "Giggles Doll, A Cameo Doll"
Composition with molded loop for ribbon

12"	$75.00	$300.00
14"	$100.00	$500.00

Ho-Ho, 1940, painted plaster, laughing mouth

5½"	$50.00	$200.00

12" composition Giggles, molded brown hair and bangs, painted blue eyes, closed mouth, fully jointed, cotton print dress, circa 1930s, $350.00. Courtesy McMasters Harris Doll Auctions.

Joy, 1932
Composition head character, wood segmented body, molded hair, painted features, label on torso

10"	$75.00	$300.00
15"	$125.00	$475.00

Margie, 1929
Composition head character, wood segmented body, molded hair, painted features, label on torso

5½"	$65.00	$250.00
9½"	$75.00	$285.00
15"	$75.00	$350.00

Pete the Pup, 1930 – 1935
Composition head character, wood segmented body, molded hair, painted features, label on torso

9"	$70.00	$265.00

Pinkie, 1930 – 1935
Composition head character, wood segmented body, molded hair, painted features, label on torso

10"	$100.00	$375.00

Composition body

10"	$75.00	$285.00

Popeye, 1935
Composition head character, wood segmented body, molded hair, painted features, label on torso

14"	$75.00	$300.00

Pretty Bettsie
Composition head, molded hair, painted side-glancing eyes, open/closed mouth, composition one-piece body and limbs, wooden neck joint, molded and painted dress with ruffles, shoes, and socks, triangular red tag on chest marked *"Pretty Bettsie//Copyright J. Kallus"*

18"	$125.00	$500.00

Scootles, 1925+
Rose O'Neill design, all-composition, no marks, painted side-glancing eyes, paper wrist tag

8"	$200.00	$975.00* all original with hang tag
13"	$135.00	$425.00
15"	$185.00	$650.00
22"	$375.00	$1,500.00

Composition, sleep eyes

15"	$175.00	$700.00

Black composition

12"	$750.00*

"The Selling Fool," 1926
Wood segmented body, hat represents radio tube, composition advertising doll for RCA Radiotrons

16"	$200.00	$800.00

HARD PLASTIC AND VINYL
Baby Mine, 1962 – 1964
Vinyl and cloth, sleep eyes

16"	$25.00	$100.00
19"	$35.00	$125.00

On Miss Peep hinged body

16"	$35.00	$135.00

Ho Ho, *Rose O'Neill,* laughing mouth, squeaker, tag

White, 7"	$35.00	$200.00
Black, 7"	$65.00	$275.00

Miss Peep, 1957 – 1970s+
Pin jointed shoulders and hips, vinyl

15"	$35.00	$75.00
18"	$50.00	$100.00

Black

18"	$65.00	$125.00

1970s+, ball-jointed shoulders, hips

17"	$12.50	$50.00
21"	$25.00	$70.00

Miss Peep, Newborn, 1962, vinyl head and rigid plastic body

18"	$10.00	$40.00

Pinkie, 1950s

10 – 11"	$75.00	$150.00

Scootles, 1964, vinyl

14"	$50.00	$195.00
27"	$135.00	$535.00
Boxes 16"		$405.00*

Composition

AMERICAN, **unknown maker, or little known manufacturer.**

First price is for poorer quality, worn doll; second price is for excellent doll original or appropriate dress. More for exceptional dolls with elaborate costume or accessories.

Baby, 1910+

Wigged or molded hair, painted or sleep eyes, composition or cloth body with bent legs

12"	$65.00	$225.00
18"	$75.00	$300.00

Dionne Quintuplets, ca. 1934+, all-composition, jointed five-piece baby or toddler body, molded hair or wig, with painted or sleep eyes, closed or open mouth

7 – 8"	$35.00	$140.00
13"	$65.00	$250.00

Child

Costumed in ethnic or theme outfit, all composition, sleep or painted eyes, mohair wig, closed mouth, original costume

Lesser quality

9 – 11"	$15.00	$75.00

Better quality

9 – 11"	$25.00	$145.00

Dream World, ca. 1939, painted eyes

9 – 11"	$45.00	$185.00

Early child, ca. 1910 – 1920, unmarked, cork-stuffed cloth body, painted features, may have molded hair

12"	$35.00	$145.00
18"	$50.00	$200.00

Early Child, character face, ca. 1910 – 1920

12"	$50.00	$200.00
18"	$75.00	$300.00

MaMa doll, ca. 1922+, wigged or painted hair, sleep or painted eyes, cloth body, with crier and swing legs, lower composition legs and arms

16"	$70.00	$250.00
20"	$90.00	$350.00
24"	$115.00	$450.00

Patsy-type girl, 1928+, molded and painted bobbed hair, sleep or painted eyes, closed pouty mouth, composition or hard stuffed cloth body

14"	$70.00	$250.00
19"	$80.00	$300.00

With molded hair loop

15"	$50.00	$200.00

Shirley Temple-type girl, 1934+, all-composition, five-piece jointed body, blond curly wig, sleep eyes, open mouth, teeth, dimples

16"	$100.00	$400.00
19"	$125.00	$450.00

8" unmarked baby (Dionne Quint look-alike), molded and painted hair, painted brown side-glancing eyes, closed mouth, jointed at head, legs, and arms, bent baby legs, replaced white cotton gown and bonnet, circa 1950s, $50.00. Courtesy Carol Stover.

8½" unmarked doll (sometimes called Worlds Fair dolls) with brown mohair wig, painted features with side-glancing eyes, inexpensively molded, fully jointed, molded shoes, inexpensive cotton costume, circa 1939, $75.00. Courtesy Carol Stover.

8½" unmarked doll (Patsyette look-alike, sold by Vogue as Twinsie), molded and painted brown hair, brown painted eyes, good quality, fully jointed flannel pants and cap, blue felt top, original unmarked box, circa 1930s – 1940s, $150.00. Courtesy Carol Stover.

12" Carmen Miranda-type Dream World Doll, molded hair, painted face with side-glancing eyes, closed mouth, inexpensive fully jointed body, attached green taffeta costume, velvet turban with fruit trim, original unmarked box, doll unmarked, circa 1930s, $125.00. Courtesy Carol Stover.

Others

Animal head doll, ca. 1930s, all-composition on Patsy-type five-piece body, could be wolf, rabbit, cat, monkey

    9½" $55.00 $210.00

Denny Dimwitt, Toycraft Inc, ca. 1948, all-composition, nodder, painted clothing

    11½" $65.00 $225.00

Jackie Robinson, complete in box

    13" $300.00 $1,000.00

Kewty, 1930, made by Domec of Canada, all-composition Patsy-type, molded bobbed hair, closed mouth, sleep eyes, bent left arm

    13½" $80.00 $350.00

Lone Ranger, *"TLR Co, Inc.//Doll Craft Novelty Co. NYC,"* cloth body, hat marked

    20" $1,400.00* in original box

Louis Vuitton, 1955, ceramic, composition, with labeled case and wardrobe

    19" $2,200.00*

Maiden America, *"1915, Kate Silverman,"* all-composition, patriotic ribbon

    8½" $45.00 $185.00

Miss Curity, composition, eye shadow, nurse's uniform

    18" $150.00 $500.00

Monica Studios, See that category.

Pinocchio, composition and wood character

    16½" $125.00 $425.00

Puzzy, 1948, *"H of P"*

    15" $100.00 $400.00

Raleigh, Jessie McCutcheon, 1916 – 1920, Chicago, IL. All-composition, painted or sleep eyes, painted and molded hair or wigged, cloth or composition bodies, some with metal spring joints, unmarked

    Baby

    11½" $100.00 $400.00

    13½" $125.00 $500.00

    Child

    16½" $165.00 $650.00

    18½" $235.00 $950.00

Refugee, Madame Louise Doll Co. ca. 1945, represents victims of WWII

    20" $550.00* MIB

Reliable Toy Company Limited, 1920 – 1991, Toronto, Canada

Made composition, hard plastic, and vinyl dolls, some dolls with license from American doll manufacturers. First price for dolls with flaws; second price for all-original dolls, near mint. Add more for unusual characters.

    Child

    12" $50.00 $175.00

    17" $65.00 $250.00

Santa Claus, composition molded head, composition body, original suit, sack

19"	$150.00	$500.00

Sizzy, 1948, "H of P"

14"	$75.00	$300.00

Thumbs-Up, to raise money for ambulances during WWII, see photo first edition

8"	$50.00	$175.00

Uncle Sam, various makers
All original, cloth body

13"	$900.00*

Ca. 1918, straw-filled

30"	$450.00*

Whistler, composition head, cotton body, composition arms, open mouth

14½"	$125.00	$225.00

GERMAN

Composition head, composition or cloth body, wig or molded and painted hair, closed or open mouth with teeth, dressed. May be Amusco, Sonneberger Porzellanfabrik, or others.

19" unmarked doll, molded and painted reddish curls, tin sleep eyes, closed mouth, fully jointed inexpensive body, re-dressed in vintage cotton dress with zipper, circa 1930s, $75.00. Courtesy Carol Stover.

Character Baby
Cloth body

18"	$95.00	$350.00

Composition baby body, bent limbs

16"	$125.00	$425.00

Child
Composition shoulder head, cloth body, composition arms

20"	$150.00	$300.00

Socket head, all-composition body

19"	$125.00	$425.00
21"	$175.00	$500.00

Petzold, Dora made character child, ca. 1920s, cloth body

19"	$175.00	$575.00

NEAPOLITAN

Adult, finely modeled character face, stick or wire bodies, elaborately dressed

13 – 14"	$1,300.00	$1,800.00
16"	$1,700.00	$2,000.00

Cosmopolitan

Ginger, ca. 1955, hard plastic, bent knees

7½"	$40.00	$150.00

Straight leg

7½"	$50.00	$200.00

Little Miss Ginger, ca. 1957, vinyl, rooted hair, sleep eyes, teen doll, tagged clothes

10½"	$50.00	$190.00

---

* at auction

20" vinyl, soft vinyl head, Candy Fashion doll, rooted saran hair, sleep eyes with lashes, closed mouth, jointed at neck, shoulders, hips, and knees, high-heeled feet, sold at food markets with four matching ensembles in box, marked on head "21HH/K74," circa 1950s, $200.00. Courtesy Carol Stover.

Deluxe Topper, Deluxe Premium, also uses names Topper Toys and Topper Corp. Made mechanical dolls, battery operated, ca. 1955 – 1972. These play dolls are collectible because so few survived intact.

First price is for played-with doll, second price is for complete doll, in excellent-to-mint condition.

HARD PLASTIC OR VINYL

Baby

Baby Boo, 1965, battery operated

21"	$120.00	$200.00

Baby Catch A Ball, 1969 (Topper Toys), battery operated

18"	$128.00* MIB

Baby Magic, 1966, blue sleep eyes, rooted saran hair, magic wand has magnet that opens/closes eyes

18"	$100.00	$200.00

Baby Peek 'N Play, 1969, battery operated

18"	$12.00	$45.00

Baby Tickle Tears

14"	$9.00	$35.00

Suzy Cute, move arm and face changes expressions

7"	$15.00	$90.00

8½" vinyl Penny Brite, blond rooted hair, painted side-glancing eyes, five-piece jointed body, cotton red and white dress, hair bow, plastic shoes, original plastic swing lid box printed "Penny Brite" on front, doll marked "Deluxe Reading Corp.//Elizabeth, N.J.//Patent Pending," circa 1963, $45.00. Courtesy Carol Stover.

Child or Adult

Betty Bride, 1957, also called Sweet Rosemary, Sweet Judy, Sweet Amy, one-piece vinyl body and limbs, more if many accessories

30"	$25.00	$90.00

Candy Fashion, 1958, made by Deluxe Premium, a division of Deluxe Reading, sold in grocery stores, came with three dress forms, extra outfits

21"	$25.00	$200.00

Dawn Series, circa 1969 – 1970s, all-vinyl doll with additional friends, Angie, Daphne, Denise, Glori, Jessica, Kip, Long Locks, Majorette, Maureen, black versions of Van and Dale. Accessories available, included Apartment, Fashion Show, outfits

Dawn

6"	$15.00	$200.00 MIB

Car

	$150.00*	

Glori, red dress

6"	$180.00* MIP	

Dawn & other outfits
Loose, but complete $10.00+
    NRFP $25.00+
Fashion Show Stage in box
                $50.00 $75.00
Go Gos
Private Ida, 1965, one of the Go Gos
    6" $6.00 $45.00
Tom Boy, 1965, one of the Go Gos
    6" $12.00 $45.00
Little Miss Fussy, battery operated
    18" $6.00 $35.00
Little Red Riding Hood, 1955, vinyl, synthetic hair, rubber body, book, basket
    23" $50.00 $125.00
Penny Brite, circa 1963+, all-vinyl, rooted blond hair, painted eyes, bendable and straight legs, extra outfits, case, furniture available
Marks: "A – 9/B150 (or B65) DELUXE READING CORP.//c. 1963."
    8" $40.00 $125.00
Outfit, NRFP $25.00 $40.00
Kitchen set $100.00
Suzy Homemaker, 1964, hard plastic and vinyl, jointed knees
Mark: "Deluxe Reading Co."
    21" $12.00 $45.00
Suzy Smart, ca. 1962, vinyl, sleep eyes, closed mouth, rooted blond ponytail, hard plastic body, The Talking School Doll, desk, chair, easel
    25" $50.00 $300.00

Eegee

1917+, Brooklyn, NY. E.G. Goldberger made composition and cloth dolls, imported bisque heads from Armand Marseille, made character head composition, mama dolls, babies, carnival dolls, and later the company made hard plastic and vinyl dolls.

First price for played-with doll, second price for completely original excellent condition doll.

> *Marks:*
> *Trademark, EEGEE,*
> *or circle with the words,*
> *"TRADEMARK*
> *//EEGEE//Dolls//MADE*
> *IN USA"*
> *Later changed to just*
> *initials, E.G.*

COMPOSITION
Add more for exceptional doll, tagged, extra outfits, or accessories.
Baby, cloth body, bent limbs
    16" $25.00 $100.00
Child, open mouth, sleep eyes
    14" $40.00 $160.00
    18" $55.00 $210.00
MaMa Doll, ca. 1920s – 1930s, composition head, sleep or painted eyes, wigged or molded hair, cloth body with crier, swing legs, composition lower arms and legs
    16" $75.00 $250.00
    20" $100.00 $350.00

* at auction

Miss Charming, 1936, all-composition, Shirley Temple look-alike

19"	$125.00	$450.00

Miss Charming, pin-back button $50.00

HARD PLASTIC AND VINYL

Andy, 1963, vinyl, teen-type, molded and painted hair, painted eyes, closed mouth

12"	$9.00	$35.00

Annette, 1963, vinyl, teen-type fashion, rooted hair, painted eyes

11½"	$15.00	$55.00

Child, 1966, marked *"20/25 M/13"*

19"	$10.00	$50.00

Child, walker, all-vinyl rooted long blond hair or short curly wig, blue sleep eyes, closed mouth

25"	$15.00	$50.00
28"	$20.00	$65.00
36"	$25.00	$85.00

Babette, 1970, vinyl head, stuffed limbs, cloth body, painted or sleep eyes, rooted hair

15"	$10.00	$40.00
25"	$18.00	$65.00

Baby Care, 1969, vinyl, molded or rooted hair, sleep or set glassine eyes, drink and wet doll, with complete nursery set

18"	$12.00	$45.00

Baby Carrie, 1970, rooted or molded hair, sleep or set glassine eyes with plastic carriage or carry seat

24"	$15.00	$60.00

Baby Luv, 1973, vinyl head, rooted hair, painted eyes, open/closed mouth, marked *"B.T. Eegee,"* cloth body, pants are part of body

14"	$10.00	$35.00

Baby Susan, 1958, *marked "Baby Susan" on head*

8½"	$4.00	$20.00

Baby Tandy Talks, 1963, pull string activates talking mechanism, vinyl head, rooted hair, sleep eyes, cotton and foam-stuffed body and limbs

14"	$10.00	$35.00
20"	$20.00	$65.00

Ballerina, 1964, vinyl head and hard plastic body

31"	$25.00	$100.00

1967, vinyl head, foam-filled body

18"	$8.00	$30.00

Barbara Cartland, painted features, adult

15"	$15.00	$52.00

Beverly Hillbillies, Clampett family from 1960s TV sitcom

Car	$80.00	$350.00

Granny Clampett, gray rooted hair

14"	$20.00	$65.00

Fields, W. C., 1980, vinyl ventriloquist doll by Juro, division of Goldberger

30"	$65.00	$210.00

Flowerkins, 1963

Marked "F-2" on head; seven dolls in series.

Boxed 16"	$15.00	$60.00

Gemmette, 1963, rooted hair, sleep eyes, jointed vinyl, dressed in gem colored dress, includes child's jeweled ring, Misses Amethyst, Diamond, Emerald, Ruby, Sapphire, and Topaz

15½"	$15.00	$50.00

Georgie, Georgette, 1971, vinyl head, cloth bodies, redheaded twins

22"	$12.00	$50.00

Gigi Perreau, 1951, early vinyl head, hard plastic body, open/closed smiling mouth

17"	$175.00	$700.00

Karena Ballerina, 1958, vinyl head, rooted hair, sleep eyes, closed mouth, hard plastic body, jointed knees, ankles, neck, shoulders, and hips, head turns when walks

21"	$12.00	$45.00

Little Debutantes, 1958, vinyl head, rooted hair, sleep eyes, closed mouth, hard plastic body, swivel waist, high-heeled feet

18"	$15.00	$50.00
20"	$20.00	$75.00

My Fair Lady, 1958, all-vinyl, fashion type, swivel waist, fully jointed

20"	$15.00	$75.00

Parton, Dolly, 1978

11½"	$5.00	$25.00
18"	$12.00	$45.00

Posi Playmate, 1969, vinyl head, foam-filled vinyl body, bendable arms and legs, painted or rooted hair, sleep or painted eyes

12"	$5.00	$20.00

Puppetrina, 1963+, vinyl head, cloth body, rooted hair, sleep eyes, pocket in back for child to insert hand to manipulate doll's head and arms

22"	$45.00	$90.00

Shelly, 1964, Tammy-type, grow hair

12"	$5.00	$18.00

Sniffles, 1963, vinyl head, rooted hair, sleep eyes, open/closed mouth, *marked "13/14 AA-EEGEE"*

12"	$5.00	$20.00

Susan Stroller, ca. 1955, vinyl head, hard plastic walker body, rooted hair, closed mouth

20"	$35.00	$75.00
23"	$45.00	$90.00
26"	$50.00	$100.00

Tandy Talks, 1961, vinyl head, hard plastic body, freckles, pull string talker

20"	$15.00	$55.00

Effanbee

Effanbee Doll Company, 1910+, New York, NY. Bernard E. Fleischaker and Hugo Baum founders. Trademark *"EFFANBEE DOLLS//THEY WALK//THEY TALK//THEY SLEEP"* registered in 1918. Made dolls in composition and later hard plastic and vinyl. The new management recently introduced limited edition collectible dolls such as Patsy Joan, Skippy, Wee Patsy, and others.

Marks:
Some marked on
shoulder plate,
"EFFANBEE
//BABY DAINTY"
or "EFFANBEE
//DOLLS//WALK,
TALK, SLEEP"
in oval

18" cloth Pat-o-Pat, hand-painted mask face, side-glancing eyes, yarn ringlet wig, hands clap together when you push chest, turning head, original organdy print dress and bonnet, wrist tag printed "Effanbee/Pat-o-Pat Doll," circa 1940, $425.00. Courtesy Shirley's Doll House, Wheeling, IL.

16" cloth body Effanbee Doll Club prototype of Baby Grumpy, molded vinyl face with furrowed brow, molded and painted red hair, painted features, vinyl hands, cotton gown and bonnet, doll tag marked "Effanbee/176/Baby Grumpy/ 1917, 1988, Effanbee, N.Y., N.Y.," circa 1988, $75.00. Courtesy Shirley's Doll House, Wheeling, IL.

First price indicates played-with doll in good condition, but with flaws; second price indicates doll in excellent condition with appropriate or original clothes. More for exceptional doll with wardrobe or accessories.

BISQUE

Mary Jane, ca. 1920

Some with bisque heads, others all-composition; bisque head, manufactured by Lenox Potteries, NJ, for Effanbee, sleep eyes, composition body, wooden arms and legs, wears Bluebird pin

20"	$525.00	$700.00

EARLY COMPOSITION

Babies

Baby Bud, 1918+

All-composition, painted features, molded hair, open/closed mouth, jointed arms, legs molded to body. One finger goes into mouth.

6"	$50.00	$195.00
Black	$65.00	$225.00

Baby Dainty, 1912+

Name given to a variety of dolls, with composition heads, cloth bodies, some toddler types, some mama-types with crier

12 – 14"	$80.00	$245.00
15"	$125.00	$400.00
Vinyl		
10"	$10.00	$40.00

Baby Effanbee, ca. 1925

Composition head, cloth body

12 – 13"	$45.00	$165.00

Baby Evelyn, ca. 1925

Composition head, cloth body

17"	$75.00	$275.00

Baby Grumpy, 1915+, also later variations

Composition character, heavily molded and painted hair, frowning eyebrows, painted intaglio eyes, pin-jointed limbs, cork-stuffed cloth body, gauntlet arms, pouty mouth

Mold #172, 174, 176

11½"	$85.00	$325.00
14½"	$125.00	$425.00

Baby Grumpy Gladys, 1923, composition shoulder head, cloth body

Marked in oval, "Effanbee/Baby Grumpy/ copr. 1923"

15"	$85.00	$350.00

Grumpy Aunt Dinah, black, cloth body, striped stocking legs

14½"	$110.00	$425.00

19", 17", 19½" composition American Children with human hair wigs, girls have blue sleep eyes, boy painted brown eyes, five-piece composition bodies, original clothing, girls marked "Effanbee//American//Children," on back of head, boy unmarked, circa late 1930s, $650.00, $1,050.00, $1,500.00, respectively. Courtesy McMasters Harris Doll Auctions.

Grumpykins, 1927, composition head, cloth body, composition arms, some with cloth legs, others with composition legs

12"	$75.00	$300.00
Black	$85.00	$375.00

Grumpykins, Pennsylvania Dutch Dolls, ca. 1936, dressed by Marie Polack in Mennonite, River Brethren, and Amish costumes

12"	$85.00	$300.00

Bubbles, ca. 1924+

Composition shoulder head, open/closed mouth, painted teeth, molded and painted hair, sleep eyes, cloth body, bent-cloth legs, some with composition toddler legs, composition arms, finger of left hand fits into mouth, wore heart necklace. *Various marks including "Effanbee//Bubbles//Copr. 1924//Made in U.S.A."*

16"	$100.00	$375.00
22"	$125.00	$525.00
25"	$200.00	$750.00

Lamkin, ca. 1930+

Composition molded head, sleep eyes, open mouth, cloth body, crier, chubby composition legs, with feet turned in, fingers curled, molded gold ring on middle finger

16"	$150.00	$475.00

Pat-o-Pat, 1925+

Composition head, painted eyes, cloth body with mechanism which, when pressed causes hands to clap

13"	$50.00	$150.00
15"	$80.00	$200.00

Characters, 1912+

Composition, heavily molded hair, painted eyes, pin-jointed cloth body, composition arms, cloth or composition legs. *Some marked "Deco"*

Cliquot Eskimo, ca. 1920

Painted eyes, molded hair, felt hands, mohair suit

18"	$150.00	$525.00

Coquette, Naughty Marietta, ca. 1915+

Composition girl, molded bow in hair, side-glancing eyes, cloth body

12"	$100.00	$400.00

Harmonica Joe, 1923

Cloth body, with rubber ball when squeezed, provides air to open mouth with harmonica

15"	$85.00	$350.00

25" composition shoulder head, Lovums, molded and painted hair, brown sleep eyes with real lashes, painted upper and lower lashes, open mouth with two upper and lower teeth, original white organdy gown and bonnet, composition arms and legs, cloth body, unplayed with condition, original box, marked on back of shoulder plate "Effanbee//Lovums//©// Pat. No 1.283.558," circa late 1930s, $675.00. Courtesy McMasters Harris Doll Auctions.

15" composition Barbara Joan from American Children collection by Deweese Cochran, auburn human hair braided wig, sleep eyes, open mouth with four teeth, fully jointed body, red check dress, marked on back of head "Effanbee," on body "Effanbee//Anne-Shirley," circa 1936 – 1939, $700.00. Courtesy Jo Barckley.

Irish Mail Kid, 1915, or Dixie Flyer
Composition head, cloth body, arms sewn to steering handle of wooden wagon

10"	$125.00	$350.00

Johnny Tu-face, 1912
Composition head with face on front and back, painted features, open/closed crying mouth, closed smiling mouth, molded and painted hair, cloth body, red striped legs, cloth feet, dressed in knitted romper and hat

16"	$150.00	$325.00

Pouting Bess, 1915
Composition head with heavily molded curls, painted eyes, closed mouth, cloth cork stuffed body, pin jointed. *Mark: "166" on back of head*

15"	$85.00	$350.00

Whistling Jim, 1916
Composition head, with heavily molded hair, painted intaglio eyes, perforated mouth, cork stuffed cloth body, black sewn-on cloth shoes, wears red striped shirt, blue overalls. *Mark, label: "Effanbee//Whistling Jim//Trade Mark"*

15"	$85.00	$350.00

LATE COMPOSITION

American Children, 1936 – 1939+
All-composition, designed by Dewees Cochran, open mouth, separated fingers can wear gloves. *Marks: heads may be unmarked, "Effanbee//Anne Shirley" on body*

Barbara Joan

15"	$350.00	$700.00

Barbara Ann

17"	$1,400.00* MIB	

Barbara Lou

21"	$450.00	$900.00

Closed mouth, separated fingers, sleep or painted eyes. *Marks: "Effanbee//American//Children" on head; "Effanbee//Anne Shirley" on body*

Boy

17"	$400.00	$1,600.00

Gloria Ann, paper purse tag reads *"Gloria Ann"*

18½"	$400.00	$1,600.00

Peggy Lou, paper purse tag, holds gloves, reads, *"Peggy Lou"*

20½"	$500.00	$1,800.00

14" composition Skippy cowboy, molded hair, painted brown, painted blue eyes, closed mouth, cloth body with composition arms, legs, molded and painted socks and shoes, head swivels, fully jointed, original red and brown suede chaps, red plaid shirt, marked on head "Effanbee//Skippy//©//P.L. Crosby," c. 1930s, $600.00. Courtesy McMasters Harris Doll Auctions.

20" composition shoulder head Charlie McCarthy, painted hair and features, brown painted eyes, mouth opens with ten teeth painted on lower jaw, pink cloth body, composition hands and feet, stitch-jointed at shoulders, hips, and knees, original tuxedo and top hat, marked on back of shoulder plate "Edgar Bergen's Charlie McCarthy// an Effanbee Product," circa 1937, $775.00. Courtesy Shirley's Doll House, Wheeling, IL.

Anne Shirley, 1936 – 1940

Never advertised as such, same mold used for Little Lady. All-composition, more grown-up body style. *Mark: "EFFANBEE//ANNE SHIRLEY"*

14"	$75.00	$300.00
21"	$125.00	$425.00
27"	$150.00	$625.00

Movie Anne Shirley, 1935 – 1940

1934 RKO movie character, Anne Shirley from *Anne of Green Gables* movie. All-composition, marked *"Patsy"* or other Effanbee doll, red braids, wearing Anne Shirley movie costume and gold paper hang tag stating *"I am Anne Shirley."* The Anne Shirley costume changes the identity of these dolls.

Mary Lee/Anne Shirley, open mouth, head marked *"©Mary Lee,"* on marked *"Patsy Joan"* body

16"	$250.00	$500.00

Patsyette/Anne Shirley, body marked *"Effanbee// Patsyette// Doll"*

9½"	$150.00	$325.00

Patricia/Anne Shirley, body marked *"Patricia"*

15"	$200.00	$550.00

Patricia-kin/Anne Shirley, head marked *"Patricia-kin,"* body marked *"Effanbee//Patsy Jr.,"* hang tag reads *"Anne Shirley"*

11½"	$175.00	$375.00

Brother or Sister, 1943

Composition head, hands, cloth body, legs, yarn hair, painted eyes

Brother

6"	$60.00	$235.00

Sister

12"	$45.00	$175.00

Butin-nose: See Patsy family, and vinyl.

Candy Kid, 1946+

All-composition, sleep eyes, toddler body, molded and painted hair, closed mouth

13½"	$75.00	$300.00

Black

13½"	$150.00	$600.00

18" composition Majorette, sleep eyes with lashes, closed mouth, yarn hair, fully jointed, gold and white majorette costume, brass buttons, originally had high hat with gold trim, marked on head "Effanbee," circa early 1940s, $400.00. Courtesy Marge Meisinger.

Charlie McCarthy, 1937

Composition head, hands, feet, painted features, mouth opens, cloth body, legs, *marked: "Edgar Bergen's Charlie McCarthy//An Effanbee Product"*

15"	$125.00	$550.00
17 – 19"	$175.00	$775.00
19"	$2,000.00* in box, top hat, tails	

* at auction

20" composition Howdy Doody, molded and painted hair, brown eyes with no lashes, open/closed mouth has painted teeth, freckles, stuffed cloth body with composition hands, original check shirt, blue pants, scarf personalized "Howdy Doody," felt hat, boots, doll not marked, circa late 1940s, $275.00. Courtesy Marge Meisinger.

Happy Birthday Doll, ca. 1940
Music box in body, heart bracelet
17" $1,050.00*

Historical Dolls, 1939+
All-composition, jointed body, human hair wigs, painted eyes, made only three sets of 30 dolls depicting history of apparel, 1492 – 1939, very fancy original costumes, metal heart bracelet. *Head marked "Effanbee//American//Children," on body, "Effanbee//Anne Shirley."*
21" $650.00 $1,500.00+
Too few in database for reliable range.

Historical Replicas, 1939+
All-composition, jointed body, copies of sets above, but smaller, human hair wigs, painted eyes, original costumes
14" $250.00 $600.00

Honey, ca. 1947 – 1948
All-composition jointed body, human hair wig, sleep eyes, closed mouth
18" $80.00 $300.00
21" $100.00 $400.00
All hard plastic, ca. 1949 – 1955, see Vinyl and Hard Plastic later in this category.

Howdy-Doody, 1947 – 1949
Composition head, brown sleep eyes, open/closed mouth, molded and painted teeth, cloth body, plaid shirt, personalized neck scarf, *"HOWDY DOODY,"* jeans and boots, cowboy hat
Effanbee gold heart paper hang tag reads *"I AM AN//EFFANBEE //DURABLE DOLL//THE DOLL//SATIN-SMOOTH//SKIN."*
20" $65.00 $275.00
23" $75.00 $300.00

17" composition Little Lady, mohair wig, sleep eyes with lashes, closed mouth, fully jointed, wrist tag "I am Little Lady/an EFFANBEE DURABLE DOLL," original yellow dress with orchid ribbon, marked on neck "Effanbee/ U.S.A.," circa 1939, $400.00. Courtesy Mary Lu Trowbridge.

Ice Queen, 1937+
Composition, open mouth, skater outfit
17" $200.00 $850.00

Little Lady, 1939+
Used Anne Shirley mold. All-composition, wigged, sleep eyes, more grown-up body, separated fingers, gold paper hang tag. Many in formals, as brides, or fancy gowns with matching parasol. During war years yarn hair was used; may have gold hang tag with name, like Gaye or Carole.
15" $365.00* box
18" $95.00 $325.00
21" $125.00 $425.00
27" $150.00 $625.00

Lovums, ca. 1928

Composition swivel head, shoulder plate, and limbs, cloth body, sleep eyes, molded and painted hair or wigged, can have bent baby legs or toddler legs

16"	$100.00	$400.00
20"	$125.00	$450.00

Mae Starr, ca. 1928

Talking doll, composition shoulder head, cloth body, open mouth, four teeth, with cylinder records

Marked: "Mae//Starr// Doll"

29"	$200.00	$750.00

MaMa Dolls, ca. 1921+

Composition shoulder head, painted or sleep eyes, molded hair or wigged, cloth body, swing legs, crier, with composition arms and lower legs

18"	$75.00	$350.00
24"	$125.00	$400.00

Marionettes, 1937+

Puppets designed by Virginia Austin, composition, painted eyes

Clippo, clown

15"	$85.00	$300.00

Emily Ann

14"	$85.00	$300.00

Lucifer, black

15"	$525.00* mint-in-box	

Marilee, ca. 1924

Mama doll, with composition shoulder head, sleep eyes, open mouth, cloth body, crier, swing legs

Marked on shoulder plate: "Effanbee//Marilee// Copyr.//Doll" in oval

24"	$150.00	$550.00
27"	$175.00	$600.00

Portrait Dolls, ca. 1940

All-composition, Bo-Peep, Ballerina, Bride, Groom, Gibson Girl, Colonial Maid, etc.

12"	$65.00	$250.00

Rosemary, 1926

Mark: "EFFANBEE// ROSEMARY//WALK// TALK//SLEEP" in oval "MADE IN US"

18"	$100.00	$350.00
24"	$150.00	$425.00

Suzanne, ca. 1940

All-composition, jointed body, sleep eyes, wigged, closed mouth, may have magnets in hands to hold accessories. More for additional accessories or wardrobe.

14"	$100.00	$325.00

14" composition Skippy sailor, molded hair painted brown, painted blue eyes, closed mouth, cloth body with composition arms and legs, molded and painted socks and shoes, head swivels, fully jointed, original blue sailor uniform, marked "Effanbee//Skippy//©//P. L. Crosby," circa 1930s, $600.00. Courtesy McMasters Harris Doll Auctions.

9" composition Patsyette, mohair wig, painted brown eyes, closed mouth, jointed five-piece body with bent right arm, original pink dress and hat, original box printed "PATSYETTE/AN/ EFFANBEE/DURABLE/DOLL," doll marked on back "Effanbee//Patsyette//Doll," circa 1930s, $425.00. Courtesy Mary Lu Trowbridge.

9" composition Patsyette Wardrobe, painted brown eyes, closed mouth, fully jointed, bent right arm, original pink dress, jointed five-piece body, additional outfits, box printed "PATSYETTE/AN/EFFAN-BEE/DURABLE/DOLL," doll marked on back "Effanbee//Patsyette//Doll," circa 1930s, $550.00. Courtesy McMaster Doll Auctions.

14" composition Skippy soldier, molded hair painted brown, painted blue eyes, closed mouth, cloth body with composition arms, legs, molded and painted socks and shoes, head swivels, fully jointed, original uniform and box, marked on head "Effanbee//Skippy//©//P.L. Crosby," circa 1930s, $725.00. Courtesy McMasters Harris Doll Auctions.

Suzette, ca. 1939

All-composition, fully jointed, painted side-glancing eyes, closed mouth, wigged

11"	$75.00	$265.00

Sweetie Pie, 1939+

Also called Baby Bright Eyes, Tommy Tucker, Mickey, composition bent limbs, sleep eyes, caracul wig, cloth body, crier. Issued again in 1952+ in hard plastic, cloth body, and vinyl limbs, painted hair or synthetic wigs. Wore same pink rayon taffeta dress with black and white trim as Noma doll.

16"	$75.00	$300.00
20"	$85.00	$350.00
24"	$100.00	$400.00

W. C. Fields, 1929+

Composition shoulder head, painted features, hinged mouth, painted teeth. In 1980 made in vinyl. See Legend Series.

Marked: "W.C. Fields//An Effanbee Product"

17½"	$250.00	$950.00

PATSY FAMILY, 1928+

Composition through 1947, later issued in vinyl and porcelain. Many had gold paper hang tag and metal bracelet that read "Effanbee Durable Dolls." More for black, special editions, costumes, or with added accessories.

Babies

Patsy Baby, 1931

Painted or sleep eyes, wigged or molded hair, composition baby body, advertised as Babykin, came also with cloth body, in pair, layettes, trunks

Marks: on head, "Effanbee//Patsy Baby"; on body, "Effanbee //Patsy// Baby"

10 – 11"	$125.00	$350.00
11"	$475.00* boxed	

Patsy Babyette, 1932

Sleep eyes

Marked on head "Effanbee"; on body, "Effanbee//Patsy //Babyette"

9"	$100.00	$325.00

Patsy Baby Tinyette, 1934

Painted eyes, bent-leg composition body

Marked on head, "Effanbee"; on body, "Effanbee//Baby//Tinyette"

6½"	$90.00	$300.00

Quints, 1935

Set of five Patsy Baby Tinyettes in original box, from FAO Schwarz, organdy christening gowns and milk glass bottles, excellent condition

Set of five

6½"	$450.00	$1,750.00

9" composition Patsy Babyette, molded hair, sleep eyes with lashes and lashes painted under, fully jointed with bent baby legs, original organdy smocked gown, marked on back "Effanbee// Patsy Babyette," on neck "Effanbee," circa 1930s, $325.00. Courtesy Carol Stover.

Children

Patsy, ca. 1924, cloth body, composition legs, open mouth, upper teeth, sleep eyes, painted or human hair wig, with composition legs to hips. *Marked in half oval on back shoulder plate:"Effanbee//Patsy"*

15"	$100.00	$300.00

Patsy, ca. 1926, mama doll, open mouth, upper teeth, sleep eyes, human hair wig, cloth body with crier and swing legs, composition arms and lower legs. *Marked on shoulder plate in oval: "Effanbee//Patsy//Copr.// Doll"*

22"	$100.00	$400.00
29"	$150.00	$550.00

Patsy, 1928, all-composition jointed body, painted or sleep eyes, molded headband on red molded bobbed hair, or wigged, bent right arm, with gold paper hang tag, metal heart bracelet. *Marked on body: "Effanbee//Patsy//Pat. Pend.//Doll"*

14"	$225.00	$550.00

Patsy, Oriental with black painted hair, painted eyes, in fancy silk pajamas and matching shoes

14"	$350.00	$750.00

Patsy, 1946, all-composition jointed body, bright facial coloring, painted or sleep eyes, wears pink or blue checked pinafore

14"	$200.00	$450.00

Patsy Alice, ca. 1933, advertised in Effanbee's *Patsytown News* for two years

24"	$400.00	$1,200.00

No doll with this name has been positively identified.

14" composition Patsy, auburn mohair wig, brown glassine eyes, closed mouth, white dotted-Swiss dress, marked on neck in oval "EFFAN-BEE//PATSY," circa 1931, $350.00. Courtesy Marge Meisinger.

Patsy Ann, 1929, all-composition, closed mouth, sleep eyes, molded hair, or wigged. *Marked on body: "Effanbee//'Patsy-Ann'//©//Pat. #1283558"*

19"	$275.00	$600.00
19"	$875.00* boxed, tagged	

Patsy Ann, 1959, all-vinyl, full jointed, rooted saran hair, sleep eyes, freckles across nose. *Head marked "Effanbee// Patsy Ann//©1959"; body marked "Effanbee//Official Girl Scout"*

15"	$75.00	$250.00

Patsy Ann, 1959, limited edition, vinyl, sleep eyes, white organdy dress, with pink hair ribbon

Marked "Effanbee//Patsy Ann//©1959" on head; "Effanbee" on body

15"	$100.00	$285.00

9" composition Bicentennial George Washington, mohair wig, painted brown eyes, closed mouth, jointed, original blue and gold felt costume, marked on back "Effanbee//Patsyette//Doll," circa 1932, $425.00. Courtesy Shirley's Doll House, Wheeling, IL.

18" composition Little Lady, real hair wig, sleep eyes with lashes, jointed body, organdy South American dress shown in 1942 Montgomery Ward Christmas Catalog, marked on neck "Effanbee/ U.S.A.," circa 1942, $350.00. Courtesy Marge Meisinger.

Patsyette, 1931, composition
9½" $150.00 $425.00
Black, Dutch, Hawaiian
9½" $200.00 $650.00+

Patsy Fluff, 1932
All-cloth, with painted features, pink checked rompers and bonnet
16" $500.00 $1,000.00
Too few examples in database for reliable range.

Patsy Joan, 1931, composition
16" $225.00 $550.00

Patsy Joan, 1946
Marked "Effandbee" on body, with extra "d" added
17" $200.00 $500.00

Patsy Jr., 1931
All-composition, advertised as Patsykins.
Marks: "Effanbee//Patsy Jr.//Doll"
11½" $150.00 $400.00

Patsy Lou, 1930
All-composition, molded red hair or wigged.
Marks: "Effanbee//Patsy Lou" on body
22" $275.00 $625.00

Patsy Mae, 1934
Shoulder head, sleep eyes, cloth body, crier, swing legs. *Marks: "Effanbee//Patsy Mae" on head; "Effanbee//Lovums//c//Pat. No. 1283558" on shoulder plate*
29" $700.00 $1,400.00

Patsy Ruth, 1934
Shoulder head, sleep eyes, cloth body, crier, swing legs. *Marks: "Effanbee//Patsy Ruth" on head; "Effanbee//Lovums//©//Pat. No. 1283558" on shoulder plate*
26" $650.00 $1,300.00+

Patsy Tinyette Toddler, ca. 1935
Painted eyes. *Marks: "Effanbee" on head; "Effanbee// Baby//Tinyette" on body*
7¾" $100.00 $325.00+

Tinyette Toddler, tagged *"Kit & Kat"*
In Dutch costume
$800.00 for pair

Wee Patsy, 1935
Head molded to body, molded and painted shoes and socks, jointed arms and hips, advertised only as "Fairy Princess," pinback button. *Marks on body: "Effanbee//Wee Patsy"*
5¾" $150.00 $475.00
In trousseau box
$250.00 $650.00+

Related items
Metal heart bracelet, reads *"Effanbee Durable Dolls"* (original bracelets can still be ordered from Shirley's Doll House) $25.00

Metal personalized name bracelet for Patsy family
$65.00

Patsy Ann, Her Happy Times, c. 1935, book by Mona Reed King $75.00

Patsy For Keeps, c 1932, book by Ester Marian Ames $125.00

PATRICIA SERIES, 1935, all sizes advertised in *Patsytown News*

All-composition slimmer bodies, sleep eyes, wigged, later WWII-era Patricia dolls had yarn hair and cloth bodies

Patricia, wig, sleep eyes, marked, *"Effanbee Patricia"* body

15"	$225.00	$525.00

Patricia Ann, wig, marks unknown

19"	$375.00	$750.00

Too few in database for reliable range.

Patricia Joan, wig, marks unknown, slimmer legs

16"	$325.00	$650.00

Too few in database for reliable range.

Patricia-Kin, wig. *Mark: "Patricia-Kin"* head; *"Effanbee//Patsy Jr."* body

11½"	$275.00	$450.00

Patricia Lou, wig, marks unknown

22"	$300.00	$600.00

Too few in database for reliable range.

Patricia Ruth

Head marked: "Effanbee//Patsy Ruth," no marks on slimmer composition body

27"	$700.00	$1,350.00
27"	$3,600.00*	

PATSY RELATED DOLLS AND VARIANTS

Betty Bee, tousel head, 1932

All-composition, short tousel wig, sleep eyes. *Marked on body: "Effanbee//Patsy Lou"*

22"	$250.00	$400.00

Betty Bounce, tousel head, 1932+

All-composition, sleep eyes, used Lovums head on body, *marked: "Effanbee//'Patsy Ann'/ /©//Pat. #1283558"*

19"	$200.00	$350.00

Betty Brite, 1932

All-composition, short tousel wig, sleep eyes, some marked: *"Effanbee//Betty Brite"* on body and others marked on head *"© Mary-Lee"*; on body, *"Effanbee Patsy Joan"*

Gold hang tag reads *"This is Betty Brite, The lovable Imp with tiltable head and movable limb, an Effanbee doll."*

16"	$175.00	$300.00

7¾" composition White House Inn Tinyette Toddlers, molded and painted hair, painted brown eyes, closed mouths, fully jointed, original boy's felt costume with pin, girl's cotton dress felt hat, marked "Effanbee," circa 1935, $650.00 pair. Courtesy Shirley's Doll House, Wheeling, IL.

15" composition #1607 Indian, Historical Series, painted eyes, closed mouth, braided human hair wig, jointed body painted brown, fringed buckskin top and legging, beads, marked on back "Effanbee/Anne Shirley," circa 1939, $600.00. Courtesy Marge Meisinger.

12" composition Candy Kid, molded hair painted brown, sleep eyes with real lashes and painted under, closed mouth, five-piece toddler body, plaid jumper with matching bonnet, marked on head and back "Effanbee," circa 1930s, $450.00. Courtesy McMasters Harris Doll Auctions.

Butin-nose, ca. 1936+

All-composition, molded and painted hair, features, distinct feature is small nose, usually has regional or special costume; name "button" misspelled to "Butin"

8"	$85.00	$275.00

Cowboy outfit

8"	$95.00	$325.00

Dutch pair, with gold paper hang tags reading: *"Kit and Kat"*

8"	$250.00	$525.00

Oriental, with layette

8"	$250.00	$525.00

Mary Ann, 1932+

Composition, sleep eyes, wigged, open mouth. Marked: *"Mary Ann" on head; "Effanbee//Patsy Ann'//©//Pat. #1283558" on body*

19"	$200.00	$350.00

Mary Lee, 1932

Composition, sleep eyes, wigged, open mouth. *Marked: "©//Mary Lee" on head; "Effanbee//Patsy Joan" on body.*

16½"	$225.00	$325.00

MiMi, 1927

All-composition, blue painted eyes, prototype of 1928 Patsy, but name change indicates a very short production run. *Marked on body: "Effanbee//MiMi//Pat.Pend//Doll"*

14"	$250.00	$600.00

Patsy/Patricia, 1940

Used a marked Patsy head on a marked Patricia body, all-composition, painted eyes, molded hair, may have magnets in hands to hold accessories. *Marked on body: "Effanbee//'Patricia'"*

15"	$300.00	$600.00

Skippy, 1929

Advertised as Patsy's boyfriend, composition head, painted eyes, molded and painted blond hair, composition or cloth body, with composition molded shoes and legs. *Marked on head: "Effanbee//Skippy//©//P. L. Crosby"; on body, "Effanbee//Patsy//Pat. Pend// Doll"*

14"	$275.00	$600.00

White Horse Inn, with pin

	$1,400.00*

RUBBER

17" composition Little Lady, brown human hair wig, blue sleep eyes with lashes, closed mouth, jointed, original dotted Swiss pinafore dress, marked on head and body "Effanbee//U.S.A.," circa 1942, $225.00. Courtesy McMasters Harris Doll Auctions.

Dy-Dee, 1934+

Hard rubber head, sleep eyes, jointed rubber bent-leg body, drink/wet mechanism, molded and painted hair. Early dolls had molded ears, after 1940 had applied rubber ears, nostrils, and tear ducts. Later made in hard plastic and vinyl.

Marked: "Effanbee//Dy-Dee Baby" with four patent numbers

* at auction

Dy-Dee Wee

9"	$75.00	$300.00

Dy-Dee-ette, Dy-Dee Ellen

11"	$50.00	$200.00

Dy-Dee Kin

13"	$65.00	$225.00

Dy-Dee Baby, Dy-Dee Jane

15"	$100.00	$400.00

Dy-Dee Lou, Dy-Dee Louise

20"	$125.00	$450.00

Dy-Dee in Layette Trunk, with accessories

15"	$150.00	$575.00

Dy-Dee Accessories

Dy-Dee marked bottle

	$7.50	$15.00

Dy-Dee pattern pajamas

	$8.00	$25.00

Dy-Dee book, *Dy-Dee Doll's Days*, c 1937, by Peggy Vandegriff, with black and white pictures

5½" x 6¾"	$25.00	$55.00

HARD PLASTIC AND VINYL

Alyssa, ca. 1960 – 1961

Vinyl head, hard plastic jointed body, walker, including elbows, rooted saran hair, sleep eyes

23"	$90.00	$225.00

Armstrong, Louis, 1984 – 1985, vinyl

15½"	$25.00	$85.00

Baby Lisa, 1980

Vinyl, designed by Astri Campbell, represents a three-month-old baby, in wicker basket with accessories

11"	$50.00	$150.00

Baby Lisa Grows Up, 1983

Vinyl, toddler body, in trunk with wardrobe

	$50.00	$150.00

Button Nose, 1968 – 1971

Vinyl head, cloth body

18"	$9.00	$35.00

Champagne Lady, 1959

Vinyl head and arms, rooted hair, blue sleep eyes, lashes, hard plastic body, from Lawrence Welk's TV show, Miss Revlon-type

21"	$75.00	$275.00
23"	$85.00	$300.00

Churchill, Sir Winston, 1984, vinyl

	$20.00	$75.00

Currier & Ives, vinyl and hard plastic

12"	$12.00	$45.00

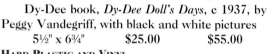

15" hard rubber Dy-Dee Baby, caracul wig over molded hair, sleep eyes with lashes, nursing mouth drink and wet doll, jointed hard rubber body with bent baby legs, flannel sleeper, in layette trunk with accessories, circa late 1930s, $575.00. Courtesy Shirley's Doll House, Wheeling, IL.

20" hard rubber Dy-Dee Baby, molded hair, sleep eyes with lashes, nursing mouth drink and wet doll, jointed hard rubber body with bent baby legs, original pink cotton gown, coat, bonnet, circa 1930s, $450.00. Courtesy Shirley's Doll House, Wheeling, IL.

18½" hard plastic Honey Walker, synthetic wig, sleep eyes with lashes, closed mouth, fully jointed, head turning walker, original cotton dress with organdy puffed sleeves, wrist tag "I Am Honey Walker...," marked on head "Effanbee," circa 1956, $425.00. Courtesy Vicki Johnson.

8½" vinyl Fluffy Brownie Scout, rooted hair, sleep eyes with molded lashes, closed mouth, jointed, original brown cotton scout dress missing yellow ribbon scarf, felt cap with orange insignia, circa 1954, $75.00. Courtesy Carol Stover.

Disney dolls, 1977 – 1978
Snow White, Cinderella, Alice in Wonderland, and Sleeping Beauty

14"	$45.00	$185.00
16½"	$85.00	$325.00

Fluffy, 1954+, all-vinyl

10"	$10.00	$35.00
Black	$12.00	$45.00
Girl Scout	$15.00	$75.00

Gumdrop, 1962+
Vinyl, jointed toddler, sleep eyes, rooted hair

16"	$9.00	$35.00

Hagara, Jan
Designer, all-vinyl, jointed, rooted hair, painted eyes
Christina, 1984

15"	$50.00	$200.00
Larry, 1985	$25.00	$95.00
Laurel, 1984		
15"	$40.00	$150.00
Lesley, 1985	$20.00	$85.00

Half Pint, 1966 – 1983
All-vinyl, rooted hair, sleep eyes, lashes

11"	$8.00	$30.00

Happy Boy, 1960
Vinyl, molded hair, tooth, freckles, painted eyes

11"	$10.00	$45.00

Hibel, Edna
Designer, 1984 only, all-vinyl
Flower Girl

11"	$40.00	$165.00
Contessa	$50.00	$185.00

Honey, 1949 – 1958
Hard plastic (see also composition), saran wig, sleep eyes, closed mouth
Marked on head and back, "Effanbee," had gold paper hang tag that read: "I am//Honey//An//Effanbee//Sweet/ /Child"
Honey, ca. 1949 – 1955, all hard plastic, closed mouth, sleep eyes

14"	$250.00	$500.00
17"	$300.00	$600.00

Honey Walker, 1952+
All hard plastic with walking mechanism; Honey Walker Junior Miss, 1956 – 1957, hard plastic, extra joints at knees and ankles permit her to wear flat or high-heeled shoes. Add $50.00 for jointed knees, ankles.

14"	$65.00	$350.00
19"	$175.00	$425.00

Humpty Dumpty, 1985

	$25.00	$75.00

Katie, 1957, molded hair

8½"	$15.00	$50.00

Legend Series, vinyl

1980, W.C. Fields,		$40.00	$200.00
1981, John Wayne, cowboy		$50.00	$300.00
1982, John Wayne, cavalry		$50.00	$350.00
1982, Mae West		$25.00	$100.00
1983, Groucho Marx		$20.00	$95.00
1984, Judy Garland, Dorothy		$20.00	$90.00
1985, Lucille Ball		$40.00	$120.00
1986, Liberace		$17.50	$95.00
1987, James Cagney		$15.00	$70.00

Lil Sweetie, 1967

Nurser with no lashes or brow	16"	$25.00	$45.00

Limited Edition Club, vinyl

1975, Precious Baby		$115.00	$350.00
1976, Patsy Ann		$85.00	$300.00
1977, Dewees Cochran		$40.00	$135.00
1978, Crowning Glory		$35.00	$105.00
1979, Skippy		$75.00	$265.00
1980, Susan B. Anthony		$35.00	$75.00
1981, Girl with Watering Can		$25.00	$70.00
1982, Princess Diana		$25.00	$100.00
1983, Sherlock Holmes		$40.00	$150.00
1984, Bubbles		$25.00	$100.00
1985, Red Boy		$25.00	$85.00
1986, China head		$17.50	$60.00
1987 – 1988, Porcelain Grumpy (2,500)		$125.00	
Vinyl Grumpy		$50.00	

Martha and George Washington, 1976 – 1977
All-vinyl, fully jointed, rooted hair, blue eyes, molded lashes

	11" pair	$40.00	$155.00

Mickey, 1956 – 1972
All-vinyl, fully jointed, some with molded hat, painted eyes

	10"	$20.00	$75.00

Miss Chips, 1966 – 1981
All-vinyl, fully jointed, side-glancing sleep eyes, rooted hair

	17"	$9.00	$35.00
Black	17"	$12.00	$45.00

Noma, The Electronic Doll, ca. 1950
Hard plastic, cloth body, vinyl limbs, battery-operated talking doll wore pink rayon taffeta dress with black and white check trim

	27"	$125.00	$375.00

Polka Dottie, 1954
Vinyl head, with molded pigtails on fabric body, or with hard plastic body

	21"	$60.00	$165.00
Latex body			
	11"	$30.00	$120.00

Presidents, 1984+
Abraham Lincoln

	18"	$15.00	$50.00

George Washington
16"	$15.00	$50.00

Teddy Roosevelt
17"	$17.50	$75.00

Franklin D. Roosevelt, 1985
	$15.00	$75.00

Prince Charming or Cinderella, Honey
All-hard plastic
16"	$165.00	$425.00

Pun'kin, 1966 – 1983
All-vinyl, fully jointed toddler, sleep eyes, rooted hair
11"	$15.00	$30.00

Rootie Kazootie, 1954
Vinyl head, cloth or hard plastic body, smaller size has latex body
11"	$30.00	$120.00
21"	$60.00	$165.00

Roosevelt, Eleanor, 1985, vinyl
14½"	$15.00	$70.00

Santa Claus, 1982+, designed by Faith Wick
"Old Fashioned Nast Santa," No. 7201, vinyl head, hands, stuffed cloth body, molded and painted features, *marked "Effanbee//7201 c//Faith Wick"*
18"	$25.00	$75.00

Suzie Sunshine, 1961 – 1979
Designed by Eugenia Dukas, all-vinyl, fully jointed, rooted hair, sleep eyes, lashes, freckles on nose. Add $25.00 more for black.
18"	$25.00	$60.00

Sweetie Pie, 1952, hard plastic
27"	$65.00	$325.00

Tintair, 1951, hard plastic, hair color set, to compete with Ideal's Toni
15"	$250.00	$400.00

Twain, Mark, 1984, all-vinyl, molded features
16"	$20.00	$70.00

Wicket Witch, 1981 – 1982, designed by Faith Wick
No. 7110, vinyl head, blond rooted hair, painted features, cloth stuffed body, dressed in black, with apple and basket. *Head marked: "Effanbee//Faith Wick//7110 19cc81"*
18"	$25.00	$75.00

Ethnic

This category describes dolls costumed in regional dress to show different nationalities, facial characteristics, or cultural background. Examples are dolls in regional costumes that are commonly sold as souvenirs to tourists. A well-made beautiful doll with accessories or wardrobe may be more.

Celluloid
8"	$20.00	$55.00
15"	$65.00	$150.00

Cloth
8"	$50.00	$175.00
13"	$65.00	$200.00

Composition Child

8"	$65.00	$185.00
13"	$75.00	$250.00

Native American Indian

8"	$65.00	$225.00
13"	$75.00	$300.00
23"	$85.00	$350.00

Skookum, 1913+, designed by Mary McAboy, painted features, with side-glancing eyes, mohair wigs, cloth figure wrapped in Indian blanket, with folds representing arms, wooden feet, later plastic, label on bottom of foot. Box marked *"Skookum Bully Good."*

First price indicates incomplete, but still very good; second price is excellent to mint with box.

6"	$25.00	$75.00
10 – 12"	$135.00	$230.00
16 – 18"	$150.00	$300.00
33"	$950.00	$1,550.00+

Hard Plastic, regional dress, unmarked or unknown maker

7"	$5.00	$15.00
12"	$7.50	$30.00

Baitz, Austria, 1970s, painted hard plastic, painted side-glancing eyes, open "o" mouth, excellent quality, tagged and dressed in regional dress

8"	$40.00	$75.00

Vinyl

6"	$10.00	$35.00
12"	$15.00	$65.00

8" hard plastic unmarked doll, mohair wig, sleep eyes with molded lashes, strung and jointed body, sewn-on felt Lapland costume, circa 1950s, $45.00. Courtesy Carol Stover.

Freundlich, Ralph A.

Ralph A. Freundlich, 1923+, New York City. Formerly Jeanette Doll Co., then Ralph Freundlich, Inc. Made composition dolls, some with molded caps in military uniform.

Baby Sandy, ca. 1939 – 1942, all-composition, jointed toddler body, molded hair, painted or sleep eyes, smiling mouth

8"	$75.00	$300.00
12"	$100.00	$400.00
15"	$125.00	$500.00

Dummy Dan, ventriloquist doll, Charlie McCarthy look-alike

15"	$40.00	$150.00
21"	$90.00	$350.00

General Douglas MacArthur, ca. 1942, all-composition, jointed body, bent arm salutes, painted features, molded hat, jointed, in khaki uniform, with paper tag

18"	$85.00	$350.00

18" composition General MacArthur, molded and painted hair on gilt-edged hat, painted features, saluting right arm, gabardine uniform, hang tag "General Mac-Arthur, Made in 1942," circa 1942, $350.00. Courtesy Shirley's Doll House, Wheeling, IL.

Military dolls, ca. 1942+, all-composition, molded hats, painted features, original clothes, with paper tag

Soldier, Sailor, WAAC, or WAVE

15"	$65.00	$275.00

Orphan Annie and her dog, Sandy

12"	$85.00	$325.00

Pinocchio, composition and cloth, with molded hair, painted features, brightly colored cheeks, large eyes, open/closed mouth

Tagged: "Original as portrayed by C. Collodi"

16"	$125.00	$500.00

Red Riding Hood, Wolf, Grandma, 1930s, composition, set of three, in schoolhouse box, original clothes

9½"	$250.00	$800.00

Pig Baby, 1930s, composition pig head, with painted features on unmarked five-piece body. Freundlich presumed maker of similar composition cat, rabbit, and monkey dolls

9"	$155.00*

Gabriel

THE LONE RANGER SERIES

Vinyl action figures with horses, separate accessory sets available.

Dan Reed on Banjo, blond hair, figure on palomino horse

9"	$15.00	$50.00

Butch Cavendish on Smoke, black hair, mustache, on black horse

9"	$20.00	$80.00

Lone Ranger on Silver, masked figure on white horse

9"	$25.00	$100.00

Little Bear, Indian boy

6"	$25.00	$100.00

Red Sleeves, vinyl Indian figure, black hair, wears shirt with red sleeves

9"	$25.00	$100.00

Tonto on Scout, Indian on brown and white horse

9"	$20.00	$80.00

Gene

1995. Designed by Mel Odom marketed through Ashton Drake.

Bird of Paradise	1997	$130.00
Breathless	1999	$100.00
King's Daughter NALED	1997	$285.00
Midnight Romance	1997	$175.00
Monaco, 2nd	1995	$160.00
Premier, 1st	1995	$795.00

15½" vinyl Gene Premiere doll, blond curled hair, blue eye-shadow, drop earrings, dressed in black velveteen jacket with rhinestone buttons, gold satin long skirt with black lace overskirt, original box and certificate, circa 1995, $650.00. Courtesy Carol Stover.

Red Venus, 3rd
1995 $80.00
Song of Spain
1999 $100.00
Gene Specials
Atlantic City Beauty Convention
1996 $750.00
Broadway Medley, Convention
1998 $750.00
Covent Garden, NALED
1998 $105.00
Dream Girl, Convention
1998 $250.00
Holiday Benefit Gala, LE 25
1998 $265.00
Las Vegas Showgirl, 50
1997 $2,000.00
Moments to Remember, MDCC 250
2000 $300.00
My Favorite Witch, Convention
1997 $1,350.00
Night at Versailles, FAO Schwarz
1997 $250.00
On the Avenue, FAO Schwarz
1998 $180.00
Santa Fe Celebration, 250
1999 $600.00
Gene Convention pack
2002 $400.00+*
Cindy Lorimer repaint
2002 $250.00 – $900.00*
Gene's green flight outfit, limited
2002 $710.0*

15½" vinyl, Modern Doll Convention 2000, blue eyes, ice blue shadow, midnight blue velvet and brocade sheath with gold accents, pearl earrings, original box and certificate, $225.00. Courtesy Carol Stover.

Gibbs, Ruth

Ca. 1940s+, Flemington, NJ. Made dolls with china and porcelain heads and limbs, pink cloth bodies. Dolls designed by Herbert Johnson.

Godey's Lady Book Dolls
Pink-tint shoulder head, cloth body
 Boxed
  7" $75.00 $210.00
 Caracul wig, original outfit
  9½" $200.00 $295.00
 Hard plastic, mint-in-box, with identification
  11" $200.00

*Marks:
RG on back
shoulder blade
Box labeled:
"GODEY LIT-
TLE LADY
DOLLS,"
Dolls designed by
Herbert Johnson.*

Gilbert Toys

Honey West, 1965, vinyl, vinyl arms, hard plastic torso and legs, rooted blond hair, painted eyes, painted beauty spot near mouth, head marked *"K73"* with leopard

11½"	$60.00	$125.00

The Man From U.N.C.L.E. characters from TV show of the 1960s. Other outfits available. (For photo, see *Doll Values, third edition.*)

Ilya Kuryakin (David McCallum)

12¼"	$25.00	$100.00

Napoleon Solo (Robert Vaughn)

12¼"	$25.00	$100.00

James Bond, Secret Agent 007, character from James Bond movies

12¼"	$20.00	$75.00
Costume only	$180.00*	

Girl Scout Dolls

1920+, listed chronologically. First price for played-with doll missing accessories; second price is for mint doll.

1920s Girl Scout doll in Camp Uniform
Pictured in Girls Scout 1920 handbook, all-cloth, mask face, painted features, wigged, gray green uniform

13"	$250.00	$600.00+

Too few in database for reliable range.

Grace Corry, Scout 1929
Composition shoulder head, designed by Grace Cory, cloth body with crier, molded hair, painted features, original uniform

Mark on shoulder plate: "by Grace Corry"; body stamped "Madame Hendren Doll//Made in USA"

13"	$350.00	$700.00+

Too few in database for reliable range.

Averill Mfg. Co, ca. 1936
Believed to be designed by Maud Tousey Fangel, all-cloth, printed and painted features

16"	$100.00	$400.00+

Too few in database for reliable range.

Georgene Novelties, ca. 1940
All-cloth, flat-faced painted features, yellow yarn curls, wears original silver green uniform with red triangle tie

Hang tag reads: "Genuine Georgene Doll//A product of Georgene Novelties, Inc., NY//Made in U.S.A."

15"	$100.00	$400.00

Georgene Novelties, ca. 1949 – 1954
All-cloth, mask face, painted features and string hair

13½"	$75.00	$250.00

1954 – 1958
Same as previous listing, but now has a plastic mask face

13½"	$35.00	$100.00

Terri Lee, 1949 – 1958
Hard plastic, felt hats, oilcloth saddle shoes

16"	$125.00	$450.00
Outfit only	$160.00*	

---

* at auction  254

Tiny Terri Lee, 1956 – 1958
Hard plastic, walker, sleep eyes, wig, plastic shoes
 10" $65.00 $225.00

Ginger, ca. 1956 – 1958, made by Cosmopolitan for Terri Lee, hard plastic, straight-leg walker, synthetic wig
 7½" – 8" $100.00 $250.00
 7½" $385.00*

Vogue, 1956 – 1957+
Ginny, hard plastic, straight-legged walker with sleep eyes and painted eyelashes; in 1957 had bending leg and felt hat
 8" $225.00 $325.00
Brownie, boxed
 8" $1,124.00*

Uneeda, 1959 – 1961
Ginny look-alike, vinyl head, hard plastic body, straight-leg walker, Dynel wig, *marked "U" on head*
 8" $50.00 $150.00

Effanbee, Patsy Ann, 1959+
All-vinyl jointed body, saran hair, with sleep eyes, freckles on nose, Brownie or Girl Scout
 15" $95.00 $350.00

Effanbee Suzette, ca. 1960
Jointed vinyl body, sleep eyes, saran hair, thin body, long legs
 15" $95.00 $350.00

Effanbee Fluffy, 1964 – 1972
Vinyl dolls, sleep eyes, curly rooted hair, Brownie had blond wig; Junior was brunette. Box had clear acetate lid, printed with Girl Scout trademark, and catalog number
 8" $65.00 $175.00

Effanbee Fluffy Cadette, 1965
 11" $75.00 $300.00

Effanbee Pun'kin Jr., 1974 – 1979+
All-vinyl, sleep eyes, long straight rooted hair Brownie and Junior uniforms
 11½" $25.00 $75.00

Hallmark, 1979
All-cloth, Juliette Low, from 1916 handbook, wearing printed 1923 uniform
 6½" $25.00 $65.00

Jesco, ca. 1985, Katie
All-vinyl, sleep eyes, long straight rooted hair, look-alike Girl Scout, dressed as Brownie and Junior
 9" $25.00 $75.00

Madame Alexander, 1992
Vinyl, unofficial Girl Scout, sleep eyes
 8" $180.00*

8" hard plastic Terri Lee Brownie, blond synthetic wig, sleep eyes with molded lashes, closed mouth, head turning walker, brown cotton uniform with snaps in front, vinyl belt, original box printed "Official Brownie Scout Doll," unmarked doll using same mold as Cosmopolitan's Ginger, circa 1956, $250.00. Courtesy Carol Stover.

17" Advance Doll and Toy Co., Wanda the Walking Doll, glued on synthetic wig, sleep eyes with lashes, closed mouth, key winds rollers on bottom of unremovable shoes, arms swing and head turns when doll walks, blue cotton original dress with sash "Wanda the Unaided Walking Doll," original box printed "Wanda the Walking Doll," doll unmarked, circa 1954, $150.00. Courtesy Carol Stover.

8" Rosebud of England Little Miss Rosebud, mohair wig, blue sleep eyes, painted lashes, jointed body, Scottish kilt and velvet jacket, tam, marked on back "Miss Rosebud" in script, "Made in England" on upper back, circa 1950s, $85.00. Courtesy Sandy Johnson Barts.

Numerous companies made hard plastic dolls, ca. 1948 through the 1950s; dolls have all hard plastic jointed bodies, sleep eyes, lashes, synthetic wig, open or closed mouths. Marks: none, letters, little known, or other unidentified companies.

14"	$65.00	$250.00
18"	$75.00	$300.00
24"	$85.00	$325.00

ADVANCE DOLL & TOY COMPANY

Ca. 1954+. Made heavy walking hard plastic dolls, metal rollers on molded shoes, named Winnie and Wanda. Later models had vinyl heads.

19"	$45.00	$150.00
24"	$75.00	$200.00

ARTISAN NOVELTY COMPANY

Ca. 1950s, hard plastic, wide crotch
Raving Beauty

19"	$75.00	$250.00

DUCHESS DOLL CORPORATION

Ca. 1948 – 1950s. Made small hard plastic adult dolls, mohair wigs, painted or sleep eyes, jointed arms, stiff or jointed neck, molded and painted shoes, about 7 – 7½" tall, costumes stapled onto body. Elaborate costumed, exceptional dolls may be more.

7"	$7.50	$20.00

FORTUNE DOLL COMPANY

Pam, hard plastic, sleep eyes, synthetic wig, closed mouth

8"	$20.00	$65.00

FURGA, ITALY

Simonna outfit, MIB, 1967
$330.00*

IMPERIAL CROWN TOY CO. (IMPCO)

Ca. 1950s, made hard plastc or vinyl dolls, rooted hair, synthetic wigs

Vinyl

16"	$20.00	$65.00

Hard plastic

20"	$50.00	$150.00

KENDALL COMPANY

Miss Curity, ca. 1953

Hard plastic, jointed only at shoulders, blond wig, blue sleep eyes, molded-on shoes, painted stockings, uniform sheet vinyl, *"Miss Curity"* marked in blue on hat

7½"	$10.00	$50.00

RODDY OF ENGLAND, CA. 1950 – 1960s

Made by D.G. Todd & Co. Ltd., Southport, England. Hard plastic walker, sleep or set eyes.

12½"	$25.00	$100.00

Walking Princess, tagged

11½"	$15.00	$50.00

ROSEBUD OF ENGLAND, CA. 1950S – 1960S
Started in Raunds, Northamptonshire, England, by T. Eric Smith shortly after WWII.

Miss Rosebud, hard plastic, various shades of blue sleep eyes, glued-on mohair wig, jointed at the neck and hips. Marked *"Miss Rosebud"* in script on her back and head and *"MADE IN ENGLAND"* on her upper back. More for rare examples or mint-in-box dolls.

7½"	$35.00	$85.00

ROSS PRODUCTS
Tina Cassini, designed by Oleg Cassini. Hard plastic, marked on back torso, *"TINA CASSINI"*; clothes tagged *"Made in British Crown Colony of Hong Kong."*

12"	$50.00	$200.00
Costume, MIB	$50.00	$125.00

Hartland Industries

1950s+. Made action figures and horses; many figures from Warner Brothers television productions.

TELEVISION OR MOVIE CHARACTERS, 8"
Annie Oakley, 1953 – 1956, by Gail Davis in *Annie Oakley*
　　8"　　$200.00* with horse
Bret Maverick, ca. 1958, by James Garner in *Maverick*
　　8"　　$750.00* MIB
Clint Bonner, 1957 – 1959, by John Payne in *The Restless Gun*
　　8"　　$135.00　　$250.00
Colonel Ronald MacKenzie, ca. 1950s, by Richard Carlson, in *MacKenzies' Raiders*
　　8"　　$810.00* with horse
Dale Evans, ca. 1958, #802, with horse, Buttermilk in *The Roy Rogers Show*
　　8"　　$375.00* MIB
Gil Favor, ca. 1950s, in *Rawhide*
　　8"　　$685.00* with horse
Jim Hardie, 1958, played by Dale Roberson in *Tales of Wells Fargo*
　　8"　　$225.00 – $275.00*
Josh Randall, ca. 1950s, by Steve McQueen in *Wanted Dead or Alive*
　　8"　　$615.00* with horse
Major Seth Adams, 1957 – 1961, #824, by Ward Bond in *Wagon Train*
　　8"　　$200.00* with horse
Marshall Johnny McKay, *Lawman*
　　8"　　$520.00*
Paladin, 1957 – 1963, by Richard Boone in *Have Gun, Will Travel*
　　8"　　$610.00* with horse
Roy Rogers, ca. 1955, and Trigger in *The Roy Rogers Show*
　　8"　　$485.00* MIB with Trigger
Sgt. William Preston, ca. 1958, #804, by Richard Simmons in *Sgt. Preston of the Yukon*
　　8"　　$700.00* with horse
Will Barclay "Bat" Masterson, 1958 – 1960, by Gene Barry in *Bat Masterson*
　　8"　　$310.00*
Wyatt Earp, 1955 – 1961 by Hugh O'Brien in *Life and Legend of Wyatt Earp*
　　8"　　$190.00* with horse

Other 8" Figures

8"	$380.00*	

Brave Eagle, #812, and his horse, White Cloud
Buffalo Bill, #819, Pony Express Rider
Chief Thunderbird, and horse, Northwind
Cochise, #815, with pinto horse from *Broken Arrow*
Jim Bowie, #817, with horse, Blaze
General George Custer, #814, and horse, Bugler
General George Washington, #815 and horse, Ajax
General Robert E. Lee, #808, and horse, Traveler
Lone Ranger, #801, and horse, Silver
Tonto, #805, and horse, Scout

All others	8"	$125.00	$225.00

Baseball 8" Figures

Dick Groat with bat & hat	$1,000.00*	
Duke Snider	$255.00*	
Ernie Banks, #920	$430.00*	
Hank Aaron, #912	$245.00*	
Harvey Keunn	$325.00*	
Willie Mays	$245.00*	
Yogi Berra, boxed	$280.00*	
Ted Williams	$135.00*	

Hasbro

Ca. 1960s+, Hassenfeld Bros. Toy manufacturer, also makes plastic or plastic and vinyl dolls and action figures.

First price for doll in played with condition, or missing some accessories; second price for mint doll.

Adam, 1971, Boy for "World of Love" Series, all-vinyl, molded painted brown hair, painted blue eyes, red knit shirt, blue denim jeans. *Mark: "Hasbro//U.S. Pat Pend//Made in//Hong Kong"*

9"	$5.00	$18.00

Aimee, 1972, rooted hair, amber sleep eyes, jointed vinyl body, long dress, sandals, earrings

18"	$25.00	$85.00

Dolly Darling, 1965

4½" Boy Trap	$240.00*

Flying Nun

5"	$135.00*

Jem: See Jem section, following this category.

Leggie, 1972

10"	$12.00	$50.00
Black	$15.00	$60.00

Little Miss No Name, 1965

15"	$75.00	$225.00

Marks:
1964 – 1965
Marked on right lower back:
G.I. Joe ™//COPYRIGHT 1964//BY HASBRO ®//PATENT PEND-ING//MADE IN U.S.A.//GIJoe®
1967
Slight change in marking:
COPYRIGHT 1964//BY HASBRO ®//PATENT PENDING// MADE IN U.S.A.// GIJoe®
This mark appears on all four armed service branches, excluding the black action figures.

Peteena Poodle, 1966
    9½" $195.00*
Real Baby, 1984, J. Turner
    18" $75.00*
Show Biz Babies, 1967
Mama Cass Elliott, 4¼" $180.00*
Denny Doherty, 4½" $125.00*
Monkees, set of four
    4" $40.00 $120.00
Storybook, 1967, 3"
Goldilocks $12.50 $50.00
Prince Charming $15.00 $60.00
Rumpelstiltskin $15.00 $55.00
Sleeping Beauty $12.50 $50.00
Snow White and Dwarfs
    $20.00 $75.00
    Sweet Cookie, 1972, vinyl, with cooking accessories
    18" $35.00 $125.00
That Kid, 1967
    21" $22.50 $95.00
World of Love Dolls, 1971
White   9" $100.00*
Black   9" $25.00 $110.00

15½" vinyl Little Miss No Name in original window-pane box, "the Doll with the Tear....I need someone to love me. I want to learn to play, please take me home with you and brush my tear away," circa 1965, $300.00. Courtesy Leslie Tannenbaum.

G.I. JOE
G.I. Joe Action Figures, 1964
Hard plastic head with facial scar, painted hair and no beard. First price indicates doll lacking accessories or nude; second price indicates mint doll in package. Add more for pristine package.
    G.I. Joe Action Soldier, flocked hair, Army fatigues, brown jump boots, green plastic cap, training manual, metal dog tag, two sheets of stickers
    11½" $120.00 $450.00
Painted hair, red
    $140.00 $300.00
Black, painted hair
    $325.00 $1,300.00
    Green Beret
    Teal green fatigue jacket, four pockets, pants, Green Beret cap with red unit flashing, M-16 rifle, 45 automatic pistol with holster, tall brown boots, four grenades, camouflage scarf, and field communication set
    11" $275.00 $1,500.00
    G.I. Joe Action Marine
    Camouflage shirt, pants, brown boots, green plastic cap, metal dog tag, insignia stickers, and training manual
    11" $80.00 $300.00

"HOME FOR THE HOLIDAYS" SOLDIER

11½" vinyl GI Joe Action Soldier, "Home for the Holidays/Limited Edition" with cotton uniform, dog tags and accessories, original box, circa 1996, $45.00. Courtesy Shirley's Doll House.

G.I. Joe Action Sailor

Blue chambray work shirt, blue denim work pants, black boots, white plastic sailor cap, dog tag, rank insignia stickers

$75.00	$250.00

G.I. Joe Action Pilot

Orange flight suit, black boots, dog tag, stickers, blue cap, training manual

	$125.00	$300.00
Dolls only	$50.00	$95.00

G.I. Joe Action Soldier of the World, 1966

Figures in this set may have any hair and eye color combination, no scar on face, hard plastic heads

Australian Jungle Fighter	$255.00	$1,050.00
British Commando, boxed	$300.00	$1,150.00
French Resistance Fighter	$150.00	$1,200.00
German Storm Trooper	$400.00	$1,200.00
Japanese Imperial Soldier	$175.00	$1,400.00
Russian Infantryman		
Boxed	$350.00	$1,100.00
Doll, no box	$75.00	$250.00

Talking G.I. Joe, 1967 – 1969

Talking mechanism added, semi-hard vinyl head

Marks: "G.I. Joe®//Copyright 1964//By Hasbro®//Pat. No. 3,277,602//Made in U.S.A.

Talking G.I. Joe Action Soldier

Green fatigues, dog tag, brown boots, insignia, stripes, green plastic fatigue cap, comic book, insert with examples of figure's speech

$150.00	$300.00

Talking G.I. Joe Action Sailor

Denim pants, chambray sailor shirt, dog tag, black boots, white sailor cap, insignia stickers, Navy training manual, illustrated talking comic book, insert examples of figure's speech

$200.00	$1,000.00

Talking G.I. Joe Action Marine

Camouflage fatigues, metal dog tag, Marine training manual, insignia sheets, brown boots, green plastic cap, comic, and insert

$60.00	$800.00

Talking G.I. Joe Action Pilot

Blue flight suit, black boots, dog tag, Air Force insignia, blue cap, training manual, comic book, insert

$150.00	$1,000.00

G.I. Joe Action Nurse, 1967

Vinyl head, blond rooted hair, jointed hard plastic body, nurse's uniform, cap, red cross armband, white shoes, medical bag, stethoscope, plasma bottle, two crutches, bandages, splints. *Marks: "Patent Pending//©1967 Hasbro®//Made in Hong Kong"*

Boxed	$1,200.00	$1,850.00
Dressed	$200.00	$1,000.00
Nude	$40.00	$150.00

G.I. Joe, Man of Action, 1970 – 1975
    Flocked hair, scar on face, dressed in fatigues with Adventure Team emblem on shirt, plastic cap. *Marks: "G.I. Joe®//Copyright 1964//By Hasbro®// Pat. No. 3, 277, 602//Made in U.S. A."*

	$15.00	$75.00
Talking	$45.00	$175.00

G.I. Joe, Adventure Team
    Marks: "©1975 Hasbro ®//Pat. Pend. Pawt. R.I." Flocked hair and beard, six team members:

    Air Adventurer, orange flight suit
        $75.00 $285.00
    Astronaut, talking, white flight suit, molded scar, dog tag pull string
        $115.00 $450.00
    Land Adventurer, black, tan fatigues, beard, flocked hair, scar
        $90.00 $350.00
    Land Adventurer, talking, camouflage fatigues
        $115.00 $450.00
    Sea Adventurer, light blue shirt, navy pants
        $75.00 $300.00
    Talking Adventure Team Commander, flocked hair, beard, green jacket, and pants
        $115.00 $450.00
    G.I. Joe Land Adventurer, flocked hair, beard, camouflage shirt, green pants
        $70.00 $150.00
    G. I. Joe Negro Adventurer, flocked hair
        $175.00 $750.00
    G. I. Joe, "Mike Powers, Atomic Man"
        $25.00 $55.00
    G.I. Joe Eagle Eye Man of Action
        $40.00 $125.00
    G.I. Joe Secret Agent, unusual face, mustache
        $115.00 $450.00
    Sea Adventurer w/Kung Fu Grip
        $80.00 $145.00
    Bulletman, muscle body, silver arms, hands, helmet, red boots
        $55.00 $125.00

Others
    G.I. Joe Air Force Academy, Annapolis, or West Point Cadet
        11" $125.00 $400.00
    G.I. Joe Frogman, Underwater Demolition Set
        11" $300.00*
    G.I. Joe Secret Service Agent, limited edition of 200
        11" $275.00*
Accessory Sets, mint, no doll included
    Adventures of G.I. Joe
        Adventure of the Perilous Rescue $250.00
        Eight Ropes of Danger Adventure $200.00
        Fantastic Free Fall Adventure $275.00

* at auction

Hidden Missile Discovery Adventure	$150.00
Mouth of Doom Adventure	$150.00
Adventure of the Shark's Surprise	$200.00

Accessory Packs or Boxed Uniforms and Accessories

Air Force, Annapolis, West Point Cadet	$200.00
Action Sailor	$350.00
Astronaut	$250.00
Crash Crew Fire Fighter	$275.00
Deep Freeze with Sled	$250.00
Deep Sea Diver	$250.00
Frogman Demolition Set	$375.00
Fighter Pilot, no package	$285.00*
Green Beret	$450.00
Landing Signal Officer	$250.00
Marine Jungle Fighter	$850.00
Marine Mine Detector	$275.00
Military Police	$325.00
Pilot Scramble Set	$275.00
Rescue Diver	$350.00
Secret Agent	$150.00
Shore Patrol	$300.00
Ski Patrol	$350.00

G.I. Joe Vehicles and Other Accessories, mint in package

Amphibious Duck, green plastic, Irwin	$600.00
Armored Car, green plastic, one figure	$150.00
Crash Crew Fire Truck, blue	$1,400.00
Desert Patrol Attack Jeep, tan, one figure	$1,400.00
Footlocker, with accessories	$400.00+
Iron Knight Tank, green plastic	$1,400.00
Jet Aeroplane, dark blue plastic	$550.00
Jet Helicopter, green, yellow blades	$350.00
Motorcycle and Side Car, by Irwin	$225.00
Personnel Carrier and Mine Sweeper	$700.00
Sea Sled and Frogman	$400.00
Space Capsule and Suit, gray plastic	$425.00
Staff Car, four figures, green plastic, Irwin	$900.00

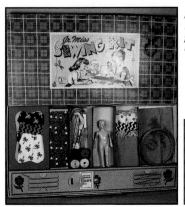

8" plastic doll in Hassenfeld Bros. (Hasbro) Jr. Miss Sewing set, inexpensive plastic molded body with painted eyes and mouth, swinging arms, in original box with sewing set, circa 1955, $35.00 set.

> *Marks:*
> On head: "HASBRO, INC."
> *On back:*
> "COPYRIGHT 1985 (or 1986 or 1987) HAS-
> BRO, INC." *followed by either* "CHINA" *or*
> "MADE IN HONG KONG."
> *Not all are marked on head.*

* at auction

12" vinyl, Jem outrageous fashion Shana On Stage Fashion Music is Magic, $25.00 mint/complete fashion; right wearing On Stage Fashion, Love's Not Easy, mint/complete fashion $65,00, nude, $40.00, circa 1985 – 1986. Courtesy Linda Holton.

JEM, 1986 – 1987

Jem dolls were patterned after characters in the animated television Jem series, ca. 1985 – 1988, and include a line of 27 dolls. All-vinyl fashion type with realistically proportioned body, jointed elbows, wrists, and knees, swivel waist, rooted hair, painted eyes, open or closed mouth, and hole in bottom of each foot.

All boxes say *"Jem"* and *"Truly Outrageous!"* Most came with cassette tape of music from Jem cartoon, plastic doll stand, poster, and hair pick. All 12½" tall, except Starlight Girls, 11".

First price is for excellent to near mint doll wearing complete original outfit; anything less is of lower value. Second price is for never removed from box doll (NRFB) which includes an excellent quality box. For an "Audition Contest" labeled box, add $10.00. A rule of thumb to calculate loose dolls which have been dressed in another outfit is the price of the mint/complete outfit plus the price of mint loose nude doll.

Jem and Rio	Stock No.	Mint	NRFB
Jem/Jerrica 1st issue	4000	$30.00	$40.00
Jem/Jerrica, star earrings	4000	$35.00	$45.00
Glitter 'n Gold Jem	4001	$60.00	$125.00
Rock 'n Curl Jem	4002	$20.00	$30.00
Flash 'n Sizzle Jem	4003	$40.00	$56.00
Rio, 1st issue	4015	$25.00	$35.00
Glitter 'n Gold Rio	4016	$25.00	$35.00
Glitter 'n Gold Rio, pale vinyl	4016	$125.00	$150.00
Holograms			
Synergy	4020	$45.00	$60.00
Aja, 1st issue	4201/4005	$45.00	$60.00
Aja, 2nd issue	4201/4005	$90.00	$125.00
Kimber, 1st issue	4202/4005	$40.00	$50.00
Kimber, 2nd issue	4202/4005	$75.00	$90.00
Shana, 1st issue	4203/4005	$275.00*	
Shana, 2nd issue	4203/4005	$225.00	$300.00
Danse	4208	$45.00	$60.00
Video	4209	$25.00	$35.00
Raya	4210	$150.00	$175.00
Starlight Girls, 11", no wrist or elbow joints			
Ashley	4211/4025	$40.00	$55.00
Krissie	4212/4025	$35.00	$65.00
Banee	4213/4025	$25.00	$40.00

* at auction

Misfits

Pizzazz, 1st issue	4204/4010	$50.00	$65.00
Pizzazz, 2nd issue	4204/4010	$55.00	$75.00
Stormer, 1st issue	4205/4010	$50.00	$65.00
Stormer, 2nd issue	4205/4010	$60.00	$75.00
Roxy, 1st issue	4206/4010	$50.00	$65.00
Roxy, 2nd issue	4206/4010	$50.00	$65.00
Clash	4207/4010	$25.00	$35.00
Jetta	4214	$40.00	$55.00

Accessories

Glitter 'n Gold Roadster	$150.00	$250.00
Rock 'n Roadster	$65.00	$90.00
KJEM Guitar	$25.00	$40.00
New Wave Waterbed	$35.00	$50.00
Backstager	$25.00	$35.00
Star Stage	$30.00	$45.00
MTV jacket (promo)	$90.00	$125.00

Jem Fashions

Prices reflect NRFB (never removed from box or card), with excellent packaging. Damaged boxes or mint and complete, no packaging prices are approximately 25 percent less.

On Stage Fashions, 1st year, "artwork" on card

Award Night	4216/4040	$30.00
Music is Magic	4217/4040	$30.00
Dancin' the Night Away	4218/4040	$25.00
Permanent Wave	4219/4040	$25.00
Only the Beginning	4220/4040	$20.00
Command Performance	4221/4040	$35.00
Twilight in Paris	4222/4040	$25.00
Encore	4223/4040	$35.00

On Stage Fashions, 2nd year, "photo" on card

Award Night	4216/4040	$35.00
Music is Magic	4217/4040	$35.00
Permanent Wave	4219/4040	$30.00
Encore	4223/4040	$30.00
Friend or Stranger	4224/4040	$50.00
Come On In	4225/4040	$55.00
There's Melody Playing	4226/4040	$280.00
How You Play Game	4227/4040	$85.00*
Love's Not Easy	4228/4040	$100.00
Set Your Sails	4229/4040	$35.00

Flip Side Fashions, 1st year "artwork" on box

Up & Rockin'	4232/4045	$20.00
Rock Country	4233/4045	$35.00
Gettin' Down to Business	4234/4045	$40.00
Let's Rock this Town	4235/4045	$30.00
Music in the Air	4236/4045	$35.00
Like a Dream	4237/4045	$30.00
Sophisticated Lady	4238/4045	$30.00
City Lights	3129/4045	$20.00

* at auction

Flip Side Fashions, 2nd year "photo" on box

Gettin' Down to Business	4234/4045	$45.00
Let's Rock this Town	4235/4045	$35.00
Music in the Air	4236/4045	$40.00
Sophisticated Lady	4238/4045	$35.00
Putting it All Together	4240/4045	$75.00
Running Like the Wind	4241/4045	$125.00
We Can Change It	4242/4045	$125.00
Broadway Magic	4243/4045	$200.00
She Makes an Impression	4244/4045	$90.00
Lightnin' Strikes	4245/4045	$45.00

Smashin' Fashions, 1st year "artwork" on card (includes Rio fashions)

Rappin'	4248/4051	$40.00
On the Road with Jem	4249/4051	$25.00
Truly Outrageous	4250/4051	$125.00
Makin' Mischief	4251/4050	$30.00
Let the Music Play	4252/4050	$30.00
Outta My Way	4253/4050	$20.00*
Just Misbehavin'	4254/4050	$65.00
Winning Is Everything	4255/4050	$31.00*

Smashin' Fashions, 2nd year, "photo" on card (Misfits fashions only)

Let the Music Play	4252/4050	$35.00
Just Misbehavin'	4254/4050	$75.00
Gimme, Gimme, Gimme	4256/4050	$50.00*
You Can't Catch Me	4257/4050	$102.00*
We're Off & Running	4258/4050	$35.00
You Gotta' Be Fast	4259/4050	$45.00
There Ain't Nobody Better	4260/4050	$50.00
Designing Woman	4261/4050	$35.00

Rio Fashion, 2nd year only, "photo" on card

Rappin'	4248/4051	$45.00
On the Road with Jem	4249/4051	$30.00
Truly Outrageous	4250/4051	$150.00
Time Is Running Out	4271/4051	$25.00
Share a Little Bit	4272/4051	$125.00
Congratulations	4273/4051	$30.00
Universal Appeal	4274/4051	$25.00
It Takes a Lot	4275/4051	$25.00
It All Depends on Mood	4276/4051	$15.00

Glitter 'n Gold Fashions, 2nd year only, "photo" on boxes

Fire and Ice	4281/4055	$55.00
Purple Haze	4282/4055	$30.00
Midnight Magic	4283/4055	$30.00
Gold Rush	4284/4055	$60.00
Moroccan Magic	4285/4055	$75.00
Golden Days/Diamond Nights	4286/4055	$50.00

Music Is Magic Fashion, 2nd year only, "photo" on boxes

Rock'n Roses	4296/4060	$35.00
Splashes of Sound	4297/4060	$25.00

* at auction

24 Carat Sound	4298/4060	$35.00
Star Struck Guitar	4299/4060	$85.00
Electric Chords	4300/4060	$25.00
Rhythm & Flash	4301/4060	$35.00

Horsman, E.I.

1865 – 1980+, New York City. Founded by Edward Imeson Horsman, distributed, assembled, and made dolls, merged with Aetna Doll and Toy Co., and in 1909 obtained first copyright for a complete doll with his Billiken. Later made hard plastic and vinyl dolls.

14" bisque Tinie Baby, molded hair, blue sleep eyes, painted upper and lower lashes, pouty mouth, cloth body, composition hands, original white gown and bonnet, marked on head "© 1924 by//E.I. Horsman Co. 116// Made in Germany, circa 1920s," $650.00. Courtesy McMasters Harris Doll Auctions.

> *Marks:*
> *"E.I. H.//CO."*
> *and "CAN'T*
> *BREAK 'EM"*

COMPOSITION

First price is for played-with doll, or missing some clothing or accessories; second price is for doll in excellent condition, add more for exceptional doll.

Baby, 1930s – 1940s
15"	$50.00	$125.00

Baby Bumps, 1910 – 1917
Composition head, cloth cork stuffed body, blue and white cloth label on romper, copy of K*R #100 Baby mold
11"	$65.00	$250.00
Black	$75.00	$300.00

Baby Butterfly, ca. 1913
Oriental baby, composition head, hands, painted features
13"	$225.00	$650.00

Billiken, 1909
Composition head, molded hair, slanted eyes, smiling closed mouth, on stuffed mohair or velvet body. *Marks: Cloth label on body. "Billiken" on right foot.*
12"	$100.00	$400.00

Betty Ann, rubber arms and legs
19"	$100.00	$350.00

Betty Jane, all-composition
25"	$100.00	$300.00

Body Twist, 1930, all-composition, with jointed waist
11"	$65.00	$225.00

Brother, 1937, *marked: "Brother//1937//Horsman//©"*
21"	$225.00*

Bright Star, 1937 – 1946, all-composition
19"	$75.00	$300.00

Campbell Kids, 1910+
By Helen Trowbridge, based on Grace Drayton's drawings, composition head, painted and molded hair, side-glancing painted eyes, closed smiling mouth, composition arms, cloth body and feet. *Mark: "EIH a 1910"; cloth label on sleeve, "The Campbell Kids// Trademark by //Joseph Campbell// Mfg. by E.I. Horsman Co."*
14"	$85.00	$325.00+

Left: 18" composition Ella Cinders, painted black hair, painted open closed mouth, composition limbs with stuffed body, jointed at hips and shoulders, original cotton dress, marked on head "©//1925//M.N.S.," circa 1925, $950.00. Courtesy Shirley's Doll House, Wheeling, IL.

Right: 24" composition flange head Dolly Rosebud, mohair wig, blue sleep eyes with real lashes, painted upper and lower lashes, open mouth with three upper teeth, cloth torso, composition arms and legs, original pink bonnet and dress tagged "Dolly Rosebud," marked on head "©//E.I.H. Co. Inc.," circa 1930s, $400.00. Courtesy McMasters Doll Auction.

1930 – 1940s, all-composition

13"	$100.00	$350.00

Child, all-composition

14"	$65.00	$185.00

Cotton Joe, black

13"	$100.00	$400.00

Dimples, 1927 – 1930+

Composition head, arms, cloth body, bent-leg body, or bent-limb baby body, molded dimples, open mouth, sleep or painted eyes, *marked "E.I. H."*

16 – 18"	$70.00	$250.00
20 – 22"	$90.00	$350.00

Laughing Dimples, open/closed mouth with painted teeth

22"	$710.00*

Dimples, toddler body

20"	$100.00	$385.00
24"	$150.00	$425.00

Dolly Rosebud, 1926 – 1930

Mama doll, composition head, limbs, dimples, sleep eyes

18"	$50.00	$175.00

Ella Cinders, 1928 – 1929

Based on a cartoon character, composition head, black painted hair or wig, round painted eyes, freckles under eyes, open/closed mouth, cloth body. Also came as all-cloth. *Mark: "1925//MNS"*

14"	$100.00	$400.00
18"	$175.00	$650.00

Gene Carr Kids, 1915 – 1916

Composition head, molded and painted hair, painted eyes, open/closed smiling mouth with teeth, big ears, cloth body, composition hands, original outfit. *Cloth tag reads: "MADE GENE CARR KIDS U.S.A.//FROM NEW YORK WORLD'S//LADY BOUNTIFUL COMIC SERIES//By E.I. HORSMAN CO. NY. 13½""*

Blink	$90.00	$360.00
Carnival Kids	$75.00	$300.00
Lizzie	$90.00	$360.00

Left: 13" composition latex Twin Doll, molded and painted hair, painted blue eyes, closed mouth, latex arms and legs foam rubber filled, soft body, turning head, cooing voice box, original cowgirl costume, felt hat, holster with metal pistol, hang tag "A Genuine Horsman Art Doll," doll unmarked, $125.00. Courtesy Carol Stover.

*Right: 20" composition doll possibly Horsman, red mohair wig, sleep eyes with lashes, open mouth with teeth, jointed, wig and body restored, marked "*20" on back, circa 1930s, $150.00. Courtesy Carol Stover.*

Mike	$90.00	$360.00
Skinney	$90.00	$360.00
Snowball, black	$135.00	$550.00
Polly Pru, 13"	$85.00	$325.00

Gold Medal doll, 1930s, composition head and limbs, upper and lower teeth, cloth body

21"	$50.00	$200.00

HEbee-SHEbees, 1925 – 1927
Based on drawings by Charles Twelvetrees, all-bisque or all-composition, painted features, molded undershirt and booties or various costumes. *Marks: on all-bisque, "Germany," and paper sticker on tummy, "COPYRIGHT BY//HEbee SHEbe//TRADEMARK//CHAS. TWELVETREES"*
Composition

10½"	$125.00	$450.00

Jackie Coogan, "The Kid," 1921 – 1922
Composition head, hands, molded hair, painted eyes, cloth body, turtleneck sweater, long gray pants, checked cap. *Button reads: "HORSMAN DOLL// JACKIE// COOGAN// KID// PATENTED"*

13½"	$135.00	$465.00+
15½"	$160.00	$550.00+

Jeanie Horsman, 1937
Composition head and limbs, painted molded brown hair, sleep eyes, cloth body, *mark: "Jeanie© Horsman"*

14"	$65.00	$225.00

Jo Jo, 1937
All-composition, blue sleep eyes, wigged, over molded hair, toddler body. *Mark: "HORSMAN JO JO//©1937"*

13"	$75.00	$250.00

Mama Dolls, 1920+
Composition head, arms, and lower legs, cloth body with crier and stitched hip joints so lower legs will swing, painted or sleep eyes, mohair or molded hair

14 – 15"	$50.00	$185.00
19 – 21"	$75.00	$285.00

| Rosebud | $75.00 | $275.00 |
| Peggy Ann | $85.00 | $350.00 |

Naughty Sue, 1937, composition head, jointed body

| 16" | $100.00 | $400.00 |

Peterkin, 1914 – 1930+

Cloth or composition body, character face, molded hair, painted or sleep eyes, closed smiling mouth, rectangular tag with name *"Peterkin"*

| 11" | $75.00 | $300.00 |
| 13½" | $85.00 | $350.00 |

Roberta, 1937, all-composition

| 16" | $115.00 | $450.00 |

Sweetums, cloth body, drink and wet, box, accessories

| 15" | $75.00 | $225.00 |

Tynie Baby, ca. 1924 – 1929

Bisque or composition head, sleep or painted eyes, cloth body, some all-bisque

Marks: "©1924//E.I. HORSMAN//CO. INC." or "E.I.H. Co. 1924" on composition or "©1924 by//E I Horsman Co. Inc//Germany// 37" incised on bisque head

All-bisque, with wardrobe, cradle

| 6" | $1,785.00* | |
| 9" | $1,800.00 | $2,500.00 |

Bisque, head circumference

| 9" | $150.00 | $600.00 |
| 12" | $200.00 | $800.00 |

Composition

| 15" | $75.00 | $300.00 |

12" vinyl Mary Poppins, rooted wig, painted eyes with lashes at side, jointed, original costume, coat, hat, marked "Horsman," circa 1965, $25.00. Courtesy Carol Stover.

HARD PLASTIC AND VINYL

First price is for doll in excellent condition, but with flaws; second price is for mint-in-box doll. Add more for accessories or wardrobe.

Angelove, 1974, plastic/vinyl made for Hallmark

| 12" | $10.00 | $25.00 |

Answer Doll, 1966, button in back moves head

| 10" | $8.00 | $15.00 |

Baby First Tooth, 1966

Vinyl head, limbs, cloth body, open/closed mouth with tongue and one tooth, molded tears on cheeks, rooted blond hair, painted blue eyes. *Mark: "©Horsman Dolls Inc.//10141"*

| 16" | $20.00 | $40.00 |

Baby Tweaks, ca. 1967

Vinyl head, cloth body, inset eyes, rooted saran hair. *Mark: "54//HORSMAN DOLLS INC.//Copyright 1967/67191" on head*

| 20" | $15.00 | $30.00 |

Ballerina, 1957, vinyl, one-piece body and legs, jointed elbows

| 18" | $15.00 | $50.00 |

10½" hard plastic Cindy, blond rooted hair, sleep eyes, closed mouth, pierced ears, painted fingernails and toenails, red and white check shirt, blue jeans with red and white check cuffs, mint in box, circa 1950s, $125.00. Courtesy Sharon Kolibaba.

* at auction

Betty, 1951, all-vinyl, one-piece body and limbs

14"	$15.00	$60.00

Vinyl head, hard plastic body

16"	$15.00	$25.00

Betty Ann, vinyl head, hard plastic body

19"	$15.00	$60.00

Betty Jane, vinyl head, hard plastic body

25"	$20.00	$75.00

Betty Jo, vinyl head, hard plastic body

16"	$15.00	$30.00

Bright Star, ca. 1952+, all hard plastic

15"	$125.00	$450.00

Bye-Lo Baby, 1972
Reissue, molded vinyl head, limbs, cloth body, white nylon organdy bonnet dress. *Mark: "3 (in square)//HORSMAN DOLLS INC.//©1972"*

14"	$15.00	$55.00

1980 – 1990s

14"	$8.00	$25.00

Celeste, portrait doll, in frame, eyes painted to side

12"	$10.00	$35.00

Christopher Robin

11"	$10.00	$35.00

Cinderella, 1965, vinyl head, hard plastic body, painted eyes to side

11½"	$8.00	$30.00

Cindy, 1950s, all hard plastic, *"170"*

15"	$50.00	$175.00+
17"	$65.00	$200.00+

1953, early vinyl

18"	$20.00	$60.00

1959, lady-type with jointed waist

19"	$25.00	$95.00

Walker

16"	$60.00	$225.00

Cindy Kay, 1950s+, all-vinyl child with long legs

15"	$25.00	$80.00
20"	$35.00	$125.00
27"	$60.00	$225.00

Crawling Baby, 1967, vinyl, rooted hair

14"	$8.00	$25.00

Disney Exclusives, 1981
Cinderella, Snow White, Mary Poppins, Alice in Wonderland

8"	$10.00	$40.00

Elizabeth Taylor, 1976

11½"	$15.00	$45.00

Floppy, 1958, vinyl head, foam body and legs

18"	$8.00	$25.00

Flying Nun, 1965, TV character portrayed by Sally Field

12"	$50.00	$125.00

Gold Medal Doll, 1953, vinyl, molded hair

26"	$45.00	$185.00

1954, vinyl, boy

15"	$20.00	$75.00

Hansel & Gretel, 1963
Vinyl head, hard plastic body, rooted synthetic hair, closed mouth, sleep eyes
Marks: "MADE IN USA" on body, on tag, "HORSMAN, Michael Meyerberg, Inc.," "Reproduction of the famous Kinemins in Michael Myerberg's marvelous Technicolor production of Hansel and Gretel"

15"	$50.00	$200.00

Jackie, 1961
Vinyl doll, rooted hair, blue sleep eyes, long lashes, closed mouth, high-heeled feet, small waist, nicely dressed. Designed by Irene Szor who says this doll named Jackie was not meant to portray Jackie Kennedy. *Mark: "HORSMAN//19©61//BC 18"*

25"	$35.00	$125.00

Lullabye Baby, 1967 – 1968, vinyl bent-leg body, rooted hair, inset blue eyes, drink and wet feature, musical mechanism, Sears 1968 catalog, came on suedette pillow, in terry-cloth p.j.s. *Mark: "2580//B144 8 //HORSMAN DOLLS INC//19©67"*

12"	$4.00	$15.00

Mary Poppins, 1965

12"	$30.00	$125.00
16"	$40.00	$150.00
26", '66	$50.00	$200.00
36"	$90.00	$350.00

In box with Michael and Jane, 1966

12" and 8"	$150.00

Police Woman, ca. 1976, vinyl, plastic fully articulated body, rooted hair

9"	$10.00	$35.00

Poor Pitiful Pearl, 1963
From cartoon by William Steig. *Marked on neck: "Horsman 1963."*

11"	$40.00	$145.00
17"	$45.00	$175.00*

Tynie Baby, ca. 1950s, vinyl, boxed

15"	$30.00	$110.00

Mary Hoyer Doll Mfg. Co.

1937+, Reading, PA. Designed by Bernard Lipfert, all-composition, later hard plastic, then vinyl, swivel neck, jointed body, mohair or human hair wig, sleep eyes, closed mouth, original clothes, or knitted from Mary Hoyer patterns.

Marks: "THE MARY HOYER DOLL" or "ORIGINAL MARY HOYER DOLL"

Composition, less for painted eyes

14"	$105.00	$425.00

Hard Plastic

14"	$125.00	$525.00
14"	$1,100.00 Bride	

14" hard plastic, blond synthetic wig, sleep eyes with lashes and painted under, pink flocked dotted nylon dress, straw bonnet, marked on back "Original Mary//Hoyer Doll" in circle, circa 1950s, $900.00. Courtesy Shirley's Doll House, Wheeling, IL.

Gigi, circa 1950, with round Mary Hoyer mark found on 14" dolls, only 2,000 made by the Frisch Doll Company

| | 18" | $1,600.00* tagged and boxed |

Vinyl, circa 1957+

Vicky, all-vinyl, high-heeled doll, body bends at waist, rooted saran hair, two larger sizes 12" and 14" were discontinued

| | 10½" | $25.00 | $100.00 |

Margie, circa 1958, toddler, rooted hair, made by Unique Doll Co.

| | 10" | $15.00 | $75.00 |

Cathy, circa 1961, infant, made by Unique Doll Co.

| | 10" | $10.00 | $25.00 |

Janie, circa 1962, baby

| | 8" | $10.00 | $25.00 |

14" hard plastic, auburn synthetic wig, sleep eyes with lashes and lashes painted under, Alice in Wonderland blue cotton dress, marked on back "Original Mary/ /Hoyer Doll" in circle, circa 1950s, $800.00. Courtesy Shirley's Doll House, Wheeling, IL.

Ideal Novelty and Toy Co.

1906 – 1980+, Brooklyn, NY. Produced their own composition dolls in early years.

CLOTH

> **Marks:**
> *Various including* "IDEAL" *(in a diamond),* "US of A: IDEAL NOVELTY," *and* "TOY CO. BROOKLYN, NEW YORK," *and others.*

Dennis the Menace, 1976

All-cloth, printed doll, comic strip character by Hank Ketcham, blond hair, freckles, wearing overalls, striped shirt

| | 7" | $5.00 | $15.00 |
| | 14" | $7.50 | $20.00 |

Peanuts Gang, 1976 – 1978

All-cloth, stuffed printed dolls from Peanuts cartoon strip by Charles Schulz, Charlie Brown, Lucy, Linus, Peppermint Patty, and Snoopy

| | 7" | $5.00 | $20.00 |
| | 14" | $8.00 | $25.00 |

16" composition Uneeda Kid, painted blue eyes, closed mouth, cloth body, composition lower arms and legs, molded boots, original bloomer suit and yellow slicker, Uneeda Biscuits box, right sleeve tag "Uneeda Kid Mark//Pat'd Dec 5, 1914, circa 1914, $475.00. Courtesy McMasters Harris Doll Auctions.

Snow White, 1938

Cloth body, mask face, painted eyes, black human hair wig, variation of red and white dress with small cape, Snow White and Seven Dwarfs printed on it. No other marks.

| | 16" | $150.00 | $550.00 |

Strawman, 1939

All-cloth, scarecrow character played by Ray Bolger in *Wizard of Oz* movie. Yarn hair, all original, wearing dark jacket and hat, tan pants, round paper hang tag

| | 17" | $250.00 | $1,000.00 |
| | 21" | $400.00 | $1,500.00 |

COMPOSITION

Composition Baby Doll, 1913+

Composition head, molded hair or wigged, painted or sleep eyes, cloth or composition body. May have Ideal diamond mark or hang tag. Original clothes.

12"	$25.00	$100.00+
16"	$40.00	$150.00+
20"	$50.00	$200.00+
24"	$65.00	$250.00+

Composition Child or Toddler, 1915+

Composition head, molded hair, or wigged, painted or sleep eyes, cloth or composition body. May have Ideal diamond mark or hang tag. Original clothes.

13"	$35.00	$125.00+
15"	$40.00	$150.00+
18"	$50.00	$200.00+

Composition Mama Doll, 1921+

Composition head and arms, molded hair or wigged, painted or sleep eyes, cloth body with crier and stitched swing leg, lower part composition

16"	$50.00	$250.00+
20"	$75.00	$300.00+
24"	$85.00	$350.00+

Buster Brown, 1929

Composition head, hands, legs, cloth body, tin eyes, red outfit. *Mark: "IDEAL" (in a diamond)*

16"	$75.00	$300.00

13" composition Snow White, mohair wig, sleep eyes with lashes, open mouth with teeth, original dress with red velvet bodice and rayon printed "Snow White" skirt, marked on back "Shirley Temple//13," circa 1938, $300.00. Courtesy McMasters Harris Doll Auctions.

Charlie McCarthy, 1938 – 1939

Hand puppet, composition head, felt hands, molded hat, molded features, wire monocle, cloth body, painted tuxedo
Mark: "Edgar Bergen's//©CHARLIE MCCARTHY//MADE IN U.S.A."

8"	$15.00	$60.00

Cinderella, 1938 – 1939

All-composition, brown, blond, or red human hair wig, flirty brown sleep eyes, open mouth, six teeth, same head mold as Ginger, Snow White, Mary Jane with dimple in chin, some wore formal evening gowns of organdy and taffeta, velvet cape, had rhinestone tiara, silver snap shoes. Sears catalog version has Celanese rayon gown. *Marks: none on head; "SHIRLEY TEMPLE//13" on body*

13"	$85.00	$325.00
16"	$90.00	$350.00
20"	$95.00	$375.00
22"	$100.00	$400.00
25"	$105.00	$425.00
27"	$110.00	$450.00

Cracker Jack Boy, 1917

Composition head, gauntlet hands, cloth body, molded boots, molded hair, wears blue or white sailor suit, cap, carries package of Cracker Jacks

14"	$100.00	$375.00

25" composition Deanna Durbin, human hair wig, sleep eyes, open mouth with teeth, five-piece body, original flower print dress, marked on head "Deanna Durbin//Ideal Doll" and "Ideal Doll//25" on back, circa 1938, $400.00. Courtesy McMasters Harris Doll Auctions.

Deanna Durbin, 1938 – 1941

All-composition, fully jointed, dark brown human hair wig, brown sleep eyes, open mouth, six teeth, felt tongue, original clothes, pin, reads: *"DEANNA DURBIN//A UNIVERSAL STAR."* More for fancy outfits. *Marks: "DEANNA DURBIN//IDEAL DOLL" on head; "IDEAL DOLL//21" on body*

15"	$125.00	$550.00
18"	$190.00	$800.00
21"	$200.00	$900.00
25"	$225.00	$1,100.00

Flexy, 1938 – 1942

Composition head, gauntlet hands, wooden torso and feet, flexible wire tubing for arms and legs, original clothes, paper tag. *Marks: "IDEAL DOLL//Made in U.S. A." or just "IDEAL DOLL" on head.*

Black Flexy, molded and painted hair, painted eyes, closed smiling mouth, tweed patched pants, felt suspenders

13½"	$85.00	$325.00

Baby Snooks, based on a character by Fannie Brice, designed by Kallus, molded and painted hair, painted eyes, open/closed mouth with teeth

13½"	$70.00	$275.00

Clown Flexy, looks like Mortimer Snerd, painted white as clown

13½"	$60.00	$225.00

Mortimer Snerd, Edgar Bergen's radio show dummy, molded and painted blond hair, smiling closed mouth, showing two teeth

13½"	$70.00	$275.00

Soldier, closed smiling mouth, molded and painted features, in khaki uniform

13½"	$65.00	$250.00

Sunny Sam and Sunny Sue, molded and painted hair, girl bobbed hair, pouty mouth, boy as smiling mouth

13½"	$65.00	$250.00

Flossie Flirt, 1924 – 1931

Composition head, limbs, cloth body, crier, tin flirty eyes, open mouth, upper teeth, original outfit, dress, bonnet, socks, and shoes

Mark: "IDEAL" in diamond with "U.S. of A."

14"	$60.00	$225.00+
18"	$65.00	$250.00+
20"	$70.00	$275.00+
22"	$75.00	$300.00+
24"	$80.00	$350.00+
28"	$100.00	$400.00+

20" composition Pinocchio, molded and painted features and body, felt hat, segmented wooden body, marked on front "Pinocchio/Des.© by Walt Disney/Made by Ideal Novelty & Toy Co," on back "©W.D.P./ Ideal Doll/Made in USA," circa 1939, $350.00. Courtesy Marge Meisinger.

Jiminy Cricket, 1940

8½", composition head and wood segmented body, yellow suit, black coat, blue felt trim on hat, felt collar, ribbon necktie, carries a wooden umbrella

Marks: "JIMINY CRICKET//IDEAL" and "BY IDEAL NOVELTY & TOY CO." on foot

9"	$125.00	$500.00

Judy Garland, 1939 – 1940, as Dorothy from *The Wizard of Oz*

All-composition, jointed, wig with braids, brown sleep eyes, open mouth, six teeth, designed by Bernard Lipfert, blue or red checked rayon jumper, white blouse

12" composition Liberty Boy, molded hair and doughboy costume, missing felt hat, details painted, moving legs, unmarked but most marked "Ideal" in a diamond on back, circa 1918, $250.00. Courtesy Shirley's Doll House.

Marks: "IDEAL" on head plus size number, and "USA" on body

13"	$250.00	$1,000.00+
15½"	$300.00	$1,200.00+
18"	$350.00	$1,400.00+

Judy Garland, 1940 – 1942

Teen, all-composition, wig, sleep eyes, open mouth, four teeth, original long dress. *Hang tag reads: "Judy Garland// A Metro Goldwyn Mayer//Star//in// 'Little Nellie//Kelly.'" Original pin reads "JUDY GARLAND METRO GOLDWYN MAYER STAR."*

Marks: "IN U.S.A." on head, "IDEAL DOLLS," a backwards "21" on body

15"	$175.00	$700.00
21"	$250.00	$1,000.00

Liberty Boy, 1918+ (Dough Boy)

All-composition, molded Army uniform, painted features, molded hair, felt hat with gold cord, Ideal diamond mark on back

12"	$65.00	$250.00

Pinocchio, 1939

Composition head, wood segmented body, painted features, clothes, yellow felt cap. *Marks: "PINOCCHIO//Des. a by Walt Disney //Made by Ideal Novelty & Toy Co" on front, "© W.D.P./ /ideal doll//made in USA" on back*

8"	$75.00	$300.00
11"	$115.00	$450.00
20"	$125.00	$550.00

Princess Beatrix, 1938 – 1943

Represents Princess Beatrix of the Netherlands, composition head, arms, legs, cloth body, flirty sleep eyes, fingers molded into fists, original organdy dress and bonnet

14"	$45.00	$175.00
16"	$50.00	$200.00
22"	$65.00	$250.00
26"	$75.00	$300.00

Seven Dwarfs, 1938

Composition head and cloth body, or all-cloth, painted mask face, head turns, removable clothes, each dwarf has name on cap, pick, and lantern

Cloth

12"	$50.00	$175.00

Composition

12"	$65.00	$250.00

Dopey, 1938

One of Seven Dwarfs, a ventriloquist doll, composition head and hands, cloth body, arms, and legs, hinged mouth with drawstring, molded tongue, painted eyes, large ears, long coat, cotton pants, felt shoes sewn to leg, felt cap with name, can stand alone. *Mark: "IDEAL DOLL" on neck*

20"	$200.00	$800.00

Snoozie, 1933+

Composition head, painted hair, hard rubber hands and feet, cloth body, open yawning mouth, molded tongue, sleep eyes, designed by Bernard Lipfert. *Marks: "©B. Lipfert//Made for Ideal Doll & Toy Corp. 1933" or "©by B. Lipfert" or "IDEAL SNOOZIE//B. LIPFERT" on head*

14"	$40.00	$150.00
16"	$65.00	$250.00
18"	$75.00	$300.00
20"	$90.00	$350.00

Snow White, 1938+

All-composition, jointed body, black mohair wig, flirty glass eyes, open mouth, four teeth, dimple in chin, used Shirley Temple body, red velvet bodice, rayon taffeta skirt pictures seven Dwarfs, velvet cape, some unmarked. *Marks: "Shirley Temple/18" or other size number on back*

11½"	$125.00	$500.00
13 – 14"	$135.00	$550.00
19"	$150.00	$600.00
22"	$165.00	$650.00
27"	$175.00	$700.00

Snow White, 1938 – 1939, as above, but with molded and painted bow and black hair, painted side-glancing eyes. Add 50 percent more for black version. *Mark: "IDEAL DOLL" on head*

14½"	$50.00	$200.00
17½"	$100.00	$400.00
19½"	$150.00	$600.00

Soozie Smiles, 1923

Two-headed composition doll with smiling face, sleep or painted eyes, and crying face with tears, molded and painted hair, cloth body and legs, composition arms, original clothes, tag, also in gingham check romper

15 – 17"	$75.00	$300.00

Tickletoes, 1928 – 1939

Composition head, rubber arms, legs, cloth body, squeaker in each leg, flirty sleep eyes, open mouth, two painted teeth, original organdy dress, bonnet, paper hang tag. *Marks: "IDEAL" in diamond with "U.S. of A." on head*

14"	$45.00	$250.00
17"	$75.00	$275.00
20"	$95.00	$300.00

Uneeda Kid, 1916

Advertising doll, carries package of Nabisco crackers, some have molded yellow hats, wears yellow rain coat, molded black boots

Painted eyes
11"	$75.00	$300.00

Sleep eyes
16"	$125.00	$475.00

ZuZu Kid, 1966 – 1967
Composition head, molded hair, composition hands, feet, cloth body, jointed hip, shoulders, girl in yellow with brown star clown costume, hat, holds small box ZuZu gingersnaps, licensed by National Biscuit Co.

15½"	$115.00	$450.00

HARD PLASTIC AND VINYL
Baby
11"	$15.00	$45.00
14"	$20.00	$65.00

Child
14"	$10.00	$35.00

April Shower, 1969
Vinyl, battery operated, splashes hands, head turns
14"	$8.00	$28.00

Baby Coos, 1948 – 1953, also Brother and Sister Coos
Designed by Bernard Lipfert, hard plastic head, stuffed magic skin body, jointed arms, sleep eyes, molded and painted hair, closed mouth, or cloth and vinyl body. Many magic skin bodies deteriorated or tuned dark. *Marks on head, "16 IDEAL DOLL// MADE IN U.S. A." or unmarked*

14"	$15.00	$75.00
16"	$25.00	$100.00
18"	$30.00	$125.00
20"	$40.00	$150.00
22"	$45.00	$175.00
27"	$50.00	$200.00
30"	$55.00	$250.00

Baby Crissy, 1973 – 1976
All-vinyl, jointed body, legs and arms foam filled, rooted auburn grow hair, two painted teeth, brown sleep eyes. *Mark: "©1972//IDEAL TOY COPR.//2M 5511//B OR GHB-H-225" on back*

White 24"	$35.00	$150.00
24"	$420.00* MIB	

Baby Pebbles, 1963 – 1964
Character from the Flintstone cartoons, Hanna Barbera Productions, vinyl head, arms, legs, soft body, side-glancing blue painted eyes, rooted hair with topknot and bone, leopard print nightie and trim on flannel blanket. Also as an all-vinyl toddler, jointed body, outfit with leopard print.

Baby
14"	$75.00	$225.00

Toddler
16"	$50.00	$200.00
16"	$265.00* MIB	

Tiny Pebbles, 1964 – 1966, smaller version, came with plastic log cradle in 1965.

Toddler
12"	$40.00	$150.00

14" soft vinyl Honey Moon, white string hair, painted features, blue eyes, original blue and silver costume with removable clear plastic space helmet, marked "© 1965-C.T.-N.Y.N.S./Ideal Toy/Corp/ HM/4-2-2H," circa 1965, $55.00. Courtesy Shirley's Doll House.

8" vinyl Little Betsy Wetsy, rooted curly saran hair, sleep eyes, nursing mouth, jointed body with bent baby legs, drinks and wets, blue cotton dress, marked on head and back "IDEAL DOLL/8," circa 1957, $75.00. Courtesy Carol Stover.

Bamm-Bamm, 1964

Character from Flintstone cartoon, Hanna Barbera Productions, all-vinyl head, jointed body, rooted blond saran hair, painted blue side-glancing eyes, leopard skin suit, cap, club

12"	$35.00	$150.00
16"	$50.00	$200.00

Belly Button Babies, 1971

Me So Glad, Me So Silly, Me So Happy, vinyl head, rooted hair, painted eyes, press button in belly to move arms, head, and bent legs; both boy and girl versions

White	9½"	$7.50	$35.00+
Black	9½"	$10.00	$45.00+

Betsy McCall, 1952 – 1953: See that section.

Betsy Wetsy, 1937 – 1938, 1954 – 1956, 1959 – 1962, 1982 – 1985

Hard rubber head, soft rubber body, sleep or painted eyes, molded hair, open mouth for bottle, drinks, wets, came with bottle, some in layettes. *Marks: "IDEAL" on head, "IDEAL" on body*

11"	$35.00	$125.00
13½"	$180.00*	
15"	$40.00	$150.00

Bizzie-Lizzie, 1971 – 1972

Vinyl head, jointed body, rooted blond hair, sleep eyes, plugged into power pack, she irons, vacuums, uses feather duster, two D-cell batteries

White	18"	$10.00	$50.00
Black	18"	$15.00	$65.00

Bonny Braids, 1951 – 1953

Comic strip character, daughter of Dick Tracy and Tess Trueheart, vinyl head, jointed arms, "Magic Skin" rubber one-piece body, open mouth, one tooth, painted yellow hair, two yellow saran pigtails, painted blue eyes, coos when squeezed, long white gown, bed jacket, toothbrush, Ipana toothpaste. *Mark: "©1951//Chi. Tribune//IDEAL DOLL//U.S.A." on neck*

Baby

11½"	$35.00	$125.00
14"	$250.00*	

Toddler, 1953, vinyl head, jointed hard plastic body, open/closed mouth with two painted teeth, walker

11½"	$35.00	$150.00
14"	$40.00	$200.00

Butterick Sew Easy Designing Set, 1953

Plastic mannequin of adult woman, molded blond hair, came with Butterick patterns and sewing accessories

14"	$20.00	$65.00

Captain Action® Superhero, 1966 – 1968

Represents a fictional character who changes disguises to become a new identity, vinyl articulated figure, dark hair and eyes

Captain Action 1967 Promo
12"	$100.00	$400.00

Batman disguise
	$30.00	$150.00

Silver Streak box only
	$400.00*

Capt. Flash Gordon accessories
	$40.00	$150.00

Phantom disguise only
	$50.00	$200.00

Steve Canyon disguise
	$50.00	$200.00

Superman set w/dog
	$35.00	$175.00

Lone Ranger outfit only
	$30.00	$150.00

Spiderman disguise only
	$30.00	$150.00

Tonto outfit only
	$30.00	$150.00

Action Boy
9"	$65.00	$250.00

Robin Accessories
	$35.00	$150.00
Special Ed.	$75.00	$300.00
Dr. Evil	$40.00	$250.00

Dr. Evil Lab Set
	$200.00	$2,000.00

Super Girl
11½"	$75.00	$300.00

Chelsea, 1967 (Jet Set Doll)

Vinyl head, posable body, rooted straight hair, mod fashions, earrings, strap shoes
24"	$15.00	$50.00

Clarabelle, 1954, clown from *Howdy Doody* TV show,

mask face, cloth body, dressed in satin Clarabelle outfit with noise box and horn, later vinyl face
16"	$25.00	$90.00
20"	$30.00	$110.00

Crissy®, Beautiful Crissy, 1969 – 1974

All-vinyl, dark brown eyes, long hair, turn knob in back to make hair grow, some with swivel waist (1971), pull string to turn head (1972), pull string to talk (1971). Reissued ca. 1982 – 1983.

14" hard plastic Toni, auburn wig, sleep eyes with lashes, closed mouth, jointed body, original dress with yellow dotted Swiss bodice, red skirt, marked "P-90//Ideal Doll// Made in USA," on head, and "Ideal Doll//P-90" on back, circa 1950s, $200.00.

13" vinyl Bonnie Braids, molded hair with saran braids, sleep eyes with lashes, open/closed mouth with painted teeth, plastic walker body, original white pique dress, original box and wrist tag, marked on head "COPR.1951/CHICAGO TRIBUNE/IDEAL DOLL," circa 1953, $300.00. Courtesy McMasters Harris Doll Auctions.

14" hard plastic Toni, blond wig, sleep eyes with lashes, closed mouth, jointed body, original yellow and blue dress embroidered trim, marked "P-90//Ideal Doll// Made in USA" on head and "Ideal Doll//P-90" on back, circa 1950s, $250.00. Courtesy Carol Stover.

17½" vinyl Talking Crissy, growing auburn hair, brown sleep eyes with lashes, open closed smiling mouth with painted teeth, pull string and doll says 12 sentences, jointed body, orange rayon dress, original box, marked on neck "© 1969/ITC/GH – 17-H120," circa 1971, $65.00. Courtesy Carol Stover.

First year hair grew to floor length. More for black version.

1969, white
17½"	$25.00	$110.00

Black, MIB
17½"	$455.00*

Crissy's Friends & Family

Brandi, 1972 – 1973; Kerry, 1971; Tressy, 1970 (Sears Exclusive); Crissy's Friends, vinyl head, painted eyes, rooted growing hair, swivel waist
17½"	$40.00	$150.00+

Cinnamon, Velvet's Little Sister, 1972 – 1974, vinyl head, painted eyes, rooted auburn growing hair, orange polka dotted outfit, additional outfits sold separately. *Marks: "©1971//IDEAL TOY CORP.//G-H-12-H18//HONG KONG//IDEAL 1069-4 b" head; "©1972//IDEAL TOY CORP.//U.S. PAT-3-162-976//OTHER PAT. PEND.//HONG KONG" on back*

White
13½"	$12.00	$50.00

Black
13½"	$15.00	$55.00

Cricket, 1971 – 1972 (Sears Exclusive); Dina, 1972 – 1973; Mia, 1971, vinyl, members of the Crissy® family, growing hair dolls, painted teeth, swivel waist
15"	$50.00	$200.00

Tara, 1976, all-vinyl black doll, long black rooted hair that "grows," sleep eyes, marked "©1975//IDEAL TOY CORP//H-250//HONG KONG" on head and "©1970//IDEAL TOY CORP//GH-15//M5169-01//MADE IN HONG KONG" on buttock
15½"	$45.00	$390.00

Velvet, 1971 – 1973, Crissy's younger cousin, vinyl head, body, grow hair, talker, pull-string, marked "©1969//IDEAL TOY CORP.//GH-15-H-157" on head ©1971//IDEAL TOY CORP.//TV15//US PAT 3162973//OTHER PATENTS PEND." on back
15"	$20.00	$125.00

Velvet, 1974, non-talker, other accessories, grow hair
15"	$9.00	$35.00

Daddy's Girl, 1961
Vinyl head and arms, plastic body, swivel

waist, jointed ankles, rooted saran hair, blue sleep eyes, closed smiling mouth, preteen girl, label on dress reads *"Daddy's Girl."* *Marks: "IDEAL TOY CORP.//g-42-1" on head, "IDEAL TOY CORP.//G-42" on body*

38"	$300.00	$1,200.00
42"	$350.00	$1,400.00

Davy Crockett and his horse, 1955 – 1956
All-plastic, can be removed from horse, fur cap, buckskin clothes

4½"	$13.00	$50.00

Diana Ross, 1969
From the Supremes (singing group), all-vinyl, rooted black bouffant hair-do, gold sheath, feathers, gold shoes, or chartreuse mini-dress, print scarf, and black shoes

17½"	$75.00	$300.00
17½"	$535.00* MIB	

Dorothy Hamill, 1978
Olympic skating star, vinyl head, plastic posable body, rooted short brown hair, comes on ice rink stand with skates; also extra outfits available

11½"	$20.00	$60.00

Evel Knievel, 1974 – 1977
All-plastic stunt figure, helmet, more with stuntcycle

7"	$7.50	$25.00

Harmony, ca. 1972
Vinyl, battery operated, makes music with guitar

21"	$45.00	$100.00

Harriet Hubbard Ayer, 1953, Cosmetic doll
Vinyl stuffed head, hard plastic (Toni) body, wigged or rooted hair, came with eight-piece H. H. Ayer cosmetic kit, beauty table and booklet. *Marks: "MK 16//IDEAL DOLL" on head "IDEAL DOLL//P-91" on body*

14"	$30.00	$175.00
16"	$35.00	$200.00
19"	$40.00	$225.00
21"	$45.00	$275.00

Hopalong Cassidy, 1949 – 1950
Vinyl stuffed head, vinyl hands, molded and painted gray hair, painted blue eyes, one-piece body, dressed in black cowboy outfit, leatherette boots, guns, holster, black felt hat. *Marked: "Hopalong Cassidy" on buckle*

18"	$20.00	$80.00
23"	$25.00	$100.00
27"	$40.00	$150.00

Plastic, with horse, Topper

4½"	$10.00	$40.00

Howdy Doody, 1950 – 1953
Television personality, hard plastic head, red molded and painted hair, freckles, ventriloquist doll, mouth operated by pull string, cloth body and limbs, dressed in cowboy outfit, scarf reads *"HOWDY DOODY."* *Mark: "IDEAL" on head*

19"	$100.00	$200.00
24"	$125.00	$250.00

28" vinyl Lori Martin, long rooted dark hair, blue sleep eyes with lashes, closed mouth, jointed body, original dungarees and check shirt with ribbon "National Velvet's Lori Martin," marked on head "Metro Goldwyn Mayer Inc./Mfg. By/Ideal Toy Corp/38," circa 1961, $750.00. Courtesy McMasters Harris Doll Auctions.

1954, with vinyl hands, wears boots, jeans

18"	$100.00	$200.00
20"	$125.00	$250.00
25"	$150.00	$300.00

Judy Splinters, 1949 – 1950
Vinylite TV character

18"	$75.00	$200.00

Kissy, 1961 – 1964

Vinyl head, rigid vinyl toddler body, rooted saran hair, sleep eyes, jointed wrists, press hands together and mouth puckers, makes kissing sound, original dress, panties, t-strap sandals. *Marks: "©IDEAL CORP.//K-21-L" on head "IDEAL TOY CORP.// K22//PAT. PEND." on body*
White

22½"	$40.00	$155.00

Black

22½"	$45.00	$175.00

Kissy Baby, 1963 – 1964, all-vinyl, bent legs

22"	$55.00	$240.00

Tiny Kissy, 1963 – 1968, smaller toddler, red outfit, white pinafore with hearts. *Marks: "IDEAL CORP.//K-16-1" on head "IDEAL TOY CORP./K-16-2" on body*
White

16"	$20.00	$80.00

Black

16"	$25.00	$90.00

Loni Anderson, 1981, star of TV sitcom, *WKRP in Cincinnati*

Vinyl, posable fashion doll packaged with picture of Loni Anderson. This doll was featured in Ideal's 1981 catalog in a red dress, white high heels, blond wig, unsure how many produced

11½"	$10.00	$50.00

Lori Martin, 1961, character from *National Velvet* TV show

All-vinyl, swivel waist, jointed body, including ankles, blue sleep eyes, rooted dark hair, individual fingers, dressed shirt, jeans, black vinyl boots, felt hat. *Marks: "Metro Goldwyn Mayer Inc.//Mfg. by//IDEAL TOY CORP//38" on head, "©IDEAL TOY CORP.//38" on back*

30"	$175.00	$750.00
38"	$200.00	$800.00
42"	$2,000.00 store display	

Magic Skin Baby, 1940, 1946 – 1949

Hard plastic head, one-piece molded latex body and legs, jointed arms, sleep eyes, molded and painted hair, some with fancy layettes or trunks, latex usually darkened

13 – 14"	$25.00	$50.00
15 – 16"	$20.00	$75.00
17 – 18"	$25.00	$100.00
20"	$35.00	$125.00

Marama, 1940: See Shirley Temple section.

Left: 15" hard plastic Mary Hartline, sleep eyes with lashes and shadow, blond side-part wig, jointed body, red cotton costume monogrammed "Mary Hartline," white leatherette boots, original hang tag "This Is/Ideal's Official/Mary Hartline/Doll," marked on HEAD "P-91//IDEAL DOLL//MADE IN U.S.A." on back "IDEAL DOLL//P-91," circa 1952, $650.00. Courtesy Ann Wencel.

Mary Hartline, 1952, from TV personality on Super Circus show

Hard plastic, fully jointed, blond nylon wig, blue sleep eyes, lashes, black eyeshadow over and under eye, red, white, or green drum majorette costume and baton, red heart paper hang tag, with original box. *Marks: "P-91//IDEAL DOLL//MADE IN U.S.A." on head, "IDEAL DOLL//P-91 or IDEAL//16" on body*

7½"	$35.00	$125.00
16"	$300.00	$650.00
23"	$375.00	$750.00

19" vinyl Magic Hair Crissy, brown rooted hair, painted eyes, closed mouth, poseable body, in original lace camisole and satin skirt, teenage characteristics, marked "©1977/IDEAL TOY CORP./ M.H.C. – 19-H28//HONG KONG," circa 1977, $35.00. Courtesy Carol Stover.

Miss Clairol, Glamour Misty, 1965 – 1966

Vinyl head and arms, rigid plastic legs, body, rooted platinum blond saran hair, side-glancing eyes, high-heeled feet. Teen doll had cosmetics to change her hair. All original. *Marks: "©1965//IDEAL TOY CORP//W-12-3" on neck, "©1965 IDEAL" in oval on lower rear torso*

12"	$10.00	$40.00

Miss Curity, 1953

Hard plastic, saran wig, sleep eyes, black eyeshadow, nurse's outfit, navy cape, white cap, Bauer & Black first aid kit and book, curlers, uses Toni body. *Mark: "P-90 IDEAL DOLL, MADE IN U.S.A." on head*

14½"	$200.00	$600.00

Miss Ideal, 1961

All vinyl, rooted nylon hair, jointed ankles, wrists, waist, arms, legs, closed smiling mouth, sleep eyes, original dress, with beauty kit and comb. *Marks: "©IDEAL TOY CORP.//SP-30-S" head; "©IDEAL TOY CORP.//G-30-S" back*

25"	$100.00	$375.00
30"	$125.00	$475.00

Miss Revlon, 1956 – 1959

Vinyl, hard plastic teenage body, jointed shoulders, waist, hips, and knees, high-heeled feet, rooted saran hair, sleep eyes, lashes, pierced ears, hang tag, original dress. Some came with trunks. *Mark: "VT 20//IDEAL DOLL"*

15"	$100.00	$350.00

18" vinyl Pattite dolls, rooted golden auburn and brown hair, sleep eyes with lashes, closed mouth, strung five-piece bodies, original cotton dresses, original hang tag "IDEAL Pettite," marked "IDEAL TOY CORP/G – 18," circa 1960, $700.00 each. Courtesy Marge Meisinger.

10½" vinyl Little Miss Revlon, rooted synthetic wig, sleep eyes with molded lashes, pierced ears with pearl earrings, jointed body with swivel waist, high heel feet, painted nails and toes, in cotton Calypso skirt and blouse trimmed with rick-rack, marked on head "IDEAL TOY CORP/VT – 10½," circa 1959, $175.00. Courtesy Carol Stover.

	18"	$150.00	$500.00
	20"	$200.00	$600.00
	23"	$225.00	$700.00
1957			
	26"	$75.00	$300.00

Little Miss Revlon, 1958 – 1960

Vinyl head and strung body, jointed head, arms, legs, swivel waist, high-heeled feet, rooted hair, sleep eyes, pierced ears with earrings, original clothes, with box, many extra boxed outfits available

10½"	$75.00	$175.00

Mysterious Yokum, Li'l Honest Abe, 1953

Son of comic strip character, Li'l Abner, hard plastic head, body, "Magic Skin" arms and legs, painted eyes, molded hair, forelock, wears overalls, one suspender, knit cap, and sock

$20.00	$80.00

Palooka, Joan, 1953

Daughter of comic strip character, Joe Palooka, vinyl, head, "Magic Skin" body, jointed arms and legs, yellow molded hair, topknot of yellow saran, blue painted eyes, open/closed mouth, smells like baby powder, original pink dress with blue ribbons, came with Johnson's baby powder and soap. *Mark: "©1952//HAM FISHER//IDEAL DOLL" on head*

14"	$50.00	$250.00

Patti Playpal and related dolls, 1959 – 1962

All-vinyl, jointed wrists, sleep eyes, curly or straight saran hair, bangs, closed mouth, blue or red and white check dress with pinafore, three-year-old size, reissued in 1981 and 1982 from old molds, more for redheads. *Mark: "IDEAL TOY CORP.//G 35 OR B-19-1" on head*

White

35"	$80.00	$350.00

Black

35"	$90.00	$375.00

Pattite, 1960

All-vinyl, rooted saran hair, sleep eyes, red and white check dress, white pinafore with her name on it, looks like Patti Playpal

18"	$150.00	$300.00
18"	$1,060.00*	MIB

Bonnie Play Pal, 1959

Patti's three-month-old sister, made only one year, vinyl, rooted blond hair, blue sleep eyes, blue and white check outfit, white shoes and socks

24"	$70.00	$275.00

Johnny Play Pal, 1959
Vinyl, blue sleep eyes, molded hair, Patti's three-month-old brother
24"	$70.00	$275.00

Penny Play Pal, 1959
Vinyl jointed body, rooted blond or brown curly hair, blue sleep eyes, wears organdy dress, vinyl shoes, socks, Patti's two-year-old sister, made only one year. *Marks: "IDEAL DOLL//32-E-L" or "B-32-B PAT. PEND." on head, "IDEAL" on back*
32"	$100.00	$400.00

Peter Playpal, 1960 – 1961
Vinyl, gold sleep eyes, freckles, pug nose, rooted blond or brunette hair, original clothes, black plastic shoes. *Marks: "©IDEAL TOY CORP.// BE-35-38" on head, "©IDEAL TOY CORP.//W-38//PAT. PEND." on body*
38"	$375.00	$850.00
Walker		
38"	$450.00	$900.00

Suzy Play Pal, 1959
Vinyl, jointed body, rooted curly short blond saran hair, blue sleep eyes, wears purple dotted dress, Patti's one-year-old sister
28"	$80.00	$375.00

Plassie, 1942
Hard plastic head, molded and painted hair, composition shoulder plate, composition limbs, stuffed pink oilcloth body, blue sleep eyes, original dress, bonnet. *Mark: "IDEAL DOLL//MADE IN USA//PAT.NO. 225 2077" on head*
16"	$25.00	$100.00
19"	$35.00	$125.00
24"	$45.00	$175.00

Samantha, 1965 – 1966, from TV show *Bewitched*
Vinyl head, body, rooted saran hair, posable arms and legs, wearing red witch's costume, with broom, painted side-glancing eyes, other costume included negligee. *Mark: "IDEAL DOLL//M-12-E-2" on head*
12"	$45.00	$175.00
All original, with broom		
	$300.00	$600.00
Mint-in-box	$1,500.00 –	$2.000.00

Tabitha, 1966, baby from TV show *Bewitched*, vinyl head, body, rooted platinum hair, painted blue side-glancing eyes, closed mouth, came in pajamas. *Mark: "©1965//Screen Gems, Inc.//Ideal Toy Corp.//T.A. 18-6//H-25" on head*
14"	$40.00	$150.00

8" vinyl Pepper, rooted synthetic hair, painted side-glancing eyes, freckles, plastic body and flexible limbs, flat feet, original blue dress with red buttons, marked on head "IDEAL TOY CORP./G-9 – 1," circa 1963, $50.00. Courtesy Carol Stover.

38" Peter Playpal and 35" Patti Playpal, rooted wigs, sleep eyes, closed mouths, five-piece vinyl bodies, original cotton outfits, marked on head "IDEAL TOY CORP.// BE-35-38," circa 1959, $775.00, $675.00 respectively. Courtesy McMasters Harris Doll Auctions.

16" hard plastic Saucy Walker, saran braided wig, flirty sleep eyes with lashes, open/closed mouth, head turning walker, holes in chest for crier, original cotton dress, original box, "Ideal's Saucy Walker Doll," marked on neck and back "IDEAL DOLL/W 16," circa 1952, $300.00. Courtesy McMasters Harris Doll Auctions.

22" hard plastic Saucy Walker, saran braided wig, flirty sleep eyes with lashes, open/closed mouth, head turning walker, holes in chest for crier, original cotton dress, hang tag "Ideal's Walking Flirting Doll," marked on neck and back "IDEAL DOLL/W 22," circa 1952, $325.00. Courtesy Vicki Johnson.

All original	$150.00	$300.00
Mint-in-box	$1,000.00 – $1,500.00	

Saucy Walker, 1951 – 1955

All hard plastic, walks, turns head from side to side, flirty blue eyes, crier, open/closed mouth, teeth, holes in body for crier, saran wig, plastic curlers, came as toddler, boy, and "Big Sister"

16"	$60.00	$225.00
22"	$85.00	$325.00
Black		
16"	$50.00	$200.00
Big Sister, 1954		
25"	$40.00	$200.00
1960 – 1961		

All-vinyl, rooted saran hair, blue sleep eyes, closed smiling mouth, walker, original print dress, pinafore, box. *Marks: "©IDEAL TOY CORP.//T28X-60" or "IDEAL TOY CO.//BYE S 285 B" on head, "IDEAL TOY CORP.//T-28 Pat. Pend." on body*

28"	$50.00	$200.00
32"	$65.00	$250.00

Smokey Bear, 1953+

Bakelite vinyl face and paws, rayon plush stuffed body, vinyl forest ranger hat, badge, shovel, symbol of US National Forest Service, wears Smokey marked belt, twill trousers, came with Junior Forest Ranger kit. Issued on 50th anniversary of Ideal's original teddy bear.

18"	$35.00	$185.00
25"	$45.00	$200.00
1957, Talking		
	$25.00	$100.00

16" vinyl head and limbs Thumbelina, rooted saran hair, painted eyes, open/closed mouth, cloth body with wind knob in back makes doll wiggle, original nylon gown with ribbon "Tiny Thumbelina," original case with layette, marked on head "IDEAL TOY CORP./OTT – 16," circa 1961, $350.00. Courtesy Shirley's Doll House.

Snoozie, 1949
1933 doll reissued in vinyl, cloth body with Swiss music box

11"	$20.00	$75.00
14"	$182.00*	
20"	$40.00	$150.00

1958 – 1965
All-vinyl, rooted saran hair, blue sleep eyes, open/closed mouth, cry voice, knob makes doll wiggle, close eyes, crier, in flannel pajamas

14"	$12.00	$45.00

1964 – 1965
Vinyl head, arms, legs, soft body, rooted saran hair, sleep eyes, turn knob, she squirms, opens and closes eyes, and cries. *Marks: "©1965//IDEAL TOY CORP//YTT-14-E" on head, "IDEAL TOY CORP//U.S. PAT. NO. 3,029,552" on knob on back*

20"	$15.00	$60.00

19" vinyl Tiffany Taylor, rooted hair changes colors blond to brown, painted eyes, jointed arms, legs, and head, high heel feet, gold swim suit, original box, marked on back "Ideal (in oval) Hollis NY 11429/2M-5854-01/1," circa 1974, $75.00. Courtesy Carol Stover.

Sparkle Plenty, 1947 – 1950
Hard plastic head, "Magic Skin" body may be dark, yarn hair, character from Dick Tracy comics

14"	$100.00	$250.00
14"	$700.00*	

Tammy and Her Family
Tammy, 1962+, vinyl head, arms, plastic legs and torso, head joined at neck base. *Marks: "©IDEAL TOY CORP.//BS12" on head, "©IDEAL TOY CORP.//BS-12//1" on back*

White	12"	$15.00	$110.00
NRFB	12"	$200.00*	
Pos'n	12"	$25.00	$65.00
Mom	12"	$20.00	$80.00
Ted	12"	$30.00	$100.00
Pepper	9"	$20.00	$65.00
Clothing (MIP)		$20.00	$75.00

Thumbelina, 1961 – 1962
Vinyl head and limbs, soft cloth body, painted eyes, rooted saran hair, open/closed mouth, wind knob on back moves body, crier in 1962

16"	$125.00	$300.00
19"	$760.00*	

1982 – 1983
All-vinyl one-piece body, rooted hair, comes in quilted carrier, also black

7"	$20.00	$75.00

1982, 1985
Reissue from 1960s mold, vinyl head, arms, legs, cloth body, painted eyes, crier, open mouth, molded or rooted hair, original with box

18"	$8.00	$30.00

12" vinyl Tammy, rooted hair, painted side-glancing eyes, jointed body, flat feet, original blue cotton dress, marked on head "©IDEAL TOY CORP/BS – 12/1," circa 1962, $55.00. Courtesy Carol Stover.

17" soft vinyl Posie, marked "IDEAL DOLL//VP – 17" on head, "IDEAL DOLL" on back, hard plastic body, jointed bent knees, walker, rooted saran hair, flirty blue sleep eyes, came with curlers, wears short blue dress, white socks/shoes, box says "Ideal's//Posie//Doll/ /with exclusive//MAGIC KNEE ACTION//The walking doll of a hundred life-like poses," mint-in-box, circa 1954 – 1956, $250.00. Courtesy Iva Mae Jones.

14" hard plastic Toni, auburn wig, sleep eyes with lashes, closed mouth, jointed body, original yellow cotton dress with rick-rack trim, marked "P-90//Ideal Doll// Made in USA," on head and "Ideal Doll//P-90" on back, circa 1950s, $250.00. Courtesy Carol Stover.

Thumbelina, Ltd. Production Collector's Doll, 1983 – 1985

Porcelain, painted eyes, molded and painted hair, beige crocheted outfit with pillow booties, limited edition 1,000

18"	$20.00	$75.00
24"	$25.00	$100.00

Tiny Thumbelina, 1962 – 1968

Vinyl head, limbs, cloth body, painted eyes, rooted saran hair, wind key in back makes body head move, original tagged clothes

Marks: "IDEAL TOY CORP.//OTT 14" on head, "U.S. PAT. # 3029552" on body

14"	$465.00* MIB

Tiffany Taylor, 1974 – 1976

All-vinyl, rooted hair, top of head turns to change color, painted eyes, teenage body, high-heeled, extra outfits available

	19"	$20.00	$75.00+
Black	19"	$25.00	$85.00+

Toni, 1949, designed by Bernard Lipfert

All hard plastic, jointed body, Dupont nylon wig, usually blue eyes, rosy cheeks, closed mouth, came with Toni wave set and curlers in original dress, with hang tag. Marks: "IDEAL DOLL//MADE IN U.S.A." on head, "IDEAL DOLL" and P-series number on body

P-90	14"	$125.00	$450.00
P-91	16"	$175.00	$600.00
P-92	19"	$185.00	$650.00
P-93	21"	$200.00	$700.00
P-94	22½"	$225.00	$800.00

Tuesday Taylor, 1976 – 1977, vinyl, poseable body, turn head to change color of hair, clothing tagged "IDEAL Tuesday Taylor"

11½"	$20.00	$65.00

Whoopsie, 1978 – 1981, vinyl, reissued in 1981. Marked: "22//©IDEAL TOY CORP//HONG KONG//1978//H298"

13"	$6.00	$25.00

Wizard of Oz Series, 1984 – 1985

Tin Man, Lion, Scarecrow, Dorothy, and Toto, all-vinyl, six-piece posable bodies

9"	$9.00	$35.00

Batgirl, Mera Queen of Atlantis, or Super Girl, 1967 – 1968

All-vinyl, posable body, rooted hair, painted side-glancing eyes, dressed in costume

MIB	11½"	$900.00

Wonder Woman

11½"	$25.00	$75.00

First price indicates played with or missing accessories doll; second price is for mint condition doll.

Baby Bundles
White   16" $4.00 $15.00

Baby Yawnie, 1974
Vinyl head, cloth body
          15" $5.00 $20.00

Blythe, 1972
Pull string to change color of eyes, "mod" clothes
          11½" $300.00 $1,300.00
          11½" $2,920.00* MIB

Bob Scout, 1974
          9" $20.00 $60.00

Butch Cassidy or Sundance Kid
          4" $4.00 $15.00

Charlie Chaplin, 1973
All-cloth, walking mechanism
          14" $25.00 $90.00

Cover Girls, 1978
Posable elbows and knees, jointed hands
Dana, black
          12½" $15.00 $50.00
Darci, blond
          12½" $15.00 $60.00
Darci, brunette
          12½" $17.00 $65.00
Darci, redhead
          12½" $20.00 $80.00
Erica, redhead
          12½" $35.00 $100.00

Crumpet 1970, vinyl and plastic
          18" $10.00 $100.00

Dusty, 1974, vinyl teenage doll
          11" $10.00 $20.00
Skye, black, teenage friend of Dusty
          11" $8.00 $25.00

Gabbigale, 1972
White   18" $5.00 $20.00
Black   18" $8.00 $35.00

Garden Gals, 1972, hand bent to hold watering can
          6½" $2.00 $6.00

Hardy Boys, 1978,   Shaun Cassidy, Parker Stevenson
          12" $15.00 $60.00

Indiana Jones, 1981
          12" $50.00 $150.00

12½" vinyl Darci auburn rooted hair, long turquoise gown, plastic stand, jointed hands, posable elbows and knees, circa 1978, $20.00. Private collection.

11½" hard plastic Blythe, pull string opens, closes eyes, and changes color from blue to yellow to green to pink, closed mouth, black synthetic wig, large head, small body, vinyl arms, circa 1972, $300.00 to $700.00 played with condition. Courtesy Kathleen Kelly.

International Velvet, 1976, Tatum O'Neill
11½"	$8.00	$25.00

Jenny Jones and baby, 1973, all-vinyl
Jenny, 9", Baby, 2½"
set	$8.00	$25.00

Rose Petal, 1984, scented
7"	$10.00	$20.00

Six Million Dollar Man Figures, 1975 – 1977
TV show starring Lee Majors
Bionic Man, Big Foot
13"	$7.00	$25.00

Bionic Man, Masketron Robot
13"	$8.00	$30.00

Bionic Woman, Robot
13"	$27.00	$85.00

Jaime Sommers, Bionic Woman
13"	$25.00	$100.00

Oscar Goldman, 1975 – 1977, with exploding briefcase
13"	$15.00	$50.00

Steve Austin, The Bionic Man
13"	$35.00	$150.00

Steve Austin, Bionic Grip, 1977
13"	$25.00	$95.00

Star Wars Figures, 1974 – 1978
Large size action figures
First price indicates doll played with or missing accessories; second price is for mint-in-box/package doll. Complete doll in excellent condition would be somewhere in between. Never removed from box would bring greater prices.

Ben-Obi-Wan Kenobi
12"	$25.00	$95.00

Boba Fett
13"	$55.00	$175.00

C-3PO
12"	$40.00	$185.00

Chewbacca
12"	$40.00	$145.00

Darth Vader
12"	$60.00	$250.00

Han Solo
12"	$125.00	$500.00

IG-88
15"	$100.00	$550.00

Jawa
8½"	$25.00	$100.00

Leia Organa
11½"	$65.00	$275.00

Luke Skywalker
12"	$65.00	$275.00

R2-D2, robot
7½"	$45.00	$175.00

Stormtrooper
12"	$50.00	$235.00

Steve Scout, 1974, black
9"	$20.00	$70.00

Strawberry Shortcake, ca. 1980 – 1986
5"	$6.00	$50.00
Lime Chiffon		$16.00*
Peach Blush, mechanical		$2,200.00*
Berry Happy Home		$760.00*

Sweet Cookie, 1972
18"	$8.00	$30.00

Terminator, Arnold Schwarzenegger, 1991, talks
13½"	$6.00	$25.00

Klumpe

Caricature figures made of felt over wire armature with painted mask faces, produced in Barcelona, Spain, from about 1952 to the mid-1970s. Figures represent professionals, hobbyists, Spanish dancers, historical characters, and contemporary males and females performing a wide variety of tasks. Of the 200 or more different figures, the most common are Spanish dancers, bull fighters, and doctors. Some Klumpes were imported by Effanbee in the early 1950s. Originally the figures had two sewn-on identifying cardboard tags.

11" felt Napoleon, circa 1960, $110.00. Courtesy Sondra Gast.

10½" unmarked cloth Klumpe-type cowboy, painted features, yellow plaid shirt, brown hat, wears guns, circa 1950s – 1960s, $78.00. Courtesy Christine McWilliams.

Average figure
10½"	$25.00	$100.00

Elaborate figure, MIB with accessories
10½"		$250.00+

Knickerbocker

CLOTH

Clown
17"	$5.00	$25.00

Disney characters
Donald Duck, Mickey Mouse, etc., all-cloth
10½"	$125.00	$425.00

Mickey Mouse, ca. 1930s, oilcloth eyes
15"	$3,100.00*

Pinocchio, cloth and plush
13"	$65.00	$250.00

10" composition Pinocchio, molded and painted hair, painted features with watermelon mouth, molded mouth, arms with composition hands, cloth suit and cap, wrist tag, "Walt Disney's Pinocchio," circa 1930s, $900.00. Courtesy McMasters Harris Doll Auctions.

Seven Dwarfs, 1939+
14"	$65.00	$260.00

Snow White, all-cloth
16"	$95.00	$365.00

Holly Hobby, 1970s, cloth, later vinyl

Cloth
9"	$7.00	$25.00
26"	$25.00	$100.00

Vinyl
16"	$15.00	$35.00

COMPOSITION

"Blondie" comic strip characters

Composition, painted features, hair

Alexander Bumsted
9"	$100.00	$375.00

Dagwood Bumsted
14"	$175.00	$650.00

Child, 1938+
15"	$55.00	$285.00

Mickey Mouse, 1930s – 1940s

Composition, cloth body
18"	$300.00	$1,100.00

Jiminy Cricket, all-composition
10"	$125.00	$495.00

Pinocchio, all-composition
13"	$125.00	$400.00
14"	$1,500.00* in original labeled box	

Seven Dwarfs, 1939+
9" each	$75.00	$275.00

Sleeping Beauty, 1939+, bent right arm
15"	$100.00	$425.00
18"	$130.00	$495.00

Snow White, 1937+, all-composition, bent right arm, black wig
15"	$110.00	$435.00
20"	$125.00	$475.00

Molded hair and ribbon. *Mark: "WALT DISNEY//1937//KNICKERBOCKER"*
13"	$75.00	$360.00

Set of seven Dwarfs, Snow White, mohair wigs, beards
9 – 11"	$1,300.00*	

HARD PLASTIC AND VINYL

Bozo Clown
14"	$7.00	$25.00
24"	$17.00	$60.00

Cinderella

Two faces, one sad; one with tiara
16"	$5.00	$20.00

11" all-cloth Mickey Mouse Cowboy, molded composition shoes, fleece chaps, felt hat, toy rope and gun, circa 1936, $3,900.00. Courtesy McMasters Harris Doll Auctions.

Flintstone characters

6"	$3.00	$10.00
17"	$9.00	$43.00

Kewpies: See Antique Kewpie section.

Little House on the Prairie, 1978

12"	$6.00	$22.00

"Little Orphan Annie" comic strip characters, 1982

Little Orphan Annie, vinyl

6"	$5.00	$17.50

Daddy Warbucks

7"	$5.00	$17.50

Punjab

7"	$4.00	$18.00

Miss Hannigan

7"	$4.00	$18.00

Molly

5½"	$4.00	$12.00

Soupy Sales, 1966

Vinyl and cloth, non-removable clothes

13"	$35.00	$135.00

Two-faced dolls, 1960s

Vinyl face masks, one crying, one smiling

12"	$5.00	$18.00

Lawton Doll Co.

Wendy Lawton, 1979+, Turlock, CA.

Price indicates complete mint-in-box doll; dolls missing accessories or with flaws would be priced less.

Childhood Classics

Alice in Wonderland

1983		$3,000.00+

Anne of Green Gables

1986	14"	$1,600.00+

Hans Brinker

1985	14"	$850.00

Heidi

1984	14"	$850.00

June Amos & Mary Anne

1996	16"	$1,305.00*

Little Women, set of four

1994 – 1995	15"	$1,525.00*

Li'l Princess

1989	14"	$850.00

Pollyanna

1986	14"	$800.00

Christmas Dolls

Christmas Joy

1988		$800.00

Noel

1989		$450.00

* at auction

Christmas Angel	1990	$450.00
Yuletide Carole	1991	$450.00

Disney World Specials

1st Main Street			$450.00
2nd Liberty Square (250)			$400.00
3rd Tish			$400.00
4th Karen (50)			$800.00
5th Goofy Kid (100)			$800.00
6th Melissa & Her Mickey			$750.00
7th Christopher, Robin, Pooh		12"	$750.00

Guild Dolls

Ba Ba Black Sheep	1989	$750.00
Lavender Blue	1990	$450.00

Special Editions

Marcella & Raggedy Ann	1988	$795.00
Flora McFlimsey	1993	$1,000.00

Other Specials

Beatrice Louise, UFDC, 1998 Luncheon		$975.00*
Josephine, UFDC Regional	12"	$750.00
Little Colonel, Dolly Dears, Birmingham, AL		$425.00
1st WL Convention, Lotta Crabtree		$1,300.00+

Marx

9" vinyl Veronica, Betty, and Jughead comic characters, Jughead has molded hair, Betty and Veronica are wigged, painted features, mint in box, circa 1975, $30.00 each. Courtesy McMasters Harris Doll Auctions.

ARCHIE AND FRIENDS

Characters from comics, vinyl, molded hair or wigged, painted eyes, in package

Archie	8½"	$10.00	$30.00
Betty	8½"	$10.00	$30.00
Jughead	8½"	$10.00	$30.00
Veronica	8½"	$10.00	$30.00

* at auction

JOHNNY APOLLO DOUBLE AGENT

    Vinyl, trench coat, circa 1970s

        12" $25.00 $50.00

MISS SEVENTEEN, 1961

    Hard plastic, high heeled, fashion-type doll, modeled like the German Bild Lilli, Barbie doll's predecessor, came in black swimsuit, black box, fashion brochure pictures 12 costumes, she was advertised as "A Beauty Queen."

        18" $175.00 $300.00

    Costume only $36.00* MIP

MISS MARLENE

    Hard plastic, high heeled, Barbie-type, ca. 1960s, blond rooted wig

        7" $170.00* in original box, costume

MISS TODDLER

    Also know as Miss Marx, vinyl, molded hair, ribbons, battery operated walker, molded clothing

        18" $75.00 $155.00

JOHNNY WEST FAMILY OF ACTION FIGURES, 1965 – 1976

    Adventure or Best of the West Series, rigid vinyl, articulated figures, molded clothes, came in box with vinyl accessories and extra clothes. Had horses, dogs, and other accessories available. First price indicates played with, missing some accessories; second price for complete in box; more if never removed from box or special sets.

    Bill Buck, brown molded-on clothing, 13 pieces, coonskin cap

        11½" $35.00 $125.00

    Captain Tom Maddox, blue molded-on clothing, brown hair, 23 pieces

        11½" $25.00 $90.00

    Chief Cherokee, tan or light color molded-on clothing, 37 pieces

        11½" $25.00 $100.00

    Daniel Boone, tan molded-on clothing, coonskin cap

        11½" $30.00 $115.00

    Fighting Eagle, tan molded-on clothes, with Mohawk hair, 37 pieces

        11½" $45.00 $135.00

    General Custer, dark blue molded-on clothing, yellow hair, 23 pieces

        11½" $25.00 $85.00

    Geronimo, light color molded-on clothing

        11½" $50.00 $95.00

    Orange body

        11½" $50.00 $125.00

11½" rigid vinyl articulated Sam Cobra an outlaw, with 26 accessories in box, circa 1975+, $100.00.

11½" rigid vinyl articulated Princess Wildflower with papoose in vinyl cradle, 22 piece vinyl accessories, from Johnny West Best of the West series, circa 1965 – 1976, $150.00 each. Courtesy Chad Moyer.

Jamie West, dark hair, molded-on tan clothing, 13 accessories

| 9" | $20.00 | $45.00 |

Jane West, blond hair, turquoise molded on clothing, 37 pieces

| 11½" | $20.00 | $50.00 |
| Orange body | $25.00 | $45.00 |

Janice West, dark hair, turquoise molded-on clothing, 14 pieces

| 9" | $20.00 | $45.00 |

Jay West, blond hair, tan molded-on clothing, 13 accessories, later brighter body colors

| 9" | $25.00 | $100.00 |

Jed Gibson, c. 1973, black figure, molded-on green clothing

| 12" | $100.00 | $260.00 |

Johnny West, brown hair, molded-on brown clothing, 25 pieces

| 12" | $25.00 | $100.00 |

Johnny West, with quick draw arm, blue clothing

| 12" | $20.00 | $55.00 |

Josie West, blond, turquoise molded-on clothing, later with bright green body

| 9" | $20.00 | $45.00 |

Princess Wildflower, off-white molded-on clothing, with papoose in vinyl cradle, 22 pieces of accessories

| 11½" | $50.00 | $130.00 |

Sam Cobra, outlaw, with 26 accessories

| 11½" | $25.00 | $100.00 |

Sheriff Pat Garrett (Sheriff Goode in Canada), molded-on blue clothing, 25 pieces of accessories

| 11½" | $75.00 | $125.00 |

Zeb Zachary, dark hair, blue molded-on clothing, 23 pieces

| 11½" | $30.00 | $110.00 |

KNIGHT AND VIKING SERIES, CA. 1960S

Action figures with accessories

Gordon, the Gold Knight, molded-on gold clothing, brown hair, beard, mustache

| 11½" | $35.00 | $125.00 |

Sir Stuart, Silver Knight, molded-on silver clothing, black hair, mustache, goatee

| 11½" | $35.00 | $125.00 |

Brave Erik, Viking with horse, ca. 1967, molded-on green clothing, blond hair, blue eyes

| 11½" | $50.00 | $125.00 |

Odin, the Viking, ca. 1967, brown molded-on clothing, brown eyes, brown hair, beard

| 11½" | $50.00 | $125.00 |

SINDY

Ca. 1963+, in England by Pedigree, a fashion-type doll, rooted hair, painted eyes, wires in limbs allow her to pose, distributed in U.S. by Marx c. 1978 – 1982.

11"	$50.00	$110.00
Pedigree	$75.00	$150.00
Pedigree Sindy Majorette, box		$480.00*

Gayle, Sindy's friend, black vinyl

| 11" | $50.00 | $115.00 |
| **Outfits** | $35.00 | $100.00 |

SOLDIERS, CA. 1960S

Articulated action figures with accessories

Buddy Charlie, Montgomery Wards, exclusive, a buddy for GI Joe, molded-on military uniform, brown hair

11½"	$35.00	$100.00

Stony "Stonewall" Smith, molded-on Army fatigues, blond hair, 36-piece accessories

11½"	$25.00	$100.00

OTHERS

Freddy Krueger, 1989, vinyl, pull string talker horror movie *Nightmare on Elm Street* character played by Robert England

18"	$20.00	$50.00

PeeWee Herman, 1987 TV character, vinyl and cloth, ventriloquist doll in gray suit, red bow tie

18"	$10.00	$30.00

PeeWee Herman, pull string talker

18"	$10.00	$36.00

Mattel

Baby Beans, 1971 – 1975

Vinyl head, bean bag dolls, terry cloth or tricot bodies filled with plastic and foam

12"	$15.00	$70.00

Talking

12"	$10.00	$40.00

Baby First Step, 1965 – 1967

Battery operated walker, rooted hair, sleep eyes, pink dress

18"	$50.00	$150.00

Talking

18"	$60.00	$300.00

Baby Go Bye-Bye and Her Bumpety Buggy, 1970

Doll sits in car, battery operated, 12 maneuvers

11"	$25.00	$100.00

Baby's Hungry, 1967 – 1968

Battery operated, eyes move and lips chew when magic bottle or spoon is put to mouth, wets, plastic bib

17"	$7.00	$30.00

Baby Love Light

Battery operated

16"	$5.00	$18.00

Baby Pattaburp, 1964 – 1966

Vinyl, drinks milk, burps when patted, pink jacket, lace trim

16"	$50.00	$200.00

18" vinyl Baby First Step, battery-operated walker, blue sleep eyes, rooted blond hair with side part, rigid vinyl body, original dress, box reads, "I really walk all by myself - New//She Skates" with red skates on white shoes, circa 1965 – 1967, $30.00. Courtesy McMasters Harris Doll Auctions.

10¾" vinyl Talking Buffy and Mrs. Beasley, painted eyes, blond wig in ponytails, original red and white dress, with Mrs. Beasley in aqua and white dotted dress, yellow rickrack trim, glasses, in box that reads "TV's Talking Buffy and Mrs. Beasley," boxed, all original, $150.00 – 350.00. Courtesy McMasters Harris Doll Auctions.

Baby Play-A-Lot, 1972 – 1973
Posable arms, fingers can hold things, comes with 20 toys, moves arm to brush teeth, moves head, no batteries, has pull string and switch

16"	$5.00	$22.00

Baby Say 'N See, 1967 – 1968
Eyes and lips move while talking, white dress, pink yoke

17"	$20.00	$175.00

Baby Secret, 1966 – 1967
Vinyl face and hands, stuffed body, limbs, red hair, blue eyes, whispers 11 phrases, moves lips

18"	$15.00	$75.00

Baby Small Talk, 1968 – 1969
Says eight phrases, infant voice, additional outfits available

10¾"	$15.00	$55.00

Black

10¾"	$20.00	$60.00

In Nursery Rhyme outfit

10¾"	$20.00	$65.00

Baby Tender Love, 1970 – 1973
Baby doll, realistic skin, wets, can be bathed

Newborn

13"	$20.00	$65.00

Talking

16"	$10.00	$35.00

Boxed

16"	$180.00*	

Molded hairpiece, 1972

11½"	$9.00	$30.00

Brother, sexed

11½"	$25.00	$50.00

Baby Walk 'n Play, 1968

11"	$4.00	$12.00

Baby Walk 'n See

18"	$5.00	$18.00

Barbie: See that section.

Bozo, 1964

18"	$20.00	$85.00

Big Jim Series
Vinyl action figures, many boxed accessory sets available

Big Jim, black hair, muscular torso

9½"	$20.00	$115.00

Big Josh, dark hair, beard

9½"	$9.00	$35.00

Dr. Steele, bald head, silver tips on right hand

9½"	$8.00	$50.00

15½" vinyl Drowsy, cloth body, pull-string talker, droopy eyelids, blue painted eyes, closed mouth, rooted blond synthetic hair, pink sleeper with white dots, eyelet lace at neck and sleeves, in box that reads, "I talk, I say 11 different things, A Chatty Doll by Mattel," circa 1965 – 1974, $65.00. Courtesy McMasters Harris Doll Auctions.

Buffy and Mrs. Beasley, 1967 & 1974

Characters from TV sitcom, *Family Affair*. Buffy, vinyl, rooted hair, painted features, holds small Mrs. Beasley, vinyl head, on cloth body

6½" $75.00 $185.00

Talking Buffy, vinyl, 1969 – 1971, holds tiny 6" rag Mrs. Beasley

10¾" $50.00 $350.00

Mrs. Beasley, 1967 – 1974, talking vinyl head, cloth body, square glasses, blue polka-dot dress

22" $175.00 $500.00

Mrs. Beasley, 1973, non-talker

15½" $25.00 $75.00

Captain Kangaroo, 1967

Sears only, talking character, host for TV kids program

19" $10.00 $50.00

Captain Laser, 1967

Vinyl, painted features, blue uniform, silver accessories, batteries operate laser gun, light-up eyes

12" $70.00 $265.00

Casper, the Friendly Ghost, ca. 1964

16" $35.00 $100.00+

1971

5" $15.00 $60.00

Chatty Cathy Series

Chatty Cathy, 1960 – 1963, vinyl head, hard plastic body, pull string activates voice, dressed in pink and white checked or blue party dresses, 1963 – 1965, says 18 new phrases, red velvet and white lace dress, extra outfits available

Blond

20" $100.00 $350.00

Blond Pigtail, boxed

20" $610.00*

Black

20" $885.00*

Charmin' Chatty, 1963 – 1964

Talking doll, soft vinyl head, closed smiling mouth, hard vinyl body, long rooted hair, long legs, five records placed in left side slot, one-piece navy skirt, white middy blouse, with red sailor collar, red socks and saddle shoes, glasses, five disks; extra outfits and 14 more disks available

24" $55.00 $300.00

20" soft vinyl Chatty Cathy, blue sleep eyes, open/closed mouth with painted teeth, blond rooted hair, hard plastic body, pull string activates voice, red dress with white pinafore, original box and accessories, doll marked on back "Mattel, Inc. Toymakers," circa 1960, $425.00. Courtesy McMasters Harris Doll Auctions.

23" vinyl Scooba Doo, rooted blond hair, heavy eyeshadow, closed mouth, pale lips, cloth body with pull string talker, says 11 phrases, wears striped top, gold necklace, advertised in 1964 Sears catalog, $75.00+. Courtesy Oleta Woodside.

16" cloth Shrinkin' Violette, felt features, long thick yellow yarn hair, pull string talker mouth moves, eyelids flutter, says 11 phrases, marked "Copyright 1963 by The Funny Company," circa 1964, $250.00. Courtesy Sue Amidon.

Chatty Baby, 1962 – 1964, red pinafore over rompers

18"	$20.00	$75.00

Tiny Chatty Baby, 1963 – 1964
Smaller version of Chatty Baby, blue rompers, blue, white striped panties, bib with name, talks, other outfits available

15½"	$20.00	$90.00
Black		
15½"	$25.00	$100.00

Tiny Chatty Brother, 1963 – 1964
Boy version of Tiny Chatty Baby, blue and white suit and cap, hair parted on side

15½"	$20.00	$75.00

Cheerful Tearful, 1966 – 1967
Vinyl, blond hair, face changes from smile to pout as arm is lowered, feed her bottle, wets and cries real tears

7"	$25.00	$100.00

Dancerina, 1969 – 1971
Battery operated, posable arms, legs, turns, dances with control knob on head, pink ballet outfit

24"	$60.00	$175.00

Baby Dancerina, 1970
Smaller version, no batteries, turn-knob on head, white ballet outfit

16"	$50.00	$125.00
Black		
16"	$85.00	$175.00

Teeny Dancerina

12"	$8.00	$30.00

Debbie Boone, 1978

11½"	$12.00	$40.00

Dick Van Dyke, 1969
As Mr. Potts in movie, *Chitty Chitty Bang Bang,* all-cloth, flat features, talks in actor's voice
Mark: "© Mattel 1969" on cloth tag

24"	$18.00	$85.00

Drowsy, 1965 – 1974
Vinyl head, stuffed body, sleepers, pull-string talker

15½"	$35.00	$175.00
15½"	$200.00* MIB	

Dr. Dolittle, 1968
Character patterned after Rex Harrison in movie version, talker, vinyl with cloth body

24"	$15.00	$50.00
All vinyl		
6"	$4.00	$20.00

Gramma Doll, 1970 – 1973
Sears only, cloth, painted face, gray yarn hair, says ten phrases, talker, foam-filled cotton

11"	$5.00	$20.00

* at auction

Grizzly Adams, 1971

10"	$20.00	$80.00

Guardian Goddesses, 1979

11½"	$10.00	$50.00

Herman Munster, 1965

Cloth doll, talking TV character, *The Munsters*

21"	$25.00	$150.00

Julia, 1969, TV character nurse, from *Julia*

Twist 'N Turn

11½"	$80.00	$250.00

Talking

11½"	$75.00	$200.00

Talking, new hairstyle

11½"	$65.00	$185.00

Liddle Kiddles, 1966+

Small dolls of vinyl over wire frame, posable, painted features, rooted hair and came with bright costumes and accessories, packaged on 8½" x 9½" cards.

2" vinyl Kiddle Kolognes, in 4½" tall bottles, Violet Kologne, circa 1968 – 1970, $40.00 each. Courtesy McMasters Harris Doll Auctions.

Mark: "1965// Mattel Inc.// Japan" on back

First price is for complete doll and accessories, excellent condition; second price (or one price only) is for mint complete doll and accessories. Add more for mint in package (or card) and never removed from package. Less for worn dolls with missing accessories.

1966, First Series

3501 Bunson Bernie	3"	$50.00	$60.00
3502 Howard "Biff" Boodle	3½"	$55.00	$75.00
3503 Liddle Diddle	2¾"	$45.00	$150.00
3505 Babe Biddle	3½"	$165.00	$225.00
3506 Calamity Jiddle	3"	$45.00	$160.00
3507 Florence Niddle	2¾"	$65.00	$75.00
3508 Greta Griddle	3"	$85.00	$95.00
3509 Millie Middle	2¾"	$45.00	$55.00
3510 Beat A Diddle	3½"	$155.00	$180.00

1967, Second Series

3513 Sizzly Friddle	3"	$50.00	$80.00
3514 Windy Fiddle	2¾"	$200.00	$225.00
3515 Trikey Triddle	2¾"	$140.00	$160.00
3516 Freezy Sliddle	3½"	$130.00	$150.00
3517 Surfy Skiddle	3"	$50.00	$60.00
3518 Soapy Siddle	3½"	$55.00	$75.00
3519 Rolly Twiddle	3½"	$180.00	$200.00
3548 Beddy Bye Biddle (with robe)		$60.00	$70.00
3549 Pretty Priddle	3½"	$50.00	$65.00

1968, Third Series

3587 Baby Liddle	2¾"	$175.00	$200.00

3551 Telly Viddle	3½"	$50.00	$200.00
3552 Lemons Stiddle	3½"	$60.00	$75.00
3553 Kampy Kiddle	3½"	$50.00	$200.00
3554 Slipsy Sliddle	3½"	$60.00	$200.00
Storybook Kiddles, 1967 – 1968		$120.00	$260.00
Skediddle Kiddles, 1968 – 1970	4"		$75.00
Kiddles 'N Kars, 1969 – 1970	2¾"		$177.50*
Tea Party Kiddles, 1970 – 1971	3½"		$135.00
Lucky Locket Kiddles, 1967 – 1970	2"		$50.00+
Kiddle Kolognes, 1968 – 1970	2"	$20.00	$125.00
Kola Kiddles, 1968 – 1969	2"	$20.00	$75.00
Sweet Treat Kiddles, 1969 – 1970	2"	$35.00	$125.00
Liddle Kiddle Playhouses, 1966 – 1968		$30.00	$75.00+

Mork & Mindy, 1979

	9"	$10.00	$30.00

Osmond Family
Donny or Marie Osmond, 1978

	12"	$12.00	$45.00

Jimmy Osmond, 1979

	10"	$15.00	$60.00

Scooba Doo, 1964
Vinyl head, rooted hair, cloth body, talks in Beatnik phrases, blond or black hair, striped dress

	23"	$25.00	$125.00

Shogun Warrior
All plastic, battery operated

	23½"	$65.00	$250.00

Shrinkin' Violette, 1964 – 1965
Cloth, yarn hair, pull-string talker, eyes close, mouth moves

	16"	$50.00	$380.00 *

Sister Belle, 1961 – 1963
Vinyl, pull string talker, cloth body

	16"	$35.00	$75.00

Star Spangled dolls
Uses Sunshine Family adults, *marked "1973"*

Pioneer Daughter		$12.00	$40.00

Sunshine Family, The
Vinyl, posable, come with Idea Book, Father, Mother, Baby

Steve	9"	$10.00	$40.00
Stephie	7½"	$10.00	$40.00
Sweets	3½"	$10.00	$40.00

Tatters, 1965 – 1967
Talking cloth doll, wears rag clothes

	19"	$30.00	$125.00

Teachy Keen, 1966 – 1970
Sears only, vinyl head, cloth body, ponytail, talker, tells child to use accessories included, buttons, zippers, comb

	16"	$9.00	$30.00

Tinkerbelle, 1969, talking, patter pillows

	18"	$7.00	$22.00

* at auction

Tippee Toes, 1968 – 1970

Battery operated, legs move, rides accessory horse, tricycle, knit sweater, pants

17"	$40.00	$80.00
Tricycle/horse	$10.00	$40.00

Welcome Back Kotter, 1973, characters from TV sitcom

Freddie "Boom Boom" Washington, Arnold Horshack

9"	$10.00	$40.00

Vinnie Barbarino (John Travolta)

9"	$25.00	$80.00

Gabe Kotter

9"	$5.00	$25.00

Zython, 1977

Has glow-in-the-dark head. Enemy in *Space 1999* series.

$25.00	$100.00

Action Jackson, 1971 – 1972

Vinyl head, plastic body, molded hair, painted black eyes, action figure, many accessory outfits. *Mark: "©Mego Corp//Reg. U.S. Pat. Off.//Pat. Pend.//Hong Kong//MCMLXXI"*

8" vinyl Batman with molded head, painted eyes and blue mask, detachable cape, body suit, gloves, and vinyl boots, circa 1974, $150.00 with box. Courtesy Carol Stover.

8"	$5.00	$30.00
Black		
8"	$10.00	$55.00
Dinah-mite, Black		
	$10.00	$40.00

Batman, 1979

8"	$355.00* MOC

Arch enemy

8"	$4.00	$15.00

Mobile Bat Lab, 1975

$350.00* original box

Captain and Tennille

Daryl Dragon and Toni Tennille, 1977, recording and TV personalities, Toni Tennille doll has no molded ears

12½"	$10.00	$40.00

Cher, 1976

TV and recording personality, husband Sonny Bono, all-vinyl, fully jointed, rooted long black hair, also as grow-hair doll

Growing Hair Cher, 1976

12"	$60.00	$225.00
Sonny/Cher Theatre in the Round		$225.00*
Star Brite costume		$130.00*

Sonny Bono

12"	$12.00	$45.00

---

* at auction

CHiPs 1977

California Highway Patrol TV show, Jon Baker (Larry Wilcox), Frank "Ponch" Poncherello (Erik Estrada)

8"	$5.00	$20.00

Diana Ross, 1977

Recording and movie personality, all-vinyl, fully jointed, rooted black hair, long lashes

12½"	$40.00	$135.00

Farrah Fawcett, 1977

Model, movie, and television personality, starred as Jill in *Charlie's Angels*, vinyl head, rooted blond hair, painted green eyes

12½"	$25.00	$60.00

Flash Gordon Series, ca. 1976

Vinyl head, hard plastic articulated body

Dale Arden

9"	$25.00	$125.00

Dr. Zarkov

9½"	$25.00	$100.00

Flash Gordon

9½"	$25.00	$100.00

Ming, the Merciless

9½"	$20.00	$65.00

Happy Days Series, 1976

Characters from *Happy Days* TV sitcom, Henry Winkler starred as Fonzie, Ronnie Howard as Richie, Anson Williams as Potsie, and Donny Most as Ralph Malph

Fonzie

8"	$15.00	$75.00

Fonzie with motorcycle

		$125.00*

Richie, Potsie, Ralph, each

8"	$15.00	$80.00

Jaclyn Smith, 1977

Vinyl

12½"	$50.00	$250.00* MIB

Joe Namath, 1970

Football player, actor, soft vinyl head, rigid vinyl body, painted hair and features

12"	$25.00	$100.00
Outfit, MIP	$32.50	

KISS, 1978

Rock group, with Gene Simmons, Ace Frehley, Peter Cris, and Paul Stanley, all-vinyl, fully jointed, rooted hair, painted features and makeup

12½"	$100.00 each	$660.00* set of four

Kristy McNichol, 1978. Actress, starred in TV show, *Family*. All-vinyl, rooted brown hair, painted eyes. *Marked on head: "©MEGO CORP.//MADE IN HONG KONG." Marked on back: "©1977 MEGO CORP.//MADE IN HONG KONG."*

9"	$8.00	$35.00

Laverne and Shirley, 1977

TV sitcom; Penny Marshall played Laverne, Cindy Williams played Shirley, also, from the same show, David Lander as Squiggy, and Michael McKean as Lenny, all-vinyl, rooted hair, painted eyes

	11½"	$15.00	$50.00

Our Gang, 1975

From *Our Gang* movie shorts, that replayed on TV, included characters Alfalpha, Buckwheat, Darla, Mickey, Porky, and Spanky

	6"	$7.00	$25.00

Planet of the Apes

Planet of the Apes Movie Series, ca. 1970s

Astronaut	8"	$30.00	$120.00
Ape Soldier	8"	$800.00* Palitoy, MOC	
Cornelius	8"	$25.00	$100.00
Dr. Zaius	8"	$25.00	$100.00
Zira	8"	$25.00	$100.00

Planet of the Apes TV Series, ca. 1974

Alan Verdon	8"	$20.00	$75.00
Galen	8"	$140.00* Palitoy	
General Urko	8"	$40.00	$150.00
General Urko	8"	$950.00* MOC	
General Ursus	8"	$50.00	$450.00
Peter Burke	8"	$40.00	$150.00

Star Trek

Star Trek TV Series, ca. 1973 – 1975

Captain Kirk	8"	$15.00	$100.00
Dr. McCoy	8"	$20.00	$145.00
Klingon	8"	$200.00* Palitoy	
Lt. Uhura	8"	$15.00	$110.00
Mr. Scott	8"	$20.00	$85.00
Mr. Spock	8"	$20.00	$80.00

Star Trek Movie Series, ca. 1979

Acturian	12½"	$25.00	$100.00
Captain Kirk	12½"	$15.00	$60.00
Ilia	12½"	$15.00	$60.00
Mr. Spock	12½"	$25.00	$100.00

Star Trek Aliens, ca. 1975 – 1976

Andorian	8"	$80.00	$325.00
Cheron	8"	$35.00	$130.00
Mugato	8"	$75.00	$300.00
Talos	8"	$65.00	$250.00
The Gorn	8"	$50.00	$170.00* MOC
The Romulan	8"	$150.00	$690.00* MOC

Starsky and Hutch, 1976

Police TV series, Paul Michael Glaser as Starsky, David Soul as Hutch, Bernie Hamilton as Captain Dobey, Antonio Fargas as Huggy Bear, also included a villain, Chopper, all-vinyl, jointed waists

	7½"	$12.00	$45.00

Mego

Suzanne Somers, 1978
Actress, TV personality, starred as Chrissy in *Three's Company,* all-vinyl, fully jointed, rooted blond hair, painted blue eyes, long lashes

12½"	$15.00	$45.00

Waltons, The, 1975
From TV drama series, set of two 8" dolls per package, all-vinyl

John Boy and Mary Ellen	$12.00	$40.00
Mom and Pop	$10.00	$35.00
Grandma and Grandpa	$12.00	$40.00

Wonder Woman Series, ca. 1976 – 1977
Vinyl head, rooted black hair, painted eyes, plastic body

Lt. Diane Prince	12½"	$40.00	$150.00
Nubia	12½"	$25.00	$75.00
Nurse	12½"	$10.00	$40.00
Queen Hippolyte	12½"	$25.00	$100.00
Steve Trevor	12½"	$25.00	$100.00
Wonder Woman	12½"	$40.00	$240.00* MIB

Molly'es

Mollye Goldman, 1920+, International Doll Co., Philadelphia, PA. Designed and created clothes for cloth, composition, hard plastic, and vinyl dolls. Name marked only on vinyls; others may have had paper hang tags. She used dolls made by other companies. Also designed clothes for other makers.

First price is for doll in good condition, but with flaws; second price is for doll in excellent condition, original clothes. More for exceptional doll with fancy wardrobe or accessories.

7" plastic Dress Me doll, red mohair wig, painted features, fixed head and legs, jointed arms, molded shoes, original box and hang tag "International Doll Company," doll unmarked, circa 1950s, $35.00. Courtesy Carol Stover.

CLOTH, fine line painted lashes, pouty mouth

Child

15"	$40.00	$135.00
18"	$45.00	$150.00
24"	$65.00	$200.00
29"	$85.00	$300.00

Internationals

13"	$27.00	$85.00
15"	$45.00	$135.00
27"	$75.00	$275.00

Girl/Lady

16"	$50.00	$175.00
21"	$75.00	$275.00

COMPOSITION

Baby

15"	$40.00	$150.00
21"	$55.00	$225.00

Cloth body

18"	$20.00	$75.00

Toddler

15"	$50.00	$250.00
21"	$75.00	$285.00

Child

15"	$50.00	$175.00
18"	$70.00	$250.00

Girl/Lady, add more for ball gown

16"	$80.00	$325.00	
21"	$130.00	$500.00	

HARD PLASTIC

Baby

14"	$25.00	$85.00	
20"	$40.00	$135.00	

Cloth body

17"	$25.00	$75.00	
25"	$35.00	$125.00	

Child

14"	$40.00	$175.00	
18"	$75.00	$375.00	
25"	$100.00	$425.00	

Girl/Lady

17"	$75.00	$300.00	
20"	$80.00	$375.00	
25"	$100.00	$425.00	

VINYL

Baby

8½"	$6.00	$20.00	
12"	$5.00	$25.00	
15"	$9.00	$40.00	

Child

8"	$7.00	$20.00	
10"	$9.00	$30.00	
15"	$15.00	$50.00	

Girl/Lady

Little Women

9"	$9.00	$35.00	

Monica Dolls

Ca. 1941 – 1951. Monica Dolls from Hollywood, designed by Hansi Share, made composition and later hard plastic with long face and painted or sleep eyes, eyeshadow, unique feature is very durable rooted human hair. Did not have high-heeled feet and unmarked, but wore paper wrist tag reading *"Monica Doll, Hollywood."* Composition dolls had pronounced widow's peak in center of forehead.

Composition, 1941 – 1949

Painted eyes, Veronica, Jean, and Rosalind were names of 17" dolls produced in 1942.

11"	$75.00	$295.00
17"	$175.00	$650.00
20 – 21"	$250.00	$850.00

Hard plastic, 1949 – 1951, sleep eyes, Elizabeth, Marion, or Linda

14"	$150.00	$550.00
18"	$200.00	$700.00

20" composition, light brown human hair wig rooted into scalp with widow's peak, painted blue eyes with eyeliner and shadow, five-piece jointed body, original cotton gown, hang tag "Monica//Doll//Hollywood," doll unmarked, circa 1941 – 1949, $600.00. Courtesy Jo Barckley.

5½" bisque, mohair wig, painted features, jointed arms, fixed legs and head, red taffeta Queen of Hearts #157 gown with white net overskirt, original box, circa 1940s, $75.00. Courtesy Carol Stover.

6½" bisque, mohair wig, painted features, jointed arms, fixed legs and head, yellow taffeta gown with pink overskirt and green felt hat with feather, original box "# 189 A BREEZY GIRL AND ARCH TO WORSHIP ME THROUGH MARCH," circa 1940s, $75.00. Courtesy Carol Stover.

1936+, San Francisco, CA. Started by Rowena Haskin (Nancy Ann Abbott). Painted bisque, mohair wig, painted eyes, head molded to torso, jointed limbs, either sticker on outfit or hang tag, in box, later made in hard plastic.

First price for played-with or missing accessories doll; second price for mint or mint-in-box. Add 30 percent or more for black dolls. Selected auction prices reflect once-only extreme high prices and should be noted accordingly. Painted bisque baby prices vary with outfits.

BABY ONLY, 1936+

Pink/blue mottled or sunburst box with gold label, gold foil sticker on clothes "Nancy Ann Dressed Dolls," marked "87," "88," or "93," "Made in Japan," no brochure

Baby			
	3½" – 4½"	$100.00	$400.00
with cradle			
	3¾"	$1,525.00*	

BABY OR CHILD

1937

Child marked "Made in Japan," "1146," "1148," or "Japan," sunburst box with gold label, gold foil sticker on clothes read "Nancy Ann Dressed Dolls," no brochure

Baby			
	3½" – 4½"	$275.00	$700.00
Child			
	5"	$500.00	$1,200.00

1938

Marked "America" (baby marked "87," "88," or "93" "Made in Japan"), colored box, sunburst pattern with gold label, gold foil sticker on clothes: "Judy Ann," no brochure

Baby			
	3½" – 4½"	$200.00	$325.00
Child			
	5"	$200.00	$500.00

1938

Marked "Judy Ann USA" and "Story Book USA" (baby marked "Made in USA" and "88, 89, and 93 Made in Japan"), colored box, sunburst pattern with gold or silver label, gold foil sticker on clothes: "Storybook Dolls," no brochure

	3½"– 4½"	$225.00	$325.00
	5"	$200.00	$300.00

Complete with teddy bear, dress tagged "*Judy Ann*," blue box, silver dots, marked "*Japan 1146*"

5"	$160.00	$650.00

Judy Ann mold

	$100.00	$500.00

Storybook mold

	$100.00	$350.00

Jointed bisque
Pussy Cat, Pussy Cat, complete with pet

5"	$100.00	$300.00

1939

Child, molded socks and molded bangs (baby has star-shaped hands), colored box with small silver dots, silver label, gold foil sticker on clothes, "*Storybook Dolls*," no brochure

5½" hard plastic Monday's Child, mohair wig, sleep eyes, jointed arms and legs, moveable head, printed taffeta gown, yellow felt hat, original box, marked "STORY-BOOK/DOLL/USA/PATENT/PEN," circa 1950s, $75.00. Courtesy Carol Stover.

Baby

3½" – 4½"	$75.00	$150.00

Child

5"	$125.00	$225.00

Spring, molded sock, molded bang

5"	$2,645.00*	

1940

Child has molded socks only (baby has star-shaped bisque hands), colored box with white polka dots, silver label, gold foil sticker on clothes, "*Storybook Dolls*," has brochure

Baby

3½" – 4½"	$60.00	$135.00

Child

5"	$50.00	$200.00

1941 – 1942

Child has pudgy tummy or slim tummy; baby has star-shaped hands or fist, white box with colored polka dots, with silver label, gold foil bracelet with name of doll and brochure

Baby

3½" – 4½"	$65.00	$125.00

Child

5"	$20.00	$75.00

1943 – 1947

Child has one-piece head, body, and legs, baby has fist hands, white box with colored polka dots, silver label, ribbon tie or pin fastener, gold foil bracelet with name of doll and brochure

6½" hard plastic, mohair wig, sleep eyes with painted lashes, moving head, arms, and legs, gold taffeta gown with flowered organdy overskirt, picture hat, circa 1950s, $50.00. Courtesy Carol Stover.

Left: 8" hard plastic Muffie, synthetic wig, sleep eyes with painted lashes, no brows, toddler walker, original flowered organdy dress, blue straw hat, marked "Storybook/Dolls/California," circa 1954, $180.00. Courtesy Carol Stover.

Right: 8" hard plastic Muffie, brunette synthetic ponytail style wig, sleep eyes with painted lashes and brows, toddler head turning walker, original brown dotted cotton dress, yellow straw hat, marked "Storybook/Dolls/California/Muffie," circa 1955, $180.00. Courtesy Carol Stover.

Baby

	3½" – 4½"	$60.00	$125.00
Child			
	5"	$25.00	$65.00

1947 – 1949

Child has hard plastic body, painted eyes, baby has bisque body, plastic arms and legs, white box with colored polka dots with *"Nancy Ann Storybook Dolls"* between dots, silver label, brass snap, gold foil bracelet with name of doll and brochure. More for special outfit.

Baby

	3½" – 4½"	$45.00	$90.00

Ca. 1949

Hard plastic, both have black sleep eyes, white box with colored polka dots and *"Nancy Ann Storybook Dolls"* between dots, silver label, brass or painted snaps, gold foil bracelet with name of doll and brochure

Baby

	3½" – 4½"	$40.00	$75.00
Child			
	5"	$15.00	$50.00

Ca. 1953

Hard plastic, child has blue sleep eyes, except for 4½" girls; baby has black sleep eyes, white box with colored polka dots, some with clear lids, silver label, gripper snap, gold foil bracelet with name of doll and brochure

Baby

	3½" – 4½"	$40.00	$75.00*
			only in christening dress
Child			
	5"	$925.00*	

SPECIAL DOLLS

Mammy and Baby, *marked "Japan 1146"* or America mold

	5"	$150.00	$1,200.00
Storybook USA			
	5"	$125.00	$500.00

Topsy, bisque black doll, jointed leg

All-bisque $75.00 $400.00

Plastic arms $50.00 $150.00

Topsy, all-plastic, painted or sleep eye

        $30.00 $100.00

White boots, bisque jointed leg dolls

   5"   Add $50.00

SERIES DOLLS, DEPENDING ON MOLD MARK

All-Bisque

   Around the World Series

     Chinese $300.00 $1,200.00

     English Flower Girl

        $150.00 $400.00

     Portuguese $200.00 $450.00

     Poland $200.00 $450.00

     Russia $200.00 $1,200.00

     Other Countries

        $100.00 $400.00

   Masquerade Series

     Ballet Dancer $200.00 $800.00

     Cowboy $200.00 $800.00

     Pirate $200.00 $800.00

   Sports Series

        $300.00 $1,200.00

   Flower Series (bisque)

        $175.00 $400.00

   Margie Ann Series

     Margie Ann $60.00 $175.00

      Margie Ann in other outfits

        $125.00 $350.00

   Powder & Crinoline Series

        $60.00 $175.00

Bisque or Plastic

   Operetta or Hit Parade Series

        $60.00 $175.00

Hard Plastic

   Big and Little Sister Series, or Commencement Series (except baby)

        $30.00 $100.00

   Bridal, Dolls of the Day, Dolls of the Month, Fairytale, Mother Goose, Nursery Rhyme, Religious, and Seasons Series, painted or sleep eye

        $20.00 $75.00

OTHER DOLLS

   Audrey Ann, toddler, marked *"Nancy Ann Storybook 12"*

     6" $250.00 $975.00

   Nancy Ann Style Show, ca. 1954

   Hard plastic, sleep eyes, long dress, unmarked

     18" $300.00 $600.00

   Long pink floral organdy costume

     18" $1,100.00*

8" vinyl Lori-Ann, rooted blond hair, sleep eyes with molded lashes, toddler walking body with jointed arms, original cotton riding outfit, felt hat, wrist tag "500," marked on neck "Nancy Ann," circa 1958, $180.00. Courtesy Marge Meisinger.

* at auction

Vinyl head, plastic body, all original, complete

18"	$300.00	$500.00

Muffie, 1953 – 1956

1953, hard plastic, wig, sleep eyes, strung straight leg, non-walker, painted lashes

8"	$75.00	$350.00
8"	$870.00* MIB with extra outfit	

1954, hard plastic walker, molded eyelashes, brows

8"	$65.00	$185.00

1955 – 1956, vinyl head, molded or painted upper lashes, rooted saran wig, walker or bent-knee walker

8"	$60.00	$165.00

Davy Crockett, 1955, walker, molded and painted lashes, all original

8"	$175.00*

Muffie, 1968+, reissued, hard plastic

8"	$45.00	$105.00

Lori Ann

Vinyl

7½"	$45.00	$175.00+

Debbie

Hard plastic in school dress, name on wrist tag/box

10"	$100.00	$400.00 MIB

Vinyl head, hard plastic body

10"	$25.00	$110.00 MIB

Hard plastic walker

10½"	$40.00	$160.00 MIB

Vinyl head, hard plastic walker

10½"	$23.00	$90.00 MIB

Little Miss Nancy Ann, 1959

Nude

8½"	$25.00	$100.00 MIB

Day dress

	$25.00	$50.00 MIB

Other outfits

	$30.00	$75.00 MIB

Miss Nancy Ann, 1959, marked *"Nancy Ann,"* vinyl head, rooted hair, rigid vinyl body, high-heeled feet

Nude

10½"	$25.00	$85.00 MIB

Day dress

	$25.00	$50.00 MIB

Other outfits

	$30.00	$75.00 MIB

Baby Sue Sue, 1960s, vinyl

Doll only

	$35.00	$1750.00+ MIB

Outfit

	$50.00	$75.00 MIB

---

* at auction

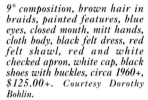

9" composition, brown hair in braids, painted features, blue eyes, closed mouth, mitt hands, cloth body, black felt dress, red felt shawl, red and white checked apron, white cap, black shoes with buckles, circa 1960+, $125.00+. Courtesy Dorothy Bohlin.

9" composition, Elizabethan Lady, royalty, dark hair up in curls, painted features, blue eyes, closed smiling mouth, cloth body, molded hands, bell-shaped purple brocade gown, matching hat, white ruffle around neck, necklace, circa 1950+, $175.00. Courtesy Dorothy Bohlin.

8½" composition, dark brown mohair wig, painted features, blue eyes, closed mouth, cloth body, mitt hands, red/white/green plaid dress, red shoes, straw hat, hang tags read "OLD COTTAGE TOYS//HANDMADE IN GREAT BRITAIN" and "as//selected//for//the DESIGN//CENTRE//LONDON," all original with box, circa 1950+, $165.00. Courtesy Dorothy Bohlin.

Late 1940s on, England

Mrs. M.E. Fleischmann made dolls with hard composition type heads, felt body, some with wire armature, oval hang tag has trademark "Old Cottage Dolls," special characters may be more.

7½"	$35.00	$125.00+
9"	$50.00	$175.00+
Mary Stuart, MIB		$280.00*
Tweedle Dee or Tweedle Dum, circa 1968		
10"	$200.00	$350.00

Pleasant Company

1986+, Middleton, WI. Pleasant Rowland started the company by making vinyl play dolls with cloth bodies, synthetic hair, and sleep eyes. Each doll was sold with a book placing it in a specific time perod. Each doll has many accessories, additional wardrobe, and books. The set includes Felecity, 1774, Williamsburg, Virginia; Kirsten, 1854, American frontier; Samantha, 1904, Victorian era; Josefina, 1824, a Hispanic in New Mexico; Addy, 1864, African American; Kit, 1934, Depression era; Molly,

19" vinyl American Girl Today, synthetic blond hair, sleep eyes, open/closed mouth with painted teeth, vinyl moving head, arms and legs, soft cloth body, original knit top and tights, vinyl jumper, tie shoes, wrist tag, box, circa 1999, $82.00 (retail). Courtesy Carol Stover.

1944, W.W.II; and the American Girl of Today that can be ordered with choice of hair, eye, and skin color. Mattel bought the company in 1998.

18"	$65.00	$82.00 (retail)

Raggedy Ann & Andy

1915+. Designed by Johnny Gruelle in 1915, made by various companies. Ann wears dress with apron; Andy, shirt and pants with matching hat.

P.J. VOLLAND, 1920 – 1934

Early dolls marked *"Patented Sept. 7, 1915."* All-cloth, tin or wooden button eyes, painted features. Some have sewn knee or arm joints, sparse brown or auburn yarn hair, oversize hands, feet turned outward.

Raggedy Ann and Andy

15 – 16"	$350.00	$1,700.00

Beloved Belindy, 1926 – 1930, painted face, **1931 – 1934,** print face

15"	$600.00	$2,300.00

Pirate Chieftain and other characters

18"	$500.00	$2,500.00
18"	$4,000.00 MIB	

EXPOSITION, 1935

Raggedy Ann, no eyelashes, no eyebrows, outline nose, no heart, satin label on hem of dress

18"	$3,000.00*

Too few in database for reliable range.

MOLLYE GOLDMAN, 1935 – 1938

Marked on chest *"Raggedy Ann and Andy Dolls Manufactured by Molly'es Doll Outfitters."* Nose outlined in black, red heart on chest, reddish-orange hair, multicolored legs, blue feet, some have oilcloth faces

15"	$225.00	$900.00
17"	$275.00	$1,100.00
21"	$350.00	$1,500.00

Did not make Beloved Belindy

GEORGENE NOVELTIES, 1938 – 1962

Ann has orange hair and a top knot, six different mouth styles; early ones had tin eyes, later ones had plastic, six different noses, seams in middle of legs and arms to represent knees and elbows. Feet turn forward, red and white striped legs. All have hearts that say *"I love you"* printed on chest. Tag sewn to left side seam, several variations, all say *"Georgene Novelties, Inc."*

Raggedy Ann or Andy, 1930s – 1960s

1930s

15"	$90.00	$350.00
18"	$180.00	$750.00

Ca. 1938

19"	$4,350.00* pair

1940s

13"	$1,665.00* pair	
18"	$85.00	$325.00
21"	$100.00	$400.00

1950s

18"	$50.00	$300.00

1960 – 1963

15"	$25.00	$110.00
18"	$35.00	$150.00

Awake/Asleep, pair

1940s

12"	$175.00	$650.00

Beloved Belindy, 1940 – 1944

18"	$125.00	$750.00

KNICKERBOCKER, 1962 – 1982

Printed features, hair color change from orange to red; there were five mouth and five eyelash variations, tags were located on clothing back or pants seam.

Raggedy Ann or Andy, 1960s

15"	$75.00	$350.00
30 – 36"	$150.00	$600.00

Raggedy Ann Talking, 1960s

	$70.00	$265.00

Beloved Belindy, ca. 1965

15"	$1,600.00* MIB

Raggedy Ann, 1970s

12"	$12.00	$45.00
15"	$15.00	$80.00
24"	$25.00	$135.00
30 – 36"	$50.00	$300.00

Talking, 1974

12"	$25.00	$100.00

Raggedy Ann, 1980s

16"	$7.00	$25.00
24"	$15.00	$55.00
30 – 36"	$35.00	$110.00

Camel with Wrinkled Knees

15"	$45.00	$175.00

NASCO/BOBBS-MERRILL, 1972

Cloth head, hard plastic doll body, printed features, apron marked *"Raggedy Ann"*

24"	$45.00	$150.00

BOBBS-MERRILL CO., 1974

Ventriloquist dummy, hard plastic head, hands, foam body, printed face

30"	$50.00	$175.00

APPLAUSE TOY COMPANY, 1981 – 1983, HASBRO (PLAYSKOOL), 1983+

8"	$2.00	$15.00
17"	$5.00	$50.00
48"	$25.00	$175.00

16" cloth Volland Raggedy Ann and 17" Raggedy Andy with brown yarn hair, button eyes, painted lower lashes, triangle nose, smiling mouth, cloth bodies with red/white striped legs and brown feet turned out, original cotton outfits, "Patented Sept. 7, 1915" stamped on back, circa 1920s, $1,350.00 and $750.00 respectively. Courtesy McMasters Harris Doll Auctions.

32" cloth Raggedy Ann & Andy by Myrtle Silsby of George Novelty Co., tagged cloth bodies, metal disc eyes, yarn wigs, red and white striped legs, original cotton costumes, circa 1946, $650.00. Courtesy McMasters Harris Doll Auctions.

9" cloth Benjamin Franklin, tagged "Bernard Ravca//Benjamin Franklin," sculptured stockinette face, painted side-glancing eyes, cloth Constitution rolled up under arm, brown felt coat and short pants, red stockings, red vest, pilgrim shoes, glasses, white gloves, circa pre-1930s, $250.00. Courtesy Nelda Shelton.

Ca. 1924 – 1935+, Paris and New York. Stitched stockinette characters, label reads *"Original Ravca//Fabrication Francaise"* or hang tag reads *"Original Ravca."* Some all-cloth or gesso/papier-mâché.

CLOTH — STOCKINETTE

Celebrities, Occupations, or Literary characters

7"	$38.00	$135.00
9½"	$40.00	$155.00
12"	$55.00	$210.00
17"	$75.00	$365.00

Queen Elizabeth

36"	$850.00*	Ravca cloth label on wrist

Military figures, such as Hitler, Mussolini

9"	$250.00	$1,300.00
20"	$450.00	$2,600.00
27"	$1,000.00	$5,000.00+

Peasants/Old People

7"	$23.00	$100.00
9"	$25.00	$135.00
12"	$35.00	$165.00
15"	$50.00	$235.00
23"	$75.00	$275.00

GESSO — PAPIER-MÂCHÉ

12"	$100.00	$435.00
15"	$150.00	$625.00
17"	$250.00	$1,000.00

Remco Industries

Ca. 1960 – 1974. One of the first companies to market with television ads. First price is for played-with doll; second price is for mint-in-box.

Addams Family, 1964

Lurch

5½"	$15.00	$55.00

Morticia

4¾"	$128.00*

Uncle Fester

4½"	$15.00	$50.00

Baby Crawl-Along, 1967

20"	$7.00	$20.00

Baby Glad 'N Sad, 1967

Vinyl and hard plastic, rooted blond hair, painted blue eyes

14"	$5.00	$15.00

Baby Grow a Tooth, 1968

Vinyl and hard plastic, rooted hair, blue sleep eyes, open/closed mouth, one tooth, grows her own tooth, battery operated

	15"	$6.00	$20.00
Black			
	14"	$8.00	$25.00

Baby Know It All, 1969

	17"	$4.00	$20.00

Baby Laugh A Lot, 1970

Rooted long hair, painted eyes, open/closed mouth, teeth, vinyl head, hands, plush body, push button, she laughs, battery operated

	16"	$5.00	$20.00

Baby Stroll A Long, 1966

	15"	$4.00	$15.00

Beatles, 1964

Vinyl and plastic, Paul McCartney, Ringo Starr, George Harrison, and John Lennon. Paul 4⅞", all others 4½" with guitars bearing their names

Set of 4			
		$125.00	$1,790.00* MIB
John Lennon			
		$40.00	$150.00

Dave Clark Five, 1964

Set of five musical group, vinyl heads, rigid plastic bodies

Set			
		$50.00	
Dave Clark			
	5"	$8.00	$15.00

Other band members have name attached to leg

	3"	$4.00	$10.00

Heidi and friends, 1967, in plastic case

Rooted hair, painted side-glancing eyes, open/closed mouth, all-vinyl, press button and dolls wave

Heidi			
	5½"	$10.00	$67.00
Herby			
	4½"	$10.00	$43.00
Jan, Oriental			
	5½"	$13.00	$50.00
Pip			
	5½"	$13.00	$50.00
Winking Heidi, 1968			
	5½"	$7.00	$35.00

6" vinyl Spunky, marked "#A211//Remco Inc.//Spunky," blue painted side-glancing eyes, glasses, open/closed mouth with painted teeth, rooted red hair, white leather vest, red canvas pants, white shoes, circa 1968, $25.00. Courtesy Nelda Shelton.

4½" vinyl Beatles, Paul McCartney, John Lennon, George Harrison, and Ringo Starr, synthetic dark wigs, molded and painted features, open/closed mouths with teeth, oversized heads, on rigid vinyl bodies with molded black suits and shoes, Paul McCartney is larger at 4⅞" tall, plastic instruments bear name of individual members, circa 1964, $105.00 for single figure, $400.00 for set.
Courtesy Sarah Munsey.

Jeannie, I Dream of
6"	$20.00	$65.00

Jumpsy, 1970, vinyl and hard plastic, jumps rope, rooted blond hair, painted blue eyes, closed mouth, molded-on shoes and socks
14"	$5.00	$20.00

Black
14"	$7.00	$25.00

Laurie Partridge, 1973
19"	$40.00	$125.00

L.B.J., 1964
5½"	$9.00	$25.00

Littlechap Family, 1963+
Vinyl head, arms, jointed hips, shoulders, neck, black molded and painted hair, black eyes, box

Set of four boxed together	$200.00	$480.00
Dr. John Littlechap		
14½"	$20.00	$75.00
Judy Littlechap		
12"	$25.00	$65.00
Libby Littlechap		
10½"	$35.00	$70.00
Lisa Littlechap		
13½"	$15.00	$45.00
Littlechap Accessories		
Dr. John's Office		
	$75.00	$325.00 MIP
Bedroom		
	$25.00	$110.00 MIP
Family room		
	$25.00	$110.00 MIP
Dr. John Littlechap's outfits		
Golf outfit		$30.00 MIP
Medical		$65.00 MIP
Suit		$50.00 MIP
Tuxedo		$70.00 MIP

Lisa's outfits
    Evening dress $90.00 MIP
    Coat, fur trim $50.00 MIP
Libby's, Judy's outfits
    Jeans/sweater $30.00 MIP
    Dance dress $45.00 MIP

Mimi, 1973

Vinyl and hard plastic, battery operated singer, rooted long blond hair, painted blue eyes, open/closed mouth, record player in body, sings *I'd Like to Teach the World to Sing,* song used for Coca-Cola® commercial; sings in different languages

    19" $20.00 $75.00
Black
    19" $25.00 $85.00

Lily Munster, #1822, 1964, vinyl, one-piece body, played by Yvonne DeCarlo

    4¾" $105.00*

Grandpa Munster, #1821, 1964, vinyl head, one-piece plastic body

    4¾" $65.00 $110.00

Orphan Annie, 1967

    15" $150.00* MIB

Sweet April, 1971

Vinyl

    5½" $4.00 $15.00
Black
    5½" $5.00 $20.00

Tippy Tumbles, 1968

Vinyl, rooted red hair, stationary blue eyes, does somersaults, batteries in pocketbook

    16" $14.00 $55.00

Tumbling Tomboy, 1969

Rooted blond braids, closed smiling mouth, vinyl and hard plastic, battery operated

    17" $3.00 $15.00

Richwood Toys Inc.

Sandra Sue, ca. 1940s, 1950s. Hard plastic, walker, head does not turn, slim body, saran wigs, sleep eyes. Some with high-heeled feet, only marks are number under arm or leg. All prices reflect outfits with original socks, shoes, panties, and accessories.

First price is for played with doll, incomplete costume; second price is for complete mint-in-box doll.

Sandra Sue, 8"

    Flat feet, in camisole, slip, panties, shoes, and socks
                   $40.00 $175.00
    In school dress
                   $50.00 $200.00+
    In party/Sunday dress
                   $80.00 $225.00

* at auction

8" hard plastic Sandra Sue twins, saran wig, sleep eyes, non-walking, jointed, original full length slips, original box, circa 1950s, $395.00. Courtesy Marge Meisinger.

Left: 8" hard plastic Sandra Sue, saran wig, sleep eyes, non-walking, jointed, original Heidi cotton costume, original box, circa 1950s, $250.00. Courtesy Marge Meisinger.

Special coat, hat, and dress, limited editions, Brides, Heidi, Little Women,

Majorette	$75.00+	$225.00
Sport or play clothes	$35.00	$150.00
MIB Twin Sandra Sues		$395.00

Too few in database for reliable range.

High-heeled feet, camisole, slip, panties, shoes, socks

	$35.00	$125.00
In school dress	$35.00	$150.00
In party/Sunday dress	$65.00	$175.00

Special coat, hat and dress, limited editions, Brides, Heidi, Little Women,

Majorette	$65.00	$175.00
Sport or play clothes	$30.00	$125.00
MIB Twin Sandra Sues		$350.00

Too few in database for reliable range.

Sandra Sue Outfits: mint, including all accessories

School dress	$5.00	$15.00
Party dress	$15.00	$25.00
Specials	$35.00	$50.00
Sport sets	$15.00	$25.00

Cindy Lou, 14"

Hard plastic, jointed dolls were purchased in bulk from New York distributor, fitted with double-stitched wigs by Richwood.

All prices include shoes, socks, panties, slips, and accessories.

In camisole, slip, panties, shoes, and socks

	$45.00	$165.00+
In school dress	$75.00	$175.00+
In party dress	$95.00	$225.00
In special outfits	$85.00+	$250.00
In sports outfits	$65.00	$175.00

Cindy Lou Outfits: mint, including all accessories

School dress	$35.00
Party dress	$45.00
Special outfit	$50.00
Sports clothes	$35.00

Roldan

Roldan characters are similar to Klumpe figures in many respects. They were made in Barcelona, Spain, from the early 1960s until the mid-1970s. They are made of felt over a wire armature with painted mask faces. Like Klumpe, Roldan figures represent professionals, hobbyists, dancers, historical characters, and contemporary males and females performing a wide variety of tasks.

Some, but not all Roldans, were imported by Rosenfeld Imports and Leora Dolores of Hollywood. Figures originally came with two sewn-on identifying cardboard tags. Roldan characters most commonly found are doctors, Spanish dancers, and bull fighters. Roldan characters tend to have somewhat smaller heads, longer necks, and more defined facial features than Klumpe.

9½" felt cloth doctor character, with Roldan marked paper tag, circa 1960s, circa $125.00. Courtesy Sharon Kolibaba.

Common figures $30.00 $100.00+
Elaborate figure, MIB with accessories
         $250.00

Sasha

1965 – 1986+. Sasha dolls were created by Swiss artist, Sasha Morgenthaler, who handcrafted 20" children and 13" babies in Zurich, Switzerland, from the 1940s until her death in 1975. Her handmade studio dolls had cloth or molded bodies, five different head molds, and were hand painted by Sasha Morgenthaler. To make her dolls affordable as children's playthings, she licensed Götz Puppenfabric (1964 – 1970) in Germany and Frido Trendon Ltd. (1965 – 1986) in England to manufacture 16" Sasha dolls in series. The manufactured dolls were made of rigid vinyl with painted features. Götz Dolls, Inc. was granted a new license in 1994 and is currently producing them in Germany.

Price range reflects rarity, condition, and completeness of doll, outfit, and packaging, and varies with geographic location. First price is for doll without original clothing and/or in less than perfect condition; second price is for mint-in-box (or tube).

12" vinyl Frido-Trendon Ltd., Baby White Bird, #508, circa 1975 – 1986, came as sexed girl and unsexed baby, clothing was also sold as a separate outfit, $300.00. Courtesy Dorisanne Osborn.

ORIGINAL STUDIO SASHA DOLL, CA. 1940S – 1974

Made by Sasha Morganthaler in Switzerland. Some are signed on soles of feet, have wrist tags, or wear labeled clothing.

    20" $2,000.00 $9,000.00 – $14,000.00

16" vinyl, blue checked gingham dress, brunette, circa 1969 – 1970, used crayon tube package, $225.00. Courtesy Sally DeSmet.

GÖTZ SASHA DOLL, 1964 – 1970, GERMANY

Girls or boys, two face molds. Marked *"Sasha Series"* in circle on neck and in three-circle logo on back. Three different boxes were used. Identified by wrist tag and/or booklet.

16"	$600.00	$1,500.00

FRIDO-TRENDON LTD., 1965 – 1986, ENGLAND

Unmarked on body, wore wrist tags and current catalogs were packed with doll

Child, 1965 – 1968, packaged in wide box

16"	$100.00	$1,000.00

Child, 1969 – 1972, packaged in crayon tubes

16"	$100.00	$600.00

Sexed Baby, 1970 – 1978, cradle, styrofoam cradles package or straw box and box

White or black

$100.00	$300.00

Unsexed Baby, 1978 – 1986, packaged in styrofoam wide or narrow cradles or straw basket and box

$100.00	$300.00

Child, 1973 – 1975, packaged in shoe box style box

16"	$100.00	$400.00

Child, 1975 – 1980, black, white, shoe box style box

16"	$100.00	$300.00

Child, 1980 – 1986, black, white, packaged in photo box with flaps

$100.00	$250.00

#1 Sasha Anniversary doll

16"	$175.00	$300.00

117S, Sasha "Sari" 1986, black hair, estimated only 400 produced before English factory closed January 1986

16"	$450.00	$700.00

130E Sasha "Wintersport" 1986, blond hair

16"	$400.00	$600.00

330E Gregor Sandy (hair) "Hiker"

16"	$1,225.00*

Limited Editions

Made by Trendon Sasha Ltd. in England, packaged in box with outer sleeve picturing individual doll. Limited edition Sasha dolls marked on neck with date and number. Number on certificate matches number on doll's neck.

1981 "Velvet," girl, light brown wig, 5,000 production planned

$300.00	$450.00

1982 "Pintucks" girl, blond wig, 6,000 production planned

$300.00	$450.00

16" vinyl, red pinafore outfit, circa 1980 – 1986, $250.00. Courtesy Dorisanne Osborn.

1983 "Kiltie" girl, red wig, 4,000 production planned
$350.00 $500.00

1984 "Harlequin" girl, rooted blond hair, 4,000 production planned
$200.00 $350.00

1985 "Prince Gregor" boy, light brown wig, 4,000 production planned
$250.00 $400.00

1986 "Princess Sasha" girl, blond wig, 3,500 production planned, but only 350 were made
$1,000.00 $1,500.00

GÖTZ DOLLS INC., 1995 +, GERMANY

They received the license in September 1994; dolls introduced in 1995.

Child, 1995 – 1996

Marked *"Götz Sasha"* on neck and *"Sasha Series"* in three circle logo on back. About 1,500 of the dolls produced in 1995 did not have mold mark on back. Earliest dolls packaged in generic Götz box, currently in tube, wear wrist tag, Götz tag, and have mini-catalog.

16½" $300.00 retail

Baby, 1996

Baby, unmarked on neck, marked *"Sasha Series"* in three circle logo on back. First babies were packaged in generic Götz box or large tube, currently packaged in small "Baby" tube. Wears Sasha wrist tag, Götz booklet and current catalog.

12" $150.00 retail

1934+, Ideal Novelty Toy Corp., New York. Designed by Bernard Lipfert, 1934 – 1940s. Composition head and jointed body, dimples in cheeks, green sleep eyes, open mouth, teeth, mohair wig, tagged original dress, center-snap shoes. Prototype dolls may have paper sticker inside head and bias trimmed wig.

First price is for incomplete or played-with doll. Second price is for doll in excellent to mint condition, all original. Add more for exceptional dolls or special outfits like Ranger or Wee Willie Winkie.

COMPOSITION

Shirley Temple		
11"	$400.00	$975.00
13"	$350.00	$750.00
16"	$400.00	$800.00
17"	$200.00	$875.00
18"	$250.00	$2,690.00*
20"	$300.00	$1,100.00
22"	$375.00	$1,200.00
27"	$450.00	$1,750.00
Baby Shirley		
18"	$400.00	$1,200.00
21"	$400.00	$1,500.00

18" composition Ideal Littlest Rebel, mohair wig, hazel sleep eyes, open mouth with teeth, jointed, original red dotted dress with organdy apron, collar, and cuffs, circa 1935, $1,000.00.   Courtesy Marge Meisinger.

* at auction

25" composition Ideal Wee Willie Winkie, mohair wig, sleep eyes, open mouth with teeth, jointed, original plaid skirt and twill top with brass buttons, missing hat, circa 1937, $1,000.00. Courtesy Marge Meisinger.

15" composition Ideal The Little Colonel, with mohair wig, sleep eyes, open mouth with teeth, jointed, original pink organdy dress NRA tagged, bonnet, pin, original box (not shown), circa 1934, $1,200.00. Courtesy Marge Meisinger.

> **Marks:**
> SHIRLEY TEMPLE//IDEAL NOV. & TOY on back of head
> and SHIRLEY TEMPLE on body. Some marked only on head
> and with a size.

Hawaiian, "Marama," Ideal used the composition Shirley Temple mold for this doll representing a character from the movie *Hurricane*, black yarn hair, wears grass skirt, Hawaiian costume

18"	$400.00	$950.00

Shirley at the Organ, special display stand with composition Shirley Temple at non-functioning organ, music provided by record

$3,500.00+

Too few in database for reliable range.

Accessories:

Button, three types		$125.00
Buggy, wicker or wood		
	$500.00	$575.00
Dress, tagged	$125.00 – $575.00	
Satin pajama, tagged		$670.00
Trunk	$175.00 – 225.00	

VARIANTS

Japanese, unlicensed Shirley dolls

All-bisque

6"	$65.00	$250.00

Celluloid

5"	$45.00	$185.00
8"	$65.00	$245.00

Celluloid, Dutch Shirley Temple, ca. 1937+. All-celluloid, open crown, metal pate, sleep eyes, dimples in cheeks. Marked: *"Shirley Temple"* on head, may have additional marks, dressed in Dutch costume.

13"	$90.00	$350.00
15"	$100.00	$400.00

Composition Japanese, heavily molded brown curls, painted eyes, open/closed mouth with teeth, body stamped *"Japan"*

7½"	$75.00	$300.00

VINYL

First price indicates doll in excellent condition with flaws; second price is for excellent condition doll, original clothes, accessories. The newer the doll the more perfect it must be to command higher prices.

1957

All-vinyl, sleep eyes, synthetic rooted wig, open/closed mouth, teeth, came in two-piece slip and undies, tagged Shirley Temple, came with gold plastic script pin reading *"Shirley Temple,"* marked on back of head: *"ST//12"*

12"	$135.00	$350.00

1958 – 1961

Marked on back of head: *"S.T.//15," "S.T.//17,"* or *"S.T.//19,"* some had flirty ("Twinkle") eyes; add more for flirty eyes or 1961 Cinderella, Bo Peep, Heidi, and Red Riding Hood

15"	$100.00	$400.00
17"	$115.00	$475.00
19"	$125.00	$525.00

1960, Jointed wrists, marked *"ST-35-38-2"*

35 – 36"	$550.00	$2,100.00

1972, Montgomery Wards reissue, plain box

17"	$50.00	$225.00

1973, red dot "Stand Up and Cheer" outfit, box with Shirley pictures, extra outfits available

16"	$45.00	$165.00

1982 – 1983

8"	$8.00	$30.00
12"	$9.00	$35.00

1984, by Hank Garfinkle, *marked "Doll Dreams & Love"*

36"	$75.00	$250.00

1994+, Shirley Temple Dress-Up Doll, Danbury Mint, similar to 1987 doll; no charge for doll, get two outfits bimonthly

16"	$30.00	$60.00

1996 Danbury Mint, Little Colonel, Rebecca/Sunnybrook Farm, and Heidi

16"	$25.00, retail at Target stores

PORCELAIN

1987+, Danbury Mint

16"	$65.00	$90.00

1990+, Danbury Mint, designed by Elke Hutchens, in costumes from *The Little Princess, Bright Eyes, Curly Top, Dimples,* and others. *Marked on neck: "Shirley Temple//1990."*

20"	$150.00	$240.00

1997 Toddler, Danbury Mint, designed by Elke Hutchens, porcelain head, arms, legs, cloth body, pink dress, more dolls in the toddler series include Flower Girl and others

20"	$129.00 retail

16½" vinyl Ideal, Stand Up and Cheer, blond rooted hair, brown painted eyes, open/closed mouth with painted teeth, jointed plastic body, red polka dot nylon dress, marked on head "1972 Ideal Toy Corp/ST – 14-H-213-Hong Kong," circa 1973, $225.00. Courtesy Marge Meisinger.

Sun Rubber

Ca. 1930s+, Barberton, OH.

Betty Bows, 1953

Molded hair with loop for ribbon, drink and wet baby, jointed body

11"	$103.00*

Sun Rubber

Psyllium, 1937
Molded painted hard rubber, moving head, blue pants, white suspenders, black shoes and hat

10"	$3.00	$15.00

Ruth E. Newton, vinyl child, molded clothes, squeaker

8"	$35.00	$90.00

18" vinyl Bannister Baby, sleep eyes, molded and painted hair, open mouth for bottle, a drink and wet baby, with crier and blows bubbles, bent-limb baby body, missing accessories, circa 1954, $95.00. Courtesy Shirley Funsten.

Terri Lee

16" hard plastic Terri Lee, synthetic wig, painted features, five-piece jointed body, original tagged yellow dress and bonnet, original box, marked on back "Terri Lee," circa 1950s, $700.00. Courtesy McMasters Harris Doll Auctions.

1946 – 1962, Lincoln, NE, and Apple Valley, CA. First dolls composition, then hard plastic and vinyl. Closed pouty mouth, painted eyes, wigged, jointed body.

First price indicates played-with doll or missing accessories; second price is mint-in-box. More for fancy costume, additional wardrobe.

Terri Lee
Composition, 1946 – 1947

16"	$80.00	$375.00+

Painted hard plastic, 1947 – 1950

16"	$125.00	$500.00
16"	$1,625.00* Pat. Pending	

Hard plastic, 1951 – 1962

16"	$150.00	$400.00

Terri Lee

16"	$2,500.00* MIB	

Vinyl, less if sticky

16"	$80.00	$250.00

Talking

16"	$150.00	$600.00

Benji, painted plastic, brown, 1947 – 1958, black lamb's wool wig

16"	$150.00	$600.00

Connie Lynn, 1955, hard plastic, sleep eyes, caracul wig, bent-limb baby body

19"	$125.00	$400.00

Gene Autry, 1949 – 1950, painted plastic

16"	$450.00	$1,800.00

Jerri Lee, hard plastic, caracul wig

16"	$125.00	$500.00
Vinyl 16"	$1,500.00	

16" hard plastic Jerri Lee, caracul wig, painted features, five-piece jointed body, original tagged tuxedo, original box, additional accessories including pajamas, robe, slippers, marked on back "Terri Lee," circa 1950s, $600.00. Courtesy McMasters Harris Doll Auctions.

* at auction

Linda Lee, 1950 – 1951, vinyl
    12" $20.00 $75.00
1952 – 1958, vinyl baby
    10" $45.00 $145.00
Mary Jane, Terri Lee look-alike, hard plastic walker
    16" $50.00 $265.00
Patty Jo, Bonnie Lou, black
    16" $150.00 $600.00
    16" $3,825.00*
Tiny Terri Lee, 1955 – 1958
    10" $50.00 $175.00
Accessories
Terri Lee Outfits:
  Girl Scout/Brownie uniform$50.00
  Heart Fund $325.00
  Plaid skirt, coat, hat $660.00*
  School dress $150.00
  Shoes $35.00
  Winter outfit, fur trim $660.00*
Jerri Lee Outfits:
  Gene Autrey $865.00*

16" composition Terri Lee black Bonnie Lou, chestnut brunette hair evenly curled around head, mannequin wig style, black single stroke brows, brown eyes/white highlights, five painted lashes above, three painted lashes below, red accent dots in nose, all original, pink outfit, satin bows, red and white plaid mint-in-box Terri Lee Toddler box with porthole lid. This doll would date circa 1947, before Jackie Ormes began painting the Patty Jo faces on black Terri Lee dolls, $3,800.00. Courtesy Pat Rather.

Robert Tonner

Left: 18" vinyl, Kitty Collier 2000 Modern Doll Convention, limited edition, synthetic wig, sleep eyes, painted features, jointed body, black velvet sparkle sheath, circa 2000, $125.00. Courtesy Carol Stover.

Right: 8" hard vinyl, Pocahontas, Kripplebush Kids #20907, sleep eyes, black braided wig, tan leather-like fringed dress and boots, jointed body, wrist tag "Robert Tonner Kripplebush Kids," circa 2000, $55.00 retail. Courtesy Marge Meisinger.

Ca. 1991.
Ann Estelle, 1999, a Mary Engelbreit character, hard plastic, blond wig, glasses
    10" $69.00 retail
Betsy McCall, see Betsy McCall section.
Kripplebush Kids, 1997, hard plastic, Marni, Eliza, Hannah
    8" $55.00 retail
Tyler Wentworth, 1999, fashion-type, long, straight, brunette, blond, or red hair
    16" $79.99 retail
Kitty Collier, 2000, blond, brunette, or red head
    18" $89.00 (retail)

Trolls portray supernatural beings from Scandinavian folklore. They have been manufactured by various companies including Helena and Martii Kuuslkoski who made Fauni Trolls, ca. 1952+ (sawdust filled cloth dolls); Thomas Dam, 1960+; and Scandia House, later Norfin®; Uneeda Doll and Toy Wishniks®; Russ Berrie; Ace Novelty; Treasure Trolls; Applause Toys; Magical Trolls; and many other companies who made lesser quality vinyl look-alikes, mostly unmarked, to take advantage of the fad. Most are all-vinyl or vinyl with stuffed cloth bodies.

Troll Figures

2½"	$3.00	$15.00
5"	$7.00	$25.00
7"	$10.00	$40.00
10"	$15.00	$55.00
12"	$17.00	$65.00
15"	$22.00	$85.00

Troll Animals

Cow, unmarked

6"	$50.00	$125.00

Donkey, Dam, 1964

9"	$40.00	$150.00

Monkey, Thomas Dam

7"	$230.00*

Mouse, Thomas Dam

5"	$170.00*

Tailed Troll, Thomas Dam

6½"	$190.00*

Uneeda

1917+, New York City. Made composition head dolls, including Mama dolls and made the transition to plastics and vinyl.

COMPOSITION

Rita Hayworth, as "Carmen," ca. 1939

From *The Loves of Carmen* movie, all-composition, red mohair wig, unmarked, cardboard tag

14"	$135.00	$500.00

HARD PLASTIC AND VINYL

Baby Dollikins, 1960

Vinyl head, hard plastic jointed body with jointed elbows, wrists, and knees, drink and wet

21"	$45.00	$200.00 MIB

Baby Trix, 1965

19"	$7.00	$25.00

Bareskin Baby, 1968

12½"	$5.00	$20.00

Blabby, 1962+

14"	$7.00	$25.00

Coquette, 1963+

16"	$5.00	$20.00

Black

16"	$9.00	$36.00

* at auction

10½" vinyl Suzette (Tiny Teen), rooted wig, blue sleep eyes with molded lashes, holes for pearl earrings, jointed rigid vinyl body and waist, high heel feet, original camisole lingerie set, in box, marked on head "Uneeda," circa 1957, $135.00. Courtesy Carol Stover.

Dollikin, 1957+, multi-joints, *marked "Uneeda//2S"*
19"	$135.00	$225.00
21"	$405.00* Ballerina	

Fairy Princess, 1961
32"	$35.00	$100.00

Freckles, 1960, vinyl head, rigid plastic body, *marked "22" on head*
32"	$20.00	$75.00

Freckles, 1973
Ventriloquist doll, vinyl head, hands, rooted hair, cotton stuffed cloth body
30"	$17.00	$60.00

Jennifer, 1973
Rooted side-parted hair, painted features, teen body, mod clothing
18"	$7.00	$20.00

Magic Meg, w/Hair That Grows
Vinyl and plastic, rooted hair, sleep eyes
16"	$10.00	$45.00

Pir-thilla, 1958
Blows up balloons, vinyl, rooted hair, sleep eyes
12½"	$4.00	$12.00

Purty, 1973
Long rooted hair, vinyl, plastic, painted features
11"	$7.00	$25.00

Pollyanna, 1960, for Disney
11"	$9.00	$35.00
17"	$200.00* MIB	
31"	$40.00	$125.00

Saranade, 1962
Vinyl head, hard plastic body, rooted blond hair, blue sleep eyes, red and white dress, speaker in tummy, phonograph and records came with doll, used battery
21"	$25.00	$100.00

Suzette (Carol Brent)
12"	$25.00	$125.00

Tiny Teen, 1957 – 1959
Vinyl head, rooted hair, pierced ears, six-piece hard plastic body, high-heeled feet to compete with Little Miss Revlon, wrist tag
10½"	$25.00	$100.00

14" composition Rita Hayworth as Carmen, mohair wig, sleep eyes with lashes, shadow and lashes painted under, jointed body, original taffeta costume with black lace mantilla and overskirt, wrist tag "The Carmen Doll/Inspired By/Rita Hayworth's/The Loves/ Of Carmen," doll unmarked, circa 1948, $500.00. Courtesy McMasters Harris Doll Auctions.

Vinyl

Ca. 1950s+. By the mid-1950s, vinyl (polyvinylchloride) was being used for dolls. Material that was soft to the touch and processing that allowed hair to be

8" Baby Susan sold by both Marlon Creations and Egee, molded and painted hair, sleep eyes with molded lashes, drinking and wetting doll, jointed with bent baby legs, marked on neck "Baby Susan," circa 1950s, $55.00. Courtesy Toni Ferry.

10½" unmarked bride, unknown manufacturer, rooted synthetic hair, sleep eyes with molded lashes and heavy lashes painted in corners, jointed body and waist, painted nails and toes, high heel feet, original nylon bridal gown with tulle overskirt and veil, circa 1950s, $45.00. Courtesy Carol Stover.

rooted were positive attractions. Vinyl became a desirable material and the market was soon deluged with dolls manufactured from this product. Many dolls of this period are of little known manufacturers, unmarked, or marked only with a number. With little history behind them, these dolls need to be mint-in-box and complete to warrant top prices. With special accessories or wardrobe values may be more.

UNKNOWN MAKER

Baby

Vinyl head, painted or sleep eyes, molded hair or wig, bent legs, cloth or vinyl body

12"	$2.50	$10.00
16"	$3.00	$12.00
20"	$5.00	$20.00

Child

Vinyl head, jointed body, painted or sleep eyes, molded hair or wig, straight legs

14"	$5.00	$14.00
22"	$6.00	$25.00

Adult

Vinyl head, painted or sleep eyes, jointed body, molded hair or wig, smaller waist with male or female modeling for torso

8"	$5.00	$25.00
18"	$20.00	$75.00

KNOWN MAKER

Baby Barry

Alfred E. Newman

20"	$35.00	$175.00

Captain Kangaroo

19"	$20.00	$125.00
24"	$50.00	$215.00

Christopher Robin

18"	$40.00	$135.00

Daisy Mae

14"	$35.00	$175.00

Emmett Kelly (Willie the Clown)

15"	$25.00	$160.00
21"	$70.00	$275.00

Li'l Abner

14"	$30.00	$150.00
21"	$50.00	$200.00

Mammy Yokum, 1957

Molded hair

14"	$30.00	$125.00
21"	$50.00	$225.00

Yarn hair
14"	$30.00	$150.00
21"	$50.00	$250.00

Nose lights up
23"	$85.00	$325.00

Pappy Yokum, 1957
14"	$25.00	$100.00
21"	$50.00	$225.00

Nose lights up
23"	$85.00	$325.00

DEE & CEE, Canada
Calypso Bill, 1961, black, vinyl, *marked "DEE CEE"*
16"	$50.00 *

GLAD TOY/BROOKGLAD
Poor Pitiful Pearl, circa 1955
Vinyl, some with stuffed one-piece vinyl bodies, others jointed
13"	$360.00 * MIB	
17"	$50.00	$95.00

HIMSTEDT, ANNETTE, 1986+
Distributed by Timeless Creations, a division of Mattel, Inc. Swivel rigid vinyl head with shoulder plate, cloth body, vinyl limbs, inset eyes, real lashes, molded eyelids, holes in nostrils, human hair wig, bare feet, original in box.

Barefoot Children, 1986, 26"
Bastian	$200.00	$800.00
Beckus	$400.00	$1,500.00
Ellen	$200.00	$900.00
Fatou	$275.00	$1,100.00
Kathe	$200.00	$800.00
Lisa	$200.00	$800.00
Paula	$175.00	$800.00

Blessed Are the Children, 1988, 31"
Friederike	$1,025.00*	
Kasimir	$1,000.00*	
Makimura	$350.00	$1,400.00
Malin	$350.00	$1,600.00
Michiko	$400.00	$1,500.00

Reflections of Youth, 1989 – 1990, 26"
Adrienne	$200.00	$900.00
Jule, 1992, 26"		$1,400.00*
Kai	$215.00	$900.00
Neblina, 1991, 27½"		$1,400.00*

8" Plastic Molded Arts baby, molded and painted hair, sleep eyes with molded lashes, drinking and wetting doll, jointed with bent baby legs, original box marked "PMA," doll unmarked, circa mid-1950s, $65.00 MIB. Courtesy Toni Ferry.

20" unmarked doll, sleep eyes with molded lashes, rooted hair, closed mouth, blow molded vinyl body with high heel feet, red jersey swim suit, long molded fingers with separate thumb similar to Ice Capades dolls, circa 1960s, $20.00. Courtesy Carol Stover.

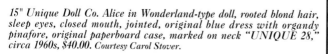

15" Unique Doll Co. Alice in Wonderland-type doll, rooted blond hair, sleep eyes, closed mouth, jointed, original blue dress with organdy pinafore, original paperboard case, marked on neck "UNIQUE 28," circa 1960s, $40.00. Courtesy Carol Stover.

* at auction

15" Shindana Kim Jeans 'n Things, painted eyes, closed mouth, long black hair, jointed vinyl body, wears blue jumpsuit, red stipped knit dickey and cap, "© 1969//Shindan a Toys//Division of Operation Bootstrap USA," circa 1975, $75.00. Courtesy Cornelia Ford.

PLAYMATES, 1985+

Made animated talking dolls using a tape player in torso powered by batteries. Extra costumes, tapes, and accessories available. More for black versions.

Amazing Amy, Maddy, circa 1998, vinyl, cloth body, interactive

20"	$69.95 retail	
Cricket, circa 1986+		
25"	$50.00	$125.00
Corky, circa 1987+		
25"	$50.00	$125.00
Jill, 1987, hard plastic, jointed body		
33"	$125.00	$300.00

SAYCO

Miss America Pagenat, circa 1950s

11" $24.00*

SHINDANA

1968 – 1983, Operation Bootstrap, Los Angeles, ethnic features

14"	$30.00	$65.00

Talking Tamu, black, ethnic features

16" $50.00 $180.00

TOMY

Kimberly, 1981 – 1985, closed mouth, more for black

17" $25.00 $55.00

Getting Fancy Kimberly, 1984, open mouth with teeth

17" $35.00 $65.00

TRISTAR

Poor Pitiful Pearl, circa 1955+, vinyl jointed doll came with extra party dress

11" $100.00* MIB

WORLD OF WONDER, circa 1985 – 1987+

Fremont, CA. Made talking dolls and Teddy Ruxpin powered by batteries, had extra accessories, voice cards.

Pamela, The Living Doll, 1986+

21" $25.00 $100.00

10" unmarked baby doll possibly by Mollyee, rooted hair, sleep eyes with lashes, closed mouth, jointed, original cotton outfit with red felt vest and tam, circa 1960s, $25.00. Courtesy Carol Stover.

10½" Hawaiian baby doll, rooted curly hair, closed mouth, brown sleep eyes with molded lashes, paper flower attached to hair, jointed body with bent baby legs, original cotton two-piece sun suit with grass skirt, lei necklace, marked on neck "U/10" possibly Uneeda, circa 1950s or 1960s, $40.00. Courtesy Carol Stover.

Julie, 1987+
24"	$50.00	$125.00

Extra costume $5.00 – $30.00

Teddy Ruxpin, 1985+, animated talking bear
20"	$30.00	$80.00

Vogue Doll Co.

1930s+, Medford, MA. Jennie Graves started the company and dressed "Just Me" and Arranbee dolls in the early years, before Bernard Lipfert designed Ginny. After several changes of ownership, Vogue dolls was purchased in 1995 by Linda and Jim Smith.

GINNY FAMILY

Toddles

Composition, 1937 – 1948, name stamped in ink on bottom of shoe. Some early dolls which have been identified as "Toodles" (spelled with two o's) are blank dolls from various companies used by Vogue. Painted eyes, mohair wig, jointed body; some had gold foil labels reading *"Vogue."*

First price indicates doll in good condition, but with flaws; second price indicates doll in excellent condition with original clothes. More for fancy outfits such as Red Riding Hood or Cowboy/Cowgirl or with accessories.

8"	$125.00	$425.00

Ginny, painted hard plastic, 1948 – 1950

Marked "Vogue" on head, "Vogue Doll" on body, painted eyes, molded hair with mohair wig. Clothing *tagged "Vogue Dolls" or "Vogue Dolls, Inc. Medford Mass.,"* inkspot tag on white with blue letters.

8"	$100.00	$375.00

Ginny, hard plastic, sleep eyes, 1953
8	$125.00	$400.00

With poodle cut wig
8"	$125.00	$400.00

Outfit only $65.00 – $90.00+

8" composition Toddles Alice in Wonderland, mohair wig, painted blue side-glancing eyes, jointed, original pink dress with organdy apron, marked "Alice In Wonderland" on shoe, doll marked "Vogue" on neck and "Doll Co." on back, original box, circa 1940s, $375.00. Courtesy Carol Stover.

Ginny, 8", hard plastic walkers, 1950 – 1954

Transitional to walkers, sleep eyes, painted lashes, strung, dynel wigs, *new mark on back torso: "GINNY//VOGUE DOLLS//INC. //PAT PEND.// MADE IN U.S.A."* Coronation Queen, 1953, has elaborate braid on her costume, silver wrist tags.

Common dress	$95.00	$350.00
1950 Julie #8		$695.00*
1951 Glad, #42		$995.00*
1952 Beryl		$2,025.00*
1952 Carol Kindergarten		$925.00*

8" hard plastic Ginny Becky #62, Debutante Series," blond synthetic wig, blue sleep eyes with painted lashes and brows, jointed body, original tagged organdy dress with black velvet top, black straw hat, marked on head "Vogue," "Vogue Doll" on back, circa 1953, $525.00. Courtesy Carol Stover.

* at auction

8" hard plastic Ginny Candy Dandy Series #55, blond synthetic wig, brown sleep eyes with painted lashes and brows, jointed walking body, original tagged pink taffeta dress with black velvet top, pink and black straw hat, circa 1954, $375.00. Courtesy Carol Stover.

8" hard plastic Ginny Davy Crockett, brunette synthetic wig, sleep eyes with painted lashes and brows, jointed walking body, original suede cloth fringed outfit, coon skin hat, toy rifle, pin, circa 1954, $525.00. Courtesy Carol Stover.

1953 Pamela #60		$510.00*
Straight leg walker, 1954, painted lash		
	$85.00	$350.00

Black Ginny, 1953 – 1954

8"	$150.00	$600.00+
8"	$2,000.00* MIB	

Ginny, hard plastic, 1954 – 1956, seven-piece body, molded lash walkers, sleep eyes, Dynel or saran wigs. *Marked: "VOGUE" on head, "GINNY//VOGUE DOLLS//INC.//PAT. NO. 2687594//MADE IN U.S.A." on back of torso*

8"	$60.00	$225.00
Outfit only	$40.00+	

Davy Crockett, coonskin cap, brown jacket, pants, toy rifle, in box

8"	$935.00*

Crib Crowd, 1950

Baby with curved legs, sleep eyes, poodle cut (caracul) wig

8"	$175.00	$650.00+
Easter Bunny		
8"	$350.00	$1,400.00

Ginny, hard plastic, 1957 – 1962

Bent-knee (jointed) walker, molded lashes, sleep eyes, dynel or saran wigs. *Marked "VOGUE" on head, "GINNY//VOGUE DOLLS//INC.// PAT.NO.2687594//MADE IN U.S.A."*

8"	$45.00	$175.00
Outfit only		$40.00+

Ginny, 1960, unmarked, big walker carried 8" doll dressed just like her

36"	$350.00*

Too few in database for reliable range.

Ginny, 1963 – 1965

Soft vinyl head, hard plastic walker body, sleep eyes, molded lashes, rooted hair. *Marked: "GINNY," on head, "GINNY//VOGUE DOLLS, Inc.//PAT. NO.2687594//MADE IN U.S.A." on back*

8"	$13.00	$50.00

Ginny, 1965 – 1972

All-vinyl, straight legs, non-walker, rooted hair, sleep eyes, molded lashes. *Marked "Ginny" on head, "Ginny//VOGUE DOLLS, INC." on back*

8"	$12.00	$50.00

Ginny, 1972 – 1977

All-vinyl, non-walker, sleep eyes, molded lashes, rooted hair, some with painted lashes. *Marked "GINNY" on head, "VOGUE DOLLS©1972//MADE IN HONG KONG//3" on back, made in Hong Kong by Tonka*

8"	$12.00	$50.00

Ginny, 1977 – 1982

1977 – 1979, "Ginny From Far-Away Lands," made in Hong Kong by Lesney, all-vinyl, sleep eyes, jointed, non-walker, rooted hair, chubby body, same as Tonka doll overall. *Marked "GINNY" on head, "VOGUE DOLLS 1972//MADE IN HONG KONG//3";* painted eyes, 1980 – 1981. *Marked "VOGUE DOLLS//©GINNY-TIM//1977" on head, "VOGUE DOLLS©1977//MADE IN HONG KONG" on back*

8"	$9.00	$35.00

Sasson Ginny, 1981 – 1982

Made in Hong Kong by Lesney, all-vinyl, fully jointed, bendable knees, rooted Dynel hair, sleep eyes in 1981, painted eyes in 1982, slimmer body. *Marked "GINNY" on head, "1978 VOGUE DOLLS INC//MOONACHIE N.J.//MADE IN HONG KONG" on back*

8"	$9.00	$35.00

Ginny, 1984 – 1986

Made by Meritus® in Hong Kong, vinyl, resembling Vogue's 1963 – 1971 Ginny. *Marked "GINNY®" on head, "VOGUE DOLLS// (a star logo)//M.I.I. 1984//Hong Kong" on back.* Porcelain marked: *"GW//SCD//5184" on head, "GINNNY //®VOGUE DOLLS//INC//(a star logo) MII 1984//MADE IN TAIWAN."*

8"	$15.00	$55.00

Ginny, 1986 – 1995

Vinyl, by Dakin, soft vinyl. *Marked "VOGUE®DOLLS//©1984 R. DAKIN INC.// MADE IN CHINA" on back;* hard vinyl, *marked "VOGUE//®// DOLLS//©1986 R. DAKIN and Co.//MADE IN CHINA"*

8"	$8.00	$25.00

Ginny Baby, 1959 – 1982

Vinyl, jointed, sleep eyes, rooted or molded hair, a drink and wet doll, some *marked "GINNY BBY//VOGUE DOLLS INC."*

12"	$10.00	$40.00+
18"	$13.00	$50.00

Ginnette, 1955 – 1969, 1985 – 1986

Vinyl, jointed, open mouth, 1955 – 1956 had painted eyes, 1956 – 1969 had sleep eyes. *Marked "VOGUE DOLLS INC"*

8"	$75.00	$250.00

1962 – 1963, rooted hair Ginnette

8"	$50.00	$175.00

Jan, 1958 – 1960, 1963 – 1964

Jill's friend, vinyl head, six-piece rigid vinyl body, straight leg, swivel waist, rooted hair, *marked "VOGUE,"* called Loveable Jan in 1963 and Sweetheart Jan in 1964

10½"	$40.00	$150.00

8" hard plastic Ginny Rain or Shine #31 Nurse, blond synthetic wig, sleep eyes with painted lashes and brows, jointed walking body, original tagged white cotton nurses outfit, circa 1954, $350.00. Courtesy Carol Stover.

8" vinyl Ginny Baby, rooted blond hair, large sleep eyes with molded lashes, drinking and wetting doll, jointed, original yellow cotton dress, plastic bottle, wrist tag "Hi! I'm Ginny Baby," doll marked on back "Vogue," circa 1964, $45.00. Courtesy Carol Stover.

10½" hard plastic Jill, synthetic wig, sleep eyes with molded lashes, bent-knee walking body, pearl earrings, high-heel feet, brown cotton ensemble # 7408 with taffeta blouse, marked on back "Vogue Dolls, Inc.," circa 1957, $150.00. Courtesy Carol Stover.

16" vinyl Miss Ginny, rooted hair, sleep eyes with molded lashes and lashes painted under, pearl earrings, closed mouth, jointed plastic body with jointed swivel waist, flat feet, original tagged dress with red velvet bodice, doll unmarked, circa 1964, $90.00. Courtesy Carol Stover.

Jeff, 1958 – 1960

Vinyl head, five-piece rigid vinyl body, molded and painted hair, *marked "VOGUE DOLLS"*

11"	$25.00	$100.00

Jill, 1957 – 1960, 1962 – 1963, 1965

Seven-piece hard plastic teenage body, bent-knee walker, high-heeled doll, big sister to Ginny (made in vinyl in 1965), extra wardrobe, *marked "JILL//VOGUE DOLLS//MADEI NU.S.A.//©1957"*

10½"	$65.00	$225.00 MIB
Street dress	$15.00	$25.00
Special outfits	$50.00	$175.00

Jimmy, 1958

Ginny's baby brother, all-vinyl, open mouth, painted eye Ginnette, *marked "VOGUE DOLLS/INC."*

8"	$15.00	$60.00

Little Miss Ginny, 1965 – 1971

All-vinyl, promoted as a pre-teen, one-piece hard plastic body and legs, soft vinyl head and arms, sleep eyes; *head marked "VOGUE DOLL//19©67" or "©VOGUE DOLL//1968" and back, "VOGUE DOLL"*

12"	$10.00	$40.00

Miss Ginny, 1962 – 1965, 1967 – 1980

1962 – 1964, soft vinyl head could be tilted, jointed vinyl arms, two-piece hard plastic body, swivel waist, flat feet; 1965 – 1980, vinyl head and arms, one-piece plastic body

15 – 16"	$15.00	$45.00

GINNY EXCLUSIVES

Enchanted Doll House
1988, limited edition

$40.00	$160.00

GiGi Dolls
1987, GiGi's Favorite

$25.00	$95.00

1988, Sherry's Teddy Bear

$25.00	$95.00

Little Friends, Anchorage, AK
1990, Alaska Ginny

$22.00	$95.00

Meyer's Collectibles
1986, Fairy Godmother

$50.00	$210.00

1987, Cinderella and Prince Charming

$50.00	$210.00

1988, Clown
    $25.00 $95.00
1989, American Cowgirl
    $25.00 $95.00

Modern Doll Convention
1986, Rose Queen
    $50.00 $200.00+
1987, Ginny at the Seashore
    $18.00 $75.00+
1988, Ginny's Claim
    $20.00 $80.00+
1989, Ginny in Nashville
    $27.00 $110.00+
1990, Ginny in Orlando
    $25.00 $95.00+
1991, Ginny in Las Vegas
    $25.00 $95.00+
1992, Poodle Skirt Ginny
    $18.00 $75.00
1993, World of Elegance
    $15.00 $60.00+

Shirley's Doll House
1986, Ginny Goes Country
    $25.00 $95.00
1986, Ginny Goes to the Fair
    $25.00 $95.00
1987, black Ginny in swimsuit
    $25.00 $95.00
1987, Santa & Mrs. Claus
    $25.00 $90.00+
1988, Sunday Best, boy or girl
    $15.00 $60.00
1988, Ginny Babysits
    $15.00 $60.00

Toy Village, Lansing, MI
1989 Ashley Rose
    $35.00 $130.00

Vogue Doll Club
1990, Member Special
    $25.00 $95.00

U.F.D.C. (United Federation of Doll Clubs)
1987 Miss Unity
    $45.00 $155.00
1988 Ginny Luncheon Souvenir
    $35.00 $140.00

Vogue Review Luncheon
1989, Ginny $65.00 $250.00
1990 $30.00 $110.00

14" composition Make-up Doll, sleep eyes with lashes, closed mouth, mohair braided wig, jointed body, pink dress, tie-on skirt, jacket, cap, and make-up bag, doll unmarked, circa 1940s, $375.00. Courtesy Carol Stover.

18" vinyl Baby Dear with rooted hair, designed by Eloise Wilkin, painted eyes, closed mouth, cloth body and vinyl limbs, original christening gown and cap # 48150, box, cloth tag on back "Vogue Dolls, Inc.," on left leg "1960/E. Wilkin," circa 1962, $350.00. Courtesy Kathy Hippensteel.

1991	$25.00	$95.00+
1993, Special Christmas	$18.00	$75.00
1994, Apple of My Eye	$18.00	$75.00
1995, Secret Garden	$18.00	$75.00

Ginny Accessories

First price is played with; second price is mint-in-box or package.

Book: *Ginny's First Secret*	$35.00	$125.00+

Furniture: chair, bed, dresser, wardrobe, rocking chair

each	$18.00	$75.00
Ginny Gym	$120.00	$500.00
Ginny Name Pin	$12.00	$50.00
Ginny Pup, Steiff	$45.00	$175.00+
Ginny's House	$300.00	$1,200.00
Luggage set	$25.00	$100.00
Parasol	$4.00	$15.00
School bag	$20.00	$75.00
Shoes/shoe bag	$10.00	$40.00

COMPOSITION

Dora Lee, sleep eyes, closed mouth

11"	$100.00	$375.00

Jennie, 1940s, sleep eyes, open mouth, mohair wig, five-piece composition body

13"	$80.00	$350.00

Cynthia, 1940s, sleep eyes, open mouth, mohair wig, five-piece composition body

13"	$80.00	$350.00

HARD PLASTIC & VINYL

8" hard plastic Ginny Crystal Blue Ballet, brunette rooted hair, sleep eyes with molded lashes, jointed body, lace and blue tulle tutu, circa 2001, $39.95 retail. Courtesy Vogue Doll Co.

Baby Dear, 1959 – 1964

18" vinyl baby designed by Eloise Wilkin, vinyl limbs, cloth body, topknot or rooted hair, white tag on body *"Vogue Dolls, Inc.";* left leg stamped *"1960/E.Wilkins."* 12" size made in 1961.

18"	$125.00	$325.00
18"		$315.00*

Baby Dear One, 1962

A one-year-old toddler version of Baby Dear, sleep eyes, two teeth

Marked *"C//1961//E.Wilkin//Vogue Dolls//Inc."* on neck, tag on body, mark on right leg

25"	$125.00	$250.00

Baby Dear Musical, 1962 – 1963

12" metal, 18" wooden shaft winds, plays tune, doll wiggles

12"	$40.00	$150.00
18"	$65.00	$250.00

Baby Too Dear, 1963 – 1965

Two-year-old toddler version of Baby Dear, all-vinyl, open mouth, two teeth

17"	$65.00	$250.00
23"	$85.00	$350.00

* at auction

Brikette, 1959 – 1961; 1979 – 1980

Swivel waist joint, green flirty eyes in 22" size only, freckles, rooted straight orange hair, paper hang tag reads *"I'm //Brikette//the//red headed//imp"* marked on head *"VOGUE INC.//19©60"*

22"	$75.00	$250.00 MIB

1960, sleep eyes only, platinum, brunette, or orange hair

16"	$35.00	$125.00 MIB

1979, no swivel waist, curly blond hair, or straight blond or brunette

1980, no swivel waist, curly pink, red, purple, or blond hair

16"	$15.00	$60.00

Li'l Imp, 1959 – 1960

Brickette's little sister, vinyl head, bent knee walker, green sleep eyes, orange hair, freckles, marked *"R and B//44"* on head and *"R and B Doll Co."* on back

10½"	$20.00	$75.00

Wee Imp, 1960

Hard plastic body, orange saran wig, green eyes, freckles, marked *"GINNY//VOGUE DOLS//INC.//PAT.No. 2687594//MADE IN U.S.A."*

8"	$100.00	$400.00

Littlest Angel, 1961 – 1963; 1967 – 1980

1961 – 1963, also called Saucy Littlest Angel, vinyl head, hard plastic bent knee walker, sleep eyes, same doll as Arranbee Littlest Angel, rooted hair, *marked "R & B"*

10½"	$85.00	$200.00

1967 – 1980, all-vinyl, jointed limbs, rooted red, blond, or brunette hair, looks older

11"	$25.00	$55.00
15"	$10.00	$40.00

Love Me Linda (Pretty as a Picture), 1965

Vinyl, large painted eyes, rooted long straight hair, came with portrait, advertised as "Pretty as a Picture" in Sears and Montgomery Ward catalogs, *marked "VOGUE DOLLS/©1965"*

15"	$25.00	$65.00

Welcome Home Baby, 1978 – 1980

Newborn, designed by Eloise Wilkin, vinyl head and arms, painted eyes, molded hair, cloth body, crier, marked *"Lesney"*

18"	$35.00	$65.00+

Welcome Home Baby Turns Two, 1980

Toddler, designed by Eloise Wilkin, vinyl head, arms, and legs, cloth body, sleep eyes, rooted hair, marked *"42260 Lesney Prod. Corp.//1979//Vogue Doll"*

22"	$75.00	$200.00

11" vinyl Vogue black Li'l Imp, marked "1964 ©//Vogue//Dolls," black synthetic hair, brown sleep eyes, closed mouth, white dress with green polka dots and ribbon, matching green ribbon in hair, tagged, with box, circa 1964, $100.00. Courtesy Ana-Lisa Cervantez.

8" hard plastic Ginny Wee Imp, red synthetic wig, freckles, green sleep eyes with molded lashes, jointed walking body with bending knees, original pink candy striped pajamas and cap, pompon slippers, circa 1960, $400.00. Courtesy Carol Stover.

Ca. 1980s+. Creative designer for various companies, including Le Petit Ami, Robin Woods Company, Madame Alexander (Alice Darling), Horsman, and Playtime Productions.

Price indicates mint complete doll; anything else would bring a lesser price.

EARLY CLOTH DOLLS

Price depends on how well painted and quality of clothing and construction. The quality varies greatly in these early cloth dolls.

Children, very rare

Betsy Bluebonnet		$250.00
Enchanted Baby		$300.00
Jane		$300.00
Jessica		$250.00
Laura		$250.00

Children, rare

Mollie		$225.00
Rachel		$200.00
Rueben		$200.00
Stevie		$200.00

Children, common

City Child		$50.00
Elizabeth		$50.00
Mary Margaret		$50.00
How Do I Love Thee		$50.00

Clowns, very rare

Aladdin		$300.00
Sinbad		$300.00
Wynter		$250.00
Yankee Doodle		$300.00

Clowns, rare

Cinamette		$250.00
Happy Holiday, 1984 – 1986		$200.00
Kubla		$200.00

Clowns, common

Bon Bon		$150.00

1986, Childhood Classics

Larissa	14"	$45.00

1987

Catherine	14"	$75.00+
Christmas dolls, Nicholas & Noel, pair		
	14"	$200.00+

1988

Dickens	14"	$125.00
Kristina Kringle	14"	$125.00
Scarlett Sweetheart	14"	$75.00

1989

Anne of Green Gables	14"	$75.00
Heidi, red, white, blue	14"	$150.00
Heidi, brown outfit	14"	$75.00

Hope	14"	$100.00
Lorna Doone	14"	$50.00
Mary of Secret Garden	14"	$100.00
Scarlett Christmas	14"	$125.00
William Noel	14"	$75.00

1990 Camelot Castle Collection

Bobbi	16"	$50.00
Kyleigh Christmas	14"	$75.00
Lady Linet	14"	$35.00
Lady of the Lake	14"	$150.00
Marjorie	14"	$50.00
Meaghan (special)	14"	$150.00
Melanie, Phebe	14"	$50.00
Tessa at the Circus	14"	$75.00
Tess of the D'urbervilles	14"	$150.00

1991 Shades of Day collection

5,000 pieces each, Dawn, Glory, Stormy, Joy, Sunny, Veil, Serenity

Each	14"	$50.00

Others

Alice in Wonderland	24"	$75.00
Bette Jack	14"	$50.00
Bouquet, Lily	14"	$50.00
Delores	14"	$100.00
Eliza Doolittle	14"	$75.00
Mistress Mary	8"	$50.00
Miss Muffet	14"	$50.00
Princess & Pea	15"	$100.00
Rose, Violet	14"	$50.00
Rosemary	14"	$50.00
Sleeping Beauty Set	8"	$150.00
Tennison	14"	$50.00
Victoria	14"	$50.00

ROBIN WOODS LIMITED EDITIONS

Merri, 1991 Doll Convention Disney World, Christmas Tree doll, doll becomes the tree 14" $150.00

Mindy, Made for Disney's Robin Wood's Day, limited to 300
14" $125.00

Rainey, 1991 Robin Woods Club
14" $60.00

J.C. Penney Limited Editions

Angelina, 1990 Christmas angel
14" $150.00

Noelle, Christmas angel	14"	$150.00

Julianna, 1991, little girl holiday shopper
14" $125.00

Robin Woods Exclusives

Gina, The Earthquake Doll, The Doll Place, Ann Parsons of Burlingame, CA 14" $150.00

Anderton, Johana Gast. *Twentieth Century Dolls*. Wallace Homestead, 1971.

———. *More Twentieth Century Dolls*. Wallace Homestead, 1974.

———. *Cloth Dolls*. Wallace Homestead., 1984.

Axe, John. *Effanbee, A Collector's Encyclopedia 1949 – 1983*. Hobby House Press, 1983.

———. *The Encyclopedia of Celebrity Dolls*. Hobby House Press, 1983.

———. *Tammy and Her Family of Dolls*. Hobby House Press, 1995.

Blitman, Joe. *Francie and Her Mod, Mod, Mod, Mod World of Fashion*. Hobby House Press, 1996.

Casper, Peggy Wiedman. *Fashionable Terri Lee Dolls*. Hobby House Press, 1988.

Clark, Debra. *Troll Identification & Price Guide*. Collector Books, 1993.

Coleman, Dorothy S., Elizabeth Ann, and Evelyn Jane. *The Collector's Book of Dolls' Clothes*. Crown Publishers, 1975.

———. *The Collector's Encyclopedia of Dolls, Vol. I & II*. Crown Publishers, 1968, 1986.

Crowsey, Linda. *Madame Alexander, Collector's Dolls Price Guide #22*. Collector Books, 1997.

DeWein, Sibyl and Joan Ashabraner. *The Collector's Encyclopedia of Barbie Dolls and Collectibles*, Collector Books, 1977.

Garrison, Susan Ann. *The Raggedy Ann & Andy Family Album*. Schiffer Publishing, 1989.

Hedrick Susan, and Vilma Matchette. *World Colors, Dolls & Dress*. Hobby House Press, 1997.

Hoyer, Mary. *Mary Hoyer and Her Dolls*. Hobby House Press, 1982.

Izen, Judith. *A Collector's Guide to Ideal Dolls*. Collector Books, 1994, 1999.

Izen, Judith and Carol Stover. *Collector's Encyclopedia of Vogue Dolls*. Collector Books, 1997.

Jensen, Don. *Collector's Guide to Horsman Dolls, 1865 – 1950*. Collector Books, 2002.

Judd, Polly and Pam. *African and Asian Costumed Dolls*. Hobby House Press, 1995.

———. *Cloth Dolls, Identification and Price Guide*. Hobby House Press, 1990.

———. *Composition Dolls, Vol I & II*. Hobby House Press, 1991, 1994.

———. *European Costumed Dolls, Identification and Price Guide*. Hobby House Press, 1994.

———. *Hard Plastic Dolls, I & II*. Hobby House Press, 1987, 1994.

———. *Glamour Dolls of the 1950s & 1960s*. Hobby House Press, 1988.

———. *Santa Dolls & Figurines*. Hobby House Press, 1992.

Langford, Paris. *Liddle Kiddles*. Collector Books, 1996.

Lewis, Kathy and Don. *Chatty Cathy Dolls*. Collector Books, 1994.

Mandeville, A. Glenn. *Ginny, An American Toddler Doll*. Hobby House Press, 1994.

Mansell, Collette. *The Collector's Guide to British Dolls Since 1920*. Robert Hale, 1983.

Melille, Marcie. *The Ultimate Barbie Doll Book*, Krause Publication 1996.

Mertz, Ursula R. *The Collector's Encyclopedia of American Composition Dolls, 1900 – 1950*. Collector Books, 1999.

Morris, Thomas. *The Carnival Chalk Prize, I & II*. Prize Publishers, 1985, 1994.

Moyer, Patsy. *Doll Values*. Collector Books, 1997, 1998, 1999.

———. *Modern Collectible Dolls, Vols. I, II, III*. Collector Books, 1997, 1998, 1999.

Niswonger, Jeanne D. *That Doll Ginny*. Cody Publishing, 1978.

———. *The Ginny Doll Family*. 1996.

Olds, Patrick C. *The Barbie Doll Years*. Collector Books, 1996.

Outwater, Myra Yellin. *Advertising Dolls*. Schiffer, 1998.

Pardee, Elaine and Jackie Robertson. *Encylopedia of Bisque Nancy Ann Storybook Dolls, 1936 – 1947*. Collector Books, 2003.

Pardella, Edward R. *Shirley Temple Dolls and Fashions*. Schiffer Publishing, 1992.

Perkins, Myla. *Black Dolls*. Collector Books, 1993.

———. *Black Dolls Book II*. Collector Books, 1995.

Robison, Joleen Ashman and Kay Sellers. *Advertising Dolls*. Collector Books, 1992.

Schoonmaker, Patricia N. *Effanbee Dolls: The Formative Years, 1910 – 1929*. Hobby House Press, 1984.

———. *Patsy Doll Family Encyclopedia Vol. 1 & II*. Hobby House Press, 1992, 1998.

Smith, Patricia R. *Madame Alexander Collector Dolls*. Collector Books, 1978.

———. *Modern Collector's Dolls*. Series 1 – 8, Collector Books.

Stover, Carol J. *Small Dolls of the '40s and '50s*. Collector Books, 2002.

Sutton, Sydney Ann with Patsy Moyer. *Scouting Dolls Through the Years*. Collector Books, 2003.

Tabbat, Andrew. *Raggedy Ann and Andy, Identification Guide*. Gold Horse Publishing, 1998.

It is recommended that when contacting the references below and requesting information that you enclose a SASE (self-addressed stamped envelope) if you wish to receive a reply.

ACCESSORIES
Best Dressed Doll
P.O. Box 12689
Salem, OR 97309
800-255-2313
Catalog $3.00
e-mail: tonilady@aol.com

ALEXANDER DOLL COMPANY
The Review
PO Box 330
Mundelein, IL 60060-0330
847-949-9200
fax: 847-949-9201
www.madc.org
Official publication of the Madame Alexander Doll Club, quarterly, plus two "Shoppers," $20.00 per year.

AMERICAN CHARACTER
Tressy
Debby Davis, Collector/Dealer
3905 N. 15th St.
Milwaukee, WI 53206

ANTIQUE DOLLS
Matrix
PO Box 1410
New York, NY 10023
Can research your wants

ANTIQUE AND MODERN DOLLS
Rosalie Whyel Museum of Doll Art
1116 108th Avenue N.E.
Bellevue, WA 98004
206-455-1116
fax: 206-455-4793

AUCTION HOUSES
Call or write for a list of upcoming auctions, or if you need information about selling a collection.

McMasters Harris Doll Auctions
James and Shari McMasters
PO Box 1755
Cambridge, OH 43725
800-842-3526 or
740-432-4419
fax: 740-432-3191

Theriaults
PO Box 151
Annapolis, MD 21404
800-638-0422
www.theriaults.com

BARBIE DOLLS, MATTEL
Dream Dolls Galleries & More,
Collector/Dealer
5700 Okeechobee Blvd. #20
West Palm Beach, FL 33417
888-839-3655
e-mail: dollnmore@aol.com

Jaci Jueden, Collector/Dealer
575 Galice Rd.
Merlin, OR 97532
e-mail: jacidj@yahoo.com

Steven Pim, Collector/Dealer
3535 17th St.
San Francisco, CA 94110

BETSY MCCALL
Betsy's Fan Club
Marci Van Ausdall, Editor
PO Box 946
Quincy, CA 95971
Quarterly, $15.50 per year

CELEBRITY DOLLS
Celebrity Doll Journal
Loraine Burdick, Editor
413 10th Ave. Ct. NE
Puyallup, WA 98372
Quarterly, $10.00 per year

CHATTY CATHY, MATTEL
Chatty Cathy Collector's Club
Lisa Eisenstein, Editor
PO Box 140
Readington, NJ 08870-0140
Quarterly newsletter, $28.00
e-mail: Chatty@eclipse.net

COMPOSITION AND TRAVEL DOLLS
Effanbee's Patsy Family
Patsy & Friends Newsletter
PO Box 311
Deming, NM 88031

e-mail: moddoll@yahoo.com
Bi-monthly, $20.00 per year

CONTEMPORARY DOLL COLLECTOR
Scott Publications
30595 Eight Mile
Livonia, MI 48152-1798
Subscription: 800-458-8237

COSTUMING
Doll Costumer's Guild
Patricia Gosh and Janet
Hollingsworth, editors
5042 Wilshire Blvd
PMB573
Los Angeles, CA 90036
323-939-1482
fax: 323-939-3696
e-mail: patgosh@aol.com
Jhollwith@pacbell.net
Quarterly, $24.00
2 years, $44.00

French Fashion Gazette
Adele Leurquin, Editor
1862 Sequoia SE
Port Orchard, WA 98366

DELUXE READING
Penny Brite
Dealer/Collector
Carole Fisher
RD 2, Box 301
Palmyra, PA 17078-9738
e-mail: rcfisher@voicenet.com

DIONNE QUINTUPLETS
Quint News
Jimmy and Fay Rodolfos,
Editors
PO Box 2527
Woburn, MA 01888

Connie Lee Martin
Collector/Dealer
4018 East 17th St.
Tucson, AZ, 85711

DOLL ARTISTS
Jamie G. Anderson
10990 Greenlefe, P.O. Box 806
Rolla, MO 65402
573-364-7347
e-mail: jastudio@rollanet.org

Martha Armstrong-Hand
575 Worcester Drive
Cambria, CA 93428
805-927-3997

Betsy Baker
81 Hy-Vue Terrace
Cold Spring, NY 10516

Cynthia Barron
7796 W. Port Madison
Bainbridge Island, WA 98110
206-780-9003

Charles Batte
272 Divisadero St. #4
San Francisco, CA 94117
415-252-7440

Atelier Bets van Boxel
De Poppenstee
't Vaartje 14
5165 NB Waspik, Holland
www.poppenstee.nl
e-mail: bets@poppenstee.nl

Cheryl Bollenbach
P.O. Box 740922
Arvada, CO 80006-0922
303-216-2424
e-mail: cdboll@aol.com

Laura Clark
P.O. Box 596
Mesilla, NM 88046

Ankie Daanen Doll-Art
Anton Mauvestraat 1
2102 BA HEEMSTEDE NL
023-5477980
fax: 023-5477981

Jane Darin
5648 Camber Drive
San Diego, CA 92117
619-514-8145
www.janedarin.com
e-mail: jdarin@san.rr.com

Marleen Engeler
m'laine dolls
Noordeinde 67 1141 AH
Monnickendam
The Netherlands
31-299656814
e-mail: mlwent4.2@globalxs.nl

Judith & Lucia Friedericy
Friedericy Dolls
1260 Wesley Avenue
Pasadena, CA 91104
626-296-0065
e-mail: friedericy@aol.com

Originals by Goldie
8517 Edgeworth Drive
Capitol Heights, MD 20743
301-350-4119

Lillian Hopkins
2315 29th Street
Santa Monica, CA 90405
310-396-3266
e-mail: lilyart@compuserve.com

Marylynn Huston
101 Mountain View Drive
Pflugerville, TX 78660
512-252-1192

Joyce Patterson
FabricImages
P.O. Box 1599
Brazoria, TX 77422
409-798-9890
e-mail: clothdol@tgn.net

W. Harry Perzyk
2860 Chiplay St.
Sacramento, CA 95826

Daryl Poole
450 Pioneer Trail
Dripping Springs, TX 78620
512-858-7181
e-mail: eltummo@aol.com

The Enchantment Peddler
Kathryn Williams Klushman
Nellie Lamers
HC6 Box 0
Reeds Spring, MO 65737
417-272-3768
www.inter-linc.net/The Enchant
mentPeddlers/
e-mail: theenchantmentpeddlers
@yahoo.com

Peggy Ann Ridley
17 Ribon Road
Lisbon, ME 04250
207-353-8827

Anne Sanregret
22910 Estorial Drive, #6
Diamond Bar, CA 91765
909-860-8007

Sandy Simonds
334 Woodhurst Drive
Coppell, TX 75019
512-219-8759

Linda Lee Sutton Originals
P.O. Box 3725
Central Point, OR 97502
541-830-8384
lindaleesutton.com
e-mail: linda@lindaleesutton.com

DOLL MANUFACTURERS
Alexander Doll Company, Inc.
Herbert Brown
Chairman & CEO
615 West 131st STreet
New York, NY 10027
212-283-5900
fax: 212-283-6042

American Girl
8400 Fairway Place
P.O. Box 620190-0190
Middleton, WI 53562-0190
800-845-0005
www.americangirl.com

Collectible Concepts
Ivonne Heather, President
945 Hickory Run Land
Great Falls, VA 22066
703-821-0607
fax: 703-759-0408
e-mail: invonnehccc@aol.com

Effanbee Doll Company
(recently acquired by Tonner Doll Co.)
459 Hurley Avenue
Hurley, NY 12443
888-FNB-DOLL!
e-mail: sperry@effanbeedoll.com

Susan Wakeen Doll Co., Inc.
P.O. Box 1321
Litchfield, CT 06759
860-567-0007
fax: 908-788-1955
e-mail: pkaverud@blast.net

Robert Tonner Doll Company
www.tonnerdoll.com
459 Hurley Avenue
Hurley, NY 12443
9 a.m. to 5 p.m. EST
845-339-9537
fax: 845-339-1259
e-mail:
customerservice@tonnerdoll.com

Vogue Doll Company
P.O. Box 756
Oakdale, CA 95361-0756
209-848-0300
fax: 209-848-4423
www.voguedolls.com

DOLL READER
Cumberland Publishing, Ic.
6405 Flank Dr.
Harrisburg, PA 17112
Subscriptions: 800-829-3340
e-mail:
dollreader@palmcoastd.com

DOLL REPAIRS
Doll Doc. Associates
1406 Sycamore Road
Montoursville, PA 17754
717-323-9604

Fresno Doll Hospital
1512 N. College
Fresno, CA 93728
209-266-1108

Kandyland Dolls
PO Box 146
Grande Ronde, OR 97347
503-879-5153

Life's Little Treasures
PO Box 585
Winston OR 97496
541-679-3472

Oleta's Doll Hospital
1413 Seville Way
Modesto, CA 95355
209-523-6669

GENE – ASHTON DRAKE GALLERIES
9200 N. Maryland Ave.
Niles, IL 60714-9853
888-For-Gene

GINNY
Ginny Journal
Suzanne Smith, Editor
P.O. Box 338
Oakdale, CA 95361-0338
877-848-0300 (toll free)
www.voguedolls.com
$15.00 dues

GIRL SCOUTS
Girl Scout Doll Collector's Patch
Pidd Miller
PO Box 631092
Houston, TX, 77263

Diane Miller, Collector
13151 Roberta Place
Garden Grove, CA 92643

Ann Sutton, Collector/Dealer
2555 Prine Road
Lakeland, FL 33810-5703
e-mail: Sydneys@aol.com

HASBRO — JEM DOLLS
Linda E. Holton, Collector/Dealer
P.O. Box 6753
San Rafael, CA 94903

HITTY
Friends of Hitty Newsletter
Virginia Ann Heyerdahl, Editor
2704 Belleview Ave
Cheverly, MD 20785
Quarterly, $12.00 per year

HITTY ARTISTS
Judy Brown
506 N. Brighton Ct.
Sterling, VA 20164
703-450-0206

Ruth Brown
1606 SW Heather Dr.
Grants Pass, OR 97526

DeAnn Cote
5555 – 22nd Avenue South
Seattle, WA 98108-2912
206-763-1871
e-mail: DRCDesigne@aol.com

Patti Hale
2301 Aazure Lane
Vista, CA 92083

JANCI
Nancy Elliott & Jill Sanders
2442 Hathaway Court
Muskegon, MI 49441
e-mail: janci@gte.net

Lotz Studio
Jean Lotz
P.O. Box 1308
Lacome, LA 70445
e-mail: lotz@gs.verio.net

IDEAL
Ideal Collectors' Newsletter
Judith Izen, Editor
PO Box 623
Lexington, MA 02173
e-mail: Jizen@aol.com
Quarterly, $20.00 per year

INTERNET
eBay auction site
www.ebay.com

About.com Doll Collecting
Denise Von Patten
www.collectdolls.about.com
e-mail: denise@dollymaker.com

Internet Lists & Chat Rooms
AG Collector
For American Girl, Heidi Ott, and
other 18" play dolls, no selling, just
talk. e-mail: ag_
collector-request@lists.best.com

Barbie chat
e-mail: Fashion@ga.unc.edu

Doll Chat List
Friendly collectors talk dolls, no
flaming permitted, a great group.
E-mail is forwarded to your address
from host, no fees, to subscribe:
DollChatRequest @nbi.com then
type "subscribe" in body of message

Dolls n Stuff
e-mail: dollsnstuff
@home.ease.lsoft.com

Not Just Dollmakers
e-mail: carls@isrv.com
www.notjustdollmakers.com

Sasha
e-mail: sasha-1-Subscribe@
makelist.com

Shirley Temple
e-mail: shirleycollect
subscribe@makelist.com

Postal Rates
website: www.usps.gov

Preservation
Twin Pines
www.twinpines.com

Publications
Collectors United
711 S. 3rd Ave.
Chatsworth, GA 30705
706-695-8242
fax: 706-895-0770
e-mail: collun@Alltel.net

Contemporary Doll Collector
Scott Publications
30595 Eight Mile
Livonia, MI 48152-1798
800-458-8237

Dolls
170 Fifth Ave., 12th Fl.
New York, NY 1010
212-989-8700
fax: 212-645-8976
e-mail: snowy@lsol.net

Patsy & Friends Newsletter
P.O. Box 311
Deming, NM 88031
e-mail: sctrading@zianet.com

KLUMPE DOLLS
Sondra Gast, Collector/Dealer
PO Box 252
Spring Valley, CA 91976
fax: 619-444-4215
e-mail: klumpe@home.com

LAWTON, WENDY
Lawton Collectors Guild
PO Box 969
Turlock, CA 95381

Toni Winder, Collector/Dealer
1484 N. Vagedes
Fresno CA 93728
e-mail: TTUK77B@prodigy.com

LIDDLE KIDDLES
For a signed copy of her book,
Liddle Kiddles, $22.95 post pd.
Write: *Paris Langford*
415 Dodge Ave
Jefferson, LA 70127
504-733-0676

MODERN DOLL CONVENTION
Judith Whorton, Coordinator
17017 61st North
Wilsonville, AL 35186
205-669-6219

MUSEUMS
Arizona
Arizona Doll and Toy Museum
602 E Adams Street, Phoenix, AZ
Hours: Tue – Sat 10 – 4; Sun: 12 – 4.
www.artcom.com/museums/nv/af/
85004-23.htm

Colorado
Denver Museum of Miniatures, Dolls & Toys
1880 Gaylord St.
Denver, Colorado 80206
303-322-1053
Hours: Tues. – Sat. 10 – 4; Sun.: 12 – 4. Closed Mondays and holidays.
www.coloradokids.com/miniatures/

Louisiana
The Enchanted Mansion, A Doll Museum
190 Lee Drive
Baton Rouge, LA 70808
225-769-0005
Hours: Mon., Wed. – Sat. 10 – 5.
Closed Sun. and Tues.
www.angelfire.com/la2/enchanted
mansion

The Lois Luftin Doll Museum
120 South Washington Avenue
DeRidder, LA 70634
Hours: Tues. – Sat. 10 – 4
www.beau.lib.la.us/doll.html

New Mexico
Land of Enchantment Doll Museum
5201 Constitution Ave.
Albuquerque, NM 87110-5813
505-821-8558
fax: 505-255-1259

New York
Museum of the City of New York
1220 Fifth Avenue @ 103rd St.
New York, NY 10029
212-534-1672
Hours: Open daily.
www.mcny.org/toy.htm

Margaret Woodbury Strong Museum
1 Manhattan Square
Rochester, NY 14607
716-263-2700

Ohio
Doll & Toy Museum
700 Winchester Pike
Canal Winchester, Ohio
Hours: Wed. – Sat. 11 – 5
April – mid Dec.
home.att.net/~dollmuseum
614-837-5573

The Children's Toy & Doll Museum:
206 Gilman Street P.O. Box 4034
Marietta, OH 4575
740-373-5900
Hours: Sat. 1 – 4, May – Dec.
www.tourohio.com/TOYDOLL/

Pennsylvania
Mary Meritt Doll Museum
843 Ben Franklin Hwy
Douglassville, PA 19518
610-385-3809
Hours: Sun. 1 – 5, Weekdays, closed Tuesday, 10 – 4:30
www.merritts.com/dollmuseum/
default.asp

Rhode Island
The Doll Museum
520 Thames St.
Newport, RI 02840
610-670-6868
Hours: Mon. – Fri.,. 11 – 5, Sat. 10 – 5. Closed Sunday and Tuesday.
www.dollmuseum.com

South Dakota
Enchanted World Doll Museum
615 North Main
Mitchell, SD 57301
606-996-9896
fax: 606-996-0210

Texas
Museum of American Architecture &
Decorative Arts
7502 Fronden Rd
Houston, Texas 77074-3298
281-649-3811

Utah
McCurdy Historical Doll Museum
246 North 100 East
Provo, UT 84606
801-377-9935
Hours: Tues. – Sat., 12 – 6,
winter: 1 – 5
www.utahvalley.org/visguide/ATT
RACTS/Mccurdy.htm

Vermont
Shelburne Museum
U.S. Route 7, P.O. Box 10
Shelburne, Vermont 05482
802-985-3346
Hours: Summer: 10 – 5 daily
www.shelburnemuseum.org

Washington
Rosalie Whyel Museum of Doll Art
1116 108th Avenue N.E.
Bellevue, WA 98004
206-455-1116
fax: 206-455-4793
www.dollart.com

Wisconsin
La Crosse Doll Museum
1213 Caledonia Street
La Crosse, WI 54603
Hours: Mon. – Sat., 10 – 5,
Sun. 11 – 4
www.dollmuseum.org/
608-785-0020

The Fennimore Doll & Toy Museum
and Gift Shoppe
140 Lincoln Ave.
Fennimore, WI 53809
608-822-4100

Hours: May 7 – Dec. 14,
Mon. – Sat. 10 – 4
www.fennimore.com/dolltoy/

NANCY ANN STORYBOOK
Elaine Pardee, Collector/Dealer
3613 Merano Way
Antelope, CA 95843
916-725-7227
fax: 916-725-7447
e-mail: epardee@jps.net

ORIENTAL DOLLS
Ninsyo Journal — Jade
Japanese American Dolls Enthusiasts
406 Koser Ave
Iowa City, IA 52246
e-mail: Vickyd@jadejapandolls.com

RAGGEDY ANN
Rags Newsletter
Barbara Barth, Editor
PO Box 823
Atlanta, GA 30301
Quarterly $16.00

ROBERT TONNER DOLL CLUB
Robert Tonner Doll Company
459 Hurley Avenue
Hurley, NY 12443
e-mail:
collectorclub@tonnerdoll.com

ROLDAN DOLLS
Sondra Gast, Collector/Dealer
PO Box 252
Spring Valley, CA 91976
fax: 619-444-4215

SANDRA SUE DOLLS, RICHWOOD
TOYS INC.
Peggy Millhouse, Collector/Dealer
510 Green Hill Road
Conestoga, PA 17516
e-mail: peggyin717@aol.com

SASHA DOLLS
Friends of Sasha
Quarterly Newsletter
Dorisanne Osborn, Editor
Box 187
Keuka Park, NY 14478

SHIRLEY TEMPLE
Australian Shirley Temple Collectors News
Quarterly Newsletter
Victoria Horne, Editor
39 How Ave.
North Dandenong
Victoria, 3175, Australia
$25.00 U.S.

Lollipop News
Shirley Temple Collectors by the Sea
PO Box 6203
Oxnard, CA 93031
Membership dues: $14.00 year

Shirley Temple Collectors News
Rita Dubas, Editor
881 Colonial Road
Brooklyn NY 11209
Quarterly, $20.00 year
www.ritadubasdesign.com/shirley/
e-mail: bukowski@wazoo.com

TERRI LEE
Daisy Chain Newsletter
Terry Bukowski, Editor
3010 Sunland Dr.
Alamogordo, NM 88310
$20.00 per year, quarterly

Ann Sutton, Collector/Dealer
2555 Prine Road
Lakeland, FL 33810-5703
e-mail: Sydneys@aol.com

Betty J. Woten, Collector
12 Big Bend Cut Off
Cloudcroft, NM 88317-9411

VIDEOS
Leonard A. Swann, Jr.
SIROCCO Productions, Inc.
5660 E. Virgina Beach Blvd.,
Suite 105
Norfolk, VA 23502
757-461-8987
www.siroccovideo.com
e-mail: iswann@specialty
products.net

VOGUE
Vogue Doll Co.
PO Box 756
Oakdale, CA 95361-0756
209-848-0300
fax: 209-848-4423
www.voguedolls.com/
e-mail: info@voguecolls.com

UNITED FEDERATION OF DOLL CLUBS, INC.
10900 North Pomona Avenue
Kansas City, MO 64153
816-891-7040
fax 816-891-8360
www.ufdc.org/about.html
e-mail: ufdcinfo@ufdc.org

WOODS, ROBIN
Toni Winder, Collector/Dealer
1484 N. Vagedes
Fresno, CA 93728

Mold Index

275	E. Heubach	319	E. Heubach
277	Bähr & Pröschild	320	E. Heubach
282	Kley & Hahn	320	A. Marseille
283	M. Handwerck	321	E. Heubach
285	Kestner	322	E. Heubach
286	Bähr & Pröschild	322	A. Marseille
286	M. Handwerck	323	A. Marseille
289	Bähr & Pröschild	325	Bähr & Pröschild
291	M. Handwerck	325	Borgfeldt
291	G. Heubach	325	A. Marseille
292	Kley & Hahn	325	Kley & Hahn
293	Bähr & Pröschild	326	A. Marseille
293	F. Schmidt	327	Borgfeldt
297	Bähr & Pröschild	327	A. Marseille
297	M. Handwerck	328	Borgfeldt
300	E. Heubach	328	A. Marseille
300	Schoenhut	329	Borgfeldt
300	Schuetzmeister & Quendt	329	A. Marseille
301	Unis France	330	Unknown
301	Schoenhut	332	Bähr & Pröschild
301	Schuetzmeister & Quendt	338	E. Heubach
301	SFBJ	339	E. Heubach
301	Unis France	340	Bähr & Pröschild
302	Schoenhut	340	E. Heubach
302	E. Heubach	341	A. Marseille
303	Schoenhut	342	E. Heubach
304	Schoenhut	345	A. Marseille
305	Schoenhut	348	E. Heubach
306	Jumeau	349	E. Heubach
306	Schoenhut	350	E. Heubach
307	M. Handwerck	350	A. Marseille
307	Schoenhut	351	A. Marseille
308	Schoenhut	352	A. Marseille
309	Bähr & Pröschild	353	A. Marseille
309	Schoenhut	360	A. Marseille
310	A. Marseille	362	A. Marseille
310	Schoenhut	369	Unknown
311	Schoenhut	370	Kling
312	Schoenhut	370	A. Marseille
313	Schoenhut	371	Amberg
314	Schoenhut	372	Unknown
315	Schoenhut	372	Kling
316	Schoenhut	372	A. Marseille
317	Schoenhut	373	Kling
318	E. Heubach	377	Kling

Mold Index

1046	Alt, Beck & Gottschalck	1272	F. Schmidt
1049	Simon & Halbig	1279	Simon & Halbig
1059	Simon & Halbig	1288	Alt, Beck & Gottschalck
1064	Alt, Beck & Gottschalck	1294	Simon & Halbig
1069	Simon & Halbig	1299	Simon & Halbig
1070	Konig & Wernicke	1302	Simon & Halbig
1070	Kestner	1303	Simon & Halbig
1078	Simon & Halbig	1304	Alt, Beck & Gottschalck
1079	Simon & Halbig	1304	Simon & Halbig
1080	Simon & Halbig	1305	Simon & Halbig
1099	Simon & Halbig	1308	Simon & Halbig
1100	Catterfelder Puppenfabrik	1310	F. Schmidt
1109	Simon & Halbig	1322	Alt, Beck & Gottschalck
1112	Alt, Beck & Gottschalck	1329	Simon & Halbig
1123	Alt, Beck & Gottschalck	1339	Simon & Halbig
1127	Alt, Beck & Gottschalck	1342	Alt, Beck & Gottschalck
1129	Simon & Halbig	1346	Alt, Beck & Gottschalck
1142	Alt, Beck & Gottschalck	1348	Cuno & Otto
1159	Simon & Halbig	1349	Cuno & Otto
1160	Simon & Halbig	1352	Alt, Beck & Gottschalck
1170	Simon & Halbig	1357	Alt, Beck & Gottschalck
1180	F. Schmidt	1357	Catterfelder Puppenfabrik
1199	Simon & Halbig	1358	Alt, Beck & Gottschalck
1200	Catterfelder Puppenfabrik	1358	Simon & Halbig
1210	Alt, Beck & Gottschalck	1361	Alt, Beck & Gottschalck
1222	Alt, Beck & Gottschalck	1362	Alt, Beck & Gottschalck
1234	Alt, Beck & Gottschalck	1367	Alt, Beck & Gottschalck
1235	Alt, Beck & Gottschalck	1368	Alt, Beck & Gottschalck
1246	Simon & Halbig	1368	Averill, G.
1248	Simon & Halbig	1368	Simon & Halbig
1249	Simon & Halbig	1376	Schuetzmeister & Quendt
1250	Simon & Halbig	1388	Simon & Halbig
1253	F. Schmidt	1394	Unknown
1254	Alt, Beck & Gottschalck	1394	Borgfeldt
1256	Alt, Beck & Gottschalck	1402	Averilla, G.
1259	F. Schmidt	1428	Simon & Halbig
1260	Simon & Halbig	1448	Simon & Halbig
1262	F. Schmidt	1469	Simon & Halbig
1263	F. Schmidt	1478	Simon & Halbig
1266	F. Schmidt	1488	Simon & Halbig
1267	F. Schmidt	1489	Simon & Halbig
1269	Simon & Halbig	1498	Simon & Halbig
1270	F. Schmidt	1890	A. Marseille
1271	F. Schmidt	1892	A. Marseille
1272	Simon & Halbig	1893	A. Marseille

1894	A. Marseille	4843	
1897	A. Marseille	– 4883	Kewpie
1898	A. Marseille	4900	Schoenau & Hoffmeister
1899	A. Marseille	4900	Schoenau & Hoffmeister
1900	E. Heubach	5500	Schoenau & Hoffmeister
1900	A. Marseille	5636	G. Heubach
1901	A. Marseille	5689	G. Heubach
1902	A. Marseille	5700	Schoenau & Hoffmeister
1903	A. Marseille	5730	G. Heubach
1906	Schoenau & Hoffmeister	5777	G. Heubach
1907	Recknagel	5800	Schoenau & Hoffmeister
1909	Schoenau Hoffmeister	6688	G. Heubach
1909	A. Marseille	6692	G. Heubach
1909	Recknagel	6736	G. Heubach
1909	Schoenau & Hoffmeister	6894	G. Heubach
1912	A. Marseille	6897	G. Heubach
1912	Cuno & Otto	6969	G. Heubach
1914	A. Marseille	6970	G. Heubach
1914	Cuno & Otto	6971	G. Heubach
1914	Recknagel	7246	G. Heubach
1916	Simon & Halbig	7247	G. Heubach
1924	Recknagel	7248	G. Heubach
2015	Muller & Strasburger	7268	G. Heubach
2020	Muller & Strasburger	7287	G. Heubach
2023	Bähr & Pröschild	7345	G. Heubach
2023	B. Schmidt	7407	G. Heubach
2033	B. Schmidt	7602	G. Heubach
2048	B. Schmidt	7603	G. Heubach
2052	B. Schmidt	7604	G. Heubach
2072	Bähr & Pröschild	7622	G. Heubach
2072	B. Schmidt	7623	G. Heubach
2092	B. Schmidt	7644	G. Heubach
2094	B. Schmidt	7657	G. Heubach
2095	B. Schmidt	7658	G. Heubach
2096	B. Schmidt	7661	G. Heubach
2097	B. Schmidt	7668	G. Heubach
2500	Schoenau & Hoffmeister	7671	G. Heubach
3200	Marottes	7681	G. Heubach
3200	A. Marseille	7686	G. Heubach
3841	G. Heubach	7711	G. Heubach
4000	Schoenau & Hoffmeister	7759	G. Heubach
4515	Muller & Strasburger	7847	G. Heubach
4600	Schoenau & Hoffmeister	7850	G. Heubach
4700	Marottes	7911	G. Heubach
4700	Schoenau & Hoffmeister	7925	G. Heubach

Name Index

Name Index

Name Index